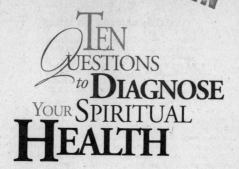

TEN QUESTIONS to DIAGNOSE YOUR SPIRITUAL HEALTH

SPIRITUAL DISCIPLINES for the CHRISTIAN LIFE

Donald S. Whitney

NAVPRESS

Bringing Tru
P.O. Box 35001, Colorado

OUR GUARANTEE TO YOU

We believe so strongly in the message of our books that we are making this quality guarantee to you. If for any reason you are disappointed with the content of this book, return the title page to us with your name and address and we will refund to you the list price of the book. To help us serve you better, please briefly describe why you were disappointed. Mail your refund request to: NavPress, P.O. Box 35002, Colorado Springs, CO 80935.

The Navigators is an international Christian organization. Our mission is to reach, disciple, and equip people to know Christ and to make Him known through successive generations. We envision multitudes of diverse people in the United States and every other nation who have a passionate love for Christ, live a lifestyle of sharing Christ's love, and multiply spiritual laborers among those without Christ.

NavPress is the publishing ministry of The Navigators. NavPress publications help believers learn biblical truth and apply what they learn to their lives and ministries. Our mission is to stimulate spiritual formation among our readers.

© 2002 by Donald S. Whitney
All rights reserved. No part of this publication may be reproduced in any form without written permission from NavPress, P.O. Box 35001, Colorado Springs, CO 80935.
www.navpress.com
ISBN 1-57683-330-5

Some of the anecdotal illustrations in this book are true to life and are included with the permission of the persons involved. All other illustrations are composites of real situations, and any resemblance to people living or dead is coincidental.

Ten Questions to Diagnose Your Spiritual Health: Unless otherwise identified, all Scripture quotations in this publication are taken from the *New King James Version* (NKJV). Copyright © 1982 Thomas Nelson Inc. Used by permission. All rights reserved. Other versions used include: the *HOLY BIBLE: NEW INTERNATIONAL VERSION®* (NIV®), Copyright © 1973, 1978, 1984 by International Bible Society, used by permission of Zondervan Publishing House, all rights reserved; the *New American Standard Bible* (NASB), © The Lockman Foundation 1960, 1962, 1963, 1968, 1971, 1972, 1973, 1975, 1977, 1995.

Spiritual Disciplines for the Christian Life: Unless otherwise identified, all Scripture quotations in this publication are taken from the *HOLY BIBLE: NEW INTERNATIONAL VERSION®* (NIV®). Copyright © 1973, 1978, 1984 by International Bible Society. Used by permission of Zondervan Publishing House. All rights reserved. Other versions used include: the *New American Standard Bible* (NASB), © The Lockman Foundation 1960, 1962, 1963, 1968, 1971, 1972, 1973, 1975, 1977, 1995.

Printed in the United States of America

1 2 3 4 5 6 7 8 9 10 / 05 04 03 02

FOR A FREE CATALOG OF
NAVPRESS BOOKS & BIBLE STUDIES,
CALL 1-800-366-7788 (USA)
OR 1-416-499-4615 (CANADA)

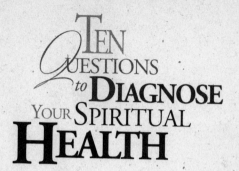

TEN
QUESTIONS
to DIAGNOSE
YOUR SPIRITUAL
HEALTH

For "Him who is able to establish you . . . ; to the only
wise God, through Jesus Christ, be the glory forever.
Amen."
(Romans 16:25,27, NASB)

And for all three generations of my girls.
May the Lord always grant you
spiritual health and growth.

CONTENTS

ACKNOWLEDGMENTS

"First, I thank my God through Jesus Christ for you all"
(Romans 1:8).

Much thanks to:

- Caffy and Laurelen, for your great patience. I love you.
- My brothers and sisters in Christ at North Pointe Baptist Church of Kansas City, for your prayers and encouragement. Your kindness repeatedly refreshed me, particularly during the last week of this project.
- My colleagues at Midwestern Baptist Theological Seminary, for your counsel and support.
- Nanci McAlister, for your consistent New Testament Christianity, even in "business," and for the "award."
- Sue Geiman, for your *long*-suffering.
- Kent Wilson, for your invitation to write the book.
- Mindy Rose, for your willing spirit on so many practical details.
- Mark and Sharon Coppenger, for the time invested to write two pages of ideas when I was stuck.
- Jim Orrick, for the creative recommendations and especially for your prayer that Wednesday night near the end.
- Rachel Sparks, for your typing. (And you, too, Jay, for running upstairs in the library late that night to help me complete that Spurgeon footnote.)
- Bob, Jenny, Josh, and Zach Hall, for your time and timely help. The food and the mowing made a hard time easier. And I wouldn't have made that flight if you hadn't printed the manuscript for me.

- Tammi Ledbetter, for finding a computer for me to use at the convention.
- The countless others who deserve thanks for their contribution to this book.

"For God is not unjust to forget your work and labor of love which you have shown toward His name, in that you have ministered to the saints, and do minister" (Hebrews 6:10).

INTRODUCTION

"DURING THE PAST YEAR, HAVE YOU HAD ANY TROUBLE SLEEPING?

"Have you experienced any breathing difficulties?

"Any changes in your eyesight?

"Relax while I test your reflexes.

"Has the nurse drawn your blood yet?

"Now for this next test . . ."

This is the way it goes during my annual physical checkup. The doctor always evaluates my bodily health by two means— questions and tests.

The English Puritans of 1550 to 1700 used to refer to ministers as "physicians of the soul." In our day, as in theirs, the timeless process of discerning one's *spiritual* health likewise involves questions and tests. My purpose in writing these pages is to act as a physician of the soul—to ask questions and suggest spiritual tests that can, by the help of the Holy Spirit, enable you to self-diagnose your spiritual health.

For health to be present, of course, there must be life. I wrote this book with the assumption that its readers would possess the eternal life given by grace to those who know God through faith in His Son, Jesus Christ. The night before He was crucified, Jesus prayed, "And this is eternal life, that they may know You, the only true God, and Jesus Christ whom You have sent" (John 17:3). Stressing the necessity of knowing Jesus, the Son of God, in order to have eternal life, the apostle John added, "He who has the Son has life; he who does not have the Son of God does not have life" (1 John 5:12).

I realize, however, that many who begin reading here will do so with a false sense of assurance that they know Jesus and that God has given them eternal life. Nothing in the world is more important than an eternal, life-giving knowledge of God through Jesus, who is the only way to the Father (see John 14:6). I urge you not to take for granted the existence of such a relationship between yourself and God. The Bible itself implores you to "make your call and election sure" (2 Peter 1:10).

Where eternal life through Christ does exist, there should be not only health but also growth. That is what this book is about—evaluating your spiritual health and growth. Throughout, remember that just as Jesus is the source of spiritual *life*, so also is He the standard of spiritual *health*. And regarding spiritual *growth*, we are to "grow up in all things into Him who is the head—Christ" (Ephesians 4:15). As Jonathan Edwards said so emphatically,

> Christians are Christlike: none deserve the name of
> Christians that are not so, in their prevailing character
> . . . . The branch is of the same nature with the stock
> and root, has the same sap, and bears the same sort of
> fruit. The members have the same kind of life with the
> head. It would be strange if Christians should not be
> of the same temper and spirit that Christ is of; when
> they are his flesh and his bone, yea are one spirit
> (1 Corinthians 6:17), and live so, that it is not they
> that live, but Christ that lives in them.[1]

So whatever the present state of your spiritual health or the rate of your spiritual growth, let's begin by "looking unto Jesus, the author and finisher of our faith" (Hebrews 12:2), and "press toward the goal for the prize of the upward call of God in Christ Jesus" (Philippians 3:14). May the Lord be pleased to use this little volume to help you "grow in the grace and knowledge of our Lord and Savior Jesus Christ. To Him be the glory both now and forever. Amen" (2 Peter 3:18).

CHAPTER ONE

SO HOLY DESIRE, EXERCISED IN LONGINGS, HUNGER-
INGS, AND THIRSTINGS AFTER GOD AND HOLINESS, IS
OFTEN MENTIONED IN SCRIPTURE AS AN IMPORTANT
PART OF TRUE RELIGION.

—JONATHAN EDWARDS

DO YOU THIRST FOR GOD?

"LORD, I WANT TO KNOW YOU MORE," SANG THE SOLOIST, JUST BEFORE the sermon. One of my seminary professors from years back, who was a guest preacher at our church that Sunday morning, sat next to me on the front pew, transfixed. As the soloist continued, I could hear my older friend sigh occasionally. When the song was over, T. W. sat motionless for so long that I thought he had forgotten he was now supposed to preach. As I turned to remind him, I saw his shoulders lift and fall with the slow draw and release of his breath. Finally, he opened his eyes and stepped thoughtfully to the pulpit. He looked down for what seemed to be a full minute before he could speak. And then he said, "Lord, I *do* want to know you more." Departing from his prepared words for a while, he spoke of his thirst for God, his longings to know Christ more intimately, to obey Him more completely. Here was a man who had followed Christ for more than fifty years and was still captivated by the sweetness of the quest. In his second half-century as a disciple of Jesus, the grace of growth still flourished in him.

It has been ten years since that Sunday morning. I've seen T. W. at least annually since then, and the things of God have not diminished their magnetic pull on his heart's aspirations. Two months ago I found myself sharing a shuttle bus ride with him from a denominational convention back to our hotel. Though nearly seventy now, and weakened by cardiac surgery, his eyes flashed as he talked for half an hour about what he was learning about prayer. Even as his body decays, his longings for God display the growing strength of his soul.

The apostle Paul must have similarly impressed others in his day. Despite his maturity in Christ and all he had seen and experienced, late in life Paul wrote of the passion that propelled him: "that I may know Him" (Philippians 3:10). What is he talking about? Didn't he already know Jesus more closely than perhaps anyone else ever would? Of course he did. But the more he knew Jesus, the more he wanted to know Him. The more Paul progressed in spiritual strength, the more thirsty for God he became.

With a similar thirst, the writer of Psalm 42:1-2 prayed, "As the deer pants for the water brooks, so pants my soul for You, O God. My soul thirsts for God, for the living God. When shall I come and appear before God?" Does this describe your thirst for God? If so, be encouraged; whatever else is transpiring in your Christian life, your soul-thirst is a sign of soul-growth.

THREE KINDS OF SPIRITUAL THIRST

Though it is not felt in every moment, in some sense there is a thirst in every soul. God did not make us to be content in our natural condition. In one way or another, to one degree or another, everyone wants more than he has now. The difference between people is the *kind* of thirsty longing in their soul.

THIRST OF THE EMPTY SOUL

The natural, that is, the unconverted man or woman, has an empty soul. Devoid of God, he is constantly in pursuit of that which will fill his emptiness. The range of his mad scramble may include money, sex, power, houses, lands, sports, hobbies, entertainment, transcendence, significance, or education, while basically "fulfilling the desires of the flesh and of the mind" (Ephesians 2:3). As Augustine attested, "Thou hast made us for Thyself, and our hearts are restless until they find their rest in Thee." Always searching and never resting, the empty soul turns from one pursuit to another, unable to find anything that will fill the God-shaped vacuum in his heart.

Thirsting and searching, the empty soul is blinded to his real need. Nothing or no one on earth fully and lastingly satisfies, but the empty soul doesn't know where to turn except to someone or something else "under the sun" (Ecclesiastes 1:9), as opposed to the One beyond the sun. Like Solomon, he discovers that no matter who or what he at first finds exciting, ultimately "all is vanity and grasping for the wind" (Ecclesiastes 1:14).

A Christian observes the man with the empty soul and knows that what he is looking for can be found only in the One who said, "whoever drinks of the water that I shall give him will never thirst" (John 4:14). Occasionally, an empty soul searches in more serious-minded or spiritual ways that lead some Christians to think he is thirsting for God. But the world has no such thirst. "There is none who understands," God inspired both King David and the apostle Paul to write, "there is none who seeks after God" (Psalm 14:2; Romans 3:11). Until and unless the Holy Spirit of God touches the spiritual tongue of the empty soul, that soul will never want to "taste and see that the Lord is good" (Psalm 34:8). Just because a man longs for something that can be found in God alone doesn't mean he's looking for God. A man may pine for peace yet have no interest in the Prince of Peace. Many who claim they are questing for

God are not thirsting for God as He has revealed Himself in Scripture, but only for God as they want Him to be, or for a god who will give them what they want.

The irony of the empty soul is that while he is perpetually dissatisfied in so many areas of his life, he is so easily satisfied in regard to the pursuit of God. His attitude toward spiritual matters is like that of the man who said to his complacent soul in Luke 12:19, "Soul, you have many goods laid up for many years; take your ease; eat, drink, and be merry." Whatever the empty soul may desire in life, he never has what the eighteenth-century pastor and theologian, Jonathan Edwards, called "holy desire, exercised in longings, hungerings and thirstings after God and holiness,"[1] as the Christian does.

The eternal tragedy is that if the empty soul never properly thirsts on earth, he will thirst in hell as did the rich man who pleaded in vain for even the tip of a moist finger to be touched to his tongue (Luke 16:24).

THIRST OF THE DRY SOUL

The difference between the empty soul and the dry soul is that one has never experienced "rivers of living water" (John 7:38), while the other has and knows what he's missing. That is not to say that the dry soul can lose the indwelling presence of the Holy Spirit; indeed, Jesus said, "the water that I shall give him will become in him a fountain of water springing up into *everlasting* life" (John 4:14, emphasis added).

How is it then that a true believer in Christ can become a dry soul when Jesus promised that "whoever drinks of the water I shall give him will never thirst" (John 4:14)?

Pastor and author John Piper was reading this verse one Monday morning and cried out, "What do You mean? I am so thirsty! My church is thirsty! The pastors whom I pray with are thirsty! O Jesus, what did You mean?"

As he meditated on the text, the illumination that seemed

to come from the Lord upon His Word was perceived by Piper
this way:

> When you drink my water, your thirst is not
> destroyed forever. If it did that, would you feel any
> need of my water afterward? That is not my goal. I do
> not want self-sufficient saints. When you drink my
> water, it makes a spring in you. A spring satisfies
> thirst, not by removing the need you have for water,
> but by being there to give you water whenever you
> get thirsty. Again and again and again. Like this morn-
> ing. So drink, John. Drink.[2]

A Christian soul becomes arid in one of three ways. The
most common is by drinking too much from the desiccating
fountains of the world and too little from "the river of God"
(Psalm 65:9). If you drink the wrong thing it can make you
even more thirsty. In particularly hot weather, my high school
football coach would give us salt tablets to help us minimize
the loss of fluids. During one game he experimented with stir-
ring salt into our drinking water, hoping the diluted form would
expedite the benefits of the salt. Bad idea. At halftime I drank
until my stomach swelled and I was too heavy to run well, yet
I was still thirsty.

Similarly, perhaps it was because the psalmist had drunk
too much of the world's briny spiritual water that he wrote twice
in one chapter about longing for God with all his heart while
closely asserting his resolve not to wander from the Lord's Word
(see Psalm 119:10,145). Too much attention to a particular sin
or sins, and/or too little attention to communion with God (two
things that often occur in tandem) inevitably shrivel the soul
of a Christian.

Another cause of spiritual dryness in the child of God is what
the Puritans used to call "God's desertions." While there are times
when God floods our souls with a sense of His presence, at other

times we dehydrate by a sense of His absence. Let me quickly say that His desertion of us is merely our *perception*, for the *reality* is just as Jesus promised: "I will never leave you nor forsake you" (Hebrews 13:5). When feeling deserted by God, however, the Christian believes himself to be in the valley of the shadow of death (Psalm 23:4), or somewhat like Jesus when He cried from the cross, "My God, My God, why have You forsaken Me?" (Matthew 27:46). The words of David in Psalm 143:6-7 describe the emotions of those who try to pray from such a spiritual desert: "I spread out my hands to You; my soul longs for You like a thirsty land. Answer me speedily, O LORD; my spirit fails! Do not hide Your face from me.".

For reasons not always made clear to us, the Lord does sometimes withdraw a conscious sense of His nearness. Because this is not the place for a lengthy treatment of the subject,[3] the best concise counsel I can offer is that of William Gurnall: "The Christian must trust in a withdrawing God."[4] When the sun goes behind a cloud, it is no less near than when its rays are felt. However, for the specific purposes of this book and chapter, remember that it is a good thing that you are able to discern the seclusion of God's presence. Such spiritual sensitivity characterizes spiritual health.

A third cause of spiritual aridity in a Christian is prolonged mental or physical fatigue. Both the cause and the cure are usually obvious enough, so I won't elaborate on them. What I do want to emphasize is that a believer may not sense spiritual growth when fatigued or burned out, but instead may brood under shadowy thoughts about the reality of his relationship with Christ. And yet, much may have been learned in the very battle that caused the fatigue, things which, when the sunlight returns to the soul, will be seen as significant spiritual turning points. Again, don't forget that the longing for fresh water is itself a sign of progress.

Regardless of the cause, the dry Christian soul is like the

believer of Psalm 42:1-2, thirsting for God "as the deer pants for the water brooks." When you are in this condition, nothing else but the living water of God Himself will do. My daughter was three when she separated herself from me while we were in a child-oriented restaurant. She wanted to play with some of the game machines instead of eating. Though she had run to the far side of the restaurant, I could see her and was on my way to bring her back to the table. Suddenly she realized she didn't know where she was or where I was. Panic-stricken, she began crying and calling for me. At that moment, the store manager could have offered her unlimited play on every machine and given her every toy prize in the place, but nothing would have appealed to her without my presence. Everything else was meaningless to her without me. Once we were reunited, for a few moments she was content just for me to hold her, just to have me back. That's the cry of the dry soul. Other things may have distracted you, but now the only thing that matters is a return of the sense of your Father's presence.

THIRST OF THE SATISFIED SOUL

Unlike the dry soul, and as self-contradictory as it may sound at the moment, the satisfied soul thirsts for God precisely because he *is* satisfied with God. He *has* "taste[d] and see[n] that the LORD is good" (Psalm 34:8), and the taste is so uniquely satisfying that he craves more.

The apostle Paul personified this in his famous exclamation, "that I may know Him" (Philippians 3:10). In the preceding lines he had been exulting in his present knowledge of and relationship with Jesus. He announced, "But what things were gain to me, these I have counted loss for Christ. Yet indeed I also count all things loss for the excellence of the knowledge of Christ Jesus my Lord, for whom I have suffered the loss of all things, and count them as rubbish, that I may gain Christ" (verses 7-8). Then, just one verse later, the apostle cried out, "that I may know Him." Paul was soul-satisfied with Jesus Christ, yet thirsty for Him still.

Thomas Shepard, founder of Harvard University and an influential New England minister, explained the cycle of satisfaction and thirst this way: "There is in true grace an infinite circle: a man by thirsting receives, and receiving thirsts for more."[5]

Knowing Christ well is so spiritually thirst quenching because no person, possession, or experience can produce the spiritual pleasure we can find in Him. Communion with Christ is incomparably satisfying because there is no disappointment in what you find in Him. Moreover, the spiritual gratification you find in Him initially is never ending. On top of these, the Lord in whom this satisfaction is found is an infinite universe of satisfaction in which one may immerse himself to explore and enjoy without limitation. So there is no lack of satisfaction in knowing Christ, but neither has God designed us so that one experience with Christ satiates all future desire for Him.

Here's how Jonathan Edwards described the relationship between the spiritual good enjoyed in fellowship with Christ and the thirst for more that it produces:

> Spiritual good is of a satisfying nature; and for that very reason, the soul that tastes, and knows its nature, will thirst after it, and a fullness of it, that it may be satisfied. And the more he experiences, and the more he knows this excellent, unparalleled, exquisite, and satisfying sweetness, the more earnestly he will hunger and thirst for more.[6]

Has your worship or devotional experience lately provided you with ravishing tastes of what A. W. Tozer called the "piercing sweetness"[7] of Christ, only to leave you with a divine discontent that desires more? Would the following prayer of Tozer's reflect your own aspirations?

O God, I have tasted Thy goodness, and it has both satisfied me and made me thirsty for more. I am painfully
conscious of my need for further grace. I am ashamed of
my lack of desire. O God, the Triune God, I want to
want Thee; I long to be filled with longing; I thirst to be
made thirsty still.[8]

Such desires, Christian brother or sister, are marks of a growing soul.

THE BLESSING OF SPIRITUAL THIRST

"How blessed are all those who long for Him," declared the prophet
Isaiah (30:18, NASB). "Blessed are those," reiterated Jesus, "who
hunger and thirst for righteousness" (Matthew 5:6). A thirsting
desire for the Lord and His righteousness is a blessing. How so?

GOD INITIATES SPIRITUAL THIRST

The reason a person thirsts for God is because the Holy
Spirit is at work within him. If you are a Christian, two people
live in your body—you and the Holy Spirit. As the apostle Paul
explained, "Do you not know that your body is the temple of
the Holy Spirit who is in you, whom you have from God, and
you are not your own?" (1 Corinthians 6:19). And the Holy
Spirit is not passive within you.

For example, just as you can choose to put thoughts in your
consciousness, so can He, and He does. For instance, as you can
decide to think for a few moments about what you should do
this evening, so He can plant thoughts in your mind about God
and the things of God. Such work is part of how He causes a
Christian to be "spiritually minded" (see Romans 8:5).[9] Another
part of that ministry is to cause you to have Godward thirsts and
longings (such as "Abba, Father," see Romans 8:15), as well as
other signs of spiritual vitality.

Charles Spurgeon, the peerless British Baptist preacher of the 1800s, elaborated on the blessing of thirsting:

> When a man pants after God, it is a secret life within which makes him do it: he would not long after God by nature. No man thirsts for God while he is left in his carnal [that is, unconverted] state. The unrenewed man pants after anything sooner than God: . . . It proves a renewed nature when you long after God; it is a work of grace in your soul, and you may be thankful for it.[10]

GOD INITIATES SPIRITUAL THIRST IN ORDER TO SATISFY IT

God does not fire a thirst for Himself in order to mock us or frustrate us. He Himself declared, "I did not say to the seed of Jacob, 'Seek Me in vain'" (Isaiah 45:19). What is true for the physical lineage of Jacob (Israel) is also true for his spiritual descendants, in other words, those who believe in Israel's Messiah, Jesus. God creates a thirst for Himself so that He can satisfy it with Himself. "For He satisfies the longing soul," is the promise of Psalm 107:9, "and fills the hungry soul with goodness." Jesus assured us that "blessed are those who hunger and thirst for righteousness, for they *shall* be filled" (Matthew 5:6, emphasis added).

Jonathan Edwards argued that Scripture plainly teaches that "the godly are designed for unknown and inconceivable happiness."[11] And, "no doubt but God will obtain his end in a glorious perfection."[12] If God has indeed made us for an unimaginable fullness of joy and has implanted longings for it, then surely

> God has made man capable of exceeding great happiness, which he doubtless did not in vain. . . . To create man with a capacity that he never intended to fill, . . . would have been to have created a large capacity when there was need but of a smaller; yea, it makes man less

happy, to be capable of more happiness than he shall
ever obtain. . . . [C]an any think that man, . . . was
intended in his creation to be left in this respect
imperfect, and as a vessel both partly empty and never
to be filled? . . . It appears that man was intended for
very great blessedness, inasmuch as God has created
man with a craving and desire that can be filled with
nothing but a very great happiness. . . . God did not
create in man so earnest a desire, when at the same
time he did not create for so much as he should desire.
. . . [A] desire that could never be satisfied would be
an eternal torment.[13]

Edwards maintained, of course, that this "craving and desire"
was a Christian's thirst for God, a longing that can be thoroughly
and finally satisfied only in the eternal, undiminished, and face-
to-face enjoyment of the Lord Himself in Heaven. Therefore,
wrote Edwards,

Seeing that reason does so undeniably evidence that
saints shall, some time or other, enjoy so great glory,
hence we learn that there is undoubtedly a future state
after death, because we see they do not enjoy so great
glory in this world. . . . [A]ll the spiritual pleasure they
enjoy in this life does but enflame their desire and thirst
for more enjoyment of God; and if they knew that there
was no future life, [it] would but increase their misery,
to consider that after this life was ended they were never
to enjoy God anymore at all. How good is God, that he
has created man for this very end, to make him happy
in the enjoyment of himself, the Almighty.[14]

Once beholding His glory, believers will testify that "they are
abundantly satisfied with the fullness of Your house, and You
give them drink from the river of Your pleasures" (Psalm 36:8).

Do you thirst for God? Thirst is a God-planned part of the growth of a soul toward its heavenly home.

PRACTICAL STEPS FOR THIRSTING AFTER THE THIRST-SLAKER

If you possess a true thirst for God, you will long to long even more. As Edwards insisted, "True and gracious longings after holiness are no idle ineffectual desires."[15]

Meditate on Scripture. Note that we are to "meditate," not merely read. Many languishing souls are assiduous Bible readers. Without the addition of meditation, warned the great man of prayer and faith George Müller, "the simple reading of the Word of God" can become information that "only passes through our minds, just as water passes through a pipe."[16]

Think of the incessant flow of information through your mind on a daily basis—all that you see, read, and hear. Most of us struggle with "information overload," unable to keep up with the constant input of data. If we are not careful, the words of the Bible can become just another gallon of words in the ever-increasing current through our thoughts. As soon as they pass by, pushed on by the pressure of the flow in the pipe, we remember little (if anything) of what we've just read, for we must immediately shift our focus to what's now before us. So much processes through our brains; if we don't absorb some of it we will be affected by none of it. And surely if we should absorb anything that courses through our thinking, it should be the inspired words from Heaven. Without absorption of the water of God's Word, there's no quenching our spiritual thirst. Meditation is the means of absorption.

Spend 25 to 50 percent of your Bible intake time meditating on some verse, phrase, or word from your reading. Ask questions of it. Pray about it. Take your pen and scribble and doodle on a pad about it. Look for at least one way you could apply it or live it. Linger over it. Soak your soul slowly in the water of the Word, and you'll find it not only refreshes you, but prompts a satisfying thirst for more.[17]

Pray through Scripture. After you read through a section of Scripture, pray through part of that same passage. Whether you read one or many chapters of the Bible per day, afterward choose a portion of your reading and, verse by verse, let the words of God become the wings of your words to Him.

While it is possible to pray through any part of Scripture, I particularly recommend, regardless of where in the Bible you have done your reading, that you turn to one of the Psalms and pray your way through as much of it as you can. The book of Psalms was the God-inspired hymnbook of Israel. In addition, twice in the New Testament (see Ephesians 5:19 and Colossians 3:16) Christians are commanded to sing psalms. Unlike any other book of the Bible, the Psalms were inspired *by* God for the express purpose of being reflected *to* God.

Say, for example, you begin praying your way through Psalm 63. The first verse is: "O God, You are my God; early will I seek You; my soul thirsts for You; my flesh longs for You in a dry and thirsty land where there is no water." You could enter into prayer by confessing that the Lord is your God, graciously thanking Him for that, then simply exulting in God as God. Next you could express your soul's thirsts and longings for Him, acknowledging what a blessing it is to have a God-given thirst for God, and so on. Perhaps then you would ask the Lord to plant a God-thirst in your children, or in someone with whom you've been sharing the gospel. On you would go through the psalm, praying about whatever the text said and whatever occurs to you as you read it. If nothing comes to mind while pausing over a verse or section of verses, go on to the next.

The poetic, visceral, and spiritually transparent elements of the Psalms often combine in ways that send the soul soaring and inflame passion for God. They deal realistically with the full range of human emotions and can take you from wherever you are spiritually and lift you heavenward. Nothing so consistently renews my longings for God and catapults me into experiential communion with Him as praying through a psalm.

Read thirst-making writers. After the God-breathed words of the Bible, read the time-tested works of those Christian writers who wrote with a thirst-making pen. If you can find the collection of Puritan prayers and devotions called *The Valley of Vision*[18] you will be blessed by reading it meditatively. Don't neglect John Bunyan's classic *Pilgrim's Progress.* Read the more devotional pieces of Puritan writers such as John Owen, Richard Sibbes, Thomas Brooks, John Flavel, and Thomas Watson. Enjoy the books and sermons of Jonathan Edwards and of Charles Spurgeon for they will be treasured as long as the church is on the earth. For more recent publications, A. W. Tozer's small books are both convicting and exhilarating; John Piper's writings are a burning blend of spirit and truth.

As He has with my friend T. W., may the Lord bless you with a great and lifelong thirst for Himself, for surely He intends to satisfy it with Himself.

CHAPTER TWO

THE SUM AND SUBSTANCE OF THE PREPARATION
NEEDED FOR A COMING ETERNITY IS THAT YOU BELIEVE
WHAT THE BIBLE TELLS YOU AND DO WHAT THE BIBLE
BIDS YOU.

—THOMAS CHALMERS

ARE YOU GOVERNED INCREASINGLY BY GOD'S WORD?

WHAT DO YOU BELIEVE TO BE THE MOST VALUABLE TANGIBLE OBJECT in the world? Perhaps you think of something like the Hope Diamond, the *Mona Lisa*, Michelangelo's sculpture of David, or the gold burial mask of King Tut's tomb. As costly as these are, the price tag on some enormous skyscraper could be higher. And yet, offer any of these to an emaciated man who is hours from dying of thirst and hunger, and the relative value of the world's greatest treasures drops to nothing. Though inexpensive and often taken for granted, ultimately it is the basics of life—things such as food and water—that are most precious. For without them, there is no life at all.

Therefore, I submit that the single most valuable item on earth is the Bible. God's Word is like water, according to

Ephesians 5:26. It is also food. As the prophet Jeremiah said to God, "Your words were found, and I ate them, and Your word was to me the joy and rejoicing of my heart" (Jeremiah 15:16). Jesus Himself proclaimed that "man shall not live by bread alone, but by every word that proceeds from the mouth of God" (Matthew 4:4). It is true that without physical food our bodies would die in a matter of days. But without soul nourishment, we perish forever.

Food and water are essential, but there are other things basic to life, and the Word of God is compared to these as well. It is called a light (Psalm 119:105), a fire and a tool (Jeremiah 23:29), a weapon (Ephesians 6:17), and seed (1 Peter 1:23). Moreover, the Word of God is perfect, sure, right, pure, true and righteous, sweeter than honey, and to be desired more than much fine gold (Psalm 19:7-10). Indeed the psalmist exclaimed, "The law of Your mouth is better to me than thousands of coins of gold and silver" (Psalm 119:72). It can convert the soul, make wise the simple, rejoice the heart, and enlighten the eyes (Psalm 19:7-9). The Bible is unlike any other book, religious or secular, "for the word of God is living and powerful, and sharper than any two-edged sword, piercing even to the division of soul and spirit, and of joints and marrow, and is a discerner of the thoughts and intents of the heart" (Hebrews 4:12).

The written words of God are closely identified with God Himself. Through them He makes Himself most clearly known and declares to us the way to Himself through Christ. Without knowledge of God, no matter how long and prosperous one's earthly existence, life is meaningless and worthless. Thus no other object on earth is as valuable as the Bible, for nothing else can provide anything as essential or eternal.

Given the incomparable value of Scripture, the Christian's need for its constant influence cannot be overstated. God's Word is the manna by which the heavenly Father feeds His children so that they can grow more into the likeness of His perfect Son. That is why the Lord has told us to "desire the pure milk of the word, that you may grow thereby" (1 Peter 2:2).

While the Pharisees of Jesus' day and certain cult groups in our own are evidence that more is needed to become Christlike than megadoses of Scripture, still it is true that little input of God's Word results in little resemblance to God's Son. So one question by which you can evaluate your spiritual health and growth is, "Are you governed increasingly by God's Word?"

LIKE THE IMPRINT OF
WORDS UPON THE AIR

Do you find yourself inquiring—consciously—how the Bible speaks to specific areas of life? Do you ask others, perhaps those in spiritual leadership or who are mature, to help you apply Scripture in particular situations? Is it your practice to actually turn the pages of the Bible in search of the will of God?

Many professing Christians bump along from Sunday to Sunday, year to year, with no recollection of changes in beliefs or practices as a result of new discoveries in the Word. They would tell you they believe the same as they did years ago. They carry a Bible to church, but they couldn't tell you the last time their daily life was altered by it. They may even be daily Bible readers, and they have heard one or more sermons per week for years. Yet with all their exposure to the Bible, generally its inspired words leave no more imprint upon their minds than spoken words do upon the air. It could never be said of them that they deliberately govern their daily lives by God's Word.

In his nineteenth-century book *Personal Declension and Revival of Religion in the Soul*, British minister Octavius Winslow further described those in this spiritual regression:

> When a professing [Christian] man can read his Bible
> with no spiritual taste, or when he searches it, not
> with a sincere desire to know the mind of the Spirit in

order to [walk] a holy and obedient walk, but with a merely curious, or literary taste and aim, it is a sure evidence that his soul is making but a retrograde movement in real spirituality. Nothing perhaps more strongly indicates the tone of a believer's spirituality, than the light in which the Scriptures are regarded by him. They may be read, and yet be read as any other book, without the deep and solemn conviction that "all Scripture is given by inspiration of God, and is profitable for doctrine, for reproof, for correction, for instruction in righteousness; that the man of God may be perfect, thoroughly furnished unto all good works" (2 Timothy 3:16-17). They may be read without a spiritual relish, without being turned into prayer, without treasuring up in the heart and reducing to daily practice its holy precepts, its precious promises, its sweet consolations, its faithful warnings, its affectionate admonitions, its tender rebukes.[1]

The person who can content himself with few or routine contacts with Scripture may be manifesting something far worse than spiritual decline. The Bible characterizes a genuine believer as not merely an admirer of God's truth, but one who *loves* it. The writer of Psalm 119 said repeatedly:

- And I will delight myself in Your commandments, which I love. (verse 47)
- My hands also I will lift up to Your commandments, which I love. (verse 48)
- Oh, how I love Your law! It is my meditation all the day. (verse 97)
- I hate the double-minded, but I love Your law. (verse 113)
- You put away all the wicked of the earth like dross; therefore I love Your testimonies. (verse 119)

- Therefore I love Your commandments more than gold, yes, than fine gold! (verse 127)
- I hate and abhor lying, but I love Your law. (verse 163)

Conversely, Scripture speaks of nonChristians as "those who perish, because they did not receive the love of the truth, that they might be saved" (2 Thessalonians 2:10). John Piper noted, "Loving the truth is a matter of perishing or being saved. Indifference to the truth is a mark of spiritual death."[2]

Are you indifferent to the truth of Scripture? Are you in retrograde? Or does God's Word have a growing influence in your life?

You are reading this because you want to become more like Jesus Christ, right? What influence did Scripture have on *His* earthly life?

THE WORD GOVERNED BY THE WORD

Jesus, the Incarnate Word of God (John 1:1), was continually governed by the inscribed Word of God. Immediately prior to His emergence into public ministry came His baptism and then the temptation by Satan. In the furnace of that temptation, Jesus Christ went to Scripture alone. Repeatedly He repulsed the tempter's crafty beguilements with the words "It is written" (see Matthew 4:1-11).

Jesus might have reasoned, "Look, Satan, you know that I'm not only a man, I am God. Fully God. God cannot be tempted. You're wasting your time." He could have argued, "Don't you realize by now that you can't win?" or "My power is greater than yours." He might have challenged Satan to a contest of supernatural abilities, similar to the confrontation between Elijah and the prophets of Baal (see 1 Kings 18:20-40). Instead Jesus found all that He needed in what God the Father had spoken. For it was here that He hurled Deuteronomy 8:3

at His wicked enemy: "Man shall not live by bread alone, but by every word that proceeds from the mouth of God" (Matthew 4:4).

Throughout the Gospels we find Jesus quoting Scripture, often asking, "Have you never read?" He knew the Scriptures intimately. Why? Because He is God, the Author of the Scriptures? Yes, but too often we attribute Jesus' mastery of the Old Testament to His divinity. Though He was undiminished deity, Jesus quoted Scriptures He had memorized as a *man,* learning them from childhood in the same kinds of ways people like ourselves can.

As it was for Jesus, it is normal for Jesus' followers to be governed by Scripture. And those who are becoming more like Jesus will, over time, live more and more "by every word that proceeds from the mouth of God."

"TO THE LAW AND TO THE TESTIMONY!"

The prophet Isaiah lived in a time not unlike our own. People commonly sought answers in all the wrong places. "To the law and to the testimony!" the prophet directed his hearers (Isaiah 8:20). "If they do not speak according to this word," he warned, "it is because there is no light in them." In other words, if people's lives aren't guided by God's revelation, it's because they are in spiritual darkness. The light of God's Spirit has never dawned within them.

As Spirit-indwelled people grow to resemble Jesus more and more, they should think more quickly and more often, "To the law and to the testimony!" This means immediately asking yourself, "What does the Bible say?" when dealing with even the most common issues, whenever you have a question about *anything.*

How should my child be educated? How would God have me vote in this political election? Should I make this purchase? What are the right reasons for choosing a church? Is this man qualified to be our new pastor? How should our church—and I—reach people with the gospel? How much time at my job is too much? What should I do with my life when I retire from my career? All of life—events and choices great or small—should be governed by the Word of God.

To live this way requires the constant consultation of Scripture. And this is exactly what the well-known words of Psalm 119:105 imply: "Your word is a lamp to my feet and a light to my path." Wherever we go, whatever decisions are before us, the way of life should be illuminated by God's Word. To live otherwise is to walk in darkness.

No Christian, of course, always and perfectly lives in accordance with Scripture. Only Jesus has done that. So we speak of being governed by Scripture as (1) a general characteristic of a true follower of Jesus, and yet (2) something that *increasingly* characterizes the growing Christian. Speaking in a practical way, you know that God's Word is growing in its influence over you when you can point to increasing numbers of beliefs and actions that have been changed because of the potency of specific texts of Scripture. You can recall times when, like Apollos in Acts 18:26, you realized that you held to doctrinal error and then changed your position as you saw "the way of God more accurately." You remember various turning points where you stopped or started some action or habit as a result of a new understanding of biblical truth.

One testimony of this in my own life has been mentioned already (at the end of chapter 1), namely, how the Bible has increasingly governed my prayer life as I have let the words of God, and especially the Psalms, give direction to my prayers.

Here is another. During my first nineteen years of pastoral ministry, I purposelessly evaluated what was or was not appropriate for worship based more upon personal preference, expedience, and "Will anyone be offended by this?" than upon what Scripture said. If I could think of nothing in the Bible against what I was considering, I assumed it was acceptable for worship. I began to see that a more deliberately biblical way of being governed by God's Word is to look for a positive indication from Scripture that the proposed element should be a part of public worship. So rather than asking, "Is there anything in the Bible *forbidding* it?" I have learned to ask, "Is there any biblical command, example, or sanction *supporting* this activity in worship?" This made a difference, for instance, in giving me intentionality about singing more psalms in worship (see Ephesians 5:19 and Colossians 3:16) than I had previously.

One more example of how the Lord has been reshaping my life to conform more to His Word has to do with my beliefs and practice about the Lord's Day. Most conservative, Bible-believing Christians I know seem to make few choices about their Lord's Day activities based on Scripture. Rather they base their choices on their culture—their family culture, church culture, or the culture of society at large. So whether they go to the mall, watch football, play golf, eat out, take a nap, work in the yard, or whatever, they do what they do more because of the traditions of their family, church, or community than because of what the Bible says. If everyone in the church talks about and watches the big NFL game on Sunday, they probably will too. Or if they do not watch the game, it's only because they don't like football or they have something else they would rather do or must do. Regardless, the decision is not made consciously for biblical reasons.

As I examined the Scriptures pertaining to this issue, my habits on the Lord's Day were transformed. The Bible has directed me on this matter in ways that are refreshing, restorative, and recreative for my soul, mind, body, and family. In summary, I have understood the Bible to teach that my greatest privilege and first responsibility on the Lord's Day is to worship Him with His people. Also, because the first day of the week is called in Scripture "the Lord's Day" (Revelation 1:10), the day should be observed uniquely for the Lord, and every activity

34

should be evaluated by that fact. However *you* choose to spend the Lord's Day, I appeal to you to base your decisions and actions on the revelation of God.

The Bible should be the measure and evaluator of all things in the life of every believer. God categorically claims that His Word can equip us for *every* good work: "All Scripture is given by inspiration of God, and is profitable for doctrine, for reproof, for correction, for instruction in righteousness, that the man of God may be complete, thoroughly equipped for every good work" (2 Timothy 3:16-17). Here are some ways you can begin to prove this enormously important truth.

DEVELOPING YOUR DEPENDENCE ON GOD'S WORD

Deepen your desire for God's Word. Do you "desire the pure milk of the word, that you may grow thereby" (1 Peter 2:2)? Without spiritual food there is no spiritual growth. And one of the best ways for acquiring a taste for God's food and cultivating this Spirit-given appetite is simply to discipline yourself to feast on it. Nothing can make us hungry for Scripture more than Scripture itself.

For starters, make sure you are in a church with heartfelt, conscience-stirring preaching that clearly comes from the pages of Scripture. At this point in my life I preach in a different church almost every Lord's Day. In some towns I ask myself, "What would I do if I lived here?" for it is evident that a famine of God's Word exists there. Maybe you live in such a place. You've had the same sparse spiritual diet from the pulpit for so long that even though you are starving, you're almost too spiritually weak to take action. Don't give up and don't fail to assume responsibility. Seek out good nourishment through radio, tapes, CDs, audio over the Internet, and so forth.

Let me say again that praying through Scripture is an excellent way to rekindle a craving for it. And once more, don't simply read the Bible, *meditate* on it. Choose at least one verse from your reading and think about it. What do the words tell you about Christ? How can you experience deeper communion with Him because of what's written there? For what situation or person could you use the passage as a basis of prayer? Try rewriting the verse in your own words. Find at least one way you could apply it. Read less, if necessary, in order to meditate more. There are astonishing promises attached to the meditation of Scripture (see Joshua 1:8; Psalm 1:1-3; James 1:25). What praying through Scripture can do to reinvigorate your prayer life, meditation on Scripture can do to revitalize all forms of your Bible intake.

And if you want guidance specifically regarding the *desire* for God's Word, pray through or meditate on Psalm 119 until you believe that your own heart is represented in that glorious chapter. Let the God-breathed words of that passage breathe the freshest of air into your soul.

Make time for God's Word. If you can't do this, you aren't dependent on Scripture—and never will be. Just as we schedule times to eat our physical food, so we must do the same for our spiritual food. From this moment forward, adopt as your own the resolution of Jonathan Edwards: "Resolved, To study the Scriptures so steadily, constantly, and frequently, as that I may find and plainly perceive myself to grow in the knowledge of the same."[3]

Read the Bible daily and do not close it until you know at least one thing God would have you do in response to your reading. This response might involve something new to believe, a habit to begin or break, a prayer to offer, a conversation to initiate, a letter or E-mail to send, a phone call to make, a spiritual discipline to practice, or something else. Read the Bible for application, not merely for information.

List at least five areas you have not recently considered from a biblical perspective. Then search the Scriptures and prayerfully consider one area each day for the next five days. Here are five major areas or segments of life, with ten categories under each as thought-starters.

- *Church:* attendance, baptism, membership, serving in, giving to, learning in, praying with, fellowship, Lord's Supper, promoting unity
- *Discipleship:* meditation on Scripture, prayer, evangelism, missions, priorities/stewardship of time, fasting, silence and solitude, journaling, learning/reading, legalism vs. consistency
- *Family:* marriage, family crisis, unconverted family members, childlessness, dealing with aging parents, parenting children, parenting teenagers, divorce, sex, family devotions
- *Money:* giving, saving, investing, controlling debt, contentment, budgeting, gambling, wasting, not loving it, simplifying with less
- *Work:* purpose, amount of, travel, attitude toward, dependability, integrity, witness at, relationships (with boss, coworkers, customers, suppliers), integration of faith with, retirement

Train yourself to ask "How does the Bible speak to this?" To do this is a manifestation of love for God and love for His will. This is to see wisdom and sweetness in the ways of God. God made us to be governed by His Spirit through His Word. Let us learn to find His glory and our joy by living in accordance with His loving design.

CHAPTER THREE

THE MORE A PERSON LOVES, THE CLOSER HE
APPROACHES THE IMAGE OF GOD.
— MARTIN LUTHER

ARE YOU
MORE LOVING?

LET ME GET RIGHT TO THE POINT. JESUS SAID THAT LOVE IS THE clearest mark of a Christian. "A new commandment I give to you," He announced in John 13:34-35, "that you love one another; as I have loved you, that you also love one another. By this all will know that you are My disciples, if you have love for one another." If you are growing in your love for others—especially in your love for Christians—then you are growing as a Christian.

Notice in God's Word the importance He places on love by Christians (emphasis added):

- "This is My commandment, that you *love one another* as I have loved you." (John 15:12)
- "These things I command you, that you *love one another*." (John 15:17)
- *Be kindly affectionate to one another with brotherly love.* (Romans 12:10)

- Owe no one anything except to *love one another,* for he who loves another has fulfilled the law. (Romans 13:8)
- *Let all that you do be done with love.* (1 Corinthians 16:14)
- For all the law is fulfilled in one word, even in this: *"You shall love your neighbor as yourself."* (Galatians 5:14)
- And *walk in love,* as Christ also has loved us and given Himself for us. (Ephesians 5:2)
- But concerning brotherly love you have no need that I should write to you, for you yourselves are taught by God to *love one another.* (1 Thessalonians 4:9)
- And let us consider one another in order to *stir up love* and good works. (Hebrews 10:24)
- *Let brotherly love continue.* (Hebrews 13:1)
- If you really fulfill the royal law according to the Scripture, *"You shall love your neighbor as yourself,"* you do well. (James 2:8)
- Since you have purified your souls in obeying the truth through the Spirit in sincere love of the brethren, *love one another fervently* with a pure heart. (1 Peter 1:22)
- And above all things *have fervent love for one another.* (1 Peter 4:8)
- For this is the message that you heard from the beginning, that we should *love one another.* (1 John 3:11)
- And this is His commandment: that we should believe on the name of His Son Jesus Christ and *love one another*, as He gave us commandment. (1 John 3:23)
- And this commandment we have from Him: that he who loves God must *love his brother also.* (1 John 4:21)
- And now I plead with you, . . . not as though I wrote a new commandment to you, but that which we have had from the beginning: that we *love one another.* (2 John 5)

Love is the badge and character of Christianity. A Christian may advance in many areas, including the ability to witness, teach, or even preach ("Though I speak with the tongues of men and of angels"), or biblical insight and knowledge ("And though I . . . understand all mysteries and all knowledge"), or faith, service, and giving ("and though I have all faith, . . . and though I bestow all my goods to feed the poor, and though I give my body to be burned"), but these mean little ("I have become sounding brass or a clanging cymbal. . . . I am nothing. . . . It profits me nothing") without growth in the most important Christian distinctive—love (1 Corinthians 13:1-3).

THE DECLINE OF LOVE

When love grows colder, our sin increasingly manifests itself and we look more *unlike* Jesus. We lose patience easily, whereas 1 Corinthians 13:4 says that "Love suffers long." Unkindness becomes common, yet love "is kind." We become sinfully envious of the advantages and privileges of others, perhaps even of those within our own family; conversely, "love does not envy." When challenged about our lack of love, we quickly and quite confidently list all the sacrifices and other proofs of our love, and yet "love does not parade itself, is not puffed up." As our hearts harden against love, we become less courteous, especially to those closest to us, in contrast to love which "does not behave rudely" (1 Corinthians 13:5). We begin to consider ourselves and our "rights" as more important than others and their needs, whereas love "does not seek its own." When love is in decline we are more easily angered, but love "is not provoked." A lack of love is often faultfinding, and it mentally keeps score of offenses, but love "thinks no evil."

We're not growing in love when we have time for projects but not for people. Love is on the downgrade when it fails to protect, whether it's the reputation of friends or coworkers, or the physical *and* spiritual health of family members. Love has cooled when it is unwilling to confront when necessary. In the church this may manifest itself by a lack of support for biblical church discipline. You do not love others if you will let them ruin their lives, their testimony, their reputation, and bring shame upon the church and the name of Christ, and you are unwilling to try to rescue them according to God's plan (see Matthew 18:15-20 and 1 Corinthians 5) from the sin that has deceived them.

Love's decline may also be typified by unconcern for the lost. We become less sensitive to the physical needs of people and less burdened by others' spiritual needs. A declining love acts but is not "without hypocrisy" (Romans 12:9). Love's decline is not "given to hospitality" (verse 13). It is too indifferent to "rejoice with those who rejoice, and weep with those who weep" (verse 15). Perhaps worst of all, it is apathetic about the rise of things in the heart and life that are *contrary* to love.

The only person who loved without fail was Jesus Christ. Neither the apostle Paul, nor the apostle John, nor your favorite hero from Christian history always lived by the 1 Corinthians 13 standard of love. Scottish pastor Maurice Roberts observed that when it comes to growing in love, "The best believers find their progress slow and their attainments meager."[1] The point, however, is not speed, but direction. Are you making convincing progress in love, however slow, or are you regressing?

WHAT KIND OF LOVE?

Some people flatter themselves about how loving they are. They know that nothing means more to them than their children. Holidays are always spent with family. They consider themselves good neighbors and devoted friends. As their family and circle of friends grow, their love grows with it, right?

The Bible alone, and not our own hearts (which the Bible

depicts in Jeremiah 17:9 as "deceitful above all things, and desperately wicked") should be our standard both to define love and to describe it in practice. Too often we wrongly classify as love what the *King James Version* of the Bible calls "natural affection" (see Romans 1:31 and 2 Timothy 3:3). In normal circumstances, parents love their children, family members love each other, and people love their friends. This is true for Christians and nonChristians alike. God made us in such a way that, even in a fallen world, we naturally love certain people, thus the term *natural* affection.

Many people, therefore, are congratulating themselves for what amounts to merely being human, and they conclude amiss that this innate love testifies of spiritual health. Natural affection, however, is just one of several pretenders to the kind of love only those indwelt by the Holy Spirit can express. In his eighteenth-century masterpiece *Religious Affections,* Jonathan Edwards warned of these imitations, referring first to true Christian love:

> 'Tis the chief of the graces of God's Spirit, and the life,
> essence and sum of all true religion; and that by
> which we are most conformed to Heaven, and most
> contrary to hell and the devil. But yet it is ill arguing
> from hence, that there are no counterfeits of it. It may
> be observed, that the more excellent anything is, the
> more will be the counterfeits of it.[2]

Besides natural affection, there is another counterfeit love. Its loving actions are only a veneer for too much self-love. Any benefits it brings to others are secondary to the question, "Does it please me first?" A man will be absolutely convinced that he loves a beautiful woman, and indeed will do almost anything for her. He adores her, thinks of her constantly, and wants nothing more than her. But the truth is, he loves her only for what she does to and for *him.* She excites, intrigues, and arouses him. He does want her to be happy, but in reality he wants her to find her happiness in bringing pleasure to him. And he continues to love her only to the degree that she continues to please him. He will do nothing for her willingly or without hypocrisy unless it brings pleasure for him to do it anyway. This kind of love is just as common in other relationships as romantic ones. With parents or children, siblings, neighbors, or friends, we can act in loving ways, but either heartlessly or only because it pleases us to do so. We do not measure our growth in Christlikeness by the vicissitudes of this kind of love.

A similar counterfeit is the "I'll love you if you'll love me" type of love. This kind of love doesn't originate from a commitment to love, nor from a desire to be like Christ, but simply dispenses love as *quid pro quo*. This is not Christian love, rather it is the epitome of worldly love. Jesus put it this way: "But if you love those who love you, what credit is that to you? For even sinners love those who love them" (Luke 6:32). Edwards portrayed those who love like this:

> They are full of dear affections to some, and full of
> bitterness toward others. They are knit to their own
> party, them that approve of them, love them and
> admire them; but are fierce against those that oppose
> and dislike them. Some show a great affection for
> their neighbors, . . . the children of God abroad; and
> at the same time are uncomfortable and churlish
> towards their wives and other near relations at home,
> and are very negligent of relative duties.[3]

Can anyone think he is growing in love and thus becoming more like Jesus when, just like those who hated Jesus, he only loves with a reciprocal love? The test of Christlikeness is not the greatness of your love toward those who love you, but the bounty of your love toward those who do not.

Then there is the counterfeit of unbalanced love. It fails to treat people as a unity of body and soul, with both elements having legitimate needs. Again, Edwards exposes the error in this love:

> Some men show a love to others as to their outward man, they are liberal of their worldly substance, and often give to the poor; but have no love to, or concern for the souls of men. Others pretend a great love to men's souls, [but] are not compassionate and charitable towards their bodies. The making of a great show of love, pity, and distress for souls, costs 'em nothing; but in order to show mercy to men's bodies, they must part with money out of their pockets. But a true Christian herein is like the love and compassion of Jesus Christ. He showed mercy to men's souls, by laboring for them in preaching the gospel to them; and showed mercy to their bodies, in going about doing good, healing all manner of sickness and diseases among the people. We have a remarkable instance of Christ's having compassion at once both to men's souls and bodies, and showing compassion by feeding both, in Mark 6:34 etc.[4]

Jesus came primarily to save sinners forever, not merely to heal their short-lived bodies. His greatest display of love for us was in His death, for through it we experience the love of God unto eternal life. And the most loving thing we can ever do for anyone is give them the words that can lead to immortality in a radiantly glorious body. But "let us not love in word or in tongue, but in deed and in truth" (1 John 3:18). Those growing in Jesus' kind of love will not only say loving words but also do loving deeds, just as He did. (See chapter 5 for more on this subject of meeting both spiritual and practical needs.)

LOVE IN REAL LIFE

Those who are growing in love will demonstrate it in at least three areas. First, their *love for other Christians* will strengthen. One of the clearest indications that we have the Spirit of God is love for others in whom He lives: "We know that we have passed from death to life, because we love the brethren" (1 John 3:14). Relationships with Christian brothers and sisters in the church become indispensable to those who share eternal life. Like Christ, true Christians have a love for nonChristians, but they have a preferential love for those who love Christ. Just as we love many people, yet have a deeper love for those in our families, so we in God's family love one another more than we love those who hate Christ and His people. And as we are able, the Bible says that we should *express* our love by doing good to all people, but particularly those in our spiritual family: "Therefore as we have opportunity, let us do good to all, especially to those who are of the household of faith" (Galatians 6:10).

A second area of growth in love is *love for the lost.* A wealthy young man once came to Jesus and asked what he must do to inherit eternal life. The young man assumed he was in fairly good standing because he had tried to keep the Ten Commandments. But after he asserted this, "Jesus, looking at him," reports Mark 10:21, *"loved him,* and said to him, 'One thing you lack: Go your way, sell whatever you have and give to the poor, and you will have treasure in heaven; and come, take up the cross, and follow Me'" (emphasis added). In showing love to this man, Jesus did not compromise His message. He made it unmistakable that to have eternal life the man must forsake his god (that is, his possessions) and put Christ first. Although there is no indication that the man became Jesus' disciple, Jesus loved him nonetheless. The more we are like Jesus, the more we manifest the fruit of the Spirit and the more loving we will be to *everyone,* including those who are cold to the things of God. Jesus said we are even to love our enemies, and not just those who love us (Luke 6:27,32).

My wife, Caffy, has spent several hours recently doing home renovation for an unconverted couple we've come to love very much. She's doing it because she wants to love them toward Christ, that is, to show a sweaty love that might gain a hearing for the gospel. She has more than enough of her own work to do, but she is, to use Puritan Ralph Venning's term, "un-selfing" at this time because of her love for God, and the gospel, and her growing love for these people who, at present, are not interested in our message.

A third area to examine when measuring your growth in love is *love for your family.* For many who are reading these lines, this will be the most brutal part of the evaluation. Nowhere are we more aware of our unloving words and ways than at home. And yet, who we really are, we are at home. Even so, we must never believe that it is impossible to grow in love toward our family members. God does not derisively give us commands such as Ephesians 5:25: "Husbands, love your wives, just as Christ also loved the church and gave Himself for her." All Christians are meant to be growing Christians, and that includes observable growth in love for family members. Over time, those in your family—your spouse, your children, your parents, your siblings—should feel that you love them more than you used to. Maybe that will be expressed in more gratitude than previously, or less anger, or more physical affection, or more patience, responsibility, generosity, frugality, or simply by having more time for them.

In some areas, of course, an unbeliever could appear to be growing in love to a degree similar to that of a Christian. For example, if I had an unconverted neighbor who would rather watch a football game on TV, but he takes his daughter to the park instead, and I'd rather read, but I take my little girl to the park, why am I manifesting Christian love and my neighbor isn't? If a nonChristian and I do the same thing—namely, give up our own desires in order to willingly spend time with our children—why is my love "Christian" and his isn't? In both cases we show love because (1) our conscience tells us to do it, and (2) we're willing to put others before ourselves.

What's different for the Christian is that he also acts as he does because he believes what he's doing is the will of God. His love is more than self-sacrifice, for it contains a vertical God-ward dimension as well as a horizontal one. The awareness that you are doing something pleasing to God adds a quality and depth to love, as well as a satisfaction in the exercise of it, that the natural affection of the world cannot reproduce.

Moreover, the motive of Christian love at its best includes another facet that worldlings are incapable of knowing. Because "the love of God has been poured out in our hearts by the Holy Spirit who was given to us" (Romans 5:5), we are able to love out of the extravagant outpouring of God's love for us. An unbeliever can only pump love from his own limited, stagnant, brackish human reserves. The Christian, on the other hand, can pour out love from the love God pours in. He can show a love to others that effervesces from the fountain of his delight in knowing God. As John Piper put it, "Love is the overflow of joy in God which gladly meets the needs of others."[5] Jonathan Edwards adds, "It is love that arises from an apprehension of the wonderful riches of free grace and sovereignty of God's love to us in Christ Jesus."[6]

So, Christian, love begins with God. We love because He first loved us. Then the more satisfaction and delight we find in His love, the more we delight in loving others. The more enjoyment we find in God as God, the more we truly enjoy being like Him by loving others. The more we grow in our joy in God, the more joy we find in the joy others find in our loving actions.

CULTIVATING LOVE

Maurice Roberts asks,

> Why is real Christian love so scarce in the world? It is
> because its cultivation requires nothing less than the
> *reversal* of every instinct in our fallen natures. Love is
> against the grain of nature. It is against *every* fiber of
> our being as sinners. But nature, in the regenerate, is
> under the higher power of grace. . . . What the unre-
> generate cannot do, true Christians may and must.[7]

Whether this chapter has comforted you or confronted you,
until you see Christ in Heaven you will always need to grow in
love. Regardless of where you are now, here are some workable
suggestions for maturing in the most Christlike of graces.

*Meditate on love as the most important distinguishing mark
of a Christian.* In his article, "The Supreme Grace of Christian
Love," Roberts wrote, "Love is the jewel among the graces of
the Christian life. We know it—and perpetually forget it."[8] But
don't just *remember* that love is the primary insignia of a Christian, *think* about it. I've known some Christians who, by the
emphasis of their lives, stress knowledge or orthodoxy over
love. While they would verbally assent to the priority of love,
they almost seem to say as an excuse not to love, "But that's not
my gift." Love is a gift from God, but not *that* kind of gift. Love
is not the sort of spiritual gift like teaching or mercy (see the lists
of gifts in Romans 12; 1 Corinthians 12; Ephesians 4) that we
can say was given to some but not to us. Instead, the Bible
insists, "He who does not love does not know God"
(1 John 4:8). Do you give primacy to the pursuit of being more
loving? If you want to grow in love, think about love. Review
the Scriptures in the introductory section of this chapter to help
in your meditation.

Let your heart be often warmed by the fire of God's love.
God is the Source of the love that flames in the Christian heart.

We must bask in His love before we can expect it to consistently blaze forth from us toward others. This means, in part, that frequently in your times of prayer and meditation on Scripture you should let some aspect of God's love—especially the Cross—allure your attention like the mesmerizing flames in a fireplace. Pray much to "be able to comprehend with all the saints what is the width and length and depth and height—to know the love of Christ which passes knowledge" (Ephesians 3:18-19). "God is love," wrote an eminent Dutch minister of the late 1600s, "and having communion with God will cause us to grow warm in love."[9]

Discover assurance that God is your Father by loving as He loves. Because "love is of God," the inspired apostle John reasons, therefore "everyone who loves is born of God" (1 John 4:7). God's nature is love, and those who have His nature are His children. I recently saw a baby alligator. If I pointed to it and claimed, "That's my child," no one would take me seriously. Any child of mine would be born with a human nature, not that of an alligator. Anyone "born of God" will have His nature, that is, His loving nature. If you love to love others because you experience genuine joy at the joy prompted in others by your actions, take heart: those who show such love are the children of God.

Delight in imitating God. This is not a mystical platitude or a new ager's aspiration. The Bible speaks plainly about imitating God by showing love: "Therefore be imitators of God as dear children. And walk in love, as Christ also has loved us and given Himself for us" (Ephesians 5:1-2). To quote Roberts again, "Love, in its essence, is likeness to God."[10] Love people at times and in ways when you can thrill at the awareness, "I am being like God as I do this!"

Identify those relationships where you most need to grow in love. Does your family come to mind first? How about someone with whom you work? A neighbor? A person at church? Target specific people as you grow in love, not just everyone in general. In particular, *who* would know that your love is more Christlike, and *how* would they know? Once these faces are in your mind, . . .

Take the initiative in showing love, especially where you have little or no expectation of love in return. Let your delight in imitating God be enough, regardless of the response your loving initiatives receive. Isn't that what Jesus did? Aren't you reading this because you want to grow more like Him?

CHAPTER FOUR

IF THE SOUL OF THE BELIEVER IS IN A HEALTHY CON-
DITION, HE WILL TAKE OCCASION TO FREQUENTLY
COME INTO GOD'S PRESENCE ON PURPOSE TO HAVE
COMMUNION WITH HIM.

—A. W. PINK

ARE YOU MORE SENSITIVE TO GOD'S PRESENCE?

WHEN WAS THE LAST TIME YOU THOUGHT, "GOD IS HERE"? PERHAPS it was during a time of unusually Spirit-anointed preaching of Holy Scripture. I recall a conference when the Lord seemed to be speaking so powerfully through the preacher of His Word that tears were coursing down my cheeks. I had been similarly moved before, but this time I didn't want to distract myself for even a couple of seconds to wipe the tears away lest I miss something from this experience with God.

Maybe you have felt God's presence in an extraordinary way during a time of passionate prayer with God's people. The Lord may have seemed so close that you were almost convinced that if you opened your eyes you would see Him.

Your Father may have been especially near in some experience in nature, as when reveling in the majestic grandeur of a Rocky Mountain vista or when awestruck while contemplating the sparkling immensity of the galaxy on a clear winter's night.

You may have perceived the nearness of the Holy One, as I have, while walking in solitude across a field or down a wooded path, hands in pockets, on a leisurely Lord's Day afternoon during leaf-turning season. Maybe you remember feeling enveloped in the presence of God in some placid place, a still moment at home without a single electronic hum anywhere and no grinding roar from any yard in the neighborhood. It could have been in the soundless serenity of a lakeside sunset when the coolness of the autumn evening carried you in reverie to the awareness of the presence of the Prince of Peace.

By contrast, you may have been thrust suddenly into a knowledge of God's closeness during an emotionally charged moment, as in a split-second, adrenaline-rushed deliverance from a car accident that appeared to be unavoidable. Or His presence may have been deeply felt in soft lamplight during tender gazes at the fingers and face of your sleeping newborn.

And surely you have known those moments in magnificent congregational worship when the Lord of glory seemed to be towering over the forest of exultant voices—those moments when God's presence is almost atmospheric.

But *how often* are you aware of the presence of God? If we take the teaching of the Bible seriously, perception of the presence of God should not be an occasional experience. I do not mean that we should frequently *feel* a supernatural presence, for that can be extremely unreliable. Nevertheless, it should not be unusual for us, wherever we are, to recognize that "God is here." As we grow closer to Him, generally speaking, we should discern His immanence more readily and more often.

"SURELY THE LORD IS IN THIS PLACE, AND I DID NOT KNOW IT"

Apparently, many professing Christians identify more with the words of Jacob "Surely the Lord is in this place, and I did not know it" (Genesis 28:16) than with the promise of Jesus when He said, "I am with you always" (Matthew 28:20). According to one survey, "Two out of every three adults (68 percent) who describe themselves as Protestant, Catholic or Christian say that *at some time* in their lives they felt as if they were in God's presence."[1] At some time? That means virtually nothing, for the same survey reveals that "more than half of all *non*Christians . . . (58 percent) also indicated that they felt they have been in His presence."[2] Furthermore, "among those who describe their church as being Protestant, Catholic or Christian, . . . one out of every eight (13 percent) has felt God's presence *one* or *two* times in their lives and 32 percent have *never* sensed His presence in their lives."[3] From those in the survey who openly described themselves as "born again Christians," the results were stunning: "one-third (32 percent) have either *never* felt God's presence or have sensed it *only once* or *twice* in their lives!"[4] (emphasis added).

What will result from a true Christian's dullness to God's company? For one thing, it necessarily means thinking less often of God, His Word, and His will. This is not a great deal different than an unbeliever who rarely thinks of God.

Insensitivity to the nearness of God certainly means less awareness that "the eyes of the LORD are in every place, keeping watch on the evil and the good" (Proverbs 15:3). That leads to thinking less of restraining sin on the one hand, or of doing good on the other. For after all, who will know? At such times we imitate Moses when "he looked this way and that way, and when he saw no one, he killed the Egyptian" (Exodus 2:12). No matter who we do *not* see, we must never forget the One whose presence is unseen yet more real than any other.

In effect, living apart from a conscious sense that the Lord is present is to live as though God really is *not* there. More pleasure is sought in things, dreams, or people than in God. A relationship with God is reduced to mere religion. The spiritual disciplines devolve into mere duty or even legalism. Public worship becomes an obligation, not a privilege. Obviously, this is not the profile of a growing Christian.

HOW DO WE DISCERN GOD'S PRESENCE?

Before proceeding, we should understand there are several meanings to the term "the presence of God." Theologians speak of:

- *The universal presence of God.* This is also called God's omnipresence, meaning that He is everywhere, and that there is no place where God is not. (See Psalm 139:5-12 and Jeremiah 23:24.) That God is everywhere, however, does not mean that God is everything. Where there is a tree, God is an infinite Person who is everywhere that tree is, but the tree is not God.
- *The Christological presence of God.* God was and is present in Jesus Christ. See John 1:1,14 and Colossians 2:9. Jesus is Immanuel, "God with us" (Matthew 1:23).
- *The indwelling presence of God.* God is present by His Holy Spirit in a unique way within Christians. See John 14:16-17. He is a second, distinct Person living with us in our bodies.
- *The perceptible presence of God.* God's presence is often perceived through His work or influence. See Luke 1:66 and Acts 11:21. This is usually what is meant when we speak of someone, say, after a powerful sermon or personal witness, "The Lord was with him."
- *The heavenly presence of God.* God's presence is manifest in Heaven as in no other place. See Matthew 6:9 and 18:10. It is the presence of God that makes it Heaven. His

glory and splendor are displayed there as nowhere else.

- *The eternal presence of God.* God's presence will either be
  forever enjoyed in Heaven or forever forfeited in hell.
  See Revelation 21:3 and 2 Thessalonians 1:9. However,
  because God is omnipresent, there is some sense in
  which He is even in hell. It is not the absence, but the
  presence of God in hell that is so terrifying and torment-
  ing. He will be present, but manifesting only His divine
  wrath and justice, without His love and mercy.

All access to the presence of God, with His universal presence excepted, is through Jesus Christ. God the Son is the way
to God the Father; no one comes to the Father except through
Jesus (see John 14:6). "For there is one God," we are taught in
1 Timothy 2:5, "and one Mediator between God and men, the
Man Christ Jesus." So when it comes to discerning the presence
of God, one must first be "Immanuelized." That is to say, you
can't reliably recognize the presence of "God with us" until you
experience "Christ in you, the hope of glory" (Colossians 1:27).
To know this indwelling presence of Christ, one must first, in
Jesus' words, "Repent, and believe in the gospel" (Mark 1:15).

God's universal presence surrounds us as the air surrounds
the soaring eagle or the Pacific engulfs the dolphin as it dives,
"for in Him we live and move and have our being" (Acts 17:28).
Even so, we could never discern the presence of God rightly
and in truth if He did not first reveal Himself to us. He has
revealed Himself generally to us through creation (Romans
1:20), but much more specifically through the Word. His self-
revealing Word has come to us in two living ways: the incarnate Word (Jesus) and the written Word (the Bible). And it is
through His Word that our experience with God, including our
perception of His presence, is mediated.

What does this mean? It means that we don't try to experience the presence of God just any way that pleases us. I am

concerned by current trends in evangelical spirituality toward mysticism, or what is sometimes called Christian mysticism. The essence of mysticism is the attempt to experience God unmediated, that is, without means. This is the belief that apart from any external assistance, you enter *directly* into an experience of the presence of God. Often this will be described as looking deep within your soul to meet the indwelling presence of God, or to imagine Him sitting with you. The problem is, as spiritual as this may sound, the Bible never commands us to do this or ever describes such an experience.[5]

Rather, what we are told to do is (1) seek Him through His Word, or (2) seek Him through experiences that are founded on His Word, or (3) seek Him through daily life in ways that are informed by His Word. In these ways, God is revealed and mediated to us through the gift He gave for that purpose: His Word.

As I read and meditate on Scripture, for example, or listen to it preached, I can expect to become aware that this is the voice of God I am hearing. As I participate in the ordained experiences of congregational worship and the Lord's Supper, by faith I can expect to find Christ's spiritual presence there. And when I'm walking in a forest or through the door to the place where I work, I can seek and sense the presence of God in such moments because the Bible informs me that God is there as well.

But this is different from the mystical way of just somehow "opening up" to the presence of God. A pagan or pantheist could do that. The difference for the Christian is that he can pursue and perceive the presence of God, not in an *im*mediate (that is, unmediated) way, but mediated through truth that is revealed by God in the Bible. That's how a man or woman can walk into the workplace and say silently, "The Lord is here. I know that because God has said He is everywhere." And based upon that truth, he or she can affirm and enjoy the presence of God there.

When we seek the presence of God mediated—directly or indirectly—through Scripture, we are not imagining God as we would like Him to be. The basis of our experience with God is God-revealed truth, not our individual, idiosyncratic opinions about God. We are then much more likely to sense the presence of God as He really is rather than as a God comprised of our preferences. (And, incidentally, we are less likely to spout the motto of those who have made God into what they want Him to be: "My God isn't like that!")

At the moment, I am sitting in a porch swing, looking at green leafy trees with the late-August afternoon sun on them. The air is still. The summer evening insect noises have just begun. A blackbird *skreees* seventy-five yards to my right, hidden in a row of trees behind my neighbor's yard. Two houses down a teenager's radio is playing indistinctly. Far away is the drone of a lawnmower. God is here. Do I know that because I can feel Him? No, a nonChristian neighbor also could have a "spiritual experience" and call the experience, which is very real, something *other* than a sense of the presence of God. But I *know* God is here and I can enjoy His presence. How do I know? The Bible tells me so. I base my experience with God upon the Word of God.

But my experience with God must go beyond just knowing He is present, closer than my own breath, nearer than my own skin. The Bible also tells me of the *character* of the God who is present. So I know that I am to seek to experience a God who is not merely present, but holy. And I know that He is merciful and patient and enjoys having me talk with Him. I know there is One keeping company with me who knows everything about me at this (and every) moment—my thoughts, my motives, my fears, my aspirations, my emotions, my anxieties, my mental and physical condition—and who loves me beyond my comprehension. I know that the One whose presence surrounds me as the universe surrounds the earth has all power and is bringing all the world to His appointed conclusion. I perceive the presence of the One who has been an earthbound man like me and understands me thoroughly, and before whom I will stand in judgment. I engage the One who gave His life—from His first breath in Bethlehem to His last heartbeat on Calvary—to atone for my sins and who rose again to bring me to His heavenly home.

This is very different from seeking the presence of a virtually unknown god, a god about whom nothing is clear, distinct, or known. That would lead me to seek an experience rather than a Person, or else not be able to distinguish a Person from a presence. Without a mediated sense of God's presence, how can I know I have indeed encountered the God of the Bible? How can I be sure that I haven't delved into the recesses of a mysterious, imaginative mind and simply manufactured an experience? How do I even reassure myself (and others) that I have not in fact encountered a demonic presence masterfully masquerading as an "angel of light" (2 Corinthians 11:14)?

In his classic book on devotion to God, *The Knowledge of the Holy*, A. W. Tozer wrote of the person who apprehends the presence of God in the correct manner. To this one

> "the practice of the presence of God" consists not of
> projecting an imaginary object from within his own
> mind and then seeking to realize its presence; it is
> rather to recognize the real presence of the One
> whom all sound theology declares to be already there,
> an objective entity, existing apart from any apprehen-
> sion of Him on the part of His creatures. The resultant
> experience is not visionary but real.[6]

So when I ask if you are more sensitive to God's presence than ever before, I'm not asking if you have had mystical experiences with an atmospheric sense of the Lord's nearness. Rather I'm inquiring whether you have increasingly paused to recognize the Lord's presence where you are and to consider who it is who is present, based upon His self-revelation. Have you been feasting on the sweetness of His presence, adoring the beauty of His presence, by delighting your mind in the revealed attributes of the omnipresent Lord?

GROWING THROUGH GOD'S DESERTIONS

I do not want to imply that to be growing spiritually means you must consistently increase your awareness of the presence of God. You can be growing when you least sense intimacy with the Lord.

In the first place, I doubt that any Christian grows more aware of God's presence every day and steadily for the rest of his life. That denies the realities of living as a sinner in a fallen world. Second, it is common for believers to have many seasons where, for their own spiritual good, God actually withdraws a conscious sense of His presence. The Puritans referred to such occasions as "God's desertions," times when we feel as though God has forgotten and forsaken us.[7] But even though God's presence is not perceived, He is no less near.

In *Pilgrim's Progress*, John Bunyan's timeless allegory on the spiritual life, the main character, Christian, travels through a dark and terrifying place called the Valley of the Shadow of Death. It is described as the worst trial through which he had yet come, and he had never felt so alone. Not only did the voice of God seem silent, but Christian also was so perplexed that "he did not know his own voice" from the blasphemies whispered to him by his spiritual enemy. "Sometimes," wrote Bunyan, "he had half a thought to go back; then again he thought he might be halfway through the Valley: . . . and that the danger of going back might be much more than for to go forward; so he resolved to go on."[8] And though Christian felt completely on his own, he was not. Pressing forward by faith alone he grew in ways he did not comprehend at the time.

If, while reading this chapter, you have thought, "I haven't been sensing God's presence much lately," take note that it's one thing to long for a sense of God's presence while not experiencing it, and another to live routinely with no awareness of His absence. There is a world of difference between Jesus crying out from the cross, "My God, My God, why have You forsaken Me?" (Matthew 27:46), and Samson saying just before his capture, "'I will go out as before, at other times,' . . . but he did not know that the LORD had departed from him" (Judges 16:20). One is known by its agony, the other by its apathy. Though you may be progressing in Christlikeness and persevering in the will of God, yet all along unaware that God is with you, take care that you do not become Samsonlike, content with or conditioned to life apart from a sense of His blessing.

John Stevenson, a British minister of the first half of the 1800s, urged the cultivation of this desire:

> The greatest of all spiritual and eternal blessings is the presence of God. On this our hearts' strongest desires ought to be fixed. This is the subject which warrants, and rewards, the most vehement importunity. Even in the greatest darkness of soul, even while the countenance of God is withdrawn, nothing can honor God more as a Creator, or gratify his heart more as a parent, than that we should make the light of his countenance the first and last object of our desires, and be restless and unhappy so long as it is turned away from us. Indeed, not to be importunate after this, proves that we are destitute of the feelings of a child, and shows that we possess little or no love to our Heavenly Father. It was this that well nigh burst the filial heart of Christ in the garden and on the Cross. His whole soul desired to enjoy the smile of his Father's countenance. He knew the goodness of his Father and he knew that the further he pressed into it the more of it he should obtain.[9]

OPENING YOUR SPIRITUAL EYES
TO HIS PRESENCE

What practical steps can we take to grow in our awareness of the continuous presence of God?

Go often to the place where God has revealed Himself most clearly—the Bible. Arguably Britain's most influential twentieth-century preacher, Martyn Lloyd-Jones said of God's Word, "The more we know it and read it, the more it will take us into the presence of God. So if you want to set the Lord always before you, spend much of your time with regular daily reading of the Bible."[10]

As obvious as this may seem at first, many who would purse their lips and nod their heads at these words would turn around and unwittingly put priority on seeking the presence of God in experiences where Scripture plays no role. Shouldn't we expect to experience God's presence *primarily* by means of that which He gave explicitly for the purpose of making Himself known to us: *His Word?*

But don't simply read from the Bible, close it, then walk away. Absorb the water of the Word of God through meditation. Otherwise, what you have read may be like rain that evaporates on a sidewalk. Linger over something from it so that it percolates into the soil of your soul. Listen long enough until you hear it for what it is—the voice of God.

Acknowledge His presence with you by talking with Him. Many wives complain that their husbands can sit in the same room with them for extended periods of time and never acknowledge their presence by speaking. Does this develop intimacy? Obviously not. When a person's prayer life is decaying by silence, is it any wonder that he or she feels unaware of the nearness of God? God is a real Person who is very present. Ignore Him and He will seem distant. Talk with Him and you will almost always feel Him closer.

As I mentioned in chapter 1, I want to commend now in this

context the practice of praying through a passage of Scripture, especially one of the Psalms. Let the words that have originated in the heart and mind of God Himself become the vehicle to carry the burdens of your heart and mind back to God. I've taught this ancient way of prayer in seminars from California to the Carolinas, and countless people have testified that praying from God's Word brings them into the presence of God as never before. Praying this way makes prayer more what it ought to be, namely, a real conversation with a real Person.

Seek Him in the manifestations of His presence given only in congregational worship. The Bible says that the body of each Christian is a temple of the Holy Spirit (1 Corinthians 6:19). But specific references to being a temple of the Holy Spirit are made far more often about the *congregation* of believers than about individual believers (for example, see 1 Corinthians 3:9,16-17). So there is a sense in which going to worship with the people of God is going to the Lord's temple where His presence abides. In a true church, His Word is preached, His Son is presented in the Lord's Supper, His Spirit ministers through many and diverse gifts, and so forth. The solitary worshiper does not have access to the presence of the Lord in exactly these ways. While there are experiences with God that are given only in private worship, it is equally true that the Lord manifests His presence in ways unique to public worship.

Continually reaffirm the truth that He is omnipresent. The truth is, God is everywhere at all times. Immanuel Himself specifically promised His people, "I am with you always" (Matthew 28:20). The Lord is with us even when we don't sense His presence. We must, however, reaffirm what we know to be true, even when we don't feel it to be true. This will help us to live more by faith than by feelings.

"God seems so far away," my strongest feelings may say to me. "Doesn't He see what's happening? Why doesn't He answer my prayers?"

Faith in the truth responds, "But God *is* here. He promised He would never leave me or forsake me. Whether I sense His presence or not, the truth is: God is here with me as much as at any moment in my life. I will believe the *truth*."

Reaffirming the truth will also prompt us to look more for evidence of the presence of God around us. The great fourth-century Christian leader Augustine is said to have been confronted one day by a man who brandished his idol and demanded, "Here is my god, where is yours?" Augustine replied, "I cannot show you my God; not because there is no God to show, but because you have no eyes to see Him."

Unlike Augustine's opponent, Christians have been given the Holy Spirit, who enlightens us to see and believe the revelation of God in creation, in Christ, and in Scripture—in ways the natural man cannot (1 Corinthians 2:9-16). However, the fact that we have eyes to see does not mean we use them to look where we ought. In other words, there is often much more evidence of the presence of God around us than we appreciate.

Take a look around for a moment and notice everything in your sight that is blue. Go ahead. When you do, you develop "blue eyes," that is, eyes sensitive to the things around you that are blue. We need to develop "God eyes." We need to develop the sensitivity to see evidence of what we know to be true, namely, that God is with us. Look for God everywhere and in everything. Say to yourself often, "The Lord is here," especially in the ordinary places of life. While sitting at the computer, or when at the gas pump, the mall, or the grocery store, remind yourself that the Lord is present. Whether you are in the car, the kitchen, or involved in the most earthy and intimate experiences of life, reaffirm the fact that God is with you.

As we develop these "God eyes," we will be more like Jesus, who always recognized His Father's presence. Spurgeon says of Him:

He fed the multitude, but it was with his Father's bread; and he healed the sick, but the Father did the works. . . . Other men remarked that the ravens were fed, but he said, "Your Heavenly Father feeds them." Other men noticed the lilies were fair to look upon, but he discerned that "God so clothes the grass of the field." The Heavenly Father was in every place, and in every thing to Jesus. . . . Refuse to see anything without seeing God in it.[11]

Let me close by addressing those who regularly find themselves in situations or places that seem totally void of God. Reaffirm your faith that the Lord is there, and ask Him to remind you the next time you are in that place or set of circumstances. Think of one object, sound, or activity that occurs in each of these situations and let it be a reminder to pray, "Lord, I do believe that You are here and I thank You for Your presence."

Regardless of how sensitive you are to the presence of God at this point in your Christian pilgrimage, the prayer of A. W. Tozer is an appropriate way to end this chapter and to begin growing onward:

Our Father, we know that Thou art present with us, but our knowledge is but a figure and shadow of truth, and has little of the spiritual savor and inward sweetness such knowledge should afford. This is for us a great loss and the cause of much weakness of heart. Help us to make at once such amendment of life as is necessary before we can experience the true meaning of the words, "In thy presence is fullness of joy." Amen.[12]

DO YOU HAVE A GROWING CONCERN FOR THE SPIRITUAL AND TEMPORAL NEEDS OF OTHERS?

ABOUT ONE HUNDRED YEARS AFTER THE DEATH AND RESURRECTION of Jesus Christ, Antoninus Pius ruled the Roman Empire. Because everyone in those days was required to worship the emperor, Christians were considered disloyal and were under constant attack as followers of an illegal religion. They weren't officially persecuted by Antoninus Pius, but they had to defend themselves incessantly against false accusations. Just as we read in the book of Acts about how Paul was often hated by those who didn't know him and that riots sometimes broke out when lives were changed by his ministry, so it was with Christians in the decades after Paul's labors. Christians were continually deflecting the false charges and undeserved blame being hurled at them.

On one of these occasions, a famous Grecian philosopher from Athens named Aristides—who had himself become a Christian—was called upon to make a defense of the Christians before Antoninus Pius. Part of his defense was this: "They love one another. The widow's needs are not ignored, and they rescue the orphan from the person who does him violence. He who has gives to him who has not, ungrudgingly and without boasting."[1]

Christianity is a religion of concern for others. Among what are called the "great religions of the world," Christianity has no parallel when it comes to demonstrating concern for people and for their needs. Whether the needs are temporal or eternal, felt or unperceived, no other religion is known for its love and compassion, not only for those within its ranks, but particularly toward those outside its circle of adherents.

The perceptive eye and the helping hand are birthmarks of the born again in Christ. Concern for others is as much a part of being a Christian as concern for self is for the nonChristian. Meeting needs is the way of Jesus. And those following Jesus can trace their progress toward His likeness by tracking their growth in their concern for the spiritual and temporal needs of others.

THE BIBLICAL NEAR-BALANCE

The Bible clearly teaches Christians to be concerned for both the spiritual and the temporal needs of people. Jesus, our Lord and example, often demonstrated this dual concern by healing bodies and teaching truth on the same occasion. This twofold emphasis on both preaching and meeting temporal needs characterized the church immediately after Pentecost: "And with great power the apostles gave witness to the resurrection of the Lord Jesus. And great grace was upon them all. Nor was there anyone among them who lacked; for all who were possessors of lands or houses sold them, and brought the proceeds of the things that were sold" (Acts 4:33-34). When the apostles James,

Peter, and John agreed that Paul and Barnabas should go as missionaries to the Gentiles, Paul reports that in addition to sending them as preachers, "They [James, Peter, and John] desired only that we should remember the poor, the very thing which I also was eager to do" (Galatians 2:10).

Evangelicals as a whole typically tend to put more time, money, and prayer into labors of missions and evangelism than in social ministries. While I believe this approach as a rule is biblically sound, we must be alert to the danger inherent in our emphasis, namely, overlooking temporal needs. For instance, James 2:15-16 asks the question, "If a brother or sister is naked and destitute of daily food, and one of you says to them, 'Depart in peace, be warmed and filled,' but you do not give them the things which are needed for the body, what does it profit?" In other words, giving a spiritual blessing (such as sharing the gospel) without meeting an urgent physical need profits no one, especially the one on the receiving end. Evangelism that ignores hollow-eyed hunger or other crying needs of the ones being evangelized is a physical contradiction to the spiritual message. To say in effect, "I love you so much and am so concerned about you that I want to give you the words of eternal life, but I don't care enough to address your basic and pressing physical need," is a denial of my supposed concern.

Even so, I rarely see such self-contradictory evangelism. Others, though, claim it is a common failure by those who believe in the necessity of the new birth. No doubt it happens, but those who swing this accusation as a club the most are often the same ones who feed the body and starve the eternal soul. They demonstrate great concern for the physical or material needs but seldom get around to sharing the gospel. Their strategy implies that the *example* of Christlike actions will somehow feed the more important spiritual need. This method is at least as deadly as the opposite error of giving only Bible verses or gospel tracts to those who have desperate temporal needs.

Humility requires us to realize that whenever the Bible presents complementary truths like these, we all tend to lean one way or the other. Take Jesus' command "God is Spirit, and those who worship Him must worship in spirit and truth" (John 4:24) as a case in point. He calls for true worship to be done both in spirit *and* truth, but most of us feel a little more at home in worship with an emphasis on spirit *or* truth. (The same unbalanced tendency is as true for churches as it is for individual Christians.) Chances are you're like me in that you are more comfortable with sharing the gospel *or* feeding the hungry, answering questions about the Bible *or* driving nails on a widow's roof, bringing comfort from Scripture *or* bringing clothes to the needy. But as we grow more like Jesus, we will see ministry to temporal needs not as competing with, but as complementing, the meeting of spiritual needs.

JESUS THE NEED-MEETER

Jesus Christ, the ultimate need-meeter, reflected the "near-balance" of filling spiritual as well as temporal needs. He laid aside His heavenly privileges and came to earth for the expressed purpose of meeting our greatest need. As He put it, "I have come that they may have life" (John 10:10).

The supreme need of every human is a spiritual one. Because we have all willingly sinned by breaking the laws of God (Romans 3:23) and have done so an infinite number of times, we face physical death (Romans 6:23), judgment (Hebrews 9:27), and the second death of eternal punishment (Revelation 21:8). But "Christ was offered once to bear the sins of many" (Hebrews 9:28). He came to provide the only hope of escape "from the wrath to come" (1 Thessalonians 1:10). Jesus said of Himself, "I am the door. If anyone enters by Me, he will be saved" (John 10:9). To all who do come to Him in repentance and faith (Mark 1:15) Jesus promised, "I give them eternal life" (John 10:28). Jesus Christ came to offer Himself as the door to life in the next world—an incomprehensibly glorious and joyous life without comparison or end. Life with God Himself.

While His primary purpose was to meet our eternal need, He was not oblivious to people's temporal needs. His method of accomplishing both aims is perfectly demonstrated in the account recorded in Mark 6:34-44. "And Jesus, when He came out, saw a great multitude and was moved with compassion for them, because they were like sheep not having a shepherd. So He began to teach them many things" (verse 34). His compassion for their hopelessness prompted Him to teach them truth from Heaven. Then, after feeding their souls, He fed their hungry stomachs in what is known as the miracle of the feeding of the five thousand.

If we saw people from Jesus' perspective, we would begin to see them as "sheep not having a shepherd." Even though many do not feel themselves to be in such a condition, they are. Even if they appear to have no temporal needs, they certainly have spiritual needs. They may appear as self-sufficient as the hardened atheist Madalyn Murray O'Hair once did. But deep within they are often like her when she wrote at least a half-dozen times in her diary the plea, "Somebody, somewhere, love me."[2] Everyone is needy, no matter how thick his or her veneer of self-sufficiency. The one universal common denominator is that everyone has spiritual needs, chief of which is the need for Jesus, the soul-shepherd.

No one who is indwelled by the Spirit of Jesus can remain unfeeling toward either the temporal or the spiritual needs of others made plain. Growth in Christlikeness involves perceiving those needs *sooner* than before, and not just when they become obvious to everyone. Increased growth in Christian maturity is revealed by a heartfelt compassion toward people, not a perfunctory, merely external response. There is no Christlikeness in throwing money at a physical need or in dutifully reading a few Bible verses to an unbeliever and apathetically sending him on his way to hell.

This is not to say that the existence of a need always equals the call to meet it. Not even Jesus responded to every need He could have met. It's true, there were occasions when He "healed all who were sick" (Matthew 8:16), but this wasn't always the case. The Gospels tell us there were many times, such as the one recorded in Luke 12:1, "when an innumerable multitude of people had gathered together, so that they trampled one another." Jesus frequently had thousands pressing around Him—all with their needs—and many of them screaming for just His touch on a dying spouse or child, pleading with Him for healing or sight, begging Him to have mercy. Yet sometimes He walked on or sailed away. But even when He did this, He was conscious of the needs. And He turned away only because He was turning *to* something else He knew to be the will of God for Him at that moment. Sometimes the growing Christian must do the same.

THE HEROES OF CHRISTIAN HISTORY

The men and women who are most admired by the church have always been those disciples of Jesus most like Him in showing love by meeting both the spiritual and temporal needs of people.

In just one of many possible fields to consider, notice how many Christians known for devotion and zeal have also been committed to the care of children and orphans. As far back as the fifth and sixth centuries, it was Christian influence that brought legal protection to the children of the Roman Empire. After the Swiss reformer Huldreich (Ulrich) Zwingli (1484–1531)—a contemporary of Luther and Calvin—broke with the Roman church, he persuaded the Council of Zürich to transform several local monasteries into orphanages.

One of the most fruitful evangelists in history, George Whitefield (1714–1770) devoted much of his income to the development of an orphanage in colonial Georgia. Think of the impact upon tens of thousands of children accomplished by the devout William Wilberforce (1759–1833), who persevered for decades in the British Parliament to begin the modern movement to end slavery. At the same time, English missionary William Carey (1761–1834) was responsible for outlawing the centuries-old practices of child sacrifice and widow burning in India. Later in the 1800s, a Christian statesman, Anthony Ashley Cooper (also known as Lord Shaftesbury) (1801–1883), led the fight against child labor practices and sought to improve treatment of the mentally ill in Great Britain.

George Müller (1805–1898) is high among the church's great champions of prayer and faith, recording more than fifty thousand specific answers to prayer in his journals. Most of these prayers, however, were for the same purpose, namely, that God would be glorified by providing the means to feed, clothe, house, and educate up to two thousand orphans at a time in nineteenth-century Bristol, England. The Lord was pleased to channel tens of millions of dollars through Müller's hands, though he never made his needs known to anyone but God.

It is often unrecognized that Charles Haddon Spurgeon (1834–1892), remembered primarily as the Prince of Preachers, built more than seventeen homes for elderly widows and an orphanage for hundreds of children of all races and backgrounds, and eventually started and/or presided over *sixty-six* ministry organizations. Most of these served in the poorer parts of London, and on occasion were funded entirely by Spurgeon himself.

Today in America, Christians in every state of the Union provide homes and education for children without parents and for unwed expectant mothers. Moreover, the followers of Jesus are the ones spearheading the effort to protect the lives of the unborn.

Throughout history, Christians have led the way in supporting widows and orphans, building hospitals, and providing disaster relief on every continent in the world. Wherever a beachhead for the gospel of Jesus Christ has been established, medicine, education, and relief for the poor have followed.

Whether the need is hunger, lack of drinking water, illiteracy, sickness, homelessness, or anything else that causes misery, Christians have been at the forefront of caring for the needs of the world.

Christianity is a religion of concern for others.

But the greatest demonstration of Christlike concern has been the effort to obey the Great Commission of Jesus and take the good news about Him to everyone in the world. Growing Christians remember that the foremost need of anyone, anywhere, anytime is salvation, to be made right with God. This was preeminent on the heart of Jesus. As we become more like Him, we'll discover that the burden on His heart is weighing heavier on ours also.

GROWING FROM HERE

Too out of balance? Have you been saying the right things, but doing nothing to meet the spiritual or temporal needs of others? What now?

Go to the Great Ophthalmologist. Jesus is often called the Great Physician. But He could also be known as the Great Ophthalmologist, or Doctor of the Eyes. During His earthly ministry He healed the blind primarily to show that His miraculous power can open the eyes of the *spiritually* blind. Our spiritual darkness is forever banished once we see "the light of the knowledge of the glory of God in the face of Jesus Christ" (2 Corinthians 4:6). If He has already given you spiritual sight, go to the Great Ophthalmologist now and ask Him to increase your sight to see more as He sees.

Last year I had eye surgery. After a five-minute laser procedure on each eye, my eyesight went from being in the worst 15 percent in America to a normal 20/20—but not immediately. Although the improvement was dramatic by the time the bandages were removed the next morning, months passed before my vision was fully corrected. I saw my ophthalmologist frequently, and under his care I came to see even better than I had with glasses.

Once we have been born again, "all things have become new" (2 Corinthians 5:17), including our spiritual vision. The Holy Spirit enlightens us to see so much in ourselves, in the Bible, and in the world that we never saw before. But our eyesight is not yet perfect. Keep going to the Great Ophthalmologist and asking Him to enable you to see the needs He wants you to meet.

As your vision becomes more Christlike, you'll begin to see temporal and spiritual needs of people that you didn't see before. You'll detect inward tears before they well in the eyes, and hollowness of heart in those who don't even themselves know how empty they are. Hurts and needs you had never noticed will begin to emerge from the most familiar people and places.

Does this describe your spiritual vision? If not, it's time for a checkup. Ask the Great Ophthalmologist to correct your spiritual myopia.

Look for the hurt in every heart and home. More than twenty years of pastoral ministry have taught me that there is a hurt in *every* heart and home. This is true even for the wealthy or those who appear most to "have it all together." I remember one particular couple I pastored for two years before I learned of their greatest hurt. I was quite close to them, for the husband was the leading layman in our church and his wife taught our women's Bible study. He was a top attorney at the international headquarters of one of the best-known corporations in the world. Despite all this earthly success and solid spiritual leadership, they carried—unknown to anyone in our church at the time—one of the heaviest burdens in our fellowship. One night, ten years earlier in another city, their teenage son experimented with drugs. This first and only occasion permanently altered his mental condition. Until then he had been a model son and student with the brightest of futures. After that night he was the source of overwhelming heartache. Because he no longer lived with his parents, no one in our church knew of the grief, the cost, and the difficulty that often dominated their private lives. Many in our church considered this couple prosperous and trouble-free, when in fact few would have exchanged circumstances with them.

I've read statistics showing that every household in the United States experiences a crisis or significant life change every six months on average. This includes events such as a birth, death, injury, serious illness, job change or transfer, car accident, financial reversal, or child leaving home. Each of these situations may result in new opportunities to meet spiritual and/or temporal needs with the love of Christ. While writing this chapter I was able to share the gospel with a friend who for three years has brushed off my attempts to talk about the things of God. But a few days after his father died, I walked over and found him quite willing to discuss eternal things and his own mortality.

Some readers can look up from this page and immediately see a world full of needs framed by their windows. You make eye contact daily with many who have acute needs for food, clothing, shelter, medical treatment, work, and the like. Others who are scanning these lines may spend their lives primarily in a world where most of the needs stay hidden, like internal bleeding. If you are in the latter group, try looking through "need filters," and the opportunities for Christlike ministry will become obvious.

Here's what I mean: look at your neighborhood, your workplace, your classes, your church, your family, with the filter of "What are his/her/their spiritual needs?" Then, "What are his/her/their temporal needs?" By looking with these filters on the eyes of your mind, you will see some needs in sharper focus. This increased perception is in itself a sign of spiritual growth. In some cases you will conclude there are needs that you, by God's grace and His Spirit, should attempt to meet.

Knowing there is a hurt in every heart and home, your filtered eyes may see pressing needs you had never seen before in relation to widows, the elderly, children, single parents, the lonely, the homebound, the disabled, the ill or infirm, or the international student. The Great Ophthalmologist may show you people who need yard or garden help, transportation, errands run, home or car repairs, cleaning, meals, computer help, snow removal, firewood, painting, roof work, gutter cleaning, childcare, or just an extra hand given in Jesus' name. Or He may help you see more clearly those who need the gospel, prayer, biblical counsel, encouragement, reproof, a listening ear, an invitation to church, discipleship, an audiotape, CD, article, book, or a simple "How-are-you-doing?" visit.

Do something for the gospel and the good of others. Would God have you see so many needs and meet none? He doesn't expect you to meet every need shown to you, for not even Jesus did that. But our fulfilling Father does expect us to find so much joy in Him that, like Jesus, we will find pleasure and satisfaction in meeting the needs of others for His sake.

Remember when Jesus washed His disciples' feet in John 13:1-17? We're told that "Jesus, knowing that the Father had given all things into His hands, and that He had come from God and was going to God, rose from supper," took a towel, and washed their feet (see verses 3-5). It was out of knowing the joy and glory He had when in Heaven with the Father, and the awareness of the pleasure and joy in God to whom He was returning, that He was willing to meet the needs of a dozen pairs of dirty feet. Find joy in God and you will find joy in doing the work of God.

Don't sit passively until you "feel led" to particular needs. Go adventurously into your world with the gospel and the love of Christ, and you'll find Him guiding you to the needs He wants you to meet. And as you become His instrument in meeting the needs of others, you'll find Him meeting many needs of your own.

CHAPTER SIX

THE CLOSER YOU ARE TO THE LORD, THE CLOSER YOU
WILL BE TO OTHER BELIEVERS.
—PETER JEFFREY

DO YOU DELIGHT
IN THE
BRIDE OF CHRIST?

AGUR, ONE OF THE ANCIENT WRITERS OF PROVERBS, ACKNOWLEDGED:

There are three things which are too wonderful for me,
Yes, four which I do not understand:
The way of an eagle in the air,
The way of a serpent on a rock,
The way of a ship in the midst of the sea,
And the way of a man with a virgin. (Proverbs 30:18-19)

I don't know much about eagles, serpents, and ships, but I
have observed (and experienced) that the ways of a man with
a woman he loves are indeed often full of wonder. In order to
fulfill the requirements mandated by Laban for his daughter's
hand in marriage, the Old Testament patriarch "Jacob served
seven years for Rachel, and they seemed only a few days to him

because of the love he had for her" (Genesis 29:20). Long years, even long distances, are irrelevant when a man delights in a woman. I was in a Texas seminary while engaged to Caffy. She was living in northwest Arkansas where we'd met while I attended law school. My delight in her made me more than willing to make the six-hour drive from Fort Worth to Fayetteville whenever possible.

On an infinitely grander scale, Jesus made an incomparable journey from Heaven and worked for more than thirty years for the delight of His eyes, the church. "Christ also loved the church," writes Paul, "and gave Himself for her, that He might sanctify and cleanse her with the washing of water by the word, that He might present her to Himself a glorious church, not having spot or wrinkle or any such thing, but that she should be holy and without blemish" (Ephesians 5:25-27).

Now suppose that the very Spirit of Jesus Christ Himself were given to dwell, not only in the body of Jesus, but also in another human. (And realize that according to the New Testament, this is what happens to all who belong to Christ—see Romans 8:9.) Obviously then, like Christ, the man or woman who has been given the Spirit of Jesus would love what Jesus loves and died for—His bride, the church. So one of the best tests of whether we belong to Christ is whether *we* delight in *His* delight, namely, the people who comprise His church. Or as the apostle John put it, "We know that we have passed from death to life, because we love the brethren" (1 John 3:14).

King David's Old Testament words are a beautiful description of this New Testament love that God's people have for each other:

> As for the saints who are in the earth,
> They are the majestic ones in whom is all my delight.
> (Psalm 16:3, NASB)

Notice the word "saints" in the first half of the verse. In the Bible, "saints" is one of the terms applied to the people of God.

Paul refers to Christians as saints in nearly every New Testament letter he wrote, using the word more than fifty times. These first-century saints were ordinary Christians, but not nominal ones. They were sincere followers of Jesus, manifesting the fruit of the Spirit (see Galatians 5:22-23). Far from perfect though, some of those he called saints were struggling with scandalous sin problems, as with the saints in the church at Corinth (see 1 Corinthians 1:2). But what was true then is true now—everyone indwelled by the Spirit of God is a saint, or as the Greek word literally means, a "holy one." Saints aren't exceptionally devoted believers now in Heaven, rather they are people who believe and live the Word of God in their workaday world—the kind of people David spoke of as "saints who are *in the earth*" (emphasis added). Yet David's delight was in such folk. He sought them out and took pleasure in their company because they loved God too.

David even waxed rhapsodical over his fellow saints, calling them "majestic ones." Other translations render the Hebrew word here as "excellent ones" or "glorious ones." Do you ever refer to your fellow believers in such magnificent terms? When you think of John the computer programmer who teaches the teenagers in your church, or Mary the homemaker who works with the children, do you say to yourself, "There's a majestic one!"? Let me remind you that God Himself inspired Israel's king to use such a description of God's people. As children of *the* Majestic One in Heaven they were His "majestic ones" in the earth, changed by the power of God. So it wasn't because of their own majesty, excellence, or glory that David delighted in them; it was because they shared with him a love for the majesty, excellence, and glory of God above all else. They loved the true Majesty, and this made them, and only them, majestic ones in David's sight.

Delighting in *Christ's* people is normal, healthy *Christ*ianity. So permit me to ask you this question to help you diagnose your spiritual health: Do *you* delight in the bride of Jesus Christ?

Do you take pleasure in those who bring pleasure to Him?

In one sense I'm asking if you delight in the church as a whole, not in each Christian in particular. After all, the bride of Christ is the church, not individual Christians. Jesus is not a polygamist. The "marriage supper of the Lamb" (Revelation 19:9) is an event with all Christians collectively, not with each believer individually. The truth of Scripture is better expressed by a congregation confessing, "We are the bride of Christ," than by a solitary Christian saying, "I am the bride of Christ." Therefore, do you delight in the church, that is, in the gathering of believers, their corporate experiences and labor?

And yet, although Jesus' joy is in one bride, she is made of millions of individual Christians with faces and names, including those of people where you live. It would be very strange to say that you love Christ's church but dislike the people in her. But the attitude of some toward the church and her members is like the character in a cartoon I once saw who smirked, "I love mankind; it's people I can't stand."

In short, delighting in "the saints who are in the earth" means finding irresistible joy in the presence and the ministry of Christ's people, both in their congregational form and as individuals. Does this describe you?

DO YOU DELIGHT IN HER WILLINGLY?

A Davidlike delight in "the saints who are in the earth" is a God-given delight poured into the soul from Heaven, not ground out from the grit of determination. It does not require setting the jaw and resolving, "I *will* delight in these people," but more of the spontaneous spirit of "I was *glad* when they said to me, 'Let us go into the house of the LORD'" (Psalm 122:1, emphasis added). When God makes a Christian, He changes the person's heart so dramatically that delighting in the followers of Jesus becomes as easy and natural for the soul as delighting in sunsets and savory food is for the senses.

Something is amiss when a person participates in the life of a church only because of the forces of "ought." Parental training, family expectations, long-term habits, the heavy weight of conscience, and a sense of duty are not the overriding compulsions of the Christlike as they arise on the Lord's Day to gather with God's own. That is not to say that rightly motivated worshipers have none of the other influences, for some of them are quite healthy. But the primary motivation for growing Christians is "want," not "ought."

Any true delight is always a willing delight, not a reluctant one. Delight in the people of God cannot be forced into the soul any more than parents can coerce their single adult son to delight in a potential mate who holds no attraction for him. Nor will anyone delight in the church primarily because we shame them for delighting in the NFL, a hobby, or something else more than the family of God. The church is not a taste to be acquired, a new preference developed by sheer resolve. Just as candy delights a child, so the child of God does not have to be persuaded to delight in the supernatural spiritual sweetness found only in God's church. Delight in the church is inborn in those who are born again.

DO YOU DELIGHT IN HER COMPANY?

Some things, simply by their nature, delight us with their company. How easy it is to delight in a baby who smiles at you over the shoulder of his or her mother. For the Christian, the presence of the "saints who are in the earth," just by virtue of their being saints, evokes delight. For what makes these people to be saints in the earth is the God in the heavens—the most delightful Being in the universe—living in them and working through them.

When authentic Christians assemble in a local church, the omnipresent God dwells in their midst in a special way. While it's true that individual Christians are called the temple of the Holy

Spirit (1 Corinthians 6:19), that kind of language is far more often spoken of believers collectively. In the following God-inspired words of the apostle Paul, each use of the word "you" is plural, referring to the entire church to whom the letter was written:

- You are the temple of God . . . the Spirit of God dwells in you. (1 Corinthians 3:16)
- For you are the temple of the living God. (2 Corinthians 6:16)
- You also are being built together into a dwelling of God in the Spirit. (Ephesians 2:22)

So the reason why growing Christians so readily delight in being with the saints of God is the real presence of God Himself living within ordinary people we know. Ultimately, you are delighted by Him in them.

This is why haters of God and church, once they come to know God through Jesus Christ, begin to show new affection for the things of God, including the people of God. As lovers of God, they become lovers of the living temples of God.

This doesn't mean that growing Christians experience spiritual elation in every encounter with fellow believers or that delighting in the church is a perfect or unmixed delight. God dwells in people who still sin, and sometimes we leave a gathering of Christians with more of the stench of sin in our nostrils than the sweet aroma of the presence of God. Occasionally our mortal bodies will sit in the worshiping congregation of saints feeling sick or exhausted, not exhilarated. At times the Christian company we keep can actually leave us bored. Overall, however, God's people, when they are with others of God's people, find their minds enlightened and their hearts warmed in ways they never do when with those who are not indwelled by the Fire of Heaven.

Recently, a group of fifteen or twenty believers I know had a meal together after church, then spent the afternoon around the tables in Christian fellowship. As they were about to leave, they decided, "Why not eat together again?" And so they did. Arriving just before 10 A.M. for worship, they didn't separate until 7 P.M. Why? Because as growing Christians do, they delighted in each other's company.

DO YOU DELIGHT IN HER ACTIVITY?

From the first days of his ministry until the end of his ministry decades later, the apostle Paul faced opposition and persecution in his work. Why did he willingly endure so many imprisonments, beatings, and stonings and for so long (see 2 Corinthians 11:23-28)? Near the end of his life, in the last of his letters included in Scripture, Paul gave the answer: "I endure all things for the sake of the elect" (2 Timothy 2:10). Like his master, Jesus, the old apostle found unequaled delight in his work on behalf of God's elect, the church.

God doesn't keep the world turning so that we can do more business, make more money, and buy more things. Rather, God keeps the planet in motion because He has not finished the work of the church, that is, building the kingdom of His Son. Because this is God's purpose, it ought to be ours as well. And if we'll see it for what it is, we will delight in it (just as God does).

In an episode of TV's *Star Trek: The Next Generation*, Captain Picard found himself near death and caught a glimpse of what his life might have been like had he made some less bold choices in his earlier years. He realized how easily he could have become "just a dreary man with a tedious job." Ultimately, however, anyone—from a starship captain on down—who lives with a this-life-only perspective is a dreary person with a tedious job because he lives and works for something that is perishing. The relatively small percentage of those who think they have exciting lives and stimulating jobs fail to see that, in light of eternity, they are trying to satisfy themselves with that which is merely temporal.

The work of Christ's church is the greatest, most soul-satisfying enterprise in the universe. Nothing compares—career, family, conquest, success, wealth, politics, retirement—nothing! Furthermore, it is the only eternally enduring work we can do. Those who aren't committed to the work of the church are not just extremely shortsighted and self-defeating, but they also forfeit an incredible privilege. To delight yourself in anything else more than in God and the work of His kingdom is like contenting yourself with watching a video of someone else's wedding ceremony when you could be on your honeymoon.

EXPRESSING YOUR DELIGHT

Delight is much more than fancy. True delight must be expressed. To say "As for the saints who are in the earth, They are the majestic ones in whom is all my delight" without feeling it and showing it is hypocrisy. Here are two of many possible suggestions for expressing your delight in the saints of God. The first suggestion relates to raising the temperature of your delight in the church and her work. The second has to do with outward change.

Grow to see the bride of Christ and her work more as Jesus does. Do you see the beauty in the bride and what she does that the world cannot see? Can you see more clearly than before what Christ loves in His bride and her labors? What He loves is the increasing clarity of His own reflection in the church and her ministry. Nothing in existence or imagination can compare with the beauty of the triune God. Christ could give no greater gift or beauty than to give His bride the beauty of His holiness. He loves to see this beauty grow in the hearts and lives of His people. Can you see in the church something of what He sees? Let's take it out of the theoretical: What are three examples of the beauty of Christ's holiness that you can identify in your local church?

This coming weekend—Lord willing—I will be in Tennessee

teaching more than a hundred people how to pray through a passage of Scripture. I believe it can change their prayer lives dramatically, which means it can change everything about their lives and make them more like Jesus. The great majority of people in that area will be consumed with thoughts about a football game. Forty-eight hours afterward, however, the game will be largely forgotten and virtually meaningless to most of them. I think about this during the build-up of hype prior to each Super Bowl. At the time, it is the dominant event in our culture, and yet its impact is so short-lived. Who played in the Super Bowl just two years ago? For two weeks before that kickoff nothing else in the world seemed as important or as glorious; today it is insignificant to, if not forgotten by, those who so anticipated it. The work done for the kingdom of God, by contrast, often seems so colorless and marginal at the time, but it has a beauty and glory that the world cannot see—yet. And its impact can last forever.

It takes eyes of faith to see this, and eyes of faith can grow in their acuity. Whereas in the body one's eyes tend to weaken as a person matures, in the spiritual realm the eyes of maturing faith become sharper and more penetrating. This is akin to what Paul wrote in 2 Corinthians 4:16: "Even though our outward man is perishing, yet the inward man is being renewed day by day." Those whose spiritual vision is becoming clearer will increasingly see the splendor and value of the work of the church versus the things that are passing away. And what looks so powerful and impressive to the world begins to appear weak and pale to the maturing Christian.

The more your eyes perceive Jesus' bride and her work in the way that He does, the more you will love her and it as He does.

Demonstrate your delight in the bride of Christ in ways that will make a real difference. The work of the local church is the work of Jesus in the world. How can anyone place a low priority on involvement with the work of Christ and think he or she is becoming more like Christ?

Where does the church of Christ that you attend need help? Chances are it makes its needs known regularly. Are you listening? Can't find your niche? Then take the initiative and create a ministry. Look for the delight found in hidden and unheralded places of service. Pursue the secret glory concealed in the mundane ministries. Give your heart and time and money and zeal to the bride for whom Christ gave His life. How long should you do this? For as long as you can say of those who have the Spirit of God, "They are the majestic ones in whom is all my delight." And for as long as Christ loves His bride.

This is how you will help to build what will last. Contrary to what man builds, "whatever God does, it shall be forever" (Ecclesiastes 3:14). Regardless of how despised or irrelevant the work of the church appears in the eyes of the world, it is a work that will gleam with God-given glory forever.

Imagine a history book written in Heaven a million years after the end of the earth. How much space will it devote to the stock market, corporate mergers, presidential elections, and sports championships? Won't it be dominated instead by actions in and through local churches, deeds that passed unnoticed at the time by people the world overlooked? The names of many mighty and noble may be mere footnotes, but the names of those who loved the Lord and ministered to His saints will fill its pages. And written in gold letters on the flyleaf may be this inscription, "For God is not unjust to forget your work and labor of love which you have shown toward His name, in that you have ministered to the saints, and do minister" (Hebrews 6:10).

Psalm 149:4 tells us that "the LORD takes pleasure in His people." Do you?

CHAPTER SEVEN

WITHOUT A DISCIPLINED LIFE YOU WILL STAGNATE AS
A CHRISTIAN.

—PETER JEFFREY

ARE THE
SPIRITUAL DISCIPLINES
INCREASINGLY
IMPORTANT TO YOU?

WE HAD A WOOD-BURNING STOVE INSTALLED AT THE WHITNEY
house last year. I've written much of this book on a yellow pad,
using a fountain pen, while sitting in my stoveside chair. When
you use a woodstove, you learn what it means to *build* a fire.

First I crumple several sheets of newspaper into "bouquets,"
tightly wadded at the bottom (for slower burning) and flared
at the top (for instant flame). Upon these I layer a dozen or so
strips of tinder. These are dry, thin pieces of wood between the
size of a physician's tongue depressor and a paint-stirring stick.
After I've made sure the damper is open and the vent in front
is set for maximum airflow, I strike a long, wooden match.
Reaching into the stove, I touch several spots in rapid succes-
sion where the paper will light quickly. To increase the draft

temporarily, I close the door within an inch of shutting it completely. The flames spread to the balled paper, which burns long enough to ignite the tinder. These pieces are burning well by the time the paper turns to ashes. Now I'm wearing fireplace gloves and ready to lay on a few sticks of kindling, which are roughly the thickness of a hammer handle, though often a little longer. When several of these are flaming happily atop the small, pulsing coals of the tinder, the stove is ready for the first of the full-size hunks of wood that will warm me all evening. The first flash of match and paper is bright and impressive, but the reason I build the fire is to enjoy the sustained heat of burning logs and slow-glowing coals.

Perhaps you are like a Christian woman I know who sometimes wonders if she is still growing spiritually, because the original God-kindled blaze of eternal life that once illuminated the darkness of her life so suddenly, seldom flames up as dramatically as when she was first converted. But what is true for the woodstove is true in this case for the Christian heart as well: just because the beginning of the combustion may briefly be more spectacular than at present doesn't mean the fire isn't growing. The initial burst of spiritual flame may be more dazzling, but the heartfire's greatest effectiveness occurs as it burns into consistency.

Nothing contributes to the growth of spiritual heat and light more than the persevering practice of the Christian spiritual disciplines. The disciplines are the bellows and the iron poker—tools in God's hands through which He stokes and blows upon the eternal fire He Himself ignites in His people.

WHAT ARE THE
SPIRITUAL DISCIPLINES?

The spiritual disciplines are the God-ordained means by which we bring ourselves before God, experience Him, and are changed into Christlikeness. The Lord is omnipresent and we often encounter Him in unexpected places and surprising ways. Nevertheless, it has pleased Him to establish specific means—the spiritual disciplines—whereby we may expect to encounter Him regularly and be transformed by Him. If the Lord might be compared to a pure, life-giving river, the spiritual disciplines would be those ways by which we come to the river to drink from, dive into, swim in, eat from, wash with, and irrigate with it.

These devotional and sanctifying practices have been categorized in many ways. One approach classifies them as personal and corporate (or congregational) disciplines, meaning some disciplines are practiced in isolation, others are practiced in community. Examples of the former are the private reading of and meditating on Scripture, individual prayer, fasting, solitude, and the keeping of a spiritual journal. Disciplines that require the presence of others include congregational worship, corporate prayer, the Lord's Supper, and fellowship. Many of the disciplines taught in the Bible can be practiced both alone *and* with the church. For instance, we can study the Bible on our own and with a group. Service for Christ's sake can be practiced individually as well as collectively. The same is true with evangelism and Christian learning.[1]

Keep in mind that the spiritual disciplines are *biblical,* that is, God-given and found in His written Word. Whatever else might be said about them, those practices originating from ourselves, derived from the culture, or discovered in other religions may not properly be considered Christian spiritual disciplines.

Remember also that the spiritual disciplines found in Christian Scripture are *sufficient.* God has revealed in the pages of the Bible every devotional and transformational practice necessary. No other ceremony, rite, ritual, religious habit, or spiritual exercise is needed for progress in Christ's likeness.

Moreover, the Spirit of God works through *each* of these disciplines *in unique ways.* What He gives through one discipline He does not duplicate in another. You cannot receive through a prayer meeting the identical blessings given through fasting, and vice versa. All the Christian spiritual disciplines are important and singularly beneficial. A discipline neglected is a blessing unclaimed.

Recognize, too, that the spiritual disciplines are *practices, not attitudes*. Do not confuse them with character qualities, Christian graces, or "the fruit of the Spirit" (Galatians 5:22-23). Prayer is a spiritual discipline; love—strictly speaking—is not. Faithful stewardship of your time and money is a discipline in a way that joy isn't. Although we must never *separate* the external practices known as the spiritual disciplines from the internal realities that are their impulse and power, we may *distinguish* them.

WHY SHOULD I PRACTICE THE SPIRITUAL DISCIPLINES?

All who consider themselves Christians are exhorted in Hebrews 12:14 to "Pursue . . . holiness, without which no one will see the Lord." Pursuing holiness is not what qualifies us to "see the Lord"; it is the Lord Himself who qualifies us for this by grace through faith in the life and death of Jesus Christ. Rather the ongoing pursuit of holiness (in other words, sanctification, god-liness, Christlikeness) is characteristic of everyone who is on the way to "see the Lord" in Heaven.

Without exception, all who have been given the *Holy* Spirit will pursue *holi*ness. His holy presence and holy ministry within us cause us to love holiness, to long for it, and at times to grieve over our lack of it. The Bible doesn't set a minimum acceptable speed for the pursuit of holiness, but it says plainly that without holiness "no one will see the Lord," regardless of profession of faith, church experience, goodness of life, or Bible knowledge. If no one will go to Heaven without pursuing holiness/Christlike-ness/godliness, then there's hardly a more important question than, "How do we pursue it?"

"Discipline yourself," answers 1 Timothy 4:7 (NASB), "for the purpose of godliness." And the way to "discipline yourself" is to engage in the disciplines commanded and modeled in the Bible. In short, the Christian spiritual disciplines are the means to godliness, to the "holiness, without which no one will see the Lord."

This is why the title of this chapter probes your growth in holiness by asking, "Are the spiritual disciplines increasingly important to you?" Of course, it's not necessarily a mark of growth when the disciplines take a greater percentage of your daily or weekly time than they used to (though that might be very significant). What does matter is whether their *influence* continues to expand in your life. Growing Christians have a growing appetite for those things that bring the sweetest enjoyment of God.

No doubt, though, when one of the spiritual disciplines gathers the dust of disregard, to pick it up and incorporate it into your routine certainly could signify growth in godliness. If, for instance, a person is not even practicing the crucial disciplines of Bible-intake and prayer, then growth in Christlikeness would definitely involve more actual time devoted to them, for these were the practices of Christ Himself and are the basic means by which God transforms us.

Those who have believed in Jesus Christ know Him to be so gratifying and desirable that they crave to be like Him. And when you want to be like Jesus, you aspire to do what Jesus did—to live as much as possible as Jesus lived. Well, Jesus practiced the spiritual disciplines; through them He purposely placed Himself before the Father. So it follows that increased devotion to the same disciplines that Jesus practiced will accompany those who are becoming like Jesus.

However, engaging in the Christian disciplines is much more than imitating Jesus' example. The spiritual disciplines are the biblical avenues of intentional communion with Christ by those who love Him. All love craves intimacy, especially your greatest love. And as you grow more intimate with Jesus, you will obviously gravitate toward the means of that intimacy. You will not think of the disciplines as mere duty, nor simply as Christlike patterns to follow, but rather as life and light from Heaven to your soul.

Intimacy with Jesus—because His beauty is ever fresh—promotes even deeper love, which in turn intensifies your desire for closer communion. So as you grow closer to Christ, you will necessarily grow in the depth, if not duration, of your experience with what ministers Christ to you. Because the spiritual disciplines are the channels of communion with Christ, there simply will be no sustained growth in Christ without them.

WHAT ARE THE DANGERS OF THE DISCIPLINES?

Do not understand me to say that the mere rise of the disciplines in your priorities automatically indicates a rise in your likeness to Christ. Both the Pharisees of Jesus' day and the cultists of our own time are legendary for intense devotion to spiritual disciplines. The Pharisees fasted twice each week, made long prayers, and spent years learning the contents of the Scriptures of the Old Covenant. Although they devoted huge amounts of time to some of the disciplines, they did so while hating the Son of God. They were exemplary in discipline, but the epitome of ungodliness. Members of cults are likewise known to give themselves to lengthy periods of prayer and fasting and to prodigious feats of religious dedication. But apart from the presence and sanctifying work of the Spirit of God within, such efforts only render a person even more culpable at the Judgment.

The spiritual disciplines are not by themselves the *marks* of Christlikeness as much as they are the *means* to it. Without understanding this distinction, it is possible for someone to practice the disciplines and be far from Christ. A chaplain reportedly asked a famous American general in the Second World War if the presence of the Bible on his bedside table indicated that he read it. He is said to have taken the Lord's name in vain while answering that he read his Bible every day. In much the same way, even true believers can spend hours each week in the disciplines and not grow spiritually if their motive is misplaced or if they equate bare devotional activity with godliness. The disciplines are not machines that make us more like Jesus if we will just use them. Only God's grace working *through* the disciplines can transform those who practice them with eyes of faith on Him.

Besides a wrongly motivated usage of the disciplines, another danger is imbalance. Strangely enough, some of those Christians most active in church are most in need of examining their relationship to the disciplines. Remember that we are called to engage in both corporate and personal spiritual disciplines. Many believers so enthusiastically engage in the corporate disciplines that they have little time to practice the personal ones. Or perhaps they content themselves with the thought that extraordinary involvement in the corporate disciplines excuses them from the personal disciplines or even renders them superfluous. In other words, "I'm always at church and get so much there; why do I need to practice those personal disciplines?"

Serving in the church is a virtue—a corporate discipline that is practiced less and less today because more and more people have a consumer's view of the church, not a family view. But some who serve so faithfully have no time for prayer or Scripture meditation, the two most important personal disciplines to practice. I know many people quite well who are among the most conscientious workers in their churches, but who never read the Bible outside the walls of the church and who never devote themselves exclusively to prayer. Working for Christ is right; it is healthy Christianity. But working for Christ in a way that leaves insufficient time to be alone with Him and His Word is spiritually unhealthy and wrong. As much as Jesus gave Himself to the daily service of the Father, He did not neglect the refreshment of His own soul by regular communion with the Father through the personal spiritual disciplines (see Matthew 14:23; Mark 1:35; Luke 4:42).

If in public worship a person really does worship, how can he content himself with only a weekly experience when such a glorious and satisfying God can be experienced in private worship all throughout the week? How can he say after encountering the Lord and His Word on Sunday, "That's enough. I don't need any more of that for a week"? How can that worshiper be a growing Christian? Jonathan Edwards was even more pessimistic: "If persons . . . are often highly affected when with others, and but little moved when they have none but God and Christ to converse with, it looks very darkly upon their religion."[2] Even a corpse can be made warm by the fire of another. But those who have been made alive to God also have a fire within them—the Holy Spirit who kindles the flame of their love for God every day of the week.

At the other extreme, those submerged in their own private "spirituality" need the balance of the corporate disciplines. While God-centered solitude and the other personal spiritual disciplines are essential for growth in Christlikeness, so are public worship and prayer, fellowship, service to and with other believers, the hearing of God's Word preached, and the communion of saints around the Lord's Supper, just as we find in the practice of Christ's people in the New Testament. Any who think it pleases God for them to seek Him in private while rejecting His people are greatly mistaken.

WHAT SHOULD I DO?

In one sense I've answered that question with book-length responses elsewhere (see note 1). Let me here make three suggestions that are always appropriate.

Devote yourself more to the pursuit of Christlikeness and the enjoyment of God through the spiritual disciplines than to the pursuit of efficiency and the completion of to-do lists. The increasing pace of life and the inexorable roll of "progress" in our culture foster neither the growth of the soul nor the improvement of relationships, either with God or with others (including family, fellow believers, and the lost). In our frustrating and futile efforts to keep up the demands of life maintenance, our souls have shriveled. We have more tasks, activities, and deadlines to accomplish than ever; we have more to organize, store, and maintain than ever; and the result is that we're becoming increasingly efficient at leading meaningless lives. What good is our multitasking, the accomplishment of more and more, and the acquisition of wealth, if we are not—by the means God has given us—becoming more like Jesus, the One we live for and the One who will evaluate our lives?

Resist the temptation to believe in microwave spirituality or shortcut Christlikeness. The subtitle of James Gleick's popular book *Faster* is *The acceleration of just about everything.*[3] One thing that will always be an exception to acceleration is the rate of growth in godliness. The increasing speed of our machines cannot stimulate a corresponding rate in the growth of our souls. Faster Internet connections do not make us like Jesus more quickly. Theologian R. C. Sproul emphasized, "There are no quick and easy paths to spiritual maturity. The soul that seeks a deeper level of maturity must be prepared for a long, arduous task. If we are to seek the kingdom of God, we must abandon any formulae that promise instant spiritual gratification."[4] But whatever time and effort is required, the pursuit of intimacy with and likeness to Jesus Christ is worth it all.

Stoke your spiritual life with at least one perceptible poke.
When a well-wooded fire in my stove burns low, usually a good nudge or two with the iron poker restores its vitality. Having now invested part of your life to read this chapter, don't turn from it without choosing at least one sharp spiritual discipline to make at least one noticeable nudge in the fire of your soul's growth.

CHAPTER EIGHT

I AM CONVINCED THAT THE FIRST STEP TOWARDS
ATTAINING A HIGHER STANDARD OF HOLINESS IS TO
REALIZE MORE FULLY THE AMAZING SINFULNESS OF
SIN.

—J. C. RYLE

DO YOU STILL GRIEVE OVER SIN?

IN 1725, THE YEAR BEFORE HE SETTLED IN NORTHAMPTON, Massachusetts, to help his grandfather pastor the church there, a young Jonathan Edwards wrote:

> I have had a vastly greater sense of my own wicked-
> ness, and the badness of my heart, than ever I had
> before my conversion. It has often appeared to me that
> if God should mark iniquity against me I should
> appear the very worst of all mankind—of all that have
> been, since the beginning of the world to this time,
> and that I should have by far the lowest place in hell.
>
> My wickedness, as I am in myself, has long
> appeared to me perfectly ineffable, and swallowing up
> all thought and imagination; like an infinite deluge or

mountains over my head. I know not how to express better what my sins appear to me to be than by heaping infinite upon infinite, and multiplying infinite by infinite. Very often, for these many years, these expressions are in my mind, and in my mouth, "Infinite upon infinite . . . Infinite upon infinite!" When I look into my heart, and take a view of my wickedness, it looks like an abyss infinitely deeper than hell.[1]

Is this normal, healthy Christianity? Or is this obsessive, unnecessary groveling? I believe that Edwards' words of grief over his sin not only indicate that he was growing in grace, but also that all growing Christians think and feel as Edwards did. Here's what I mean.

WHEN TO GRIEVE IS TO GROW

The closer you get to Christ, the more you will hate sin; for nothing is more unlike Christ than sin. Because Jesus hates sin, the more like Him you grow the more you will grow to hate sin. And the more you hate sin, the more you will grieve whenever you realize that you have embraced that which killed your Savior.

Perhaps the world has never seen a man closer to Christ than the apostle Paul in the final years of his life. And yet, having grown into such a universally recognized example of Christlikeness, having audibly heard the voice of the Lord Himself on several occasions (see Acts 9:1-6; 18:8-10), having been given the privilege of glimpsing the glories of Heaven itself (see 2 Corinthians 12:2-4), Paul wrote in one of his final letters, "Christ Jesus came into the world to save sinners, of whom I am chief" (1 Timothy 1:15). If, as I am sure he did, Paul believed this sincerely, then he could not say it coldly. He meant every word of it with a breast-beating grief over his sin.

I once heard seminary professor John Hannah say, "The closer one comes to Christ, in one sense the more miserable he becomes."[2] Those who have a Holy-Spirit-implanted love for holy truth, holy things, and the Holy One can't help but feel miserable when they are reminded of that which is unholy within them. Sometimes the growing Christian sinks under a sense of sin so miserable that he wishes he could tear open his chest, rip out his sin-blackened heart, and fling it as far from himself as possible.

But the fact that there is a struggle with sin, and a sense of grief because of sin, is good. Unbelievers have no such struggles or griefs. They may disappoint themselves for not living up to their own standards or to the standard of someone they respect. But they do not agonize over being unholy before God—a God who is holy and who calls them to holiness (see 1 Peter 1:15). As A. W. Pink explained, "It is not the absence of sin but the grieving over it which distinguishes the child of God from empty professors [of faith]."[3]

Are you aware of sins in your life that you weren't cognizant of years ago, even though you were committing those sins back then as well? As discouraging as the fresh exposure is, and as grievous as it may be to have ever-deeper layers of sin laid bare, there's something positive here. Increased sensitivity to your sin is a mark of growth. You've made spiritual progress beyond where you were years ago because back then you didn't even realize that those *were* sins. The closer you come to the light of Christ, the more sins His holy light will expose in you. In the words of nineteenth century Bible scholar Thomas D. Bernard, "Our sense of sin is in proportion to our nearness to God."[4]

Edwards was right: "The more a true saint loves God . . . the more he mourns for sin."[5]

SHOULD I CONTINUALLY GRIEVE OVER SIN?

A longtime friend of my wife and I sent an e-mail recently. In it she wondered:

Is it good to always be so aware of my sin rather than focusing solely on the love and grace of God? After all, isn't that counterproductive now that we have been forgiven? And if someone has a tendency to be overly introspective or easily discouraged, can't the frequent thought of your sinfulness push you too far toward guilt and gloom?

Excessive introspection is itself a sinful possibility. But the spirit of the age certainly doesn't incline us to go to extremes in brooding over our sin. Even at church, religious entertainment characterizes more "worship" services than conviction of sin. Sermons are much more likely to be described as upbeat than heart-searching. Guffaws are far more common in church than tears, whether tears of joy *or* of repentance.

True, the correct proportion must be assigned to both the occasions of sin in a Christian's life and the incomparable freedom of forgiveness and grace he has through Christ. It is also true that many ministers and churches overemphasize the wrath of God and the sinfulness of people, including God-forgiven people. Nevertheless, amid all the error or overemphasis on sin a person may have experienced, and despite all the joy in the Lord that should characterize a Christian, the truth remains that the more a believer in Christ experiences growth, the more he grieves over sin. As Edwards put it in *Religious Affections:* "One great difference between saints and hypocrites is this, that the joy and comfort of the former is attended with godly sorrow and mourning for sin."[6]

Jesus Himself describes true Christians not only as those who *have* mourned over their sin, but also as those who are *still* mourning: "Blessed are those who mourn [present tense], for they shall be comforted" (Matthew 5:4). This is not to say that Christians should be mourning their sin every moment, but it does mean that they should grieve over it all their lives. We do not read of the apostle Paul endlessly lamenting his sin. Often we find him greatly rejoicing, not grieving, such as when we read of him singing praise to God at midnight with Silas in the Philippian jail (see Acts 16:25). On the other hand, he wouldn't think of himself near the end of his life as the "chief" sinner on the planet unless there had been much private grief over the sins that prompted such a claim.

There is a widely mistaken notion that repentance and faith in Christ are once-only events. Thereafter, when hearing of these matters, we tend to think, "I've done that." But Christians are *lifelong* repenters and *lifelong* believers. The initial experiences of turning from sin and trusting in Christ should characterize every Christian every day to some extent. Not that the new birth should occur daily for the child of God, for that happens only once. Rather the first experiences of those newly born again—repentance and faith—are the daily stuff of Christian living.

Jeremiah Burroughs, one of the most beloved of the seventeenth-century English Puritan preachers, elaborates in his book on sin, *The Evil of Evils*:

> There's a great mistake in the world in the matter of trouble for sin. They think repentance or mourning for sin is but one act, that if once they have been troubled for sin they need never be troubled anymore. It is a dangerous mistake, for we need to know that true sorrow for sin, true repentance, is a continual act that must abide all our lives. And it is not only at that time when we are afraid that God will not pardon our sins, when we are afraid that we shall be damned for our sins, but when we come to hope that God will, yes, when we come to know that God has pardoned our sins.[7]

Because, therefore, a Christian is always looking afresh to Christ and often turning from sin, it follows that he would often grieve over the presence of this sin. Would true repentance, simply by virtue of its frequency, become heartless and mechanical?

God forbid! Lifelong repentance of sin implies some measure of lifelong grief for sin.

THE RIGHT AND WRONG WAY
TO GRIEVE OVER SIN

In 2 Corinthians 7:8-11 the Bible juxtaposes two kinds of sorrow for sin: one that is expressed "in a godly manner" and then a "sorrow of the world." The passage contrasts the "godly sorrow" as the kind that by God's grace leads to salvation with the worldly sorrow that does not result in biblical repentance. Even unbelievers can grieve over sin, but without it being "in a godly manner," that is, without it leading to the proper end—repentance and its fruits. Still, as those who have experienced the "godly sorrow" that leads to eternal life, believers can either grieve over sin as Christians ought, or improperly as worldlings do.

Godly sorrow is much more than admitting your imperfections. I've never met anyone who considered himself perfect, but relatively few are often brokenhearted because they know themselves to be nonstop offenders against the Law of God. Many professing Christians show no more sorrow for sin on their occasional or perfunctory confessions to God than a boy forced to say "I'm sorry" to his sister. As a child of God, should we feel no more deeply about our sin than this? Godly sorrow for sin does involve *sorrow*.

Godly sorrow also results in repentance, that is, a change of mind about the sin that produces a change of behavior. The apostle Paul had written to the Christians in Corinth regarding sin and he later rejoiced in this result: "Now I rejoice, not that you were made sorry [only], but that your sorrow led to repentance" (2 Corinthians 7:9). Contrast their grief for sin with the kind manifested by Esau, the brother of the Old Testament patriarch Isaac: "He could bring about no change of mind though he sought the blessing with tears" (Hebrews 12:17, NIV). Like Esau, we may weep with regret over our sins and yet have no change of mind and life, no real repentance. Godly sorrow involves true sorrow, but true sorrow without true repentance is not godly sorrow.

In addition, sorrow for sin that is "in a godly manner" is genuinely humble. Edwards reflected on how some who use the most self-effacing language to describe their sinfulness may also be the most proud:

> "I am a poor vile creature," they may say, "I am not
> worthy of the least mercy, or that God should look
> upon me! Oh, I have a dreadful wicked heart! My
> heart is worse than the devil! Oh, this cursed heart of
> mine, etc." Such expressions are very often used, not
> with a heart that is broken. . . . There are many that
> are full of expressions of their own vileness, who yet
> expect to be looked upon as eminent and bright
> saints by others, as their due.[8]

Godly sorrow in the growing Christian makes him a thousand times more aware of his pride than his humility. It sometimes causes him to wonder how God's saving grace and such pride could dwell in the same heart. His grief is such that he feels himself to be "less than the least of all the saints" (Ephesians 3:8), not a great one at all.

In the worldly sort of grief for sin, the focus is on self. Like Esau, it may betray self-pity over what has been lost as a consequence of sin (see Genesis 25:27-34; 27:36-38). It may reveal self-disappointment over the failure to keep one's own standards or those of one's family or church. Worldly sorrow may even include a self-centered fear of God's wrath or of hell. While it's right to fear these, they may be feared only out of concern for self and without any thought of God, without any grief over having offended God.

All worldly grief over sin is itself sin because its main interest is selfward. Against this, Burroughs wrote:

The chief of all is the humiliation of the soul for sin as it is against God. Then is the heart humbled rightly for sin when it apprehends how, by sin, the soul has been against the infinite, glorious First-Being of all things. All other humiliations in the world are not sufficient without this. For it is not deep enough. There can be no humiliation deep enough unless the soul is humbled for sin because it has sinned against God.[9]

King David was a great sinner, but God called him "a man after My own heart" (Acts 13:22) because he was also a great repenter. Notice the God-centeredness of his grief: "Against You, You only, have I sinned, and done this evil in Your sight—that You may be found just when You speak, and blameless when You judge" (Psalm 51:4). The entire Psalm is addressed to God and overflows with thirty-one specific references to Him in just nineteen verses. As David's example shows, godly sorrow is *Godward* sorrow. And when our focus is on God and not self, we can hope for grace and pray expectantly with David, "Restore to me the joy of Your salvation, and uphold me by Your generous Spirit" (Psalm 51:12).

There is another measure of gentle sweetness in a Christian's godly grief over sin. Godly sorrow is the misery of a lover pining for what will be. We grieve over our sin partly because we long so for a holiness that is coming, but not yet. Paul writes in Romans 8:23, "We also who have the firstfruits of the Spirit, even we ourselves groan within ourselves, eagerly waiting for the adoption, the redemption of our body." The presence of the Holy Spirit in an unholy creature causes longings for what we are promised but do not have—thoroughly holy hearts and holy minds living in holy bodies. Because of His residence, we groan over every painful reminder that holiness is not yet, that we are still awaiting what God has destined us to become—the likeness of His sinless Son (see Romans 8:29-30).

WHAT SHOULD I DO IF I
DO NOT GRIEVE OVER SIN?

John Owen ventured, "I do not understand how a man can be a true believer in whom sin is not the greatest burden, sorrow, and trouble."[10] If you are not sure your experience resonates with Owen's statement, consider the following recommendations:

Make sure you understand the gospel of the New Testament. I'm always amazed at how many churchgoing people are unclear on the gospel. Write it out, as if you were putting it in a letter or e-mail. Think paragraph or page length, not a sentence or two. In this instance, give special attention to two parts of the gospel: that which made the death of Jesus necessary, and the relationship of repentance to faith.

Ask God to show you the reality of your sin. Ask Him to show you specifics of how you sin, when you sin, where you sin, why you sin, and against whom you sin.

Pray slowly through Psalm 51, making it your own heartfelt prayer. Remember that these words are more than just David's words. God Himself inspired them (see 2 Timothy 3:16), and He preserved them as an example of grief over sin. Pray through these words until they become a reflection of your own heart.

Meditate on the fact that it was your sin that nailed the holy, sinless One from Heaven to the cross. Are you never sorrowful for causing the death of Jesus? Think of what your sin cost the most pure, loving, and gracious One who ever lived. Consider how others are now in hell for the same sins you've committed. Remember that it is the eternal and perfect law of God Himself that you have so willingly and repeatedly broken and disregarded. Realize that your every sin is a double sin because every sin is also a failure to keep the greatest of all commandments—to love God with all your heart, soul, mind, and strength (see Mark 12:28-30). "Behold the Man" (John 19:5) your sins have pierced. Then remember that the life and death of Jesus saves from sin all who repent and believe. Be driven closer to Christ by your sin. May your sin only serve to cause you to prize Christ even more.

Preach the gospel to yourself every day. I've borrowed this phrase from Jerry Bridges, who wrote:

> To preach the gospel to yourself, then, means that you continually face up to your own sinfulness and then flee to Jesus through faith in His shed blood and righteous life. It means that you appropriate, again by faith, the fact that Jesus fully satisfied the law of God, that he is your propitiation, and that God's holy wrath is no longer directed toward you. . . . You can be sure of one thing, though: When you set yourself to seriously pursue holiness, you will begin to realize what an awful sinner you are. And if you are not firmly rooted in the gospel and have not learned to preach it to yourself every day, you will soon become discouraged and will slack off in your pursuit of holiness.[11]

From this perspective of grieving for sin, there are two ways to evaluate your life—proximity to the ideal or progress toward it. You can look at what you ought to be—Christlike—and be discouraged because you are so far from it. Too much measuring yourself by the perfection of Jesus will dishearten you. Too little can breed spiritual pride. But you can also look at how far by God's grace you've come, and be hopeful. In the life of the growing Christian, there are times for both.

CHAPTER NINE

THE UNFORGIVING SPIRIT . . . IS THE NUMBER ONE
KILLER OF SPIRITUAL LIFE.

—JAMES COULTER

ARE YOU A QUICKER FORGIVER?

I WAS TWENTY-SEVEN WHEN I BECAME THE PASTOR OF A SMALL RURAL church in a southern state. I was the seventeenth pastor of that church in twenty-one years. Today that statistic tells me far more than it did when I was twenty-seven.

Although I'd grown up in a small-town church in the same state, I had no idea in those days how horribly some churches treat pastors, no matter how hard-working or loving the ministers may be. I assumed that if I loved the people, preached the Word of God to them, and gave myself to serve them, they all would respond well and be grateful. That was the most naïve mistake of my life.

A woman I'll call Patsy increasingly opposed me. Disagreement deteriorated into criticism. The criticisms became more caustic until they spewed forth in confrontive, brazen challenges. "If you had the faith you preach about," she once taunted, "you'd leave [with no place to go or to live] and trust God to provide for you." When, after twelve months, I spent my first week away from the church, she managed to arrange a meeting of some of the deacons for the purpose of getting me fired. Later she admitted "forgetting" to call those deacons who were known to be my strong supporters.

Despite her desire to see me go, when she heard second-hand that while on vacation I had interviewed with another church, she called that church and misrepresented herself in an effort to find out what I'd been doing. After I returned she asked if I'd be willing to come to a Saturday night meeting (that she had already secretly organized) "to discuss some problems in the church." I was the pastor; how could I not go?

Upon arrival I learned that I was there as the accused to stand trial and Patsy was the self-appointed prosecutor. Although most of her efforts that night were frustrated, she had done her best to humiliate me before the church and to undermine my pastoral leadership.

After fifteen months of stomach churning, the Lord opened a new door of ministry as pastor of a church where He "turned for me my mourning into dancing" (Psalm 30:11). I was there for almost fifteen years. But the stress of our pressure-cooker pastorate took its toll. Between us, Caffy and I experienced five hospitalizations, three surgeries, and the inability to have children for sixteen years.

I knew I had to be willing to forgive Patsy, but I found it hard because she had treated us in such ungodly ways. In the last month of our time there, Caffy was diagnosed with a life-threatening, stress-induced thyroid difficulty that soon required the removal of the gland. When the physician she first consulted—an unconverted man—examined her, he asked, "What are those people out there doing to you two?"

Patsy was merciless, relentless, and rapacious. Why should I forgive her? Every day for months on end, if I didn't see her in person, I saw her face in my mind. Mentally I replayed each of her attacks, only now I said the things I wished I'd said then. I might be in my car, driving; I might be trying to sleep, or even praying, and find myself gnashing my teeth at her, even bursting out in angry shouts at the Patsy in my imagination. Often I would awaken from my imaginary conversation glaring at nothing, fists clenched, stomach acid boiling, breath coming rapidly.

I can't remember ever emerging from one of these frequent episodes without an awareness that God's will was for me to forgive Patsy. Especially when her specter would invade my prayer time I would recall Jesus' words, "And whenever you stand praying, if you have anything against anyone, forgive him, that your Father in heaven may also forgive you your trespasses. But if you do not forgive, neither will your Father in heaven forgive your trespasses" (Mark 11:25-26).

I knew it was useless to pray unless I forgave Patsy. It was one thing for her to accuse me of failures as a pastor; it was another for my own conscience to accuse me before God because of her.

But at last I found the grace to let go of my bitterness. I realized that I could either continue to stoke my smoldering grudge against her and allow her to control me in absentia, or I could move toward forgiveness just as I had been forgiven by Jesus.

REAL CHRISTIANS WANT TO FORGIVE

Although my heart was a volcano of anger, by God's grace I was also inclined to forgive Patsy. I knew forgiveness to be the will of God, as well as the path back to freedom and joy. When God makes of us "a new creation" (2 Corinthians 5:17), He gives us a disposition to love and obey His will (as in Psalm 40:8). And this heart desire to do God's will—such as to forgive—beats within us even during the times when we sinfully resist it.

Three times in the Gospels Jesus directly connects our forgiveness of others with God's forgiveness of us—Mark 11:25-26 (quoted previously), Matthew 6:14-15, and also Luke 6:37, where He says, "Forgive, and you will be forgiven." He did not mean that we earn God's forgiveness for the sins we commit against Him by granting forgiveness to others for their sins against us. This would make our salvation conditional upon doing something to earn it—in this case dispensing forgiveness to others. Rather, these texts show that *a forgiving spirit characterizes those who have been forgiven.* Repenters toward God are forgivers toward others. Those who find themselves unable to forgive reveal that they've never experienced the transforming forgiveness of God. But those who are willing to forgive as God forgives may be hopeful that they have received the grace of God. And this grace causes them to truly *want* to forgive, even when the flesh rages against that impulse.

In Matthew 18:21-35, Jesus told a parable about a king and one of his servants. The servant owed an unpayable debt, but the king showed great mercy and forgave the entire amount. When the king heard that the servant had choked a fellow servant to wring from him a tiny unpaid debt, he was enraged: "You wicked servant! I forgave you all that debt because you begged me. Should you not also have had compassion on your fellow servant, just as I had pity on you?" (verses 32-33). He then condemned the servant to prison where he would spend his remaining years in a futile attempt to work off the impossible debt.

Then Jesus made His point: "So My heavenly Father also will do to you if each of you, from his heart, does not forgive his brother his trespasses" (verse 35). Unlike the servant in the story, the true servant of God will be a forgiver. Knowing that God has forgiven him a debt of sin he could never remove, he is willing to forgive others. And the grace of God causes him to want to forgive another's comparatively insignificant sins against him, not just with words but "from his heart."

The testimony of Martyn Lloyd-Jones should be the heart-cry of every Christian: "I say to the glory of God and in utter humility that whenever I see myself before God and realize even something of what my blessed Lord has done for me, I am ready to forgive anybody anything."[1]

READY TO FORGIVE VERSUS EXTENDING FORGIVENESS

Notice Lloyd-Jones' phrase, "I am *ready* to forgive anybody anything" (emphasis added). Many do not understand the difference between being ready to forgive and actually extending forgiveness.

Often after a shooting at a school or some other horrendous, large-scale massacre, well-meaning spokespeople in the community will appeal for people to forgive the murderer(s). But biblical forgiveness is never given or required where there is no repentance. Although Jesus prayed immediately after they nailed Him to a cross, "Father, forgive them, for they do not know what they do" (Luke 23:34), this wasn't an unconditional forgiveness. Otherwise these people would be forgiven of their sins without repenting and believing in the gospel—a heretical notion. "On the cross, Jesus did not forgive," Jay Adams points out, "He prayed." Referring to the martyr Stephen's prayer for the forgiveness of his persecutors in Acts 7:60, Adams continues,

> The same is true of Stephen. If forgiveness is unconditional, Jesus, Stephen, and others would have *forgiven* their murderers rather than use what, if true, would be a roundabout way to do so. At other times Jesus had no hesitancy in saying, "Your sins be forgiven you."
>
> Jesus' prayer was answered in the response to the preaching of Peter and the apostles on the day of Pentecost, and on those other occasions when thousands of Jews repented and believed the Gospel (Acts 2:37-38; 3:17-19; 4:4). They were not forgiven the

sin of crucifying the Savior apart from believing that
He was dying for their sins, but precisely by doing so
in response to the faithful preaching of the Gospel in
Jerusalem.[2]

What Christians should always do, as Jesus exemplified in
His prayer, is be *ready* to forgive. And then, when forgiveness is
sought, forgiveness can be extended.

Yes, we ought to release our sinful bitterness and hatred
whether the offender ever seeks forgiveness. Some equate this
decision with forgiveness itself. In reality though, this is only
getting ready, being willing to forgive. Then if the offender
repents, we are prepared to complete the process by saying, "I forgive you." The one who announces forgiveness where it hasn't
been sought not only discounts the importance of repentance, he
also misunderstands the requirement of Scripture. But the one
who is not willing to forgive is contradicting the Scripture, and
for the moment at least, is putting the reality of his salvation to
the test.

Leon Morris, a New Testament scholar from Australia,
noted, "We can always think of some 'good' reason why in any
particular case we need not forgive. But that is always an error."[3]
Growing Christians will recognize that error and become
quicker to say to themselves, "I'm ready to forgive."

FORGIVE AND FORGET?

The Bible doesn't contain the expression "forgive and forget."
Not only that, the Bible never commands us to forget an offense
once we have forgiven it, though sometimes forgetfulness does
result from forgiveness.

The promise of God for all who know Him through Christ
is "I will forgive their iniquity, and their sin I will remember no
more" (Jeremiah 31:34). Because God is omniscient, knowing

infallibly all the past, present, and future, He doesn't actually forget our sins. What His forgiveness means is that He will not remember them *against* us anymore. He will never bring them up again. That's the way we are to forgive others. To say "I forgive you" is not a commitment never to recall the offense, but forgiveness *is* a promise never to *use* the sin against the offender again. While we may not totally forget the offense, we are to treat the forgiven person as though we *had* forgotten it. (There may be occasions where trust needs to be rebuilt after a wrongdoing is forgiven, but forgiveness means that the offense itself will never again be the basis of a breach in the relationship.)

When I first overcame my unwillingness to forgive Patsy, it was like pulling an enemy's flaming arrow out of my chest. The removal initially seemed worse than the torment of living with the bitterness. Immediately after the extraction, however, my soul began to breathe more easily and a cleansing process began.

Not all the poison of bitterness was removed from my system immediately. Although I had passed the greatest crisis of forgiveness, her face soon reappeared in my mind and with it the mental videotapes of many of our confrontations. Here I began to learn for the first time that the readiness to forgive might not always be won in a single decisive battle. I truly wanted to forgive Patsy, but when in my mind I relived her attacks, the wounds were reopened.

Jesus teaches us, "Take heed to yourselves. If your brother sins against you, rebuke him; and if he repents, forgive him. And if he sins against you seven times in a day, and seven times in a day returns to you, saying, 'I repent,' you shall forgive him" (Luke 17:3-4). We're to take this literally; that is, we should be willing to forgive the repentant believer no matter how often he sincerely repents. But I think it would be rather unusual for a person to come in sincere humility seven times to repent for a sin willfully committed on seven different occasions in one day. And yet, when I have been offended it is not unusual at all for the *memory* of that one offense to return to my mind seven times in a single day. Just as in the situation Jesus described, I might find myself faced with the necessity to become willing to forgive at least seven times that day.

That's the way it was with my frequent recollections of Patsy's hurtful attacks. With each remembrance I had to return to the cross of Jesus and renew my willingness to forgive her. And while the fresh tearing of the wound made the process painful, the second time wasn't quite as difficult as the first, for there had been some progress in healing. The third time was less difficult than the second, and each succeeding time I had to return to this crisis of forgiveness was easier than the previous one. It wasn't long until I could think of Patsy without bitterness at all. And though she never sought my forgiveness, by God's grace I reached the place where I was ready to give it.

I believe it is because I became willing to forgive Patsy that I have virtually forgotten the things she said and did. However, sometimes we may believe we have fulfilled God's expectation of forgiveness simply because we no longer think of the offenses. In other words, life goes on, we become occupied with other things, and eventually we forget without forgiving. But even worldlings can do that. Does the return of a seldom-remembered face or event cause your stomach to churn and your jaw muscles to tighten? *Be careful that you do not think you have forgiven just because you have forgotten.*

PROBING THE HEART

"Everyone thinks forgiveness is a lovely idea," C. S. Lewis observed, "until he has something to forgive."[4] If you don't have something to forgive at present, you soon will. Here are three personal inquiries intended to encourage you to do what every Christian, by grace, wants to do "from his heart."

Are you ready to forgive? Perhaps this is better asked in

reverse: Is there anyone you are *not* ready to forgive? Is there any-one at church, at work, in your neighborhood, or in your family whose face or voice causes more of the acid of bitterness to flow out of your heart than the willingness to forgive? If so, resolving that matter is the only way forward. As King David testified in Psalm 86:5, the Lord is "ready to forgive." To grow more like Him means that we must be likewise, and in every situation.

Do you need to initiate the process of forgiveness with any-one? If you know you are the offender, the next step is clear. Repent—don't merely apologize, repent—for your offense and ask forgiveness. During my final two weeks as Patsy's pastor, I became convicted of my sin of gossiping about her sins. I tried to reason my way around asking her forgiveness by telling myself that her sins were 95 percent of the problem between us, and that my gossip was only 5 percent of the sin in this mat-ter. But I knew that regardless of what she did, I was respon-sible before God for my 5 percent and had to repent. It wasn't easy to go to Patsy and ask her forgiveness. I knew that my con-fession likely would result only in Patsy feeling more justified in her opposition to me and in her having more ammunition to use against me. Still, I wanted to do what I believed was right in God's sight and leave the consequences to Him.

You may also need to initiate the process of forgiveness with someone who has offended you. Jesus said, "If your brother sins against you, rebuke him; and if he repents, forgive him" (Luke 17:3). As obvious as the sin is to you, it is possible that the offender isn't even aware that you've been offended. In any case, if you find yourself unable to overlook the offense and to prac-tice 1 Peter 4:8, that is, "love will cover a multitude of sins," then your responsibility is to bring the offense to the person's attention and work toward reconciliation.

Do you love forgiveness? Many professing Christians are too easily offended. Some almost seem to take pride in their ability to hold a grudge or in their refusal to humble themselves or in their resistance to seeking or extending forgiveness. True Christians love forgiveness. Because of God's forgiveness of them, they think it beautiful and Godlike to give or get forgiveness. That's why the ready willingness to forgive is such a clear mark of growth in godliness. As the godly and persecuted fifth-century preacher John Chrysostom concluded, "Nothing causes us to so nearly resemble God as the forgiveness of injuries."[5]

CHAPTER TEN

YOU MAY JUDGE OF A MAN BY WHAT HE GROANS AFTER.
—C. H. SPURGEON

DO YOU YEARN FOR HEAVEN AND TO BE WITH JESUS?

As a young pastor, I was sometimes frustrated by the emphasis that elderly church members placed on Heaven. *What about now?* I wondered. *Don't you have any goals for your spiritual life, your church, or the kingdom of God at large before you die?* Now that I am nearing twice the age when I mentally muttered those semi-disparaging thoughts and am much closer to the age of the folks to whom I directed them, I am tempted to believe those thoughts were merely the musings of a zealous, but immature minister.

Those who have been on a long pilgrimage increasingly desire to reach their destination, especially one as glorious and excellent as Heaven. Those who have spent decades loving and living for Jesus naturally long to see Him. While it's obvious that such anticipation should characterize those older believers living right on the borders of Heaven, these yearnings surge in the hearts of all growing Christians.

GROWING CHRISTIANS ARE GROANING CHRISTIANS

In Romans 8:22-23, the apostle Paul calls attention to the groans of the entire creation, and especially the groans of that human part of creation indwelled by the Spirit of God, as they await the removal of the corruption they have endured since sin's entrance into the world. He wrote, "For we know that the whole creation groans and labors with birth pangs together until now. Not only that, but we also who have the firstfruits of the Spirit, even we ourselves groan within ourselves, eagerly waiting for the adoption, the redemption of our body."

Notice that the human groaners here are not exceptionally committed Christians, but simply "we also who have the first-fruits of the Spirit." In other words, every Christian, every person in whom the Holy Spirit has begun an eternal work, experiences these groans "for the adoption, the redemption of [the] body." These longings for the coming great change in body and place are simply part of a normal, healthy, growing Christian life.

Paul reiterated this fact in 2 Corinthians 5:2 when he declared, "For in this [referring to our earthly bodies] we groan, earnestly desiring to be clothed with our habitation which is from heaven." Of course, the groans of the Christian are not simply for the clothing of a new, glorified body, but for all that such a transformation represents. Six verses later, Paul again uses a kind of theological shorthand when he looks forward to when we will "be present with the Lord" (verse 8). In each of these references, the apostle specifies only one aspect of the Christian's hope, but each is representative of the believer's entire experience in eternity. So when the Christian groans for the redemption of the body, he is also groaning to be in the presence of the Lord, who will redeem (that is, glorify) his body—to live in Heaven forever and to enjoy eternal fellowship with God's people.

"Okay," interjects someone, "but what is it like in daily life when a Christian yearns to be in Heaven and with Jesus?" An excerpt from the diary of David Brainerd (1718–1747) provides a good example. Brainerd was a missionary to Indians in eighteenth-century New England. He died of tuberculosis in the home of Jonathan Edwards at age twenty-nine. Edwards published *The Life and Diary of David Brainerd*, which remains a classic of Christian devotion. An entry from 1742 is typical:

> Saturday, June 12. Spent much time in prayer this morning, and enjoyed much sweetness. Felt insatiable longings after God much of the day. I wondered how poor souls do to live that have no God. The world with all its enjoyments quite vanished. I see myself very helpless, but I have a blessed God to go to. I longed exceedingly to be dissolved and to be with Christ, to behold His glory. Oh, my weak, weary soul longs to arrive at my Father's house![1]

Notice the "sweetness" and the joy that permeate Brainerd's longings. Despite the agony of separation from something much desired and the dissatisfaction with the present whenever we yearn for something yet future, the Holy Spirit intersperses both sweetness and happiness into our groans. This is what C. S. Lewis portrayed in his retelling of the myth of Cupid and Psyche in *Till We Have Faces*. Think of a Christian's longing to be in Heaven and with Jesus, as Psyche explains to her friend Orual,

> It was when I was happiest that I longed most. It was on happy days when we were up there on the hills, the three of us, with the wind and the sunshine. . . . Do you remember? The color and the smell, and looking across at the Grey Mountain in the distance? And because it was so beautiful, it set me longing, always longing. Somewhere else there must be more of it. Everything seemed to be saying, Psyche come! But I couldn't (not yet) come and I didn't know where

I was to come to. It almost hurt me. I felt like a bird
in a cage when the other birds of its kind are flying
home. . . . The sweetest thing in all my life has been
the longing—to reach the Mountain, to find the place
where all the beauty came from.[2]

Does Psyche give voice to your soul? Do you find more and
more that the life you long for in Heaven seems more natural
to you than the one you are living on earth? Does it seem that
your deepest longings were made to be fulfilled in another
world? These are the groans of a growing Christian, one who
knows that God made us for glorious communion with Him
and that we are never at home, never fulfilled, until we are there.

GROWING CHRISTIANS
GROAN FOR HOLINESS

As I mentioned, age and experience have tempered my evaluation of the often heavenward mindset of some of those older
folks I pastored. But I remain reluctant to regard all longings
for Heaven as rightly motivated. The older I get and the more
easily my body fatigues, the more sympathetic I am to the desire
for rest—eternal rest. But even Buddhists, Muslims, and athe-
ists want that. There's nothing uniquely Christian about longing for an end to a wearying existence and the beginning of a
new and more restful one.

In a similar way, pining for lasting relief from the cares of the
world is also universal and not exclusively Christian. Every person on earth dreams of a time when he can lay his burdens
down. Should we then base our confidence that we are growing in grace on the fact we want only what everyone else in the
world, even self-confessed God-haters, wants?

Like the desires for rest and relief, yearning for reunion with
deceased loved ones is as common among *non*Christians as

Christians. Just because someone looks forward with increased hope to seeing a child or parent or spouse in Heaven does not mean he or she is growing as a Christian. Realistically, it's no mark of faith at all, but of nothing more than natural affection.

Even the eagerness to be with Jesus is not necessarily a confirmation of knowing Christ, much less of growth in His likeness. Some people want to see Jesus in the same way they would like to see the Virgin Mary or King David. Natural curiosity, or simply the desire to see someone so well known, may be the only motivation.

So the question is not merely, "Do you yearn for Heaven and to be with Jesus?" but also "For which Heaven and Jesus do you yearn?" Growing Christians increasingly long for a *holy* Heaven, not just a restful one. They look forward to *holy* relationships, not just nostalgic ones. They sigh to see a *holy* Jesus. They feel less and less at home in a sinful world because they are growing more and more homesick for a holy place, a holy people, and a God who is "holy, holy, holy" (Revelation 4:8). They ache to share in this holiness more than in Heaven's rest, relief, or reunions. Jonathan Edwards put it this way: "But neither a . . . longing to be in Heaven, nor longing to die, are in any measure so distinguishing marks of true saints, as longing after a more holy heart."[3]

In describing his own spiritual cravings, Edwards said in another place: "The Heaven I desired was a Heaven of holiness; to be with God, and to spend my eternity in divine love, and holy communion with Christ. My mind was very much taken up with contemplations of Heaven, and the enjoyments there; and living there in perfect holiness, humility and love."[4]

His younger friend David Brainerd shared Edwards' heartbeat with him and with all growing Christians. On October 26, 1744, he wrote:

My soul was exceedingly grieved for sin, and prized, and longed after holiness; it wounded my heart deeply, yet sweetly, to think how I had abused a kind God. I longed to be perfectly holy, that I might not grieve a gracious God; who will continue to love, not withstanding his love is abused.[5]

And a late twentieth-century biographer of Brainerd adds,

His often expressed desire to die was not merely a wish to escape the tribulations and trials of this life, although we cannot eliminate that motive altogether. For him the final state in Heaven was the supreme goal for living because it afforded final relief from the weight of sin which hung upon him.[6]

All this is consistent with Paul's description of a Christian in Romans 8:23, "Not only that, but we also who have the first-fruits of the Spirit, even we ourselves groan within ourselves, eagerly waiting for the adoption, the redemption of our body." To at last live in a body redeemed from sin, to exult in the breathtaking presence of Jesus Himself with a body, mind, and heart soaring free from any vestige of sin is the burning hope that obsesses the growing Christian's thoughts of eternity.

If there is anyone who would look forward to the "redemption of the body" more in a physical sense than a spiritual one it would be a Christian in circumstances like quadriplegic Joni Eareckson Tada. And yet, like all growing Christians, her greatest groans for the next life are more for holiness than health. I heard her attest:

People say, "You must be looking forward to Heaven," thinking I am looking forward to getting my new body. And after more than twenty-five years in a wheelchair, it's true that I am. But more than I am looking forward to my new body [she said with her voice choking with emotion] I am looking forward to a heart without sin.[7]

Elsewhere she added, "Most people will continue to think that getting a new body is my focus. But I can't wait to be clothed in righteousness, with not a trace of sin. . . . For me, that will be the best part of heaven."[8]

To be pure in heart and to see the Lord are the Christian's highest hopes and deepest groans, as Martyn Lloyd-Jones summarized:

> What are you looking for and hoping for in Heaven? Let me ask you a question that perhaps should come before that. Do you ever look forward to being in Heaven? . . . The person who looks forward to death simply wants to get out of life because of his troubles. That is not Christian; that is pagan. The Christian has a positive desire for Heaven, and therefore I ask: Do you look forward to being in Heaven? But, more than this, what do we look forward to when we get to Heaven? What is it we are desiring? Is it the rest of Heaven? Is it to be free from troubles and tribulations? Is it the peace of Heaven? Is it the joy of Heaven? All those things are to be found there, thank God; but that is not the thing to look forward to in Heaven. It is the face of God. "Blessed are the pure in heart: for they shall see God". . . to stand in the very presence of God—"To gaze and gaze on thee." Do we long for that? Is that Heaven to us? Is that the thing we want above everything else?[9]

GROWING CHRISTIANS GROAN FOR HOLINESS IN HEAVEN MORE THAN ANYTHING

Spiritually flourishing Christians answer Lloyd-Jones' final question in the affirmative: "Yes, we do long for the *holiness* of Heaven and the face of God above everything else."

In 2 Corinthians 5:2, Paul described the heavenly holiness we groan for as something we're also "earnestly desiring." Years before he penned these words he was given a glimpse of what awaits us in our holy home above (see 2 Corinthians 12:1-4). After that indescribable experience he could say things like, "But if I live on in the flesh, this will mean fruit from my labor; yet what I shall choose I cannot tell. For I am hard pressed between the two, having a desire to depart and be with Christ, which is far better" (Philippians 1:22-23). Despite all the unparalleled blessings Paul experienced as an apostle—miracles frequently coursing through his hands, dramatic conversions when he preached, angelic appearances, and so on, he knew firsthand that "to depart and be with Christ" is "far better." Not just better, "far better."

Consider again the intensity of the words "we groan, earnestly desiring," "to depart and be with Christ, which is far better." Paul wrote like a man who had not only tasted and seen that the Lord is good (Psalm 34:8), but like one who has found the holiness of the Lord eternally and irresistibly addictive. He couldn't get enough, and he groaned, "earnestly desiring" the one thing that could satisfy—the rapturous, full-faced enjoyment of God Himself.

It is incomparable, exclaimed Edwards:

> The enjoyment of God is the only happiness with which our souls can be satisfied. To go to Heaven, fully to enjoy God, is infinitely better than the most pleasant accommodations here. Fathers and mothers, husbands, wives, or children, or the company of earthly friends, are but shadows; but God is the substance. These are but scattered beams, but God is the sun. These are but streams, but God is the ocean.[10]

Brainerd also thirsted for the holy ocean of God more than he wanted anything else:

Tuesday, June 15 [1742]. Had the most ardent longings after God that ever I felt in my life. At noon in
my secret retirement I could do nothing but tell my
Lord, in a sweet calm, that He knew I longed for
nothing but Himself, nothing but holiness; that He
had given me these desires and He only could give me
the thing desired.[11]

Jesus said, "For where your treasure is, there your heart will
be also" (Matthew 6:21). When your treasure is in Heaven, like
Paul, Jonathan Edwards, David Brainerd, and all other growing
Christians, your heart will ache for Heaven more than for anything else. That's not to deny the many legitimate longings we
have for earthly things. The desires to get married, have children,
experience job satisfaction, and the like, may also be strong,
long-lasting, and God-ignited. But even if someone wanted one
or more of these as much as Joni Eareckson Tada yearns to walk,
maturing Christians would say with Joni that year in and year
out, nothing "outgroans" their groan for holiness in Heaven.

GROANING CHRISTIANS ARE
GROWING CHRISTIANS

I said at the outset that growing Christians will groan for Heaven
and all it holds. But the reverse is also true—groaning Christians grow.

They set their minds on things above. One of the ways Christians grow is by thinking much about great matters, subjects
that have the power to change their lives. There are no more
powerful or worthy subjects to consider than the Lord Jesus
Christ, Heaven, and the redemption of the body. Growing Christians take seriously, as well as joyously, the command to "seek
those things which are above, where Christ is, sitting at the right
hand of God. Set your mind on things above, not on things on

the earth" (Colossians 3:1-2). Their great Treasure is sitting at the right hand of God. Their greatest hopes and eternal home are among the "things above," so their thoughts are often there also. They'll soon be living there, so they want to visit as often as possible before relocating permanently.

There's no greater example of such heavenly-mindedness than the English Puritan pastor/writer Richard Baxter. He lived during most of the 1600s, though he was in terrible physical condition for nearly all his seventy-six years. He lay sick and lonely in a house far from his home all during the winter of 1646, "sentenced to Death by the Physicians." For his own use he began to write out his meditations about the Heaven he seemed so near to entering. Thus began what may be his most important book, *The Saints' Everlasting Rest*. Believing that his extended thoughts on Heaven were so beneficial, when he recovered he disciplined himself to meditate on Heaven—often while walking—for at least half an hour daily. The final product, published several decades later, was a monumental, still-in-print work that has been one of the most influential Christian books ever written.

The practice of regular "heavenly meditation," as he called it, transformed Baxter and it will transform us. While thirty minutes' meditation on one subject, in addition to the practice of the other spiritual disciplines, may sound unworkable for many in today's culture, we can adopt Baxter's intentionality. Resolving to devote *some* time on a regular basis to reflect upon the coming world and the coming One would encourage, embolden, strengthen, invigorate, illumine, ravish, and de-stress us. And anyone who cannot find time to meditate on Jesus and Heaven is either wasting time or busier than God intends.

The mind never stops. It is like a waterwheel always being turned by the river. Even when we're asleep it is turning, thinking, dreaming. Shouldn't we then put the best thoughts into our minds as much as possible? What better things to think about than Jesus and Heaven?

Groaning Christians purify themselves in anticipation of see-ing the Pure One. The apostle John wrote the inspired assur-ance that when Jesus "is revealed, we shall be like Him, for we shall see Him as He is" (1 John 3:2). Then note what he says about those who groan with this anticipation of seeing the Lord: "And everyone who has this hope in Him purifies himself, just as He is pure" (verse 3). All those ("everyone," not just some) who have this hope, who yearn for the return of Jesus, are affected by it. The second coming of the Lord is not a mere curiosity or just a matter of theological deliberation for them. All those who are sincerely longing to see a *holy* Christ appear are growing more like Christ. How do I know? It's because each one "purifies himself, just as He is pure." In other words, you are in the grip of the groan. Your longings for holiness in Heaven pull you toward holiness now. You can't just wait for holiness; you have to pursue it. As theologian J. I. Packer wrote, "The hope of a holy Heaven, to be enjoyed in the company with our holy Savior, is a potent motive to holiness now."[12]

Do you have "this hope" to "see Him as He is"? How has it affected you? How does it cause you to purify yourself? How are you growing in Christlikeness because of your view of Christ's return?

I am writing these words while on an airplane, just twenty minutes from home after four days and four long flights. The nearer I get to my destination the more I anticipate it. The closer my longing comes to reality the more I think about what and who awaits me. You are nearer the end of your journey than you were when you began this book. Are your thoughts increasingly homeward nowadays? The closer he gets to his heavenly home, the growing Christian will—for the right reasons—think more about what and who awaits him in Heaven. And he will yearn.

NOTES

INTRODUCTION

1. Jonathan Edwards, *The Works of Jonathan Edwards,* vol. 2, Perry Miller, gen. ed., *Religious Affections,* ed. John E. Smith (New Haven, Conn.: Yale University Press, 1959), pp. 346-347. If you find my book helpful and/or would enjoy the challenge of reading a deeper and much more thoughtful one on the same subject, I highly recommend Edwards' *Religious Affections.* It is available in many editions.

CHAPTER 1:
DO YOU THIRST FOR GOD?

1. Jonathan Edwards, *The Works of Jonathan Edwards,* vol. 2, Perry Miller, gen. ed., *Religious Affections,* ed. John E. Smith (New Haven, Conn.: Yale University Press, 1959), p. 104.

2. John Piper, *A Godward Life* (Sisters, Ore.: Multnomah, 1997), pp. 84-85.

3. For further reading on God's desertions, see Joseph Symonds, *The Case and Cure of a Deserted Soul* (1671; reprint ed., Morgan, Penn.: Soli Deo Gloria, 1996).

4. John Blanchard, comp., *Gathered Gold* (Welwyn, England: Evangelical Press, 1984), p. 100.

5. Thomas Shepard, *Parable of the Ten Virgins*, as quoted in Edwards, pp. 376-377.

6. Edwards, p. 379.

7. A. W. Tozer, *The Pursuit of God* (Harrisburg, Penn.: Christian Publications, 1948), p. 8.

8. Tozer, p. 20.

9. For further reading on spiritual mindedness, see Donald S. Whitney, *How Can I Be Sure I'm a Christian?* (Colorado Springs: NavPress, 1994), pp. 67-80.

10. C. H. Spurgeon, "The Panting Heart," *Metropolitan Tabernacle Pulpit*, vol. 14 (1869; reprint, Pasadena, Tex.: Pilgrim Publications, 1982), p. 417.

11. Jonathan Edwards, "Nothing Upon Earth Can Represent the Glories of Heaven," *The Works of Jonathan Edwards*, vol. 14, *Sermons and Discourses, 1723-1729*, ed. Kenneth P. Minkema (New Haven, Conn.: Yale University Press, 1997), p. 143.

12. Edwards, *Sermons and Discourses, 1723-1729*, p. 147.

13. Edwards, *Sermons and Discourses, 1723-1729*, pp. 151-152.

14. Edwards, *Sermons and Discourses, 1723-1729*, pp. 152-153.

15. Edwards, *Religious Affections*, p. 378.

16. Roger Steer, ed., *Spiritual Secrets of George Müller* (Wheaton, Ill.: Harold Shaw, 1985), pp. 62-63.

17. For further reading on scriptural meditation, see Donald S. Whitney, *Spiritual Disciplines for the Christian Life* (Colorado Springs: NavPress, 1991), pp. 43-51, 67-72.

18. Arthur Bennett, ed., *The Valley of Vision* (Edinburgh: The Banner of Truth Trust, 1975).

CHAPTER 2:
ARE YOU GOVERNED INCREASINGLY BY GOD'S WORD?

1. Octavius Winslow, *Personal Declension and Revival of Religion in the Soul* (1841; reprint, Edinburgh: The Banner of Truth Trust, 1993), pp. 17-18.

2. John Piper, *A Godward Life* (Sisters, Ore.: Multnomah, 1997), p. 107.

3. Iain Murray, *Jonathan Edwards: A New Biography* (Edinburgh: The Banner of Truth Trust, 1987), p. 40.

CHAPTER 3:
ARE YOU MORE LOVING?

1. Maurice Roberts, "The Supreme Grace of Christian Love," *The Banner of Truth,* February 1989, p. 3.

2. Jonathan Edwards, *The Works of Jonathan Edwards*, vol. 2, Perry Miller, gen. ed., *Religious Affections,* ed. John E. Smith (New Haven, Conn.: Yale University Press, 1959), p. 146.

3. Edwards, p. 368.

4. Edwards, p. 369.

5. John Piper, *Desiring God* (Portland, Ore.: Multnomah, 1986), p. 96.

6. Jonathan Edwards, *The Works of Jonathan Edwards*, vol. 4, *The Great Awakening*, ed. C. C. Goen (New Haven, Conn.: Yale University Press, 1972), p. 257.

7. Roberts, p. 4.

8. Roberts, p. 4.

9. Wilhelmus à Brakel, *The Christian's Reasonable Service,* vol. 4, trans. Bartel Elshout (Morgan, Penn.: Soli Deo Gloria, 1995), p. 61.

10. Roberts, p. 3.

CHAPTER 4:
ARE YOU MORE SENSITIVE TO GOD'S PRESENCE?

1. George Barna, *Virtual America* (Ventura, Calif.: Regal, 1994), p. 55.

2. Barna, p. 56.

3. Barna, pp. 57-58.

4. Barna, p. 58.

5. I have written more fully on this in "Unity of Doctrine and Devotion," in John H. Armstrong, ed., *The Compromised Church* (Wheaton, Ill.: Crossway, 1998), pp. 241-262.

6. A. W. Tozer, *The Knowledge of the Holy* (New York: Harper & Row, 1961), p. 82.

7. For more on this theme, I recommend a book by a contemporary writer well steeped in the Puritans: Sinclair B. Ferguson, *Deserted by God?* (Grand Rapids, Mich.: Baker, 1993).

8. John Bunyan, *The Pilgrim's Progress* (1678; reprint, Uhrichsville, Oh.: Barbour, 1993), pp. 67-68.

9. John Stevenson, "Prayer: Degrees of Boldness," *The Banner of Truth,* June 1998, p. 21.

10. Martyn Lloyd-Jones, *Enjoying the Presence of God* (Ann Arbor, Mich.: Servant, 1992), p. 133.

11. C. H. Spurgeon, "The Secret of a Happy Life," *Metropolitan Tabernacle Pulpit*, vol. 22 (1876; reprint, Pasadena, Tex.: Pilgrim Publications, 1981), p. 411.

12. Tozer, p. 80.

CHAPTER 5:
DO YOU HAVE A GROWING CONCERN FOR THE SPIRITUAL AND TEMPORAL NEEDS OF OTHERS?

1. As quoted by W. Stanley Mooneyham in "Orphans," *Baker's Dictionary of Christian Ethics,* ed. Carl F. H. Henry (Grand Rapids, Mich.: Baker, 1973), p. 477.

2. *World* (January 23, 1999), p. 13.

CHAPTER 7;
ARE THE SPIRITUAL DISCIPLINES INCREASINGLY IMPORTANT TO YOU?

1. For further reading on the personal spiritual disciplines, see Donald S. Whitney, *Spiritual Disciplines for the Christian Life* (Colorado Springs: NavPress, 1991). To learn about the corporate spiritual disciplines, see Donald S. Whitney, *Spiritual Disciplines Within the Church* (Chicago: Moody, 1996).

2. Jonathan Edwards, *The Works of Jonathan Edwards*, vol. 2, Perry Miller, gen. ed., *Religious Affections*, ed. John E. Smith (New Haven, Conn.: Yale University Press, 1959), p. 376.

3. James Gleick, *Faster* (New York: Pantheon, 1999).

4. R. C. Sproul, *The Soul's Quest for God* (Wheaton, Ill.: Tyndale, 1992), p. 7.

CHAPTER 8:
DO YOU STILL GRIEVE OVER SIN?

1. Iain Murray, *Jonathan Edwards: A New Biography* (Edinburgh: The Banner of Truth Trust, 1987), pp. 101-102.

2. Class lecture at Midwestern Baptist Theological Seminary, Kansas City, Missouri, October 22, 1998.

3. John Blanchard, comp., *More Gathered Gold* (Welwyn, England: Evangelical Press, 1986), p. 297.

4. John Blanchard, comp., *Gathered Gold* (Welwyn, England: Evangelical Press, 1984), p. 289.

5. Jonathan Edwards, *The Works of Jonathan Edwards*, vol. 2, Perry Miller, gen. ed., *Religious Affections*, ed. John E. Smith (New Haven, Conn.: Yale University Press, 1959), p. 377.

6. Edwards, p. 366.

7. Jeremiah Burroughs, *The Evil of Evils* (1654; reprint, Ligonier, Penn.: Soli Deo Gloria, 1992), p. 69.

8. Edwards, pp. 316-317.

9. Burroughs, pp. 66-67.

10. John Owen, *The Works of John Owen,* vol. 7, "The Grace and Duty of Being Spiritually Minded" (1850-1853; reprint, Edinburgh: The Banner of Truth Trust, 1965), p. 333.

11. Jerry Bridges, *The Discipline of Grace* (Colorado Springs: NavPress, 1994), pp. 58, 60.

CHAPTER 9:
ARE YOU A QUICKER FORGIVER?

1. John Blanchard, comp., *Sifted Silver* (Durham, England: Evangelical Press, 1995), p. 104.

2. Jay E. Adams, *From Forgiven to Forgiving* (Wheaton, Ill.: Victor, 1989), p. 33.

3. Leon Morris, "Forgiving Others," *Tabletalk,* February 1998, p. 52.

4. John Blanchard, comp., *Gathered Gold* (Welwyn, England: Evangelical Press, 1984), p. 108.

5. John Blanchard, comp., *More Gathered Gold* (Welwyn, England: Evangelical Press, 1986), p. 105.

CHAPTER 10:
DO YOU YEARN FOR HEAVEN AND TO BE WITH JESUS?

1. Jonathan Edwards, ed., *The Life and Diary of David Brainerd*, ed. by Philip E. Howard, Jr. (Chicago: Moody, 1949), p. 87.

2. C. S. Lewis, *Till We Have Faces* (San Diego: Harcourt, Brace & Company, 1984), pp. 74-75.

3. Jonathan Edwards, *The Works of Jonathan Edwards*, vol. 2, Perry Miller, gen. ed., *Religious Affections*, ed. John E. Smith (New Haven, Conn.: Yale University Press, 1959), p. 383.

4. Iain Murray, *Jonathan Edwards: A New Biography* (Edinburgh: The Banner of Truth Trust, 1987), p. 51.

5. John Thornbury, *David Brainerd* (Durham, England: Evangelical Press, 1996), p. 132.

6. Thornbury, p. 132.

7. Joni Eareckson Tada, testimony at the Ligonier Ministries Conference, Orlando, Florida, March 5, 1993.

8. Joni Eareckson Tada, "The Best Part of Heaven," *Moody,* March 1995, p. 32.

9. D. Martyn Lloyd-Jones, *Faith Tried and Triumphant* (Grand Rapids, Mich.: Baker Book House, 1987), p. 199.

10. Murray, p. 143.

11. Edwards, ed., *The Life and Diary of David Brainerd,* p. 88.

12. J. I. Packer, "Why I Like My Pie in the Sky," *Christianity Today,* June 18, 1990, p. 11.

SPIRITUAL
DISCIPLINES
for the
CHRISTIAN
LIFE

CONTENTS

For the glory of my Lord and Savior, Jesus Christ—
becoming like Him is the goal of the Spiritual Disciplines

For Don and Dollie Whitney,
who first taught me of Christ and of many Spiritual Disciplines

and for Caffy,
who always encourages me in the Spiritual Disciplines

FOREWORD

I was asked to write a foreword for this book before I saw it. Having now gone through it, I would in any case have volunteered for the job, so that I can go on record as urging all Christians to read what Don Whitney has written; indeed, to read it three times over, with a month's interval (certainly not less, and ideally, I think, not more) between each reading. This will not only make the book sink in, but will also give you a realistic picture of your seriousness, or lack of it, as Jesus' disciple. Your first reading will show you several particular things that you should start doing. In your second and third readings (for each of which you should choose a date on the day you complete the previous reading) you shall find yourself reviewing what you have done and how you have fared in doing it. That will be very good for you, even if the discovery comes as a bit of a shock at first.

Ever since Richard Foster rang the bell with his *Celebration of Discipline* (1978), discussing the various spiritual disciplines has become a staple element of conservative Christian in-talk in North America. This is a happy thing. The doctrine of the disciplines (Latin disciplinae, meaning courses of learning and training) is really a restatement and extension of classical Protestant teaching on the means of grace (the Word of God, prayer, fellowship, the Lord's Supper). Don Whitney's spiritual feet are blessedly cemented in the wisdom of the Bible, as spelled out by the Puritan and older evangelical masters, and he plots the path of discipline with a sure touch. The foundations he lays are evangelical, not legalistic. In other words, he calls us to pursue Godliness through practicing the disciplines out of gratitude for the grace that has saved us, not as self-justifying or self-advancing effort. What he builds on these foundations is as beneficial as it is solid. He is in truth showing us the path of life.

If, then, as a Christian you want to be really real with your God, moving beyond the stage of playing games with yourself and Him, this book provides practical help. A century and a half ago the Scottish professor "Rabbi" Duncan sent his students off to read John Owen, the Puritan, on indwelling sin with the admonition, "But, gentlemen, *prepare for the knife*." As I pass you over to Don Whitney, I would say to you, "Now, friend, *prepare for the workout*." And you will find health for your soul.

—J.I. Packer

ACKNOWLEDGMENTS

When Allan Wells of Scotland won the 100-meter dash at the 1980 Olympics in Moscow, he said, "That's for Eric Liddell." In so doing he acknowledged the inspiration and influence Liddell had been to him and to all Scotsmen since the 1924 Olympics in Paris. That's when Liddell opted out of a great chance at winning the prestigious 100-meter championship because the day of the race conflicted with his Christian convictions, only to set an Olympic record on another day in winning the gold medal in the 400 meters.

As Wells acknowledged the influence of someone who had died almost forty years before, so I want to acknowledge the influence of men I have never met except through their writings and biographies. But they are men whose thoughts and lives have profoundly changed mine.

Thanks to the Puritans. Today they are often maligned by Christians and nonChristians alike, who often know little or nothing about them. Our stereotyped perceptions of them reveal a lack of awareness of their profound contributions to spirituality and Godly living. They are spiritual giants on whose shoulders I stand.

Thanks to Jonathan Edwards, C. H. Spurgeon, and Martyn Lloyd-Jones. My life and ministry are immeasurably better because of theirs.

I also want to show my gratitude to those in my own day who have enriched my life in ways that have had a direct bearing on this book.

Thanks to Ernie Reisinger for his vision for reformation and revival, for his willingness to help a young pastor he hadn't met, and for the books.

Thanks to John Armstrong, Jim Elliff, and Tom Nettles for their friendship and for challenging me to think.

Thanks to J. I. Packer for writing theology so clearly and for communicating so winsomely the fruit of all those years of studying the Puritans.

Thanks to Jim Rahtjen for his genuine, unselfish excitement about the book and for being such a joy to work with.

Thanks to Beth Mullins for her help in entering data and for assisting with so many details.

Thanks to David Larsen for the doctoral seminar which first prompted me to organize much of this material.

Thanks to Roger and Jean Fleming for the friendship and encouragement without which this book probably would not have been written and published.

Thanks to Traci Mullins for being such an affirming editor from beginning to end.

Thanks to Glenfield Baptist Church for praying for me and for supporting me with extra love throughout the process of writing this book.

Thanks to Caffy who patiently endured so much that this book might be written.

Discipline yourself for the purpose of godliness.
1 Timothy 4:7, NASB

CHAPTER ONE

THE SPIRITUAL DISCIPLINES . . .
FOR THE PURPOSE OF GODLINESS

❖❖❖

Ours is an undisciplined age. The old disciplines are
breaking down. . . . Above all, the discipline of divine
grace is derided as legalism or is entirely unknown to
a generation that is largely illiterate in the Scriptures.
We need the rugged strength of Christian character
that can come only from discipline.

V. Raymond Edman
The Disciplines of Life

Discipline without direction is drudgery.

Imagine six-year-old Kevin, whose parents have enrolled him in music lessons. After school every afternoon, he sits in the living room and reluctantly strums "Home on the Range" while watching his buddies play baseball in the park across the street. That's discipline without direction. It's drudgery.

Now suppose Kevin is visited by an angel one afternoon during guitar practice. In a vision he's taken to Carnegie Hall. He's shown a guitar virtuoso giving a concert. Usually bored by classical music, Kevin is astonished by what he sees and hears. The musician's fingers dance excitedly on the strings with fluidity and grace. Kevin thinks of how stupid and klunky his hands feel when they halt and stumble over the chords. The virtuoso blends clean, soaring notes into a musical aroma that wafts from his guitar. Kevin remembers the toneless, irritating discord that comes stumbling out of his.

But Kevin is enchanted. His head tilts slightly to one side as he listens. He drinks in everything. He never imagined that anyone could play the guitar like this.

"What do you think, Kevin?" asks the angel.

The answer is a soft, slow, six-year-old's "W-o-w!"

The vision vanishes, and the angel is again standing in front of Kevin in his living room. "Kevin," says the angel, "the wonderful musician you saw is *you* in a few years." Then pointing at the guitar, the angel declares, "But you must practice!"

Suddenly the angel disappears and Kevin finds himself alone with his guitar. Do you think his attitude toward practice will be different now? As long as he remembers what he's going to become, Kevin's discipline will have a direction, a goal that will pull him into the future. Yes, effort will be involved, but you could hardly call it drudgery.

When it comes to discipline in the Christian life, many believers feel as Kevin did toward guitar practice—it's discipline without direction. Prayer threatens to be drudgery. The practical value of meditation on Scripture seems uncertain. The real purpose of a Discipline like fasting is often unclear.

First we must understand what we shall become. It is said of God's elect in Romans 8:29, "For those God foreknew he also predestined to be conformed to the image of his Son." God's eternal plan ensures that every Christian will ultimately conform to Christlikeness. We will be changed "when he appears" so that "we shall be like him" (1 John 3:2). This is no vision; this is *you*, Christian, in a few years.

So why all the talk about discipline? If God has predestined our conformity to Christlikeness, where does discipline fit in?

Although God will grant Christlikeness to us when Jesus returns, until then He intends for us to grow toward that Christlikeness. We aren't merely to wait for holiness, we're to pursue it. "Make every effort to live in peace with all men and to be holy," we're commanded in Hebrews 12:14, for "without holiness no one will see the Lord."

Which leads us to ask what every Christian should ask, "How then shall we pursue holiness? How can we be like Jesus Christ, the Son of God?"

We find a clear answer in 1 Timothy 4:7: "Discipline yourself for the purpose of godliness" NASB.

This verse is the theme for the entire book. In this chapter I will attempt to unpack its meaning; the rest of the book is an effort to apply it in practical ways. I will refer to the scriptural ways Christians discipline themselves in obedience to this verse as the Spiritual Disciplines. I will maintain that the only road to Christian maturity and Godliness (a biblical term synonymous with Christlikeness and holiness) passes through the practice of the Spiritual Disciplines. I will emphasize that Godliness is the goal of the Disciplines, and when we remember this, the Spiritual Disciplines become a delight instead of drudgery.

THE SPIRITUAL DISCIPLINES—
THE MEANS TO GODLINESS

The Spiritual Disciplines are those personal and corporate disciplines that promote spiritual growth. They are the habits of devotion and expe-riential Christianity that have been practiced by the people of God since biblical times.

This book examines the Spiritual Disciplines of Bible intake, prayer, worship, evangelism, service, stewardship, fasting, silence and solitude, journaling, and learning. This is by no means, however, an exhaustive list of the Disciplines of Christian living. A survey of other literature on this subject would reveal that confession, accountability, simplicity, submission, spiritual direction, celebration, affirmation, sac-rifice, "watching," and more also qualify as Spiritual Disciplines.

Whatever the Discipline, its most important feature is its purpose. Just as there is little value in practicing the scales on a guitar or piano apart from the purpose of playing music, there is little value in practic-ing Spiritual Disciplines apart from the single purpose that unites them (Colossians 2:20-23, 1 Timothy 4:8). That purpose is godliness. Thus we are told in 1 Timothy 4:7 to discipline ourselves "*for the purpose* of godliness" (emphasis added).

The Spiritual Disciplines are the God-given means we are to use in the Spirit-filled pursuit of Godliness.

Godly people are disciplined people. It has always been so. Call to mind some heroes of church history—Augustine, Martin Luther, John Calvin, John Bunyan, Susanna Wesley, George Whitefield, Lady Hunt-ingdon, Jonathan and Sarah Edwards, Charles Spurgeon, George Muller—they were all disciplined people. In my own pastoral and per-sonal Christian experience, I can say that I've never known a man or woman who came to spiritual maturity except through discipline. God-liness comes through discipline.

Actually, God uses three primary catalysts for changing us and con-forming us to Christlikeness, but only one is largely under our control. One catalyst the Lord uses to change us is people. "As iron sharpens iron, so one man sharpens another" (Proverbs 27:17). Sometimes God uses our friends to sharpen us into more Christlike living, and sometimes He uses our enemies to file away our rough, ungodly edges. Parents, children, spouses, coworkers, customers, teachers, neighbors, pastors—God changes us through these people.

Another change agent God uses in our lives is circumstances. The classic text for this is Romans 8:28: "We know that in all things God works for the good of those who love him, who have been called according to his purpose." Financial pressures, physical conditions, even the weather are used in the hands of Divine Providence to stimulate His elect toward holiness.

Then there is the catalyst of the Spiritual Disciplines. This catalyst differs from the first two in that when He uses the Disciplines, God works from the inside out. When He changes us through people and circumstances, the process works from the outside in. The Spiritual Disciplines also differ from the other two methods of change in that God grants us a measure of choice regarding involvement with them. We often have little choice regarding the people and circumstances God brings into our lives, but we can decide, for example, whether we will read the Bible or fast today.

So on the one hand, we recognize that even the most iron-willed self-discipline will not make us more holy, for growth in holiness is a gift from God (John 17:17, 1 Thessalonians 5:23, Hebrews 2:11). On the other hand, we can do something to further the process. God has given us the Spiritual Disciplines as a means of receiving His grace and growing in Godliness. By them we place ourselves before God for Him to work in us.

The New Testament was first written in Greek. The word translated "discipline" in the New American Standard Bible is the Greek word *gumnasia* from which our English words *gymnasium* and *gymnastics* derive. This word means "to exercise or discipline," which is why the King James Version renders 1 Timothy 4:7, "Exercise thyself rather unto godliness."

Think of the Spiritual Disciplines as spiritual exercises. To go to your favorite spot for prayer or journaling, for example, is like going to a gym and using a weight machine. As physical disciplines like this promote strength, so the Spiritual Disciplines promote Godliness.

There are two Bible stories that illustrate another way of thinking of the role of the Spiritual Disciplines. Luke 18:35-43 tells the story of a blind beggar named Bartimaeus and his encounter with Jesus. As Bartimaeus sat by a roadside near Jericho, a crowd of unusual numbers and excitement came near. When he asked what was happening, he was told that Jesus of Nazareth was passing by. Even a social outcast like Bartimaeus had heard the incredible stories about Jesus that had come from all over Israel during the past two or three years. Immediately he began shouting, "Jesus, Son of David, have mercy on me!" Those who were leading the procession, perhaps some of the local dignitaries, were embarrassed by the beggar's disruptive behavior and sternly told him to keep quiet. But he only cried out all the more, "Jesus, Son of David, have mercy on me!" To everyone's amazement, Jesus stopped and called for the one who was calling for Him. In response to the poor man's faith, Jesus miraculously healed Bartimaeus of his blindness.

The second Bible story is in the very next paragraph of Scripture, Luke 19:1-10. It's the famous account of the conversion of the tax collector, Zacchaeus. Perhaps it happened only minutes after the healing of Bartimaeus. Because Zacchaeus was so short, he was unable to see Jesus in the crowd. So he ran ahead and climbed into a sycamore tree in order to see Jesus when He passed by it. When Jesus came to the place, He looked up, called Zacchaeus by name, and told him to come down. The two of them went to the tax collector's house, where he believed in Christ for salvation and resolved to give half his possessions to the poor and return with interest all tax money he had wrongfully taken.

Think of the Spiritual Disciplines as ways we can place ourselves in the path of God's grace and seek Him much as Bartimaeus and Zacchaeus placed themselves in Jesus' path and sought Him. As with these two seekers, we will find Him willing to have mercy on us and to have communion with us. And in the course of time we will be transformed by Him from one level of Christlikeness to another (2 Corinthians 3:18).

The Spiritual Disciplines then are also like channels of God's transforming grace. As we place ourselves in them to seek communion with Christ, His grace flows to us and we are changed. That's why the Disciplines must become priority for us if we will be Godly.

The great British Baptist preacher of the nineteenth century, Charles Spurgeon, stressed the importance this way: "I must take care above all that I cultivate communion with Christ, for though that can never be the basis of my peace—mark that—yet it will be the channel of it."[1] The channels of peace and all that Christ gives that lead us to holiness are the Spiritual Disciplines.

Tom Landry, coach of the Dallas Cowboys football team for most of three decades, said, "The job of a football coach is to make men do what they don't want to do in order to achieve what they've always wanted to be."[2] In much the same way, Christians are called to make themselves do something they would not naturally do—pursue the Spiritual Disciplines—in order to become what they've always wanted to be, that is, like Jesus Christ. "Discipline yourself," says the Scripture, "for the purpose of godliness."

THE SPIRITUAL DISCIPLINES—THE LORD EXPECTS THEM

The original language of the words "discipline yourself for the purpose of godliness" makes it plain that this is a command of God, not merely a suggestion. Holiness is not an option for those who claim to be children of the Holy One (1 Peter 1:15-16), so neither are the means of holiness, that is, the Spiritual Disciplines, an option.

The inspired counsel of Solomon in Proverbs 23:12 is, "Apply your heart to discipline" NASB. (Although discipline in the Proverbs usually refers to chastisement from the Lord, verses like this apply to the Spiritual Disciplines when we realize that the Lord disciplines us in order to get us to discipline ourselves.) The picture brought to my mind by the word *apply* is that of applying a decal to my windshield or a bumper sticker to my car. In other words, the Lord expects us to permanently affix ourselves to those devotional practices that promote Godliness.

The expectation of disciplined spirituality is implied in Jesus' offer of Matthew 11:29: "Take my yoke upon you and learn from me." The same is true in this offer of discipleship: "Then he said to them all: 'If anyone would come after me, he must deny himself and take up his cross daily and follow me'" (Luke 9:23). These verses tell us that to be a disciple of Jesus means, at the very least, to learn from and follow Him. Learning and following involve discipline, for those who only learn accidentally and follow incidentally are not true disciples. That discipline is at the heart of discipleship is confirmed by Galatians 5:22-23, which says that spiritual self-discipline (i.e., "self-control") is one of the most evident marks of being Spirit-controlled.

The Lord Jesus not only expects these Disciplines of us, He modeled them for us. He applied His heart to discipline. He disciplined Himself for the purpose of Godliness. And if we are going to be Christlike, we must live as Christ lived.

This is the message of Dallas Willard's book *The Spirit of the Disciplines*:

> My central claim is that we *can* become like Christ by doing one thing—by following him in the overall style of life he chose for himself. If we have faith in Christ, we must believe that he knew how to live. We can, through faith and grace, become like Christ by practicing the types of activities he engaged in, by arranging our whole lives around the activities he himself practiced in order to remain constantly at home in the fellowship of his Father.[3]

So many professing Christians are so spiritually undisciplined that they seem to have little fruit and power in their lives. I've seen men and women who discipline themselves for the purpose of excelling in their profession discipline themselves very little "for the purpose of godliness." I've seen Christians who are faithful to the church of God, who frequently demonstrate genuine enthusiasm for the things of God, and who dearly love the Word of God, trivialize their effectiveness for the Kingdom of God through lack of discipline. Spiritually they are a mile wide and an inch deep. There are no deep, time-worn channels of communing discipline between them and God. They have dabbled in everything but disciplined themselves in nothing.

Consider the people who will work hard at learning to play an instrument, knowing that it takes years to acquire the skills, who will practice hard to lower their golf score or to improve their sports performance, knowing it takes years to become proficient, who will discipline themselves throughout their career because they know it takes sacrifice to succeed. These same people will give up quickly when they find the Spiritual Disciplines don't come easily, as though becoming like Jesus was not supposed to take much effort.

The undisciplined are like playwright George Kaufman, who was enduring a sales pitch from a gold-mine promoter. The salesman was praising the productivity of the mine in hopes of persuading Kaufman to buy shares in it. "Why, it's so rich you can pick up the chunks of gold from the ground."

"Do you mean," asked Kaufman, "I'd have to bend over?"[4]

The gold of Godliness isn't found on the surface of Christianity. It has to be dug from the depths with the tools of the Disciplines. But for those who persevere, the treasures are more than worth the troubles.

MORE APPLICATION

There is danger in neglecting the Spiritual Disciplines. A well-known selection from William Barclay's pen powerfully illustrates the danger. Commenting on the difference between the disciplined and the undisciplined way, he wrote,

> Nothing was ever achieved without discipline; and many an athlete and many a man has been ruined because he abandoned discipline and let himself grow slack. Coleridge is the supreme tragedy of indiscipline. Never did so great a mind produce so little. He left Cambridge University to join the army; but he left the army because, in spite of all his erudition, he could not rub down a horse; he returned to Oxford and left without a degree. He began a paper called *The Watchman* which lived for ten numbers and then died. It has been said of him: "He lost himself in visions of work to be done, that always remained to be done. Coleridge had every poetic gift but one—the gift of sustained and concentrated effort." In his head and in his mind he had all kinds of books, as he said himself, "completed save for transcription." "I am on the eve," he says, "of sending to the press two octavo volumes." But the books were never composed outside Coleridge's mind, because he would not face the discipline of sitting down to write them out. No one ever reached any eminence, and no one having reached it ever maintained it, without discipline.[5]

By neglecting the Spiritual Disciplines we face the danger of bearing little spiritual fruit. Few of us will have Coleridge's intellectual and poetic gifts, but all believers have been given spiritual gifts (1 Corinthians 12:4-7). The mere presence of spiritual gifts, however, does not guarantee abundant fruitfulness any more than Coleridge's mental gifts assured the production of poetry. Just as with natural gifts, spiritual gifts must be developed by discipline in order to bear spiritual fruit.

There is freedom in embracing the Spiritual Disciplines. Richard Foster's *Celebration of Discipline* has been the most popular book on the subject of the Spiritual Disciplines in the last half of the twentieth century. The great contribution of this work is the reminder that the Spiritual Disciplines, which many see as restrictive and binding, are actually the means to spiritual freedom. He rightly calls the Disciplines the "Door to Liberation."

We can illustrate this principle by observing the freedom that comes through mastery of any discipline. Watching a Christopher Parkening or a Chet Atkins play guitar gives the impression that these guitarists were born with the instrument attached to their bodies. They have an intimacy and a freedom with the guitar that makes playing the thing look easy. Anyone who's ever tried to play realizes that the musical freedom of such masters comes from decades of disciplined practice. Freedom through discipline is seen not only in proficient musicians, but also in all-star shortstops, expert carpenters, successful executives, well-prepared students, and moms who daily manage home and family well.

Elton Trueblood demonstrates the relationship between discipline and freedom by saying,

> We have not advanced very far in our spiritual lives if we have not encountered the basic paradox of freedom . . . that we are most free when we are bound. But not just any way of being bound will suffice; what matters is the character of our binding. The one who would be an athlete, but who is unwilling to discipline his body by regular exercise and abstinence, is not free to excel on the field or the track. His failure to train rigorously denies him the freedom to run with the desired speed and endurance. With one concerted voice, the giants of the devotional life apply the same principle to the whole of life: Discipline is the price of freedom.[6]

While Trueblood is right in calling discipline "the price" of freedom, Elisabeth Elliot reminds us that "freedom and discipline have come to be regarded as mutually exclusive, when in fact freedom is not at all the opposite, but the final *reward,* of discipline."[7] While emphasizing that discipline is the price of freedom, let us not forget that freedom is the reward of discipline.

What is this freedom of Godliness? Think again of our illustrations. For instance, a guitar virtuoso is "free" to play a difficult arrangement by Segovia while I am not. Why? Because of his years of disciplined practice. Similarly, those who are "free" to quote Scripture are those who have disciplined themselves to memorize God's Word. We may experience a measure of freedom from spiritual insensitivity through the Discipline of fasting. There is a freedom from self-centeredness found in Disciplines such as worship, service, and evangelism. The freedom of Godliness is the freedom to do what God calls us to do through Scripture and the freedom to express the character qualities of Christ through our own personality. This kind of freedom is the "reward" or result of the blessing of God upon our engagement in the Spiritual Disciplines.

But we must remember that the full-grown freedoms of discipline-nurtured Godliness don't develop overnight or during a weekend seminar. The Bible reminds us that self-control, such as that expressed through the Spiritual Disciplines, must persevere before the mature fruit of Godliness ripens. Notice the sequence of development in 2 Peter 1:6—"and to self-control, perseverance; and to perseverance, godliness." Godliness is a lifelong pursuit.

There is an invitation to all Christians to enjoy the Spiritual Disciplines. All in whom the Spirit of God dwells are invited to taste the joy of a Spiritual Disciplines lifestyle.

Remember Kevin and his guitar? His daily practice would take on an entirely new spirit once he realized where it would take him. The discipline of practice would gradually become the means to one of the greatest enjoyments of his life.

Discipline without direction is drudgery. But the Spiritual Disciplines are never drudgery as long as we practice them with the goal of Godliness in mind. If your picture of a disciplined Christian is one of a grim, tight-lipped, joyless half-robot, then you've missed the point. Jesus was the most disciplined Man who ever lived and yet the most joyful and passionately alive. He is our Example of discipline. Let us follow Him to joy through the Spiritual Disciplines.

NOTES

1. C. H. Spurgeon, "Peace By Believing," in *Metropolitan Tabernacle Pulpit* (London: Passmore and Alabaster, 1864; reprint, Pasadena, TX: Pilgrim Publications, 1970), vol. 9, page 283.

2. Tom Landry, as quoted by Ray Stedman in *Preaching Today* (Carol Stream, IL: Christianity Today, n.d.), tape number 25.

3. Dallas Willard, *The Spirit of the Disciplines* (San Francisco, CA: Harper & Row, 1988), page ix.

4. George Kaufman, as quoted in *The Little, Brown Book of Anecdotes* (Boston, MA: Little, Brown and Company, 1985), page 321.

5. William Barclay, *The Gospel of Matthew* (Philadelphia, PA: Westminster, 1958), vol. 1, page 284.

6. Elton Trueblood, as quoted in *Leadership,* vol. 10, no. 3, summer 1989, page 60.

7. Elisabeth Elliot, as quoted in *Christianity Today,* November 4, 1988, page 33, emphasis mine.

CHAPTER TWO

BIBLE INTAKE (PART 1) . . .
FOR THE PURPOSE OF GODLINESS

❖❖❖

The alternative to discipline is disaster.

Vance Havner
quoted in John Blanchard, compiler,
More Gathered Gold

In August of 1989 I had the privilege of participating in a mission trip to the bush country of East Africa. Four of us from the church I pastor lived in tents in front of a tiny, unfinished, mud-and-sticks church building six miles from the nearest settlement.

I've been overseas enough to know that many customs I have come to identify with Christianity will clash at some points with the culture of our hosts. My experiences have taught me to anticipate swallowing with difficulty some of my American expectations (not to mention a few other things!) about how Christians should live. But I was unprepared for some of my encounters with many of the professing Christians in this equatorial setting. Lying, stealing, and immorality were common and generally accepted, even among the leadership of the church. Theological understanding was as scarce as water, the disease of doctrinal error as common as malaria.

Soon I discovered one of the main reasons this church looked as though it had been started by Corinthian missionaries. No one had a Bible—not the pastor, not a deacon, no one. The pastor had only half-a-dozen sermons, all half-baked over the coals of a few Bible-story recollections. Every sixth week came the same sermon. The only real contact with Scripture happened with the occasional visit of a missionary (the

nearest one was one hundred miles away) or when an area denominational worker would preach. For almost everyone in the church, these
infrequent, vicarious brushes with the Bible were all they'd ever known.
Only one man had any measure of spiritual maturity, and that was
because he had lived most of his life elsewhere and attended a Bible-
teaching church.

The four of us pooled our resources and bought inexpensive Bibles
for many of the church members. After evangelistic visitation each day
we led Bible studies for the church in the afternoon and again at night
by flashlight. We left with prayers that the Holy Spirit would cause the
Word of God to take deep root in this dry, bush-country assembly.

Most of us shake our heads in pity at such sad conditions. It's hard
to imagine that many of us have more Bibles in our homes than entire
churches have in some Third-World situations. But it's one thing to be
unfamiliar with Scripture when you don't own a Bible; it's another thing
when you have a bookshelf full.

No Spiritual Discipline is more important than the intake of God's
Word. Nothing can substitute for it. There simply is no healthy Christian
life apart from a diet of the milk and meat of Scripture. The reasons for
this are obvious. In the Bible God tells us about Himself, and especially
about Jesus Christ, the incarnation of God. The Bible unfolds the Law of
God to us and shows us how we've all broken it. There we learn how
Christ died as a sinless, willing Substitute for breakers of God's Law and
how we must repent and believe in Him to be right with God. In the Bible
we learn the ways and will of the Lord. We find in Scripture how to live
in a way that is pleasing to God as well as best and most fulfilling for ourselves. None of this eternally essential information can be found anywhere else except the Bible. Therefore if we would know God and be
Godly, we must know the Word of God—intimately.

However, many who yawn with familiarity and nod in agreement
to these statements spend no more time with God's Word in an average
day than do those with no Bible at all. My pastoral experience bears
witness to the validity of surveys that frequently reveal that great numbers of professing Christians know little more about the Bible than
Third-World Christians who possess not even a shred of Scripture.

Some wag remarked that the worst dust storm in history would happen if all church members who were neglecting their Bibles dusted them
off simultaneously.

So even though we honor God's Word with our lips, we must confess that our hearts—as well as our hands, ears, eyes, and minds—are often far from it. Regardless of how busy we become with all things Christian, we must remember that the most transforming practice available to us is the disciplined intake of Scripture.

Bible intake is not only the most important Spiritual Discipline, it is also the most broad. It actually consists of several subdisciplines. It's much like a university comprised of many colleges, each specializing in a different discipline, yet all united under the general name of the university.

Let's examine the "colleges," or subdisciplines, of Bible intake, proceeding from the least to the most difficult.

HEARING GOD'S WORD

The easiest of the Disciplines related to the intake of God's Word is simply *hearing* it. Why consider this a Discipline? Because if we don't discipline ourselves to hear God's Word regularly, we may only hear it accidentally, just when we feel like it, or we may never hear it at all. For most of us, disciplining ourselves to hear God's Word means developing the practice of steadfastly attending a New Testament church where the Word of God is faithfully preached.

Jesus once said, "Blessed rather are those who hear the word of God and obey it" (Luke 11:28). Merely listening to God-inspired words is not the point. The purpose of all methods of Bible intake is obedience to what God says and the development of Christlikeness. But the method Jesus encourages in this verse is hearing God's Word.

Another passage emphasizing the importance of hearing is Romans 10:17: "Consequently, faith comes from hearing the message, and the message is heard through the word of Christ." This doesn't mean that a person can come to faith in Christ only by hearing Scripture, for multitudes have become believers as Jonathan Edwards did, through reading the Bible. Still this verse concerns itself with hearing. We may add, however, that most who, like Edwards, were converted while reading Scripture are also like him in that they heard the proclamation of God's Word prior to conversion. Furthermore, whereas this passage teaches that initial faith in Christ comes from hearing the inspired Word about Jesus Christ, it's also true for Christians that much of the faith we need for day-to-day living comes from hearing the Bible's message. From a scriptural word about God's provision may come the faith that a family with financial struggles needs. Hearing a biblically based sermon on the love of Christ may be God's means of granting assurance of faith to a downcast believer. I recently heard a tape-recorded message that the Lord used to give me the faith to persevere in a matter. Gifts of faith are often given to those who discipline themselves to hear the Word of God.

There are other ways we may discipline ourselves to hear God's Word in addition to the most important way, which is hearing it preached as part of a local church ministry. (I say this realizing that some do not have the opportunity to hear God's Word through the ministry of a local church.) The most obvious of these is by Christian radio and tapes. These can be used in creative ways and times while dressing, cooking, traveling, etc. If neither of these media is available in your area, consider shortwave radio and mail-order tape-lending libraries. Although shortwave radio is common overseas, most Americans don't have one and rarely think of the medium. But many of the best Bible teachers on traditional AM and FM stations in the United States also can be heard practically anywhere in the world (including the United States) on the powerful, if lesser quality signal, shortwave stations. And there are several cassette-lending libraries nationwide, each with thousands of sermons on tape. Usually they ask for payment only to cover postage costs or for a nominal rental fee per tape. Check the classified ads of Christian publications, contact the office of ministries that distribute cassette tapes, or check with several local churches to get names and addresses of some of these tape libraries.

One other text worthy of note on this subject is 1 Timothy 4:13. There the Apostle Paul instructs his young friend in the ministry: "Until I come, devote yourself to the public reading of Scripture, to preaching and to teaching." Though a lot more explanation could be given, it's enough to say that it was important in the ministry of Paul and important to the Lord, who inspired these words, for God's people to hear God's Word. Since this is so, it should become a disciplined priority for us to hear it. If someone says, "I don't need to go to church to worship God; I can worship Him on the golf course or at the lake just as well, if not better, than in church," we may agree that

God can be worshiped there. But the ongoing worship of God cannot be separated from the Word of God. We are to discipline ourselves to go and hear the Word of God.

A brief word is in order here about preparing ourselves to hear the Word of God. If you enter the typical evangelical church two minutes before the start of the worship service, it sounds almost like you've walked into a gymnasium two minutes before a basketball game. Part of my pastoral heart appreciates the good things represented by people who are glad to see and talk with each other. There is a spirit of family reunion in the air when the family of God gathers together. But I think a larger part of my heart longs for reverence and a spirit of seeking God among those who come to hear His Word.

For a while a congregation of Korean Christians used our church building for their midweek service. I was impressed by the way they entered the worship center. Whether they were first to arrive or came in after the service had already started, they immediately bowed in prayer for several moments before arranging their belongings, unbuttoning their coat, or acknowledging the presence of anyone else. This served as an effective reminder to their own hearts and to everyone else of their main purpose for that time. Most churches I'm familiar with could stand more of this kind of thing.

One of the English Puritans, Jeremiah Burroughs, wrote in 1648 the following words of counsel regarding preparation for the discipline of hearing God's Word:

> First, when you come to hear the Word, if you would sanctify God's name, you must possess your souls with what it is you are going to hear. That is, what you are going to hear is the Word of God. . . . Therefore you find that the apostle, writing to the Thessalonians, gives them the reason why the Word did them so much good as it did; it was because they did hear it as the Word of God. "And we also thank God constantly for this, that when you received the word of God which you heard from us, you accepted it not as the word of man but as what it really is, the word of God" (1 Thessalonians 2:13).[1]

So hearing the Word of God is not merely passive listening, it is a Discipline to be cultivated.

READING GOD'S WORD

If you still doubt that Christians need to be exhorted to discipline themselves to read the Bible, consider this: *USA Today* reported a poll just three months before this writing that showed only 11 percent of Americans read the Bible every day. More than half read it less than once a month or never at all.[2]

Of course, we attempt to comfort ourselves by noting that the survey included all Americans, not just professing Christians. Lamentably, little comfort may be found. A survey taken less than a year earlier by the Barna Research Group among those claiming to be "born-again Christians" disclosed these disheartening numbers: Only 18 percent—less than two of every ten—read the Bible every day. Worst of all, 23 percent—almost one in four professing Christians—say they *never* read the Word of God.[3] Consider these statistics in light of 1 Timothy 4:7, "Discipline yourself for the purpose of godliness" (NSAB).

Jesus often asked questions about people's understanding of the Scriptures, beginning with the words, "Have you not read . . . ?" He assumed that those claiming to be the people of God would have read the Word of God. And a case can be made that this question implies a familiarity with the *entire* Word of God.

When Jesus said, "Man does not live on bread alone, but on every word that comes from the mouth of God" (Matthew 4:4), surely He intended at the very least for us to read "every word."

Since "All Scripture is God-breathed and is useful for teaching, rebuking, correcting and training in righteousness" (2 Timothy 3:16), shouldn't we read it?

Revelation 1:3 tells us, "Blessed is the one who reads the words of this prophecy, and blessed are those who hear it and take to heart what is written in it, because the time is near." God promises that those who read and heed His Word will be blessed. But only those who discipline themselves to do so will receive those blessings.

The main reason, remember, for disciplining ourselves is Godliness. We have learned that the Spiritual Disciplines are scriptural paths where we may expect to encounter the transforming grace of God. The most critical Discipline is the intake of God's Word. A 1980 survey by *Christianity Today* and the Gallup Poll supported this when it concluded that no factor is more influential in shaping a person's moral and social behavior than regular Bible reading.[4] If you want to be changed, if you want to become more like Jesus Christ, discipline yourself to read the Bible.

How often should we read it? British preacher John Blanchard, in his book *How to Enjoy Your Bible*, writes,

> Surely we only have to be realistic and honest with ourselves to know how regularly we need to turn to the Bible. How often do we face problems, temptation and pressure? *Every day!* Then how often do we need instruction, guidance and greater encouragement? *Every day!* To catch all these felt needs up into an even greater issue, how often do we need to see God's face, hear his voice, feel his touch, know his power? The answer to all these questions is the same: *every day!* As the American evangelist D. L. Moody put it, "A man can no more take in a supply of grace for the future than he can eat enough for the next six months, or take sufficient air into his lungs at one time to sustain life for a week. We must draw upon God's boundless store of grace from day to day as we need it."[5]

Here are the three most practical suggestions for consistent success in Bible reading. First find the *time*. Perhaps one of the main reasons Christians never read through the entire Bible is discouragement. Most people have never read a thousand-page book before and get discouraged at the sheer length of the Bible. Do you realize that tape-recorded readings of the Bible have proven that you can read through the entire Book in seventy-one hours? The average person in the United States watches that much television in less than two weeks. In no more than fifteen minutes a day you can read through the Bible in less than a year's time. Only five minutes a day takes you through the Bible in less than three years. And yet the majority of Christians never read the Bible all the way through in their whole life. So we're back to the idea that it's primarily a matter of discipline and motivation.

Discipline yourself to find the time. Try to make it the same time every day. Try to make it a time other than just before you go to sleep. There's value in reading the Bible just before you drop off, but if this is the *only* time you read Scripture then you should try to find another time. There are at least two reasons for this. First, you will retain very little of what you read when you're so tired and sleepy. And second, if you're like me, you probably do very little evil in your sleep. You need to encounter Christ in the Scriptures when it will still have an impact on your day.

The second practical suggestion is to find a Bible-reading plan. It's no wonder that those who simply open the Bible at random each day soon drop the discipline. There are inexpensive Bible reading plans available in all Christian bookstores. Many study Bibles contain a reading schedule somewhere within the pages. Most local churches can provide you with a daily reading guide also.

Apart from a specific plan, reading three chapters every day and five on Sundays will take you through the Bible in a year's time. Read three in the Old Testament and three in the New Testament every day, and you will finish the Old Testament once and the New Testament four times in a twelve-month span.

My favorite plan involves reading in five places each day. I begin in Genesis (the Law), Joshua (History), Job (Poetry), Isaiah (the Prophets), and Matthew (the New Testament) and read an equal number of chapters in each section. A variation of this plan is to read in three places daily, starting in Genesis, Job, and Matthew, respectively. The three sections are roughly the same in length, so you will finish them all about the same time. The great advantage of such a design is its variety. Many who intend to read straight through the Bible become confused in Leviticus, discouraged in Numbers, and give up completely by Deuteronomy. But when you are reading in more than one place each day, it's easier to keep up the momentum.

Even if you don't read through the Bible in a year's time, keep a record of which books you have read. Put a check beside a chapter when you read it or by the title of a book in the table of contents when you've completed it. That way, regardless of how long it takes, or in what order they're read, you'll know when you've read every book in the Bible.

The third suggestion is to find at least one word, phrase, or verse to *meditate* on each time you read. We'll look at meditation more closely in the next chapter, but you should recognize now that without meditation you may close your Bible and not be able to remember a single thing you've read. And if that happens, your Bible reading is not likely to change you. Even with a good plan, it can become a mundane chore instead of a Discipline of joy. Take at least one thing you've read and think deeply about it for a few moments. Your insight into Scripture will deepen and you'll better understand how it applies to your life. And the more you apply the truth of Scripture, the more you'll become like Jesus.

We should all have the passion for reading God's Word of the man in this story. Evangelist Robert L. Sumner, in his book *The Wonder of the Word of God*, tells of a man in Kansas City who was severely injured in an explosion. His face was badly disfigured, and he lost his eyesight as well as both hands. He had just become a Christian when the accident happened, and one of his greatest disappointments was that he could no longer read the Bible. Then he heard about a lady in England who read braille with her lips. Hoping to do the same, he sent for some books of the Bible in braille. But he discovered that the nerve endings in his lips had been too badly damaged to distinguish the characters. One day, as he brought one of the braille pages to his lips, his tongue happened to touch a few of the raised characters and he could feel them. Like a flash he thought, "I can read the Bible using my tongue." At the time Robert Sumner wrote his book, the man had read through the entire Bible four times.[6] If he can do that, can you discipline yourself to read the Bible?

STUDYING GOD'S WORD

If reading the Bible can be compared to cruising the width of a clear, sparkling lake in a motorboat, studying the Bible is like slowly crossing that same lake in a glass-bottomed boat.

The motorboat crossing provides an overview of the lake and a swift, passing view of its depths. The glass-bottomed boat of study, however, takes you beneath the surface of Scripture for an unhurried look of clarity and detail that's normally missed by those who simply read the text. As author Jerry Bridges put it, "Reading gives us breadth, but study gives us depth."[7]

Let's look at three examples of a heart to study the Word of God. The first is the Old Testament figure Ezra: "For Ezra had devoted himself to the study and observance of the Law of the LORD, and to teaching its decrees and laws in Israel" (Ezra 7:10). There's an instructive significance to the sequence in this verse. Ezra (1) "devoted himself," (2) "to the study," (3) "and observance of the Law of the Lord," (4) "and to teaching its decrees and laws in Israel." Before he taught the Word of God to the people of God, he practiced what he learned. But Ezra's learning came from a study of the Scriptures. Before he studied, however, he first "devoted himself" to study. In other words, Ezra disciplined himself to study God's Word.

A second example is from Acts 17:11. Missionaries Paul and Silas had barely escaped with their lives from Thessalonica after their successful evangelistic work had provoked the Jews there to jealousy. When they repeated the same course of action in Berea, the Jews there responded differently: "Now the Bereans were of more noble character than the Thessalonians, for they received the message with great eagerness and examined the Scriptures every day to see if what Paul said was true." According to the next verse, the result was, "Many of the Jews believed." The willingness to examine the Scriptures is commended here as noble character.

My favorite example of a heart to study the truth of God is in 2 Timothy 4:13. The Apostle Paul is in prison and writing the last chapter of his last New Testament letter. Anticipating the coming of his younger friend Timothy, he writes, "When you come, bring the cloak that I left with Carpus at Troas, and my scrolls, especially the parchments." The scrolls and parchments Paul requested almost certainly included copies of the Scriptures. In his cold and miserable confinement, the godly apostle asked for two things: a cloak to wear so his body could be warmed and God's Word to study so his mind and heart could be warmed. Paul had seen Heaven (2 Corinthians 12:1-6) and the resurrected Christ (Acts 9:5), he had experienced the Holy Spirit's power for miracles (Acts 14:10) and even for writing Holy Scripture (2 Peter 3:16); nevertheless, he continued to study God's Word until he died. If Paul needed it, surely you and I need it and should discipline ourselves to do it.

Then why don't we? Why do so many Christians neglect the study of God's Word? R. C. Sproul said it painfully well: "Here then, is the real problem of our negligence. We fail in our duty to study God's Word not so much because it is difficult to understand, not so much because it is dull and boring, but because it is work. Our problem is not a lack of intelligence or a lack of passion. Our problem is that we are lazy."[8]

Besides laziness, part of the problem for some may be an insecurity about how to study the Bible or even where to begin. Actually, starting is not so difficult. The basic difference between Bible reading and Bible study is simply a pencil and a piece of paper. Write down observations about the text as you read and record questions that come to your mind. If your Bible has cross-references, look up the ones that relate to the verses that prompt your questions, then record your insights. (If you're unsure what cross-references are or about how to use them, ask your pastor or another mature Christian.) Find a key word in your reading and use the concordance found in the back of most Bibles to review the other references that use the word, and again note your findings. Another way to begin is to outline a chapter, one paragraph at a time. When you finish that chapter, move on to the next until you've outlined the entire book. Before long you'll have a far stronger grasp on a section of Scripture than you had by just reading it.

As you advance in the study of the Book of God, you will learn the value of in-depth word studies, character studies, topical studies, and book studies. You'll discover a new richness in the Scripture as your understanding grows of how the grammar, history, culture, and geography surrounding a text affect its interpretation.

Don't let a feeling of inadequacy keep you from the delight of learning the Bible on your own. Books, thick and thin, abound on how to study the Bible. They can provide more guidance regarding methods and tools than I can in this chapter. Don't settle only for spiritual food that's been "predigested" by others. Experience the joy of discovering biblical insights firsthand through your own Bible study!

MORE APPLICATION

If your growth in Godliness were measured by the quality of your Bible intake, what would be the result? This is an important question, for the truth is, your growth in Godliness *is* greatly affected by the quality of your Bible intake. In His magnificent High Priestly prayer of John 17, Jesus asked this of the Father for us: "Sanctify them by the truth; your word is truth" (17:17). God's plan for sanctifying us, that is, for making us holy and Godly, is accomplished by means of "the truth"— His Word. If we settle for a poor quality intake of hearing, reading, and studying God's Word, we severely restrict the main flow of God's sanctifying grace toward us.

As I say this, I realize that it would be easy to cause guilt feelings in us all (myself included) over past failures regarding the intake of God's Word. Above all, remember that Heaven's door is opened to us not by the works we do (such as the intake of God's Word), but by the work of God in Jesus Christ. Beyond that, let's apply the message of Philippians 3:13 to any previous inconsistency with our Bible intake and start "forgetting what is behind and straining toward what is ahead" in this area.

This leads us to a final application question.

What is one thing you can do to improve your intake of God's Word? Unless providentially hindered, joining a group of like-minded believers to hear God's Word preached each week should be a minimum. Many Bible-believing churches provide more than one opportunity each week to hear God's Word. You may want to consider tapes of the Bible, sermon tapes, or Bible exposition on radio as options for increased hearing of God's Word. Set goals of earnestly attempting to read the Bible every day and completing the entire Book. Also, inexpensive workbooks and study guides on every book in the Bible and a multitude of topics are available in Christian bookstores. Besides launching out individually, join a Bible study group in your church or community, or even start a group study.

Whatever way you choose, discipline yourself for the purpose of Godliness by committing to at least one way of improving your intake of the holy Word of God. For those who use their Bibles little are really not much better off than those who have no Bible at all.

Let's finish this chapter with a substantial word of encouragement. It's from a helpful booklet, *Reading the Bible*, by a Welsh pastor named Geoffrey Thomas. Whenever he writes of reading the Bible, also think of hearing and studying it as well.

Do not expect to master the Bible in a day, or a month, or a year. Rather expect often to be puzzled by its contents. It is not all equally clear. Great men of God often feel like absolute novices when they read the Word. The apostle Peter said that there were some things hard to understand in the epistles of Paul (2 Peter 3:16). I am glad he wrote those words because I have felt that often. So do not expect always to get an emotional charge or a feeling of quiet peace when you read the Bible. By the grace of God you may expect that to be a frequent experience, but often you will get no emotional response at all. Let the Word break over your heart and mind again and again as the years go by, and imperceptibly there will come great changes in your attitude and outlook and conduct. You will probably be the last to recognize these. Often you will feel very, very small, because increasingly the God of the Bible will become to you wonderfully great. So go on reading it until you can read no longer, and then you will not need the Bible any more, because when your eyes close for the last time in death, and never again read the Word of God in Scripture you will open them to the Word of God in the flesh, that same Jesus of the Bible whom you have known for so long, standing before you to take you for ever to His eternal home.[9]

NOTES

1. Peter Lewis, *The Genius of Puritanism* (Haywards Heath, Sussex, England: Carey Publications, 1979), page 54.
2. Princeton Religious Research Center, *100 Questions and Answers: Religion in America* (1989), cited in *USA Today*, February 1, 1990.
3. *Bookstore Journal*, as quoted in *Discipleship Journal*, issue 52, page 10.
4. Harold O.J. Brown, "What's the Connection Between Faith and Works?" *Christianity Today*, October 24, 1980, page 26.
5. John Blanchard, *How to Enjoy Your Bible* (Colchester, England: Evangelical Press, 1984), page 104.
6. Robert L. Sumner, as quoted in "Treasuring God's Word," *Our Daily Bread*, October 5, 1988.
7. Jerry Bridges, *The Practice of Godliness* (Colorado Springs, CO: NavPress, 1983), page 51.
8. R. C. Sproul, *Knowing Scripture* (Downers Grove, IL: InterVarsity Press, 1977), page 17.
9. Geoffrey Thomas, *Reading the Bible* (Edinburgh, Scotland: The Banner of Truth Trust, 1980), page 22.

CHAPTER THREE

BIBLE INTAKE (PART 2) ...
FOR THE PURPOSE OF GODLINESS

✤✤✤

There is discipline involved in Christian growth.
The rapidity with which a man grows spiritually
and the extent to which he grows, depends upon this
discipline. It is the discipline of the means.

Richard Halverson
in D. G. Kehl,
Control Yourself! Practicing the Art of Self-Discipline

Two brothers were walking on their father's extensive, wooded acreage when they came upon a young tree heavy with fruit. Both enjoyed as much of the delicious fruit as they wanted. When they started back, one man gathered all the remaining fruit and took it home with him. His brother, however, took the tree itself and planted it on his own property. The tree flourished and regularly produced a bountiful crop so that the second brother often had fruit when the first had none.

The Bible is like the fruit-bearing tree in this story. Merely hearing the Word of God is to be like the first brother. You may gather much fruit from the encounter and even bring home enough to feed on for a few days, but in the long run it doesn't compare with having your own tree. Through the Disciplines of reading and studying, we make the tree our own and enjoy its fruit. Among the Spiritual Disciplines we also find the tools of memorization, meditation, and application, which bountifully increase our harvest of fruit from the tree.

MEMORIZING GOD'S WORD—BENEFITS AND METHODS

Many Christians look on the Spiritual Discipline of memorizing God's Word as something tantamount to modern-day martyrdom. Ask them to memorize Bible verses and they react with about as much eagerness as a request for volunteers to face Nero's lions. How come? Perhaps because many associate all memorization with the memory efforts required of them in school. It was work, and most of it was uninteresting and of limited value. Frequently heard, also, is the excuse of having a bad memory. But what if I offered you one thousand dollars for every verse you could memorize in the next seven days? Do you think your attitude toward Scripture memory and your ability to memorize would improve? Any financial reward would be minimal when compared to the accumulating value of the treasure of God's Word deposited within your mind.

Memorization Supplies Spiritual Power

When Scripture is stored in the mind, it is available for the Holy Spirit to take and bring to your attention when you need it most. That's why the author of Psalm 119 wrote, "I have hidden your word in my heart that I might not sin against you" (verse 11). It's one thing, for instance, to be watching or thinking about something when you know you shouldn't, but there's added power against the temptation when a specific verse can be brought to your mind, like Colossians 3:2: "Set your minds on the things above, not on earthly things."

When the Holy Spirit brings a definite verse to mind like that, it's an illustration of what Ephesians 6:17 can mean when it refers to "the sword of the Spirit, which is the word of God." A pertinent scriptural truth, brought to your awareness by the Holy Spirit at just the right moment, can be the weapon that makes the difference in a spiritual battle.

There is no better illustration than Jesus' confrontation with Satan in the lonely Judean wilderness (Matthew 4:1-11). Each time the Enemy thrust a temptation at Jesus, He parried it with the sword of the Spirit. It was the Spirit-prompted recollection of specific texts of Scripture that helped Jesus experience victory. One of the ways we can experience more spiritual victories is to do as Jesus did—memorize Scripture so that it's available for the Holy Spirit to take and ignite within us when it's needed.

Memorization Strengthens Your Faith

Want your faith strengthened? What Christian doesn't? One thing you can do to strengthen it is to discipline yourself to memorize Scripture. Let's walk through Proverbs 22:17-19, which says, "Incline your ear and hear the words of the wise, and apply your mind to my knowledge; for it will be pleasant if you keep them within you, that they may be ready on your lips. So that your trust may be in the Lord, I have taught you today, even you" (NASB). To "apply your mind" to the "words of the wise" spoken of here and to "keep them within you" certainly pertains to Scripture memory. Notice the reason given here for keeping the wise words of Scripture within you and "ready on your lips." It's "so that your trust may be in the Lord." Memorizing Scripture strengthens your faith because it repeatedly reinforces the truth, often just when you need to hear it again.

Our church has sought to build a new worship center. We felt that we would most honor God if we built the building without going into debt. There were times when my faith in the Lord's provision would begin to sink. More often than not, what renewed my faith was the reminder of God's promise in 1 Samuel 2:30, "Those who honor me I will honor." Scripture memory is like reinforcing steel to a sagging faith.

Memorization and Witnessing and Counseling
On the Day of Pentecost (the Jewish holiday being celebrated when the Holy Spirit first came to dwell within Christians), the Apostle Peter was suddenly inspired by God to stand and preach to the crowd about Jesus. Much of what he said consisted of quotations from the Old Testament (see Acts 2:14-40). Although there's a qualitative difference between Peter's uniquely inspired sermon and our Spirit-led conversations, his experience illustrates how Scripture memory can prepare us for unexpected witnessing or counseling opportunities that come our way.

Recently, while I was presenting the message about Christ to a man, he said something that brought to mind a verse I had memorized. I quoted that verse and it was the turning point in a conversation that resulted in him professing faith in Christ. The same kind of thing happens frequently in counseling conversations. But until the verses are hidden in the heart, they aren't available to use with the mouth.

A Means of God's Guidance
The psalmist wrote, "Your statutes are my delight; they are my counselors" (Psalm 119:24). Just as the Holy Spirit retrieves scriptural truth from our memory banks for use in counseling others, so also will He bring it to our own minds in providing timely guidance for ourselves.

Many times when I have been trying to decide whether to say what I think in a given situation, the Lord brings Ephesians 4:29 to my mind: "Do not let any unwholesome talk come out of your mouths, but only what is helpful for building others up according to their needs, that it may benefit those who listen." I'm sure that sometimes I misunderstand the voice of the Holy Spirit, but His guidance could hardly be more clear than when He brings to mind a verse like that! But it's the result of disciplined Scripture memory.

Memorization Stimulates Meditation

One of the most underrated benefits of memorizing Scripture is that it provides fuel for meditation. When you have memorized a verse of Scripture, you can meditate on it anywhere at anytime during the day or night. If you love God's Word enough to memorize it, you can become like the writer of Psalm 119:97, who exclaimed, "Oh, how I love your law! I meditate on it all day long." Whether you're driving the car, riding the train, waiting at the airport, standing in line, rocking a baby, or eating a meal, you can benefit from the Spiritual Discipline of meditation if you have made the deposits of memorization.

The Word of God is the "sword of the Spirit," but the Holy Spirit cannot give you a weapon you have not stored in the armory of your mind. Imagine yourself in the midst of a decision and needing guidance, or struggling with a difficult temptation and needing victory. The Holy Spirit rushes to your mental arsenal, flings open the door, but all He finds is a John 3:16, a Genesis 1:1, and a Great Commission. Those are great swords, but they're not made for every battle. How do we go about filling our personal spiritual arsenal with a supply of swords for the Holy Spirit to use?

You Can Memorize Scripture

Most people think they have a bad memory, but it's not true. As we've already discovered, most of the time memorizing is mainly a problem of motivation. If you know your birthday, phone number, and address, and can remember the names of your friends, then you can memorize Scripture. The question becomes whether you are willing to discipline yourself to do it.

When Dawson Trotman, founder of the Christian organization called The Navigators, was converted to faith in Christ in 1926, he began memorizing one Bible verse every day. He was driving a truck for a lumber yard in Los Angeles at the time. While driving around town he would work on his verse for that day. During the first three years of his Christian life he memorized his first thousand verses. If he could memorize over three hundred verses a year while driving, surely we can find ways to memorize a few.

Have a Plan

There are several good prepackaged Scripture memory plans available in Christian bookstores. But you might prefer selecting verses on a particular topic where the Lord is working in your life right now. If your faith is weak, memorize verses on faith. If you're struggling with a habit, find verses that would help you experience victory over it. One man told Dawson Trotman that he was afraid that following his example of Scripture memory would make him prideful. Trotman's reply: "Then make your first ten verses on humility!" Another option is to memorize a section of Scripture, such as a psalm, rather than isolated verses.

Write Out the Verses

Make a list of the verses on a sheet of paper or write each one on a separate index card.

Draw Picture Reminders

Nothing elaborate here, just a few lines or stick figures beside each verse. But this makes the verse "visual" and puts the picture-is-worth-a-thousand-words principle to work for you. One simple picture can remind you of a couple dozen words. This is especially true if the drawing illustrates some action described in the verse. For instance, with Psalm 119:11, you might make a crude drawing of a heart with a Bible inside to remind you of treasuring God's Word in the heart. For Ephesians 6:17, a sketch of a sword is an obvious reminder. You'll find this method particularly helpful when memorizing a section of consecutive verses. I realize that you are probably no more of an artist than I am, but no one else has to see the pictures and they can make Scripture memory easier.

Memorize the Verses Word-Perfectly

There's a great temptation, especially when first learning a verse, to lower this standard. Don't settle for just getting close, or getting the "main idea." Memorize it word for word and learn the reference, too. Without an objective standard of measurement, the goal is unclear and you may tend to continue lowering the standard until you quit altogether. Moreover, if you don't have the verse memorized exactly, you lose confidence in using it in conversation and witnessing. So even though memorizing "every jot and tittle" is harder in the beginning, it's easier and more productive in the long run. Incidentally, verses you know word-perfectly are easier to review than those you don't know so accurately.

Find a Method of Accountability

Because of our tendency toward sloth, most of us need more accountability on Scripture memory than on other Disciplines. And the busier we are, the more we tend to excuse ourselves from this commitment. Some, like Dawson Trotman, have developed personalized means of accountability to this Discipline that keep them faithful. Most Christians, however, are more consistent when they meet or talk regularly with someone else—not always another Christian—with whom they review their verses.

Review and Meditate Every Day

No principle of Scripture memory is more important than the principle of review. Without adequate review you will eventually lose most of what you memorize. But once you really learn a verse, you can mentally review it in a fraction of the time it would take to speak it. And when you know a verse this well, you don't have to review but once a week, once a month, or even once every six months to keep a sharp edge on it. It's not unusual, however, to reach a point where you spend 80 percent of your Scripture memory time in review. Don't begrudge devoting so much time to polishing your swords. Rejoice instead at having so many!

A great time to review your better-known verses is while going to sleep. Since you don't need a written copy of the verses before you, you can repeat them and meditate on them while dozing off or even when you have trouble sleeping. And if you can't stay awake, it's fine, since you're supposed to be sleeping anyway. If you can't go to sleep, you're putting the most profitable and peaceful information possible into your mind, as well as making good use of the time.

As we finish this section on the Discipline of Scripture memory, remember that memorizing verses is not an end in itself. The goal is not to see how many verses we can memorize, the goal is Godliness. The goal is to memorize the Word of God so that it can transform our minds and our lives.

Dallas Willard said in this regard, "As a pastor, teacher, and counselor I have repeatedly seen the transformation of inner and outer life that comes simply from memorization and meditation upon Scripture. Personally, I would never undertake to pastor a church or guide a program of Christian education that did not involve a continuous program of memorization of the choicest passages of Scripture for people of all ages."[1]

MEDITATING ON GOD'S WORD—BENEFITS AND METHODS

One sad feature of our modern culture is that meditation has become identified more with nonChristian systems of thought than with biblical Christianity. Even among believers, the practice of meditation is often more closely associated with yoga, transcendental meditation, relaxation therapy, or the New Age Movement. Because meditation is so prominent in many spiritually counterfeit groups and movements, some Christians are uncomfortable with the whole subject and suspicious of those who engage in it. But we must remember that meditation is both commanded by God and modeled by the Godly in Scripture. Just because a cult uses the cross as a symbol doesn't mean the Church should cease to use it. In the same way, we shouldn't discard or be afraid of scriptural meditation simply because the world has adapted it for its own purposes.

The kind of meditation encouraged in the Bible differs from other kinds of meditation in several ways. While some advocate a kind of meditation in which you do your best to empty your mind, Christian meditation involves filling your mind with God and truth. For some, meditation is an attempt to achieve complete mental passivity, but biblical meditation requires constructive mental activity. Worldly meditation employs visualization techniques intended to "create your own reality." And while Christian history has always had a place for the sanctified use of our God-given imagination in meditation, imagination is our servant to help us meditate on things that are true (Philippians 4:8). Furthermore, instead of "creating our own reality" through visualization, we link meditation with prayer to God and responsible, Spirit-filled human action to effect changes.

In addition to these distinctives, let's define meditation as deep thinking on the truths and spiritual realities revealed in Scripture for the purposes of understanding, application, and prayer. Meditation goes beyond hearing, reading, studying, and even memorizing as a means of taking in God's Word. A simple analogy would be a cup of tea. You are the cup of hot water and the intake of Scripture is represented by the tea bag. Hearing God's Word is like one dip of the tea bag into the cup. Some of the tea's flavor is absorbed by the water, but not as much as would occur with a more thorough soaking of the bag. In this analogy, reading, studying, and memorizing God's Word are represented by additional plunges of the tea bag into the cup. The more frequently the tea enters the water, the more effect it has. Meditation, however, is like immersing the bag completely and letting it steep until all the rich tea flavor has been extracted and the hot water is thoroughly tinctured reddish brown.

Joshua 1:8 and the Promise of Success

There is a specific scriptural connection between success and the practice of meditation on God's Word found in Joshua 1:8. As the Lord was commissioning Joshua to succeed Moses as the leader of His people, He told him, "Do not let this Book of the Law depart from your mouth; meditate on it day and night, so that you may be careful to do everything written in it. Then you will be prosperous and successful."

We must remember that the prosperity and success the Lord speaks of here is prosperity and success in His eyes and not necessarily in the world's. From a New Testament perspective we know that the main application of this promise would be to the prosperity of the soul and spiritual success (though some measure of success in our human endeavors would ordinarily occur as well when we live according to God's wisdom). Having made that qualification, however, let's not lose sight of the relationship between meditation on God's Word and success.

True success is promised to those who meditate on God's Word, who think deeply on Scripture, not just at one time each day, but at moments throughout the day and night. They meditate so much that Scripture saturates their conversation. The fruit of their meditation is action. They do what they find written in God's Word and as a result God prospers their way and grants success to them.

How does the Discipline of meditation change us and place us in the path of God's blessing? David said in Psalm 39:3, "As I meditated, the fire burned." The Hebrew word translated "meditated" here is closely related to the one rendered "meditate" in Joshua 1:8. When we hear, read, study, or memorize the fire (Jeremiah 23:29) of God's Word, the addition of meditation becomes like a bellows upon what we've taken in. As the fire blazes more brightly, it gives off both more light (insight and understanding) and heat (passion for obedient action). "Then," says the Lord, "you will be prosperous and successful."

Why does the intake of God's Word often leave us so cold, and why don't we have more success in our spiritual life? Puritan pastor Thomas Watson has the answer: "The reason we come away so cold from reading the word is, because we do not warm ourselves at the fire of meditation."[2]

Psalm 1:1-3—The Promises

God's promises in Psalm 1:1-3 regarding meditation are every bit as generous as those in Joshua 1:8:

> Blessed is the man
>> who does not walk in the counsel of the wicked
> or stand in the way of sinners
>> or sit in the seat of mockers.
> But his delight is in the law of the LORD,
>> and on his law he meditates day and night.
> He is like a tree planted by streams of water,
>> which yields its fruit in season
> and whose leaf does not wither.
>> Whatever he does prospers.

We think about what we delight in. A couple who have found romantic delight in each other think about each other all day. And when we delight in God's Word we think about it, that is, we meditate on it, at times all throughout the day and night. The result of such meditation is stability, fruitfulness, perseverance, and prosperity. One writer said it crisply: "They usually thrive best who meditate most."[3]

The tree of your spiritual life thrives best with meditation because it helps you absorb the water of God's Word (Ephesians 5:26). Merely hearing or reading the Bible, for example, can be like a short rainfall on hard ground. Regardless of the amount or intensity of the rain, most runs off and little sinks in. Meditation opens the soil of the soul and lets the water of God's Word percolate in deeply. The result is an extraordinary fruitfulness and spiritual prosperity.

The author of Psalm 119 was confident that he was wiser than all his enemies (verse 98). Moreover, he said, "I have more insight than all my teachers" (verse 99). Is it because he heard or read or studied or memorized God's Word more than every one of his enemies and his teachers? Probably not. The psalmist was wiser, not necessarily because of more input, but because of more insight. But how did he acquire more wisdom and insight than anyone else? His explanation was,

> Your commands make me wiser than my enemies,
> for they are ever within me.
> I have more insight than all my teachers,
> for I meditate on your statutes. (Psalm 119:98-99)

It is possible to encounter a torrential amount of God's truth, but without absorption you will be little better for the experience. Meditation is absorption.

I believe meditation is even more important for spiritual fruitfulness and prosperity in our day than it was in ancient Israel. Even if the total input of God's Word were the same, we experience a flash flood of information that the psalmist could never have imagined. Combine this with some of our additional modern responsibilities and the result is a mental distraction and dissipation that choke our absorption of Scripture. I'm told that due to the information explosion, which doubles the total sum of human knowledge every few years, we've now reached a point where the average weekday edition of the *New York Times* contains more information than Jonathan Edwards would have encountered in his entire eighteenth-century lifetime. Granted, he had many time-consuming responsibilities (such as care for his horse) that we don't have to worry about. On the other hand, he never had to answer a telephone once in his entire life! Despite his inconveniences, his mind, like the psalmist's, was not as distracted by instant world news, television and radio, portable and car telephones, personal stereos, rapid transportation, junk mail, and so on. Because of these things, it's harder for us today to concentrate our thoughts, especially on God and Scripture, than it ever has been.

This is part of a long-standing mystery that has begun to clarify for me. I have often wondered how men who lived hundreds of years ago were often able to produce more by pen than most modern men can with typewriters and computers. I recently received a copy of Richard Baxter's *Christian Directory*, a practical guide relating to just about every imaginable aspect of the Christian life. This astonishing book consists of almost one thousand pages of tiny print and contains one-and-a-quarter-million words. If that isn't enough to impress you, realize that Baxter researched and wrote by hand most of this in less than two years (1664–1665). And he wouldn't have had the help of electric lights, either, much less an electric typewriter or word processor. I realize that he had no other responsibilities except his family during this two-year period, but it's still an amazing achievement. I've imagined having no other responsibilities except research and writing for two years, but I still don't think I could come close to Baxter's output. Furthermore, I'm not sure I know of anyone else who could, either. How did he do it? Did the people born then have more natural brainpower than all succeeding generations? I don't think so.

I do think men like Baxter were exceptions even in their own day. And I think the Lord's anointing was on him for this enduring task even as it was on Handel when he wrote the *Messiah* in less than a month. But I also think there is a practical difference between people like Baxter and people like us. His mind wasn't as distracted as ours, having less general information and fewer facts to clutter his thinking.

So what do we do? We can't return to the days of Richard Baxter unless we move to the jungles of Papua New Guinea. And even then we have already lived too long in the information age to escape its influence. But we can restore an order to our thinking and recapture some of the ability to concentrate—especially on spiritual truth—through biblical meditation.

In fact, this is exactly the way men like Baxter and Edwards disciplined themselves. In her winsome biography of Sarah Edwards, Elisabeth Dodds said this about Jonathan:

> When he was younger, Edwards had pondered how to make use of the time he had to spend on journeys. After the move to Northampton he worked out a plan for pinning a small piece of paper to a given spot on his coat, assigning the paper a number

and charging his mind to associate a subject with that piece of paper. After a ride as long as the three-day return from Boston he would be bristling with papers. Back in his study, he would take off the papers methodically, and write down the train of thought each slip recalled to him.[4]

We don't have to walk around bristling like a paper porcupine, but we can be transformed by the renewing of our minds (Romans 12:2) through disciplined meditation upon Scripture. We may not be as fruitfully productive as a Richard Baxter or as spiritually successful as a Jonathan Edwards. But we can be wiser than our enemies, have more insight than our teachers, experience all the promises of Joshua 1:8 and Psalm 1, and be more Godly if we will meditate biblically.

How then do we meditate Christianly?

Select an Appropriate Passage

The easiest way to decide what to meditate on is to choose the verse(s), phrase, or word that impresses you most during your encounter with Scripture. Obviously, this is a subjective approach, but any approach is going to be somewhat subjective. Besides, meditation is essentially a subjective activity, a fact that underscores the importance of basing it on Scripture, the perfectly objective resource.[5]

Our understanding of the ministry of the Holy Spirit also leads us to believe that many times He, as Author of the Book, will impress us with a certain part of Scripture because that is the very part He wants us to meditate on for that day. No doubt this approach can be misused or taken to an extreme. We must use wisdom and make sure we don't fail to meditate often on the Person and work of Jesus Christ and the great themes of the Bible.

Verses that conspicuously relate to your concerns and personal needs are clearly targets for meditation. Although we don't want to approach the Bible simply as a digest of wise advice, a collection of promises, or an "answer book," it is God's will that we give our attention to those things He has written that directly pertain to our circumstances. If you have been struggling with your thought life and you read Philippians, then you probably need to meditate on 4:8, "Finally, brothers, whatever is true, whatever is noble, whatever is right, whatever is pure, whatever is lovely, whatever is admirable—if anything is excellent or praiseworthy—think about such things." Is the salvation of a friend or family member on your mind? Should you encounter John 4, the thing to do would be to meditate on Jesus' manner of communication there and draw parallels to your own situation. Sensing distance from God or a dryness in your spiritual condition? Looking for clues to the character of God and drawing on them is a good choice.

One of the most consistent ways to select a passage for meditation is to discern the main message of (one of) the section(s) of your encounter with the Scripture and meditate on its meaning and application. For instance, recently I read Luke 11. There are ten paragraphs to that chapter in the version I was using. I chose one section, verses 5-13. The main theme of that paragraph is persistence in prayer. I reflected on that idea, especially as it is set forth in verses 9-10, which talk about asking, seeking, and knocking. This is harder to do in books like Proverbs where an individual verse is often a self-contained concept and not part of a paragraph. When in such sections, you must rely on one of the methods mentioned above to select your text for meditation.

Repeat It in Different Ways

This method takes the verse or phrase of Scripture and turns it like a diamond to examine every facet.

A meditation on Jesus' words at the beginning of John 11:25 would look like this:

> "*I* am the resurrection and the life."
> "I *am* the resurrection and the life."
> "I am *the* resurrection and the life."
> "I am the *resurrection* and the life."
> "I am the resurrection *and* the life."
> "I am the resurrection and *the* life."
> "I am the resurrection and the *life*."

Of course, the point is not simply to repeat vainly each word of the verse until they've all been emphasized. The purpose is to think deeply upon the light (truth) that flashes into your mind each time the verse is turned. It's simple, but effective. I've found it especially helpful when I have trouble concentrating on a passage or when insights come slowly from it.

Rewrite It in Your Own Words

From his earliest home-school days, Jonathan Edwards' father taught him to do his thinking with pen in hand, a habit he retained throughout his life. This practice helps you to focus your attention to the matter at hand, while stimulating your flow of thinking. Paraphrasing the verse(s) you are considering is also a good way to make sure you understand the meaning. I have a friend who says that paraphrasing verses after the fashion of the *Amplified Bible* is the most productive method of opening a text for him. The very act of thinking of synonyms and other ways of restating the inspired meaning of a part of God's Word is in itself a way of meditation.

Look for Applications of the Text

Ask yourself, "How am I to respond to this text? What would God have me do as a result of my encounter with this part of His Word?"

The outcome of meditation should be application. Like chewing without swallowing, so meditation is incomplete without some type of application. This is so important that the entire next section is devoted to applying God's Word.

Pray Through the Text

This is the spirit of Psalm 119:18: "Open my eyes that I may see wonderful things in your law." The Holy Spirit is the Great Guide into the truth (John 14:26). Meditation is more than just riveted human concentration or creative mental energy. Praying your way through a verse of Scripture submits the mind to the Holy Spirit's illumination of the text and intensifies your spiritual perception. The Bible was written under the Holy Spirit's inspiration; pray for His illumination in your meditation.

I recently meditated on Psalm 119:50: "This is my comfort in my affliction, that Thy word has revived me" (NASB). I prayed through the text along these lines:

Lord, You know the affliction I'm going through right now. Your Word promises to comfort me in my affliction. Your Word can revive me in my affliction. I really believe that is true. Your Word has revived me in affliction during the past, and I confess my faith to You that it will revive me in this experience. I pray that You will revive me now through the comfort of Your Word.

As I prayed through this text, the Holy Spirit began to bring to my mind truths from Scripture about the sovereignty of God over His Church, His providence over the circumstances in my life, His power, His constant presence and love, and so on. In this extended time of meditation and prayer, my soul was revived and I felt comforted by the Comforter.

Meditation must always involve two people—the Christian and the Holy Spirit. Praying over a text is the invitation for the Holy Spirit to hold His divine light over the words of Scripture to show you what you cannot see without Him.

Don't Rush—Take Time!

What value is there to reading one, three, or more chapters of Scripture only to find that after you've finished you can't recall a thing you've read? It's better to read a small amount of Scripture and meditate on it than to read an extensive section without meditation.

Maurice Roberts wrote these words from Scotland in 1990:

> Our age has been sadly deficient in what may be termed spiritual greatness. At the root of this is the modern disease of shallowness. We are all too impatient to meditate on the faith we profess. . . . It is not the busy skimming over religious books or the careless hastening through religious duties which makes for a strong Christian faith. Rather, it is unhurried meditation on gospel truths and the exposing of our minds to these truths that yields the fruit of sanctified character.[6]

Read less (if necessary) in order to meditate more. Although many Christians need to find the time to increase their Bible reading, there may be some who are spending all the time they can or should reading the Bible. If you could not possibly add more time to your devotional schedule for meditating on your Scripture reading, read less in order to have some unhurried time for meditation. Even though you may find moments throughout the day when you meditate on God's Word (see Psalm 119:97), the best meditation generally occurs when it's part of your main daily encounter with the Bible.

May our experience in scriptural meditation be as joyful and fruitful as that of Jonathan Edwards, who penned these lines in his journal soon after his conversion: "I seemed often to see so much light exhibited by every sentence, and such a refreshing food communicated, that I could not get along in reading; often dwelling long on one sentence to see the wonders contained in it, and yet almost every sentence seemed to be full of wonders."[7]

APPLYING GOD'S WORD—BENEFITS AND METHODS

In a study sponsored by Holman Bibles, adults were asked to name their main difficulty in reading the Bible. Their answer was "applying Scripture to concrete situations."[8] Despite our occasional struggles to understand parts of Scripture, understanding it isn't our chief problem. Most of Scripture is abundantly clear. Much more often our difficulty lies in knowing how to apply the clearly understood parts of God's Word to everyday living. What does it say about raising my children? How should Scripture influence my decisions and relationships at work? What is the biblical perspective on the upcoming choice I must make? How can I know God better? These are the kinds of questions Bible readers ask frequently; they prove the urgency of learning the Discipline of applying God's Word.

The Value of Applying God's Word

The Bible promises the blessing of God on those who apply the Word of God to their lives. The classic New Covenant statement on the value of integrating the spiritual with the concrete is James 1:22-25: "Do not merely listen to the word, and so deceive yourselves. Do what it says. Anyone who listens to the word but does not do what it says is like a man who looks at his face in a mirror and, after looking at himself, goes away and immediately forgets what he looks like. But the man who looks intently into the perfect law that gives freedom, and continues to do this, not forgetting what he has heard, but doing it—he will be blessed in what he does." Pithy and powerful is Jesus' similar statement, "Now that you know these things, you will be blessed if you do them" (John 13:17).

These verses tell us there can be a delusion in hearing God's Word. Without minimizing the sufficiency of Scripture nor the power of the Holy Spirit to work through even the most casual brush with the Bible, we can frequently be deluded about the Scripture's impact on our lives. According to James, we can experience God's truth so powerfully that what the

Lord wants us to do becomes as plain as our face in the morning mirror. But if we do not apply the truth as we meet it, we delude ourselves by thinking we have gained practical value, regardless of how wonderful the experience of discovering the truth has been. The one who "will be blessed in what he does" is the one who does what Scripture says.

For someone to "be blessed in what he does" is the equivalent of the promises of blessing, success, and prosperity given in Joshua 1:8 and Psalm 1:1-3 to those who meditate on God's Word. That's because meditation should ultimately lead to application. When God instructed Joshua to meditate on His Word day and night, He told him the purpose for meditating was "so that you may be careful to do everything written in it." The promise "then you will be prosperous and successful" would be fulfilled, not as the result of meditation only, but as God's blessing upon meditation-forged application.

Expect to Discover an Application

Because God wills for you to be a doer of His Word, you may be confident that He wants you to find an application whenever you come to the Scriptures. For the same reason you may believe that the Holy Spirit is willing to help you discern how to flesh out your insights. Therefore, open the Book expectantly. Anticipate the discovery of a practical response to the truth of God. It makes a big difference to come to the Bible with the faith that you will find an application for it as opposed to believing you won't.

The Puritan minister and writer, Thomas Watson, whose influence was so great he was called "the nursing mother of gigantic evangelical divines," encouraged anticipation about application when he said,

> Take every word as spoken to yourselves. When the word thunders against sin, think thus: "God means my sins;" when it presseth any duty, "God intends me in this." Many put off Scripture from themselves, as if it only concerned those who lived in the time when it was written; but if you intend to profit by the word, bring it home to yourselves: a medicine will do no good, unless it be applied.[9]

Because of God's inspiration of Scripture, believe that what you are reading was meant for you as well as for the first recipients of the message. Without that attitude you'll rarely perceive the application of a passage of Scripture to your personal situation.

Understand the Text

A misunderstanding about the meaning of a verse leads to misguided applications of it. For instance, some have applied the injunction of Colossians 2:21—"Do not handle! Do not taste! Do not touch!"—to prohibit just about everything imaginable. And while there may be good reasons to abstain from some of the things this verse has been used against, the text is misapplied when used that way because its meaning is misunderstood. When taken in context, it's clear that these words were actually the slogans of an ascetic group the Apostle Paul was denouncing as an enemy of the gospel. So if you were reading this verse and thought it could apply to your need to lose weight, you might be pleased to know that's an invalid application from an incorrect interpretation. (However, a different diet might be the personal application the Holy Spirit would lead you to from 1 Corinthians 9:27.)

Watson was right when he said, "Take every word as spoken to yourselves." But we cannot do that until we understand how it was intended for those who heard it first. If you take every word of God's call to Abram in Genesis 12:1-7 as spoken to yourself, you'll soon be moving to Israel. But if you understand that particular call as unique to Abram, you can still discover the timeless truths within it and apply every word to yourself. Have you followed the call of God to come to Christ? Are you willing to obey the voice of God wherever He might call you—to a new job, a new location, the mission field, etc.?

We must understand how a passage applied when it was first given before we can understand how it applies now. When Jesus said "Today you will be with me in paradise" (Luke 23:43), it's application was for the thief on the cross. Because these words are part of Scripture, however, and since "all Scripture is God-breathed and is useful," the Lord intends for them to have application to all believers. Obviously, the contemporary application is not that each Christian will die today and be with Jesus in Paradise. One way we can apply this text is in terms of preparing for death. We realize that it is possible for death to come today and then examine ourselves about our readiness for it. We also can apply it regarding the presence of Christ. As Christians, Christ is always present within us, thus He is with us today even though we are not yet in

Paradise. How does a fresh awareness of Christ's presence affect your prayers or your outlook on the rest of the day?

Jesus' promise to the thief is an example of how not every promise is meant to be applied today in exactly the same way as it originally was. Yet many other promises are general, universal, and perpetual in their application. One obvious example is John 3:16. Another is 1 John 1:9. How can we know which passages should be applied somewhat differently than when first given? Here is where a growing knowledge of Scripture through hearing, reading, and in particular, studying the Bible pays dividends. For the better we understand the Bible, the better equipped we will be to apply it.

Having said all that, I still maintain that much of Scripture is plain and straightforward in its meaning. Our problem continues to be more of a lack of action than comprehension. The words of Scripture must be understood to be applied, but until we apply them, we don't really understand them.

Meditate to Discern Application

We've already noted that meditation isn't an end in itself. Deep thinking on the truths and spiritual realities of Scripture is the key to putting them into practice. It is by means of meditation that the facts of biblical information are fleshed out into practical application.

If we read, hear, or study God's Word without meditating on it, no wonder "applying Scripture to concrete situations" is so difficult. Perhaps we could even train a parrot to memorize every verse of Scripture that we do, but if we don't apply those verses to life they won't be of much more lasting value to us than they are to the parrot. How does the Word memorized become the Word applied? It happens through meditation.

Most information, even biblical information, flows through our minds like water through a sieve. There's usually so much information coming in each day and it comes in so quickly that we retain very little. But when we meditate, the truth remains and percolates. We can smell its aroma more fully and taste it better. As it brews in our brain the insights come. The heart is heated by meditation and cold truth is melted into passionate action.

Psalm 119:15 puts it this way: "I meditate on your precepts and consider your ways." It was through meditation on God's Word that the psalmist discerned how to regard God's ways for living, that is, how to be a doer of them. It's no different for us. The way to determine how any scripture applies to the concrete situations of life is to meditate on that scripture.

Ask Application-Oriented Questions of the Text

Asking questions of the text is one of the best ways to meditate. The more questions you ask and answer about a verse of Scripture, the more you will understand it and the more clearly you will see how to apply it.

Here are some examples of application-oriented questions that can help you become a doer of God's Word:

❖ Does this text reveal something I should believe about God?
❖ Does this text reveal something I should praise or thank or trust God for?
❖ Does this text reveal something I should pray about for myself or others?
❖ Does this text reveal something I should have a new attitude about?
❖ Does this text reveal something I should make a decision about?
❖ Does this text reveal something I should do for the sake of Christ, others, or myself?

There are times when a verse of Scripture will have such evident application for your life that it will virtually jump off the page and plead with you to do what it says. More often than not, however, you must interview the verse, patiently asking questions of it until a down-to-earth response becomes clear.

Respond Specifically

An encounter with God through His Word should result in at least one specific response. In other words, after you have concluded your time of Bible intake, you should be able to name at least one definite response you have made or will make to what you have encountered. That response may be an explicit act of faith, worship, praise, thanksgiving, or prayer. It may take the form of asking someone's forgiveness or speaking a word of encouragement. The response may involve the forsaking of a sin or showing an act of love. Regardless of the nature of that response, consciously commit yourself to at least one action to take following the intake of God's Word.

How important is this? How often have you closed your Bible and suddenly realized you can't remember a thing you've read? How many Bible studies have you participated in and how many sermons have you heard where you left without any imprint of Scripture on your life at all? I've known people in as many as six Bible studies per week who grew only in knowledge but not in Christlikeness because they were not applying what they were learning. Their prayer life wasn't strong, they weren't influencing lost people with the gospel, their family life was strained. If we will begin to discipline ourselves to determine at least one specific response to the text before walking away from it, we will much more rapidly grow in grace. Without this kind of application, we aren't doers of God's Word.

MORE APPLICATION

Will you begin a plan of memorizing God's Word? If you've been a Christian for very long, you probably have already memorized much more Scripture than you realize. One of the verses you may know is Philippians 4:13: "I can do everything through him who gives me strength." Do you believe that verse is true? Do you believe that the "everything" mentioned there includes Scripture memory? Since you *can* do it, *will* you do it? When will you begin?

Will you cultivate the Discipline of meditating on God's Word? Occasional Godward thoughts are not meditation. "A man may think on God every day," said William Bridge, "and meditate on God no day."[10] God calls us through the Scriptures to develop the practice of *dwelling* on Him in our thoughts.

By now I'm sure you realize that cultivating the Discipline of meditation involves a commitment of time. Bridge, one of the older but best-ever evangelical writers on meditation, anticipated this problem of making time for meditation.

> "Oh," saith one, "I would think on God with all my heart, but meditation work is a work of time, it will cost time, and I have no time; my hands are so full of business, and so full of

employment, I have no time for this work. Meditation is not a transient thought, but it is a work of time, and will ask time, and I have no time." Mark therefore what [the psalmist] saith in Psalm 119, "Lord incline my heart unto Thy testimonies," how so? "Turn away mine eyes from beholding vanity." The way to have one's heart inclined to the testimonies of God, is to turn away one's eyes from these outward vanities. Would you therefore meditate on God and the things of God, then take heed that your hearts, and your hands, be not too full of the world and the employments thereof. . . . Friends, there is an art, and a divine skill of meditation, which none can teach but God alone. Would you have it, go then to God, and beg of God these things.[11]

Here's the question we naturally tend to ask at this point: "Will the Discipline of meditation be worth this commitment of my time?" I cannot answer better than Bridge.

It is an help to knowledge, thereby your knowledge is raised. Thereby your memory is strengthened. Thereby your hearts are warmed. Thereby you will be freed from sinful thoughts. Thereby your hearts will be tuned to every duty. Thereby you will grow in grace. Thereby you will fill up all the chinks and crevices of your lives, and know how to spend your spare time, and improve that for God. Thereby you will draw good out of evil. And thereby you will converse with God, have communion with God, and enjoy God. And I pray, is not here profit enough to sweeten the voyage of your thoughts in meditation?[12]

When you consider what the Scriptures say about meditation, and when you weigh the testimonies of some of the Godliest men and women of Church history, the importance and value of Christian meditation for progress in Christian growth is undeniable.

Ponder one more quotation on the subject. It presents a challenge about meditation. It is from Richard Baxter, the most practical of all Puritan writers. I join him in making this challenge to you regarding the cultivation of the Discipline of meditation.

If, by this means, thou dost not find an increase of all thy graces, and dost not grow beyond the stature of common Christians, and art not made more serviceable in thy place, and more precious in the eyes of all discerning persons; if thy soul enjoy not more communion with God, and thy life be not fuller of comfort, and hast it not readier by thee at a dying hour: then cast away these directions, and exclaim against me for ever as a deceiver.[13]

Will you prove yourself an "applier" of the Word? You have read many verses from the Word of God in this chapter. What will you do in response to these passages of Scripture?

Most of us would consider ourselves to be doers of the Word and not merely hearers. But remember that James 1:22 begins by saying "prove it." It says to us, "Prove yourselves doers of the word" (NASB). How will you prove that you are a doer of the Word of God as it's been presented to you here?

The Discipline of Bible intake, especially the Discipline of applying God's Word, will often be difficult for many reasons, not the least of which is spiritual opposition. J. I. Packer made the point this way:

If I were the devil, one of my first aims would be to stop folk from digging into the Bible. Knowing that it is the Word of God, teaching men to know and love and serve the God of the Word, I should do all I could to surround it with the spiritual equivalent of pits, thorn hedges, and man traps, to frighten people off. . . . At all costs I should want to keep them from using their minds in a disciplined way to get the measure of its message.[14]

Despite the difficulty and spiritual opposition, are you willing, at all costs, to begin using your mind "in a disciplined way" to feed on the Word of God "for the purpose of godliness"?

NOTES
1. Dallas Willard, *The Spirit of the Disciplines* (San Francisco, CA: Harper & Row, 1988), page 150.
2. Thomas Watson, "How We May Read the Scriptures with Most Spiritual Profit," in *Puritan Sermons* (1674; reprint, Wheaton, IL: Richard Owen Roberts, 1981), vol. 2, page 62.
3. Thomas Brooks, as quoted in *The Banner of Truth*, February 1989, page 26.

4. Elisabeth D. Dodds, *Marriage to a Difficult Man* (Philadelphia, PA: Westminster Press, 1971), pages 67-68.
5. The Bible refers to four general objects of meditation. The one mentioned much more often than any other is meditation on the content of Scripture itself. A second object of meditation is God's creation. And even though we don't have to have a Bible in our hands to dwell on the glory of God in a sunset or the creative skill of God in a sunflower, our meditation on creation should always be informed by Scripture. The Bible also speaks of meditation on God's providence and on His character. Both of these can be perceived in circumstances, but are revealed infallibly only in Scripture. My point in this is to show that the Bible doesn't limit meditation just to biblical *principles*. However, all meditation should focus either on what is revealed in Scripture or be informed by Scripture. The following chart displays all the Bible verses that explicitly refer to the objects of meditation:

God's Word:	Joshua 1:8, "on it"
	Psalm 1:2, "on his law"
	Psalm 119:15, "on your precepts"
	Psalm 119:15, "your ways"
	Psalm 119:23, "on your decrees"
	Psalm 119:48, "on your decrees"
	Psalm 119:78, "on your precepts"
	Psalm 119:97, "your law"
	Psalm 119:99, "your statutes"
	Psalm 119:148, "on your promises"
God's Creation:	Psalm 143:5, "what your hands have done"
God's Providence:	Psalm 77:12, "all your mighty deeds"
	Psalm 77:12, "on all your works"
	Psalm 119:27, "on your wonders"
	Psalm 143:5, "on all your works"
	Psalm 145:5, "on your wonderful works"
God's Character:	Psalm 63:6, "you"
	Psalm 145:5, "the glorious splendor of your majesty"

6. Maurice Roberts, "O the Depth!" *The Banner of Truth*, July 1990, page 2.
7. Jonathan Edwards, *The Works of Jonathan Edwards*, rev. Edward Hickman (1834; reprint, Edinburgh, Scotland: The Banner of Truth Trust, 1974), vol. 1, page xiv.
8. As quoted by Philip Yancey in "Breaking the Bible Barrier," *Moody*, July/August 1986, page 30.
9. Watson, page 65.
10. William Bridge, *The Works of the Reverend William Bridge* (reprint,1845; reprint, Beaver Falls, PA: Soli Deo Gloria, 1989), vol. 3, page 126.
11. Bridge, page 152.
12. Bridge, page 135.
13. Richard Baxter, *The Practical Works of Richard Baxter: Select Treatises* (Grand Rapids, MI: Baker Book House, 1981), page 90.
14. J. I. Packer, foreword to R. C. Sproul, *Knowing Scripture* (Downers Grove, IL: InterVarsity Press, 1979), pages 9-10.

CHAPTER FOUR

PRAYER . . .
FOR THE PURPOSE OF GODLINESS

❖❖❖

*We Protestants are an undisciplined people. Therein
lies the reason for much of the dearth of spiritual
insights and serious lack of moral power.*

Albert Edward Day
quoted in Ronald Klug, *How to Keep a Spiritual Journal*

The largest radio receiver on earth is in New Mexico. Pilots call it "the mushroom patch." Its real name is the Very Large Array. The "VLA" is a series of huge satellite disks on thirty-eight miles of railways. Together the dishes mimic a single telescope the size of Washington, D.C. Astronomers come from all over the world to analyze the optical images of the heavens composed by the VLA from the radio signals it receives from space. Why is such a giant apparatus needed? Because the radio waves, often emitted from sources millions of light years away, are very faint. The total energy of all radio waves ever recorded barely equals the force of a single snowflake hitting the ground.[1]

What great lengths people will go to searching for a faint message from space when God has spoken so clearly through His Son and His Word! Straining through the eyes of telescopes and the electronic ears of the VLA, they search the infinite darkness of the universe for a word. And all the while, "We have the word of the prophets made more certain, and you will do well to pay attention to it, as to a light shining in a dark place, until the day dawns and the morning star arises in your hearts" (2 Peter 1:19).

But God not only has spoken clearly and powerfully to us through Christ and the Scriptures, He also has a Very Large Ear continuously open to us. He will hear every prayer of His children, even when our prayers are weaker than a snowflake. That's why, of all the Spiritual Disciplines, prayer is second only to the intake of God's Word in importance.

The dynamic relationship of prayer to the intake of God's Word, and their prominence over all other Spiritual Disciplines, is illustrated from Christian history by Carl Lundquist:

> The New Testament church built two other disciplines upon prayer and Bible study, the Lord's Supper and small cell groups. John Wesley emphasized five works of piety by adding fasting. The medieval mystics wrote about nine disciplines clustered around three experiences: purgation of sin, enlightenment of the spirit and union with God. Later the Keswick Convention approach to practical holiness revolved around five different religious exercises. Today Richard Foster's book, *Celebration of Discipline*, lists twelve disciplines—all of them relevant to the contemporary Christian. But whatever varying religious exercises we may practice, without the two basic ones of Emmaus— prayer and Bible reading—the others are empty and powerless.[2]

If Lundquist is right, as I believe he is, then one of the main reasons for a lack of Godliness is prayerlessness.

During the 1980s, more than seventeen thousand members of a major evangelical denomination were surveyed about their prayer habits while attending seminars on prayer for spiritual awakening. Because they attended this kind of seminar, we can assume these people are above average in their interest in prayer. And yet, the surveys revealed that they pray an average of less than five minutes each day. There were two thousand pastors and wives at these same seminars. By their own admission, they pray less than seven minutes a day. It's very easy to make people feel guilty about failure in prayer, and that's not the intent of this chapter. But we must come to grips with the fact that to be like Jesus we must pray.

PRAYER IS EXPECTED

I realize that to say prayer is expected of us may make the children of a nonconformist, anti-authoritarian age bristle a bit. Those who have been brought under the authority of Christ and the Bible, however, know that the will of God is for us to pray. But we also believe that His will is good.

Jesus Expects Us to Pray

Don't think of prayer as an impersonal requirement. Realize that it is a Person, the Lord Jesus Christ, with all authority and with all love, who expects us to pray. These excerpts from His words show that He Himself expects us to pray:

- ✧ Matthew 6:5, "And when you pray. . . ."
- ✧ Matthew 6:6, "But when you pray. . . ."
- ✧ Matthew 6:7, "And when you pray. . . ."
- ✧ Matthew 6:9, "This, then, is how you should pray: . . ."
- ✧ Luke 11:9, "So I say to you: Ask . . . ; seek . . . ; knock."
- ✧ Luke 18:1, "Then Jesus told his disciples . . . they should always pray."

Suppose Jesus appeared to you personally, much as He did to the Apostle John on the Isle of Patmos in Revelation 1, and said that He expected you to pray. Wouldn't you become more faithful in prayer, knowing specifically that Jesus expected that of you? Well, the words of Jesus quoted above are as much His will for you as if He spoke your name and said them to you face to face.

God's Word Makes It Clear

In addition to the words of Jesus, the unmistakable expectation of God from the rest of the New Testament is that we pray.

Colossians 4:2, "Devote yourselves to prayer." Everyone is devoted to something. Most of us are devoted to many things. When you make something a priority, when you will sacrifice for it, when you will give time to it, you know you are devoted to it. God expects Christians to be devoted to prayer.

1 Thessalonians 5:17, "Pray continually." While "Devote yourselves to prayer" emphasizes prayer as an activity, "Pray continually" reminds us that prayer is also a relationship. Prayer is in one sense an expression of a Christian's unbroken relationship with the Father.

This verse, then, doesn't mean that we do nothing but pray, for the

Bible expects many other things of us besides prayer, including times of rest when we could not consciously pray. But it does mean that if talking with and thinking of God can't be in the forefront of your mind, it should always be peeking over and ready to take the place of what you are concentrating on. You might think of praying without ceasing as communicating with God on one line while also taking calls on another. Even while you are talking on the other line, you never lose your awareness of the need to return your attention to the Lord. So praying without ceasing means you never really stop conversing with God; you simply have frequent interruptions.

I could have chosen other New Covenant passages which indicate that God expects us to pray, but these two are especially significant because they are direct commands. This means too little time, too many responsibilities, too many kids, too much work, too little desire, too little experience, etc., do not exempt us from the expectation to pray. God expects every Christian to be devoted to prayer and to pray without ceasing.

A praying man as well as reformer of the church, Martin Luther expressed God's expectation of prayer this way: "As it is the business of tailors to make clothes and of cobblers to mend shoes, so it is the business of Christians to pray."[3]

But we must see the expectation to pray not only as a divine summons, but also as a royal invitation. As the writer of Hebrews tells us, "Let us then approach the throne of grace with confidence, so that we may receive mercy and find grace to help us in our time of need" (4:16). We can be prayer pessimists and see the expectation to pray merely as obligation, or we can be optimists who view the command to pray as an opportunity to receive the mercy and grace of God.

My wife, Caffy, expects me to call her when I travel. But that expectation is an expectation of love. She requires that I call because she *wants* to hear from me. God's expectation that we pray is like that. His command to pray is a command of love. In His love He desires to communicate with us and to bless us.

God also expects us to pray just as a general expects to hear from his soldiers in the battle. One writer reminds us that "prayer is a walkie-talkie for warfare, not a domestic intercom for increasing our conveniences."[4] God expects us to use the walkie-talkie of prayer because that is the means He has ordained not only for Godliness, but also for the spiritual warfare between His Kingdom and the kingdom of His Enemy. To abandon prayer is to fight the battle with our own resources at best, and to lose interest in the battle at worst.

This much we know—Jesus prayed. Luke tells us, "But Jesus often withdrew to lonely places and prayed" (Luke 5:16). If Jesus needed to pray, how much more do we need to pray? Prayer is expected of us because we need it. We will not be like Jesus without it.

Why, then, do so many believers confess that they do not pray as they should? Sometimes the problem is primarily a lack of discipline: Prayer is never planned; time is never allotted just for praying. While lip service is given to the priority of prayer, in reality it always seems to get crowded out by things more urgent.

Often we do not pray because we doubt that anything will actually happen if we pray. Of course, we don't admit this publicly. But if we felt certain of visible results within sixty seconds of every prayer, there would be holes in the knees of every pair of Christian-owned pants in the world! Obviously the Bible never promises this, even though God does promise to answer prayer. Prayer involves communication in the spiritual realm. Many prayers are answered in ways that cannot be seen in the material realm. Many prayers are answered in ways different from what we asked. For a variety of reasons, after we open our eyes we do not always see tangible evidence of our prayers. When we are not vigilant, this tempts us to doubt the power of God through prayer.

A lack of sensing the nearness of God may also discourage prayer. There are those wonderful moments when the Lord seems so near that we almost expect to hear an audible voice. No one needs to be prodded to pray in such times of precious intimacy with God. Usually, though, we don't feel like that. In fact, sometimes we can't *feel* the presence of God at all. While it's true that our praying (as well as all aspects of our Christian living) should be governed by the truth of Scripture rather than our feelings, nevertheless the frailty of our emotions frequently erodes our desire to pray. When the desire to pray is weakened, we can find many other things to do.

When there is little awareness of real need there is little real prayer. Some circumstances drive us to our knees. But there are periods when life seems quite manageable. Although Jesus said, "Apart from me you can do nothing" (John 15:5), this truth hits home more forcefully at some times than at others. In pride and self-sufficiency we may live for days as though prayer were needed only when something comes along that's too big for us to handle on our own. Until we see the danger and foolishness of this attitude, God's expectation for us to pray may seem irrelevant.

When our awareness of the greatness of God and the gospel is dim, our prayer lives will be small. The less we think of the nature and character of God, and the less we are reminded of what Jesus Christ did for us on the Cross, the less we want to pray. While driving today I heard a radio program where the guest, an astrophysicist, spoke of the billions of galaxies in the universe. In only a moment of meditation on this I automatically shifted into praise and prayer. Why? I became newly aware of how great God really is. And when I think of what Christ has saved me from, when I recall the shame He endured so willingly for my sake, when I remember all that salvation means, prayer is not hard. When this kind of thinking is infrequent, meaningful prayer will also be infrequent.

Another reason many Christians pray so little is because they haven't learned about prayer.

PRAYER IS LEARNED

If you are discouraged by the command to pray because you feel like you don't know how to pray well, the fact that prayer is learned should give you hope. That means that it's okay to start the Christian life without any knowledge or experience of prayer. No matter how weak or strong your prayer life is right now, you can learn to grow even stronger.

There is a sense in which prayer needs to be taught to a child of God no more than a baby needs to be taught to cry. But crying for basic needs is minimal communication, and we must soon grow beyond that infancy. The Bible says we must pray for the glory of God, in His will, in faith, in the name of Jesus, with persistence, and more. A child of God gradually learns to pray like this in the same way that a growing child learns to talk. To pray as expected, to pray as a maturing Christian, and to pray effectively, we must say with the disciples in Luke 11:1, "Lord, teach us to pray."

By Praying
If you've ever learned a foreign language you know that you learn it best when you actually have to speak it. The same is true with the

"foreign language" of prayer. There are many good resources for learning how to pray, but the best way to learn how to pray is to pray.

Andrew Murray, South African minister and author of *With Christ in the School of Prayer*, wrote, "Reading a book about prayer, listening to lectures and talking about it is very good, but it won't teach you to pray. You get nothing without exercise, without practice. I might listen for a year to a professor of music playing the most beautiful music, but that won't teach me to play an instrument."[5]

The Holy Spirit teaches praying people how to pray better. That's one of the applications of John 16:13 where Jesus said, "But when he, the Spirit of truth, comes, he will guide you into all truth." Just as a plane is guided more easily when it's airborne than when it's on the ground with its engines off, so the Holy Spirit guides us in prayer better when we are airborne in prayer than when we are not.

By Meditating on Scripture

This is one of the most compelling concepts on prayer I've ever learned. Meditation is the missing link between Bible intake and prayer. The two are often disjointed when they should be united. We read the Bible, close it, and then try to shift gears into prayer. But many times it seems as if the gears between the two won't mesh. In fact, after some forward progress in our time in the Word, shifting to prayer sometimes is like suddenly moving back into neutral or even reverse. Instead there should be a smooth, almost unnoticeable transition between Scripture input and prayer output so that we move even closer to God in those moments. This happens when there is the link of meditation in between.

At least two scriptures plainly teach this by example. David prayed in Psalm 5:1, "Give ear to my words, O LORD, consider my sighing." The Hebrew word rendered as "sighing" may also be translated "meditation." In fact, this same word is used with that meaning in another passage, Psalm 19:14: "May the words of my mouth and the meditation of my heart be pleasing in your sight, O LORD, my Rock and my Redeemer." Notice that both verses are prayers and both refer to other "words" spoken in prayer. Yet in each case meditation was a catalyst that catapulted David from the truth of God into talking with God. In 5:1 he has been meditating and now he asks the Lord to give ear to it and to consider it. In Psalm 19 we find one of the best-known statements about

Scripture written anywhere, beginning with the famous words of verse 7, "The law of the LORD is perfect, reviving the soul." This section continues through verse 11 and then David prays in verse 14 as a result of these words and his meditation.

The process works like this: After the input of a passage of Scripture, meditation allows us to take what God has said to us and think deeply on it, digest it, and then speak to God about it in meaningful prayer. As a result, we pray about what we've encountered in the Bible, now personalized through meditation. And not only do we have something substantial to say in prayer, and the confidence that we are praying God's thoughts to Him, but we transition smoothly into prayer with a passion for what we're praying about. Then as we move on with our prayer, we don't jerk and lurch along because we already have some spiritual momentum.

Those who seem to have known this secret best were the English Puritans who lived from 1550 to 1700. Permit me to quote from several Puritan writers, not only to show how remarkably common this now uncommon connection between meditation and prayer was among them, but also to secure its truth firmly into your prayer life. There's much to hold onto in this collection of well-driven nails.

Richard Baxter, pastor and author of the still-printed classic *The Reformed Pastor*, wrote,

> Thus in our meditations, to intermix soliloquy and prayer; sometimes speaking to our own hearts, and sometimes to God, is, I apprehend, the highest step we can advance to in this heavenly work. Nor should we imagine it will be as well to take up with prayer alone, and lay aside meditation; for they are distinct duties, and must both of them be performed. We need the one as well as the other, and therefore we shall wrong ourselves by neglecting either. Besides, the mixture of them, like music, will be more engaging; as the one serves to put life into the other. And our speaking to ourselves in meditation, should go before our speaking to God in prayer.[6]

John Owen, chaplain to Oliver Cromwell and the greatest theologian of the Puritans, said, "Pray as you think. Consciously embrace with your heart every gleam of light and truth that comes to your mind.

Thank God for and pray about everything that strikes you powerfully."[7]

Puritan pastor and Bible commentator Matthew Henry remarked about Psalm 19:14, "David's prayers were not his words only, but his meditations; as meditation is the best preparation for prayer, so prayer is the best issue of meditation. Meditation and prayer go together."[8]

One of the most prolific Puritan preacher-writers was Thomas Manton. In a message on Isaac's meditation in the field (refer to Genesis 24:63), he points directly to meditation as the link between Bible intake and prayer. He wrote,

> Meditation is a middle sort of duty between the word and
> prayer, and hath respect to both. The word feedeth meditation,
> and meditation feedeth prayer. These duties must always go
> hand in hand; meditation must follow hearing and precede
> prayer. To hear and not to meditate is unfruitful. We may hear
> and hear, but it is like putting a thing into a bag with holes. . . .
> It is rashness to pray and not to meditate. What we take in by
> the word we digest by meditation and let out by prayer. These
> three duties must be ordered that one may not jostle out the
> other. Men are barren, dry, and sapless in their prayers for want
> of exercising themselves in holy thoughts.[9]

William Bates, called "that most classic and cultured of the later Puritan preachers," said, "What is the reason that our desires like an arrow shot by a weak bow do not reach the mark? but only this, we do not meditate before prayer. . . . The great reason why our prayers are ineffectual, is because we do not meditate before them."[10]

Among the best of the practical Puritan writings came from the pen of William Bridge. On meditation he asserted the following:

> As it is the sister of reading, so it is the mother of prayer.
> Though a man's heart be much indisposed to prayer, yet, if he
> can but fall into a meditation of God, and the things of God, his
> heart will soon come off to prayer. . . . Begin with reading or
> hearing. Go on with meditation; end in prayer. . . . Reading
> without meditation is unfruitful; meditation without reading is
> hurtful; to meditate and to read without prayer upon both, is
> without blessing.[11]

A modern British writer, Peter Toon, in his book *From Mind to Heart*, summarizes the teaching of the Puritans on these things:

> To read the Bible and not to meditate was seen as an unfruitful
> exercise: better to read one chapter and meditate afterward than
> to read several chapters and not to meditate. Likewise to medi-
> tate and not to pray was like preparing to run a race and never
> leaving the starting line. The three duties of reading Scripture,
> meditation, and prayer belonged together, and though each
> could be done occasionally on its own, as formal duties to God
> they were best done together.[12]

About two hundred years after the Puritans came the man recognized as one of the most God-anointed men of prayer ever seen by the
world, George Muller. For two-thirds of the last century he operated an
orphanage in Bristol, England. Solely on prayer and faith, without
advertising his need or entering into debt, he cared for as many as two
thousand orphans at a single time and supported mission work throughout the world. Millions of dollars came through his hands unsolicited,
and his tens of thousands of recorded answers to prayer are legendary.

Anyone who has heard the story of George Muller ponders the secret
of his effectiveness in prayer. Although some argue for one thing as
Muller's "secret" and others argue for another, I believe we must ultimately attribute his unusually successful prayer life to the sovereignty
of God. But if we look for something transferable from his life to ours,
my vote goes for something I've never heard credited as his "secret."

In the spring of 1841, George Muller made a discovery regarding
the relationship between meditation and prayer that transformed his
spiritual life. He described his new insight this way:

> Before this time my practice had been, at least for ten years pre-
> viously, as an habitual thing, to give myself to prayer after hav-
> ing dressed in the morning. Now, I saw that the most important
> thing was to give myself to the reading of God's Word, *and to
> meditation on it*, that thus my heart might be comforted,
> encouraged, warned, reproved, instructed; and that thus, by
> means of the Word of God, *whilst meditating on it*, my heart
> might be brought into experimental communion with the Lord.

I began therefore to *meditate* on the New Testament from the beginning, early in the morning. *The first thing I did*, after having asked in a few words of the Lord's blessing upon His precious Word, *was to begin to meditate on the Word of God*, searching as it were into every verse to get blessing out of it; not for the sake of the public ministry of the Word, not for the sake of preaching on what I had meditated upon, but for the sake of obtaining food for my own soul.

The result I have found to be almost invariably this, that after a few minutes my soul has been led to confession, or to thanksgiving, or to intercession, or to supplication; so that, though I did not, as it were, give myself to prayer, *but to meditation*, yet it turned almost immediately more or less to prayer. When thus I have been for a while making confession or intercession or supplication, or have given thanks, I go on to the next words or verse, turning all, as I go on, into prayer for myself or others, as the Word may lead to it, but still continually keeping before me that food for my own soul is the object of my *meditation. The result of this is that there is always a good deal of confession, thanksgiving, supplication, or intercession mingled with my meditation*, and that my inner man almost invariably is even sensibly nourished and strengthened, and that by breakfast time, with rare exceptions, I am in a peaceful if not happy state of heart.

The difference, then, between my former practice and my present one is this: formerly, when I rose, I began to pray as soon as possible, and generally spent all my time till breakfast in prayer, or almost all the time. At all events I almost invariably began with prayer. . . . But what was the result? I often spent a quarter of an hour, or half an hour, or even an hour on my knees before being conscious to myself of having derived comfort, encouragement, humbling of soul, etc.; and often, after having suffered much from wandering of mind for the first ten minutes, or quarter of an hour, or even half an hour, I only then really began to pray.

I scarcely ever suffer now in this way. For my heart being nourished by the truth, being brought into experimental fellowship with God, I speak to my Father and to my Friend (vile though I am, and unworthy of it) about the things that He has brought before me in His precious Word. It often now astonishes me that I did not sooner see this point. . . . And yet now, since God has taught me this point, it is as plain to me as anything that the first thing the child of God has to do morning by morning is to obtain food for his inner man.

Now what is food for the inner man? *Not prayer, but the Word of God; and here again, not the simple reading of the Word of God, so that it only passes through our minds, just as water passes through a pipe, but considering what we read, pondering over it and applying it to our hearts.*

When we pray we speak to God. Now prayer, in order to be continued for any length of time in any other than a formal manner, requires, generally speaking, a measure of strength or godly desire, and the season therefore when this exercise of the soul can be most effectually performed is after the inner man has been nourished by *meditation on the Word of God*, where we find our Father speaking to us, to encourage us, to comfort us, to instruct us, to humble us, to reprove us. We may therefore profitably *meditate* with God's blessing though we are ever so weak spiritually; nay, the weaker we are, the more we need *meditation* for the strengthening of our inner man. Thus there is far less to be feared from wandering of mind than if we give ourselves to prayer without having had time previously for *meditation*.

I dwell so particularly on this point because of the immense spiritual profit and refreshment I am conscious of having derived from it myself, and I affectionately and solemnly beseech all my fellow believers to ponder this matter. By the blessing of God, I ascribe to this mode the help and strength which I have had from God to pass in peace through deeper trials, in various ways, than I have ever had before; and having now above fourteen years tried this way, I can most fully, in the fear of God, commend it.[13]

How do we learn to pray? How do we learn to pray like David, the Puritans, and George Muller? We learn to pray by meditating on Scripture, for meditation is the missing link between Bible intake and prayer.

By Praying with Others

The disciples learned to pray not only by hearing Jesus teach about prayer, but also by being with Him when He prayed. Let's not forget that the words "Lord, teach us to pray" didn't just come as a random idea. This request followed a time when the disciples accompanied Jesus in prayer (Luke 11:1). In a similar way, we can learn to pray by praying with other people who can model true prayer for us.

And I don't mean just picking up new words and phrases to use in prayer. As with all learning by example, we can acquire some bad habits as well as good ones. I've heard people who never seem to pray an original prayer. Every time they pray they say the same things. And it's obvious they are merely using shiny phrases picked like fruit from the prayers of others here and there throughout the years. Jesus said, "Do not use meaningless repetition" when praying (Matthew 6:7, NASB). These kinds of prayers are rarely from the heart. God is not the audience being addressed. In reality these prayers are offered to impress the other people who are listening.

There are always other believers who can teach us much by praying with them. But we pray with them to learn principles of prayer, not phrases for prayer. One fellow Christian may give biblical reasons to the Lord why a prayer should be answered. Another might show us how to pray through passages of Scripture. By praying with a faithful intercessor we might learn how to pray for missions. Praying regularly with others can be one of the most enriching adventures of your Christian life. Most of the great movements of God can be traced to a small group of people He called together to begin praying.

By Reading About Prayer

Reading about prayer instead of praying simply will not do. But reading about prayer *in addition to* praying can be a valuable way to learn. "As iron sharpens iron," says Proverbs 27:17, "so one man sharpens another." Read the lessons learned by veterans of the trenches of prayer and let them sharpen your weapons of the warfare of prayer. "He who walks with the wise grows wise" is the teaching of Proverbs 13:20. Reading the books of wise men and women of prayer gives us the privilege of "walking" with them and learning the insights God gave them on how to pray.

We've learned from experience how others can see things in a passage of Scripture we cannot, or how they are able to explain a familiar doctrine in a fresh way that deepens our understanding of it. In the same way reading what others have learned about prayer from their study of Scripture and their pilgrimage in grace can be God's instrument of teaching us what we'd never learn otherwise. Who hasn't learned about praying in faith after reading of George Muller's prayer life, or who hasn't been motivated to pray after reading David Brainerd's biography? Hopefully the reading of this chapter on the Discipline of prayer convinces you that you can learn to pray by reading about prayer!

Let me add a word of encouragement. No matter how difficult prayer is for you now, if you will persevere in learning how to pray you will always have the hope of an even stronger and more fruitful prayer life ahead of you.

PRAYER IS ANSWERED

I love how David addresses the Lord in Psalm 65:2: "O you who hear prayer."

Perhaps no principle of prayer is more taken for granted than this one—that prayer is answered. Try to read this promise of Jesus as though it were for the first time: "Ask and it will be given to you; seek and you will find; knock and the door will be opened to you. For everyone who asks receives; he who seeks finds; and to him who knocks, the door will be opened" (Matthew 7:7-8).

Andrew Murray comments boldly, but I think rightly, on Christ's pledge.

> "*Ask and you* shall *receive*; everyone *that asks, receives*." This is the fixed eternal law of the kingdom: if you ask and receive not, it must be because there is something amiss or wanting in the prayer. Hold on; let the Word and Spirit teach you to pray aright, but do not let go the confidence He seeks to waken: Everyone who asks receives. . . . Let every learner in the school of Christ therefore take the Master's word in all simplicity. . . . Let us beware of weakening the Word with our human wisdom.[14]

Since God answers prayer, when we "ask and receive not" we must consider the possibility that there is "something amiss or wanting" in our prayer. It may be, remember, that God has indeed answered but not in a way that is obvious to us. And it is possible that nothing is amiss in our praying, but that we haven't yet seen the answer only because God intends for us to persevere in praying about the matter awhile longer. But we must also learn to examine our prayers. Are we asking for things that are outside the will of God or would not glorify Him? Are we praying with selfish motives? Are we failing to deal with the kind of blatant sin that causes God to put all our prayers on hold? Despite what we see in response to our prayers, however, let's not become so accustomed to our shortcomings in prayer and to the perception of asking without receiving that our faith in the force of Jesus' promise is diminished. Prayer *is* answered.

My wife, Caffy, ministers as an artist and free-lance illustrator from a small studio in our home. Although she's produced hundreds of illustrations for a variety of Christian organizations, all her jobs are on an occasional basis. Frequently we pray for the Lord to open doors of opportunity for her art work. Because she had nothing on the drawing board, I recently said to her that we should start praying for some new projects. Before lunch the very next morning Caffy called me and said, "Please stop praying for the Lord to provide art work for me! I've had so many callers commissioning work this morning that it's going to take months to get it all done!" She never had so much work come her way so quickly. There were any number of things I had been praying for (regarding not just myself, but my church and others) that the Lord could have chosen to answer. I don't know why it pleased Him to choose that particular request. Were these multiple opportunities really answers to prayer or just a collection of providential coincidences? Only God knows for sure. But I agree with the man who said, "If it is coincidence, I sure have a lot more coincidences when I pray than when I don't."

God doesn't mock us with His promises to answer prayer. C. H. Spurgeon said,

> I cannot imagine any one of you tantalizing your child by exciting in him a desire that you did not intend to gratify. It were a very ungenerous thing to offer alms to the poor, and then when they hold out their hand for it, to mock their poverty with a denial. It were a cruel addition to the miseries of the sick if they were taken to the hospital and there left to die untended and uncared for. Where God leads you to pray, He means you to receive.[15]

By the scriptures about prayer and by His Spirit, God does lead us to pray. He does not lead us to pray in order to frustrate us by slamming Heaven's door in our face. Let's discipline ourselves to pray and to learn about prayer so that we may be more like Jesus in experiencing the joy of answered prayer.

MORE APPLICATION

Since prayer is expected, will you pray? I challenge you with this directly because I think we need to make some conscious decisions about our prayer life. It's time for general intentions about prayer to become specific plans. One pastor who agrees writes the following:

> Unless I'm badly mistaken, one of the main reasons so many of God's children don't have a significant prayer life is not so much that we don't want to, but that we don't plan to. If you want to take a four-week vacation, you don't just get up one summer morning and say, "Hey, let's go today!" You won't have anything ready. You won't know where to go. Nothing has been planned. But that is how many of us treat prayer. We get up day after day and realize that significant times of prayer should be a part of our life, but nothing's ever ready. We don't know where to go. Nothing has been planned. No time. No place. No procedure. And we all know that the opposite of planning is not a wonderful flow of deep, spontaneous experiences in prayer. The opposite of planning is the rut. If you don't plan a vacation you will probably stay home and watch TV. The natural, unplanned flow of spiritual life sinks to the lowest ebb of vitality. There is a race to be run and a fight to be fought. If you want renewal in your life of prayer you must *plan* to see it.[16]

For the purpose of Godliness, will you pray? Today? Will you plan to pray tomorrow? The days after that?

Since prayer is learned, will you learn to pray? Learning more about prayer often helps improve your prayer life. But just as with the practice of prayer, learning about prayer also takes some planning. Will you learn to pray by linking your Bible reading to prayer via meditation? Do you have a plan for praying with others? Are you willing to learn more about prayer by reading? What will you read? Books on the subject, as well as biographies of great prayer warriors, abound. In addition to considering some of the sources quoted in this chapter, consult your pastor or Christian bookseller for recommendations. Now, when will you start?

Since prayer is answered, will you persistently pray? Remember that the words *ask*, *seek*, and *knock* in Matthew 7:7-8 in the original language of the text are in the present, continuous tense. That means we often must pray persistently before the answers come. Starting in Luke 18:1 Jesus tells an entire parable "to show us that we should always pray and not give up." Sometimes a failure to persist in prayer proves that we were not serious about our request in the first place. At other times God wants us to persist in prayer in order to strengthen our faith in Him. Faith would never grow if all prayers were answered immediately. Persistent prayer tends to develop deeper gratitude as well. As the joy of a baby's birth is greater because of the months of anticipation, so is the joy of an answer to prayer after persistent praying. And as much as a generation that measures time in nanoseconds hates to admit its need for it, God crafts Christlike patience in us when He requires persistence in prayer.

George Muller observed,

> The great fault of the children of God is, *they do not continue in prayer; they do not go on praying; they do not persevere*. If they desire anything for God's glory, they should pray until they get it. Oh, how good, and kind, and gracious, and condescending is the One with Whom we have to do! He has given me, unworthy as I am, immeasurably above all I had asked or thought![17]

Perhaps the reason such testimonies are not more common is because so few persevere in prayer. But such a pursuit of God in prayer is worth it. It is worth any amount of frustration and discouragement with prayer. Don't let the Enemy tempt you to become silently cynical about God's willingness and ability to answer. Let a love for God cause you to prevail in prayer to Him who loves you, even when His judgments are unsearchable and His ways past tracing out (Romans 11:33).

Let's pause and get our bearings. Why this appeal to discipline ourselves to pray? It's "for the purpose of godliness." Where there is Godliness there is prayerfulness. Typically picturesque, Spurgeon said it this way: "Even as the moon influences the tides of the sea, even so does prayer . . . influence the tides of godliness."[18]

Men and women of God are always men and women of prayer. My pastoral experience concurs with the words of J. C. Ryle: "What is the reason that some believers are so much brighter and holier than others? I believe the difference, in nineteen cases out of twenty, arises from different habits about private prayer. I believe that those who are not eminently holy pray *little*, and those who are eminently holy pray *much*."[19]

Would you be like Christ? Then do as He did—discipline yourself to be a person of prayer.

NOTES

1. From a January 1990 program, "Infinite Voyage," broadcast on WTTW, the public television station in Chicago.
2. Carl Lundquist, *The Burning Heart* newsletter (St. Paul, MN: Evangelical Order of the Burning Heart, November 1984), page 2.
3. John Blanchard, comp., *Gathered Gold* (Welwyn, Hertfordshire, England:Evangelical Press, 1984), page 227.
4. From the book *Desiring God: Meditations of a Christian Hedonist* by John Piper, copyright 1986 by Multnomah Press. Published by Multnomah Press, Portland, Oregon 97266. Used by permission, page 147.
5. Andrew Murray, as quoted in *Christianity Today*, February 5, 1990, page 38.
6. Richard Baxter, *The Practical Works of Richard Baxter: Select Treatises* (Grand Rapids, MI: Baker Book House, 1981), page 103.
7. John Owen, as quoted in *The Banner of Truth*, August-September 1986, page 58.
8. Matthew Henry, *Commentary on the Whole Bible* (Old Tappan, NJ: Revell, n.d.), vol. 3, page 255.
9. Thomas Manton, *The Works of Thomas Manton* (reprint, Worthington, PA: Maranatha Publications, n.d.), pages 272-273.
10. William Bates, *The Whole Works of the Rev. W. Bates*, arr. and rev. W. Farmer (reprint, Harrisburg, PA: Sprinkle, 1990), vol. 3, page 130.
11. William Bridge, *The Works of the Reverend William Bridge* (reprint, 1845; reprint, Beaver Falls, PA: Soli Deo Gloria, 1989), vol. 3, pages 132, 154.
12. Peter Toon, *From Mind to Heart: Christian Meditation Today* (Grand Rapids, MI: Baker Book House, 1987), page 93.
13. Taken from *Spiritual Secrets of George Muller*, © 1985 by Roger Steer. American rights granted by Harold Shaw Publishers, Wheaton, IL 60189. Pages 60-62, emphasis mine.
14. Andrew Murray, *With Christ in the School of Prayer* (Old Tappan, NJ: Spire Books, 1975), page 33.

15. C. H. Spurgeon, "Thought-Reading Extraordinary," *Metropolitan Taberna-cle Pulpit* (London: Passmore and Alabaster, 1885; reprint, Pasadena, TX: Pilgrim Publications, 1973), vol. 30, pages 539-540.

16. Piper, pages 150-151, used by permission.

17. Roger Steer, *George Muller: Delighted in God!* (Wheaton, IL: Harold Shaw, 1975), page 310.

18. C. H. Spurgeon, "Prayer—The Forerunner of Mercy," in *New Park Street Pulpit* (London: Passmore and Alabaster, 1858; reprint, Pasadena, TX: Pilgrim Publications, 1981), vol. 3, page 251.

19. J. C. Ryle, *A Call to Prayer* (Grand Rapids, MI: Baker Book House, 1979), page 35.

CHAPTER FIVE

WORSHIP ...
FOR THE PURPOSE OF GODLINESS

❖❖❖

True spiritual self-discipline holds believers
in bounds but never in bonds; its effect is
to enlarge, expand and liberate.

D. G. Kehl
Control Yourself! Practicing the Art of Self-Discipline

One of the saddest experiences of my childhood happened on my tenth birthday. Invitations to the celebration were mailed days in advance to eight friends. It was going to be my best birthday ever. They all came to my house right after school. We played football and basketball outside until dark. My dad grilled hot dogs and hamburgers while my mother put the finishing touches on the birthday cake. After we had eaten all the icing and ice cream and most of the cake, it was time for the presents. Honestly, I can't recall even one of the gifts today, but I do remember the great time I was having with the guys who gave them to me. Since I had no brothers, the best part of the whole event was just being with the other boys.

The climax of this grand celebration was a gift from me to them. Nothing was too good for my friends. Cost was immaterial. I was going to pay their way to the most exciting event in town—the high school basketball game. I can still see us spilling out of my parents' station wagon with laughter on that cool evening and running up to the gymnasium. Standing at the window, paying for nine 25-cent tickets and surrounded by my friends—it was one of those simple but golden moments in life. The picture in my mind was the perfect ending to a ten-year-old boy's perfect birthday. Four friends on one side and four friends on the other, I would sit in the middle while we munched popcorn, punched each other, and cheered our high school heroes. As we went inside, I remember feeling happier than Jimmy Stewart in the closing scene of *It's a Wonderful Life*.

Then the golden moment was shattered. Once in the gym, all my friends scattered and I never saw them again the rest of the night. There was no thanks for the fun, the food, or the tickets. Not even a "Happy Birthday, but I'm going to sit with someone else." Without a word of gratitude or goodbye, they all left without looking back. So I spent the rest of my tenth birthday in the bleachers by myself, growing old alone. As I recall, it was a miserable ball game.

I tell that story, not to gain sympathy for a painful childhood memory, but because it reminds me of the way we often treat God in worship. Though we come to an event where He is the Guest of Honor, it is possible to give Him a routine gift, sing a few customary songs to Him, and then totally neglect Him while we focus on others and enjoy the performance of those in front of us. Like my ten-year-old friends, we may leave without any twinge of conscience, without any awareness of our insensitivity, convinced we have fulfilled an obligation well.

Jesus Himself reemphasized and obeyed the Old Testament command "Worship the Lord your God" (Matthew 4:10). It is the duty (and privilege) of all people to worship their Creator. "Come, let us bow down in worship," says Psalm 95:6, "let us kneel before the LORD our Maker." God clearly expects us to worship. It's our purpose! Godliness without the worship of God is unthinkable. But those who pursue Godliness must realize that it is possible to worship God in vain. Jesus quoted another Old Testament passage to warn of worshiping God vainly: "These people honor me with their lips, but their hearts are far from me. They worship me in vain" (Matthew 15:8-9).

How can we worship God without worshiping in vain? We must learn something that is essential in learning to be like Jesus—the Spiritual Discipline of worship.

WORSHIP IS . . . FOCUSING ON AND RESPONDING TO GOD

Worship is difficult to define well. Let's observe it first. In John 20:28, when the resurrected Jesus appears to Thomas and shows him the scars in His hands and side, worship is what happens when Thomas says to

Him, "My Lord and my God!" In Revelation 4:8, we're told that four creatures around the throne worship God day and night without ceasing with "Holy, holy, holy is the Lord God Almighty, who was, and is, and is to come." Then in verse 11 the twenty-four elders around the throne of God in Heaven are said to worship Him by casting their crowns at His feet, falling down before Him, and saying, "You are worthy, our Lord and God, to receive glory and honor and power, for you created all things, and by your will they were created and have their being." In the next chapter, thousands and thousands of angels, elders, and living creatures around the heavenly throne of Jesus Christ, the Lamb of God, cry out with a loud voice in worship, "Worthy is the Lamb, who was slain, to receive power and wealth and wisdom and strength and honor and glory and praise" (5:12). Immediately following comes worship from every created thing saying, "To Him who sits on the throne and to the Lamb be praise and honor and glory and power, for ever and ever!" (5:13).

Now let's describe what we've seen. The word *worship* comes from the Saxon word *weorthscype*, which later became *worthship*. To worship God is to ascribe the proper worth to God, to magnify His worthiness of praise, or better, to approach and address God as He is worthy. As the Holy and Almighty God, the Creator and Sustainer of the Universe, the Sovereign Judge to whom we must give an account, He is worthy of all the worth and honor we can give Him and then infinitely more. Notice, for instance, how those around the throne of God in Revelation 4:11 and 5:12 addressed God as "worthy" of so many things.

The more we focus on God, the more we understand and appreciate How worthy He is. As we understand and appreciate this, we can't help but respond to Him. Just as an indescribable sunset or a breathtaking mountaintop vista evokes a spontaneous response, so we cannot encounter the worthiness of God without the response of worship. If you could see God at this moment, you would so utterly understand how worthy He is of worship that you would instinctively fall on your face and worship Him. That's why we read in Revelation that those around the throne who see Him fall on their faces in worship and those creatures closest to Him are so astonished with His worthiness that throughout eternity they ceaselessly worship Him with the response of "Holy, holy, holy." So worship is focusing on and responding to God.

But we aren't yet in Heaven to see the Lord this way. How is God revealed to us here that we might focus on Him? He has revealed Himself through Creation (Romans 1:20), thus the right response to the stunning sunset or the spectacular mountain view is worship of the Creator. More specifically, God has flawlessly revealed Himself through His Word, the Bible (2 Timothy 3:16, 2 Peter 1:20-21), and His Word, Jesus Christ (John 1:1,14; Hebrews 1:1-2). Therefore, our responsibility is to seek God by means of Christ and the Bible. As the Holy Spirit opens the eyes of our understanding, we see God revealed in Scripture and respond. For example, we have just read in the Bible that God is holy. As we meditate on this and begin to discover more of what it means for God to be holy, the desire to worship Him overwhelms us. But God is most clearly revealed in Jesus Christ, for Jesus is God. If by means of meditation we will focus on the Person and work of Christ as found in the Bible, we will understand what God is like, for Jesus "has made him known" (John 1:18). And to the degree we truly comprehend what God is like, we will respond to Him in worship.

That's why both the public and private worship of God should be based upon and include so much of the Bible. The Bible reveals God to us so that we may worship Him. Bible reading and preaching are central in public worship because they are the clearest, most direct, most extensive presentation of God in the meeting. For the same reasons, Bible intake and meditation are the heart of private worship. Psalms and hymns and spiritual songs are sung either to express truth about God or in worshipful response to God. Prayer is a response to God as He is revealed in Scripture, and so is giving.

Since worship is focusing on and responding to God, regardless of what else we are doing we are not worshiping if we are not thinking about God. You may be listening to a sermon, but without thinking of how God's truth applies to your life and affects your relationship with Him, you aren't worshiping. You may be singing "Holy, holy, holy," but if you aren't thinking about God while singing it, you are not worshiping. You may be listening to someone pray, but if you aren't thinking of God and praying with them, you aren't worshiping. There is a sense in which all things done in obedience to the Lord, even everyday things at work and at home, are acts of worship. But these things are not substitutes for the direct worship of God.

Worship often includes words and actions, but it goes beyond them to the *focus* of the mind and heart. Worship is the God-centered focus and response of the inner man; it is being preoccupied with God. So no matter what you are saying or singing or doing at any moment, you are worshiping God only when you are focused on Him and thinking of Him. But whenever you do focus on the infinite worth of God, you will respond in worship as surely as the moon reflects the sun. This kind of worship isn't in vain. The same is true when . . .

WORSHIP IS . . . DONE IN SPIRIT AND TRUTH

The most profound passage on worship in the New Testament is John 4:23-24. There Jesus said, "Yet a time is coming and has now come when the true worshipers will worship the Father in spirit and truth, for they are the kind of worshipers the Father seeks. God is spirit, and his worshipers must worship in spirit and in truth."

Before we can worship in spirit and truth we must have within us the One whose name is the Holy Spirit and the "Spirit of truth" (John 14:17). He lives only within those who have come to Christ in repentance and faith. Without Him true worship will not happen. We're told in 1 Corinthians 12:3 that "no one can say, 'Jesus is Lord,' except by the Holy Spirit." That doesn't mean no one is capable of speaking such words apart from the Holy Spirit, it means no one can say them as an act of true worship unless motivated by the Holy Spirit. He is the One who reveals God to us and makes Christ irresistible, who teaches us the truth of Scripture, who makes alive hearts that were dead toward God. He is the One who makes hearts that were cold toward worship flame with passion for Christ.

Having the Holy Spirit residing within does not guarantee that we will always worship in spirit and truth, but it does mean we can. To worship God in spirit is to worship from the inside out. It means to be sincere in our acts of worship. No matter how spiritual the song you are singing, no matter how poetic the prayer you are praying, if it isn't sincere then it isn't worship, it's hypocrisy.

The balance to worshiping in spirit is to worship in truth. We are to worship according to the truth of Scripture. We worship God as He is revealed in the Bible, not as we might want Him to be. We worship Him as a God of both mercy and justice, of love and wrath, a God who both welcomes into Heaven and condemns into hell. We are to worship in response to truth. If we don't, we worship in vain.

Having made a case earlier for worshiping God in response to the truth of Scripture, I want to say more here about worshiping in spirit. Whether we are considering public or private worship, we need to realize that unless the heart is plugged in, there's no electricity for worship. One contemporary pastor and author put it bluntly: "Where feelings for God are dead, worship is dead."[1]

He illustrates that effectively as follows:

Worship is a way of gladly reflecting back to God the radiance of His worth. This cannot be done by mere acts of duty. It can be done only when spontaneous affections arise in the heart.

Consider the analogy of a wedding anniversary. Mine is on December 21. Suppose on this day I bring home a dozen long-stemmed roses for Noël. When she meets me at the door I hold out the roses, and she says, "O Johnny, they're beautiful, thank you," and gives me a big hug. Then suppose I hold up my hand and say matter-of-factly, "Don't mention it; it's my duty."

.What happens? Is not the exercise of duty a noble thing? Do not we honor those we dutifully serve? Not much. Not if there's no heart in it. Dutiful roses are a contradiction in terms. If I am not moved by a spontaneous affection for her as a person, the roses do not honor her. In fact, they belittle her. They are a very thin covering for the fact that she does not have the worth or beauty in my eyes to kindle affection. All I can muster is a calculated expression of marital duty. . . .

The real duty of worship is not the outward duty to say or do the liturgy. It is the inward duty, the command—"Delight yourself in the Lord!" (Psalm 37:4). . . .

The reason this is the real duty of worship is that this honors God, while the empty performance of ritual does not. If I take my wife out for the evening on our anniversary and she asks me, "Why do you do this?" the answer that honors her most is, "Because nothing makes me happier tonight than to be with you."

"It's my duty," is a dishonor to her.

"It's my joy," is an honor.

How shall we honor God in worship? By saying, "It's my duty?" Or by saying, "It's my joy"?[2]

So we must worship in both spirit and truth, with both heart and head, with both emotions and thought. If we worship too much just by spirit we will be mushy and soft on the truth, worshiping according to feelings. That can lead anywhere from a sleepy tolerance of anything in worship at one extreme to uncontrollable spiritual wildfire on the other. But if we worship by truth without spirit, then our worship will be taut, grim, and icily predictable.

Actually these balancing truths of worshiping in spirit and truth are complementary. It is important to realize this because frankly, all of us have at times attempted to engage in public or private worship but found no fire on the altar of our heart. Meditation on the truth, rightly done, can kindle the emotions of worship. Conversely, the right kind of heart for God longs to be guided by the truth. We must have both. Jesus said the greatest commandment involved loving God with all the heart *and* with all the mind (Mark 12:30). Otherwise, we worship in vain.

Should we stop attending worship or discontinue daily devotions if we can't seem to maintain the proper balance of spirit and truth? What if we endure a long period of spiritual dryness where practically every supposed worship experience seems little more than an exercise in hypocrisy? Why continue if we are just worshiping in vain?

No, we should not stop engaging in the forms of worship even though we don't have the feelings of worship. There are some things in which we must persevere even when we don't feel like it, just because it is the right thing to do. Remember that even our "best" worship is imperfect in some ways, however minuscule those imperfections might be. But we don't advocate the cessation of worship then because it is somehow flawed. More importantly, it is probable that the "breakthrough" in restoring the joy and freedom of worship will happen in the context of worship. People frequently tell me that they didn't feel like coming to church at a particular service, but something happened during that time that refreshed them and restored their spiritual perspective.

Every believer must cross a few spiritual deserts in his or her pilgrimage to the Celestial City. Some arid places may be traversed in an hour or a few days. Occasionally, however, you may be required to travel for weeks with an almost withered soul. Press on in worship. Cry out to God for a renewed awareness of the "streams of living water" (referring to the Holy Spirit) that Jesus promised in John 7:38 would flow in every believer. But don't stop worshiping. Never give up in the desert. You don't know how wide it is and you may be almost across.

WORSHIP IS . . . EXPECTED
BOTH PUBLICLY AND PRIVATELY

That believers are expected to participate regularly in corporate worship is given in the command of Hebrews 10:25: "Let us not give up meeting together, as some are in the habit of doing." The first exercise of the Discipline of worship is to develop the habit of faithfully assembling with other believers in meetings where the primary purpose is to worship God.

Christianity is not an isolationist religion. The New Testament describes the Church with metaphors like *body* (1 Corinthians 12:12), *building* (Ephesians 2:21), and *household* (Ephesians 2:19), each of which speaks of the relationship between individual units and a larger whole. To express and experience Christianity almost always on the individual level (that is, to the exclusion of the group level), means you will needlessly and sinfully miss much of the blessing and power of God. This verse teaches that those who "give up" the disciplined "habit" of assembling with other believers have developed an unChristian habit.

It's undeniable that "meeting together" means to worship God in the physical presence of other believers. Not only do the words themselves allow for no other interpretation, but when this letter was written to the Hebrews there was no other way they could be construed. So we cannot persuade ourselves that we are "meeting together" with other Christians by watching them worship on television. There are good reasons for the broadcast and tape recording of church worship, but none includes the idea of substituting media ministry for church attendance by those who are able.

It's also true that the quality of your private devotional life doesn't exempt you from worshiping with other believers. You may have the devotional life of a George Muller, but you need corporate worship as much as he and these Hebrews did. There's an element of worship and Christianity that cannot be experienced in private worship or by watching worship. There are some graces and blessings that God gives only in the "meeting together" with other believers.

The Puritan preacher David Clarkson explains this in an instructive sermon on "Public Worship to Be Preferred Before Private."

> The most wonderful things that are now done on earth are
> wrought in the public ordinances, though the commonness and
> spiritualness of them makes them seem less wonderful. . . .
> Here the Lord speaks life unto dry bones, and raises dead souls
> out of the grave and sepulchre of sin, . . . Here the dead hear the
> voice of the Son of God and His messengers, and those that
> hear do live. Here He gives sight to those that are born blind; it
> is the effect of the gospel preached to open the eyes of sinners,
> and to turn them from darkness to light. Here He cures diseased
> souls with a word, which are otherwise incurable by the utmost
> help of men and angels. . . . Here He dispossesses Satan, and
> casts unclean spirits out of the souls of sinners that have been
> long possessed by them. Here He overthrows principalities and
> powers, vanquishes the power of darkness, and causes Satan to
> fall from heaven like lightning. Here He turns the whole course
> of nature in the souls of sinners, makes old things pass away,
> and all things become new. Wonders these are, and would be so
> accounted, were they not the common work of the public min-
> istry. It is true indeed, the Lord has not confined himself to
> work these wonderful things only in public; yet the public min-
> istry is the only ordinary means whereby He works them.[3]

On the other hand, no matter how fulfilling or sufficient our regular public worship celebration seems, there are experiences with God that He gives only in our private worship. Jesus participated faithfully in the public worship of God at the synagogue each Sabbath and at the stated assemblies of Israel at the Temple in Jerusalem. In addition to that, however, Luke observed that "Jesus often withdrew to lonely places and prayed" (5:16). As the familiar Puritan commentator, Matthew Henry, put it, "Public worship will not excuse us from secret worship."[4]

How is it possible to worship God publicly once each week when we do not worship Him privately throughout the week? Can we expect the flames of our worship of God to burn brightly in public on the Lord's Day when they barely flicker for Him in secret on other days? Isn't it because we do not worship well in private that our corporate worship experience often dissatisfies us? "There is no way," says the Welsh Baptist, Geoffrey Thomas, "that those who neglect secret worship can know communion with God in the public services of the Lord's Day."[5]

We must not forget, however, that God expects us to worship privately so He can bless us. We minimize our joy when we neglect the daily worship of God in private. It is one of the great blessings of life that God does not limit our access to Him and enjoyment of His presence to one day per week! Daily strength, guidance, and encouragement are available to us. An invitation to grow in intimacy with Jesus Christ Himself is open every day.

Think of it: The Lord Jesus Christ is willing to meet with you privately for as long as you want, and He is willing—even eager—to meet with you every day! Suppose you had been one of the thousands who followed Jesus around for much of the last three years of His earthly life. Can you imagine how excited you would have been if one of His disciples said, "The Master wants us to tell you that He is willing to get alone with you whenever you're willing, and for as much time as you want to spend, and He'll be expecting you most every day"? What a privilege! Who would have complained about this expectation? Well, that marvelous privilege and expectation is always yours. Exercise this privilege and fulfill this expectation for the glory and enjoyment of God forever.

WORSHIP IS . . . A DISCIPLINE TO BE CULTIVATED

Jesus said, "Worship the Lord your God" (Matthew 4:10). To worship God throughout a lifetime requires discipline. Without discipline, our worship of God will be thin and inconsistent.

When I say that worship is focusing on and responding to God, I hope to convey my conviction that true worship is always covered with heartprints. Worship can't be diagramed or calculated, for it is the response of a heart in love with God. And yet, we also must be able to think of worship as a Discipline, a Discipline that must be cultivated just as all relationships must be to remain healthy and grow.

Worship is a Spiritual Discipline insofar as it is both an end and a means. The worship of God is an *end* in itself because worship, as we've defined it, is to focus on and respond to God. There is no higher goal than focusing on and responding to God. But worship is also a *means* in the sense that it is a means to Godliness. The more truly we worship God, the more we become like Him.

People become like their focus. We emulate what we think about. Children pretend they are the heroes they dream about. Teenagers dress like the sports stars or popular musicians they devote so much attention to. But these tendencies don't disappear when we become adults. Those who concentrate on "making it to the top" read the books of those "at the top," then copy their business style and personal habits. To illustrate the point on a more crude level, those who focus on pornography mimic what they see. Focusing on the world more than on the Lord makes us more worldly than Godly. But if we would be Godly, we must focus on God. Godliness requires disciplined worship.

"But I've tried it," someone screams in frustration, "and it doesn't work for me! I faithfully attend church. I've tried a daily routine of Bible reading and prayer, but I didn't experience the results I expected. Despite all I'm doing I don't seem to be growing much in Godliness." Going through a routine is not the same as rightly practicing a Spiritual Discipline. Reading the Bible every day doesn't automatically make me more Godly any more than reading the business section of the *Chicago Tribune* every day makes me a businessman. And a failure to experience what we want when we want it doesn't prove that God's means to Christlikeness are ineffective. Get counsel from those who are growing in Godliness through public and private worship. Talk to a mature Christian who has a meaningful devotional life. Review some of the earlier chapters of this book, particularly the ones on meditation and prayer. The development of any discipline, from hitting a golf ball to playing the piano, often requires outside help from those with more experience. So don't be surprised that you need help in the development of the Disciplines that lead to Christlikeness, and don't be afraid to ask for it.

Describing modern man, one has written, "He worships his work, works at his play, and plays at his worship." In defiance of this, will you cultivate the Discipline of worship?

MORE APPLICATION

Will you commit yourself to the Discipline of daily worship? "If you will not worship God seven days a week," said A. W. Tozer, "you do not worship Him on one day a week."[6] Let's not fool ourselves. Worship is not a once-a-week event. We can't expect worship to flow from our lips on the Lord's Day if we keep it dammed in our hearts throughout the week. The waters of worship should never stop flowing from our heart, for God is always God and always worthy of worship. But the flow of worship should be channeled and distilled at least daily into a distinct worship experience.

There are those who want to take the Spiritual Disciplines and practically isolate themselves from other believers. They believe their personal devotional life is superior to anything they experience in corporate worship, so they disregard the public ministry of God's Word. We should be alert to the danger of becoming unbalanced in that direction. In my pastoral ministry, however, I have encountered many more professing Christians who go to the opposite extreme. They faithfully discipline themselves to attend corporate worship, but they neglect the regular practice of privately worshiping God. There is hardly a more common pitfall on the path to Godliness. Many progress little in Christlikeness simply because they fail to discipline themselves at this very point. Don't let it happen to you.

Will you put actual worship into your acts of worship? What David Clarkson says about public worship applies to all acts of worship, both public and private.

> What you do in public worship, do it with all your might. Shake off that slothful, indifferent, lukewarm temper, which is so odious to God. . . . Think it not enough to present your bodies before the Lord. . . . The worship of the body is but the carcass of worship; it is soul worship that is the soul of worship. Those that draw near with their lips only shall find God far enough from them; not only lips, and mouth, and tongue, but mind, and heart, and affections; not only knee, and hand, and eye, but heart, and conscience, and memory, must be pressed to attend upon God in public worship. David says, not only "my flesh longs for Thee," but "my soul thirsts for Thee." Then will the Lord draw near, when our whole man waits on Him; then will the Lord be found, when we seek Him with our whole heart.[7]

The act of worship without actual worship is a miserable, hypocritical experience. So if worship wearies you, you aren't really worshiping. Imagine one of the creatures worshiping around the throne of

God saying, "I'm tired of this!" It's a thought that's never crossed their minds throughout all eternity past, nor will it ever in all eternity to come. Instead we read that they are so endlessly overwhelmed with the glory of God that "day and night they never stop" worshiping Him (Revelation 4:8). Obviously we cannot yet see and experience in worship all that they are privileged to enjoy, but we can learn from them that meaningless worship is a contradiction in terms. Since the object of our worship is the glorious and majestic God of Heaven, when worship becomes empty, the problem lies with the subject (us), not the object (God). He is worthy of all the worship, the best and most wholehearted worship, you can give Him.

The Spiritual Discipline of publicly and privately worshiping God is one of the means He has given us to receive the grace to grow in Christlikeness. As we grow stronger in the worship of God, we grow stronger in the likeness of Christ. Perhaps President Calvin Coolidge said much more than he realized when he asserted, "It is only when men begin to worship that they begin to grow."[8]

NOTES
1. From the book *Desiring God: Meditations of a Christian Hedonist* by John Piper, copyright 1986 by Multnomah Press. Published by Multnomah Press, Portland, Oregon 97266. Used by permission, page 70.
2. Piper, pages 72-73, used by permission.
3. David Clarkson, *The Works of David Clarkson* (London: James Nichol, 1864; reprint, Edinburgh, Scotland: The Banner of Truth Trust, 1988), vol. 3, pages 193-194.
4. John Blanchard, comp., *Gathered Gold* (Welwyn, Hertfordshire, England: Evangelical Press, 1984), page 342.
5. Geoffrey Thomas, "Worship in Spirit," *The Banner of Truth*, August-September 1987, page 8.
6. John Blanchard, comp., *More Gathered Gold* (Welwyn, Hertfordshire, England: Evangelical Press, 1984), page 344.
7. Clarkson, page 209.
8. Lewis C. Henry, ed., *5000 Quotations for All Occasions* (Philadelphia, PA: The Blakiston Company, 1945), page 319.

CHAPTER SIX

EVANGELISM...
FOR THE PURPOSE OF GODLINESS

❖❖❖

The present benefit of spiritual discipline is a fulfilled,
God-blessed, fruitful, and useful life. If you get
involved in spiritual gymnastics, the blessings of
godliness will carry on into eternity. Although many
people spend far more time exercising their bodies
than their souls, the excellent servant of Jesus Christ
realizes that spiritual discipline is a priority.

John MacArthur, Jr.
Qualities of an Excellent Servant

Only the sheer rapture of being lost in the worship of God is as exhilarating and intoxicating as telling someone about Jesus Christ.

Some of the most rewarding times of my life have been during mission trips when I have done nothing but talk about Christ on the streets and in homes, with one individual or group after another, all day long. The same is true in my own locale—nothing so excites me as a conversation about Christ with someone who does not know Him. It can be an equally rewarding experience for any believer.

And yet nothing causes an eye-dropping, foot-shuffling anxiety more quickly among a group of Christians like myself than talking about our responsibility to evangelize. I know many believers who feel confident that they are obeying the Lord when it comes to their intake of Scripture or to their giving or serving, but I'm sure I don't know a single Christian who would boldly say, "I am as evangelistic as I should be."

Evangelism is a broad subject, and there are many things about it I won't take the time to address in this chapter. The main idea I want to communicate about it here is that Godliness requires that we discipline ourselves in the practice of evangelism. Among the reasons we don't speak of Christ more often is fear. We'll think together about that a little later. But I'm convinced that the main reason many of us don't witness for Christ in ways that would be effective and relatively fear-free is simply because we don't discipline ourselves to do it.

EVANGELISM IS EXPECTED

Most of those reading this book will not need convincing that evangelism is expected of every Christian. All Christians are not expected to use the same *methods* of evangelism, but all Christians are expected to evangelize.

Before we go further, let's define our terms. What is evangelism? If we want to define it thoroughly, we could say that evangelism is to present Jesus Christ in the power of the Holy Spirit to sinful people, in order that they may come to put their trust in God through Him, to receive Him as their Savior, and serve Him as their King in the fellowship of His Church.[1] If we want to define it simply, we could say that New Testament evangelism is communicating the gospel. Anyone who faithfully relates the essential elements of God's salvation through Jesus Christ is evangelizing. This is true whether your words are spoken, written, or recorded, and whether they are delivered to one person or to a crowd.

Why is evangelism expected of us? The Lord Jesus Christ Himself has commanded us to witness. Consider His authority in the following:

"Therefore go and make disciples of all nations, baptizing them in the name of the Father and of the Son and of the Holy Spirit, and teaching them to obey everything I have commanded you. And surely I will be with you always, to the very end of the age" (Matthew 28:19-20).

"He said to them, 'Go into all the world and preach the good news to all creation'" (Mark 16:15).

"And repentance and forgiveness of sins will be preached in his name to all nations, beginning at Jerusalem" (Luke 24:47).

"Again Jesus said, 'Peace be with you! As the Father has sent me, I am sending you'" (John 20:21).

"But you will receive power when the Holy Spirit comes on you; and you will be my witnesses in Jerusalem, and in all Judea and Samaria, and to the ends of the earth" (Acts 1:8).

These commands weren't given to the apostles only. For example, the apostles never came to *this* nation. For the command of Jesus to be fulfilled and for America to hear about Christ, the gospel had to come here by other Christians. And the apostles will never come to your home, your neighborhood, or to the place where you work. For the Great Commission to be fulfilled there, for Christ to have a witness in that "remote part" of the earth, a Christian like you must discipline yourself to do it.

Some Christians believe that evangelism is a gift and the responsibility of only those with that gift. They appeal to Ephesians 4:11 for support: "It was he who gave some to be apostles, some to be prophets, some to be evangelists, and some to be pastors and teachers." While it is true that God gifts some for ministry as evangelists, He calls all believers to be His witnesses and provides them with both the power to witness and a powerful message. Every evangelist is called to be a witness, but only a few witnesses are called to the vocational ministry of an evangelist. Just as each Christian, regardless of spiritual gift or ministry, is to love others, so each believer is to evange*lize* whether or not his or her gift is that of evange*list*.

Think of our responsibility for personal evangelism from the perspective of 1 Peter 2:9: "But you are a chosen people, a royal priesthood, a holy nation, a people belonging to God." Many Christians who are familiar with this part of the verse don't have a clue how the rest of it goes. It goes on to say that these privileges are *yours*, Christian, "that you may declare the praises of him who called you out of darkness into his wonderful light." We normally think of this verse as establishing the doctrine of the priesthood of all believers. But it is equally appropriate to say that it also exhorts us to a kind of prophethood of all believers. God expects each of us to "declare the praises" of Jesus Christ.

EVANGELISM IS EMPOWERED

If it is so obvious to almost all Christians that we are to evangelize, how come almost all Christians seem to disobey that command so often?

Some believe they need a lot of specialized training to witness effectively. They are afraid to talk to someone about Christ until they feel confident that they have an adequate amount of Bible knowledge and could deal with any potential question or objection. The problem is that confident day never comes. What if the formerly blind man that Jesus healed in John 9 had thought that way? Would he ever have felt ready to witness to the scholarly, critical Pharisees? And yet within hours, perhaps minutes, of meeting Jesus he bravely tells them what he knows of Jesus.

Sometimes we are unable to speak of Christ because we are afraid that people will think we are strange and will reject us. When I was in law school I became friends with a fellow student in my property class. Soon realizing he was not a Christian, I became conscious of my responsibility to share the gospel with him. I did my best to model the character of Christ around him and prayed for opportunities to witness to him. One day near the end of the school year, just as the first bell rang he surprised me by asking, "Why are you always so happy?" Although class was about to start, I could have given my friend a clear testimony, even if it were only one sentence. I could have answered, "Because of Jesus Christ." Or I might have said, "I'd like to tell you why after class." But when the opportunity I'd prayed for finally came, I froze in fear that he might think less of me for my faith and said, "I don't know."

In some cases the method of witnessing we're asked to use causes our evangelophobia. If it requires approaching someone we've never met before and striking up a conversation about Christ, most people will be terrified and indicate it by their absence. Although a few enjoy it, most people tremble at the thought of going door to door to share the gospel. Even methods that call for witnessing to friends or family, if they involve a forced, confrontational, or unnatural approach, fill us with fear at sharing the best news in the world with the people we love the most.

I've never heard it expressed before, but I think the seriousness of evangelism is the main reason it frightens us. We realize that in talking with someone about Christ, Heaven and hell are at stake. The eternal destiny of the person is the issue. And even when we rightly believe that the results of this encounter are in God's hands and that we are not accountable for the person's response to the gospel, we still sense a solemn duty to communicate the message faithfully coupled with a holy dread of saying or doing anything that would be a stumbling block to this person's salvation. Many Christians feel too unprepared for this kind of challenge, or simply have too little faith and are terrified of entering into such an eternally important situation.

Researcher George Barna offers another explanation for Christians' fear of evangelism.

One dominant reason underlying the increasing reluctance of Christians to share their faith with non-Christians pertains to the faith sharing experience itself. In asking Christians about their witnessing activities, we have found that nine out of ten individuals who attempt to explain their beliefs and theology to other people come away from those experiences feeling as if they have failed. . . . The reality of human behavior is that most people avoid those activities in which they perceive themselves to be failures. As creatures seeking pleasure and comfort, we emphasize those dimensions and activities in which we are most capable and secure. Thus, despite the divine command to spread the Word, many Christians redirect their energies into areas of spiritual activity that are more satisfying and in which they are more likely to achieve success.[2]

What is success in evangelism? Is it when the person you witness to comes to Christ? Certainly that's what we want to happen. But if this is success, are we failures whenever we share the gospel and people refuse to believe? Was Jesus an "evangelistic failure" when people like the rich young ruler turned away from Him and His message? Obviously not. Then neither are we when we present Christ and His message and they turn away in unbelief. We need to learn that sharing the gospel *is* successful evangelism. We ought to have an obsession for souls, and tearfully plead with God to see more people converted, but conversions are fruit that God alone can give.

In this regard we are like the postal service. Success is measured by the careful and accurate delivery of the message, not by the response of the recipient. Whenever we share the gospel (which includes the summons to repent and believe), we have succeeded. In the truest sense, *all* biblical evangelism is successful evangelism, regardless of the results.

The power of evangelism is the Holy Spirit. From the instant that He indwells us He gives us the power to witness. Jesus stressed this in Acts 1:8 when He said, "But you will receive power when the Holy Spirit comes on you; and you will be my witnesses in Jerusalem, and in all Judea and Samaria, and to the ends of the earth." Evangelism is expected of every Christian because every Christian is empowered to evangelize. But this power to witness that Jesus promised in Acts 1:8 is often misunderstood. We are not all empowered to evangelize the same way, but all believers have been given power to be witnesses of Jesus Christ. The evidence that you've been given the power to witness is a changed life. The same Holy Spirit power that changed your life for Christ is the power to witness for Christ. So if God by His Spirit has changed your life, be confident of this: God has given you Acts 1:8 power. That means that in ways and methods compatible with your personality, temperament, spiritual gift, opportunities, etc., you do have the power to share the gospel with people. Having Acts 1:8 power also means God will empower your life and words in the sharing of the gospel in ways you will often not perceive. To put it another way, the Holy Spirit may grant much power to your witness in an evangelistic encounter without giving to you any *feeling or sense* of power in it.

The gospel we share carries with it the power of the Holy Spirit of God as well. "I am not ashamed of the gospel," said the Apostle Paul in Romans 1:16, "because it is the power of God for the salvation of everyone who believes: first for the Jew, then for the Gentile." That's why people can be converted whether they hear the gospel from a teenage teacher of a vacation Bible school class or a seminary-trained evangelist with a Ph.D., whether they read it in a book by an Oxford scholar like C. S. Lewis or in a simple tract. It is *the gospel* God blesses like no other words.

That does not mean the gospel is a kind of magic wand we can wave over unbelievers and the power of God will spring from it and automatically convert all of them. You are probably like myself in that you heard the gospel many times before you were saved. Doubtless you can think of several people who have heard the gospel repeatedly and have not experienced the new birth. God must also grant faith (Ephesians 2:8-9) with the hearing of the gospel, "because it is the power of God for the salvation of everyone who *believes*." But it is *through the gospel* that God gives the power to believe. That's the meaning of Romans 10:17: "Consequently, faith comes from hearing the message, and the message is heard through the word of Christ."

When you share the gospel, you share "the power of God for the salvation of everyone who believes." Sharing the gospel is like walking around in a thunderstorm and handing out lightning rods. You don't know when the lightning is going to strike or who it will strike, but you know what it's going to strike—the lightning rod of the gospel. And when it does, that person's lightning rod is going to be charged with the power of God and he or she is going to believe.

That's why we can be confident that some will believe if we will faithfully and tenaciously share the gospel. It is the *gospel* that is the power of God for salvation and not our own eloquent power or persua-siveness. God has His elect whom He will call and whom He has cho-sen to call *through the gospel* (Romans 8:29-30, 10:17). Otherwise we would despair at those rejecting the gospel and see them as reasons to cease evangelizing. But the power for people to be made right with God comes through the message of His Son. If we will give it, we can be assured some will respond.

There is also a power for evangelism in the one living a sincere Christian life. This power, strange as it may sound, can be illustrated by a barbecue restaurant on Highway 71, just north of Caffy's hometown of Springdale, Arkansas. This restaurant's best advertising isn't the typ-ical media variety aimed at the eye or ear. Its best advertising is directed to the *nose*. The seasoned beef and pork is barbecued where its tangy smoke can waft across the four-lane highway. Every day, people driving by who aren't even thinking about being hungry become interested in the "message" of the restaurant because of its fragrant aroma.

Paul describes the power of Godliness that way in 2 Corinthians 2:14-17: "But thanks be to God, who always leads us in triumphal pro-cession in Christ and through us spreads everywhere the fragrance of the knowledge of him. For we are to God the aroma of Christ among those who are being saved and those who are perishing. To the one we are the smell of death; to the other, the fragrance of life. And who is equal to such a task? Unlike so many, we do not peddle the word of God for profit. On the contrary, in Christ we speak before God with sin-cerity, like men sent from God." The Lord empowers the life (verses 14-16) and the words (verse 17) of the faithful believer with a power of spiritual attraction. It is the power of a fragrant aroma that God uses to attract people to the message about His Son.

The most powerful ongoing Christian witness has always been the speaking of God's Word by one who is living God's Word. In the mid-1980s Caffy started a women's Bible study in our home at the encour-agement of two new believers. To the second meeting they brought Janet, a mutual friend who was very cynical about the whole thing. In a song about her spiritual pilgrimage, she later wrote, "Sex and drugs and rock-and-roll (were) my trinity." Her thinking had been further blurred by involvement in the est cult. But something began that night that for a long time only Janet knew about. Months afterward she said that from their initial meeting an aroma from Caffy's Christian living, especially in her own home, combined with the meat of God's Word in the Bible study made her want to taste more. She couldn't get enough of the aromatic message that had changed these people's lives so beautifully. Today Janet is a fresh and living "aroma of Christ among those who are being saved and those who are perishing."

Because of the nature of the Holy Spirit and the Holy Scriptures, evangelism *is* empowered.

EVANGELISM IS A DISCIPLINE

Evangelism is a natural overflow of the Christian life. We should all be able to talk about what the Lord has done for us and what He means to us. But evangelism is also a *Discipline* in that we must discipline ourselves to get into the context of evangelism, that is, we must not just wait for witnessing opportunities to happen.

Jesus said in Matthew 5:16, "Let your light shine before men, that they may see your good deeds and praise your Father in heaven." To "let" your light shine before others means more than simply "Don't do anything to keep your light from shining." Think of His exhortation as, "Let there be the light of good works shining in your life, let there be the evidence of God-honoring change radiating from you. Let it begin! Make room for it!"

Why don't we witness more actively? As mentioned earlier, some say it's primarily because many Christians aren't adequately trained to share their faith. There is some truth to this. There are worthwhile advantages to going through some guided thinking about the specifics of sharing the gospel. But as we think again about the blind man Jesus healed in John 9:25 it should become evident that we cannot attribute our failure to witness to a lack of training. Though he had been a believer in Jesus only for a few minutes and obviously had no evangelism training at all, he was willing to tell others what Jesus had done for him ("One thing I do know. I was blind but now I see!"). Moreover, any Christian who has heard biblical preaching, participated in Bible studies, and has read the Scriptures and Christian literature for any time at all should have at least enough understanding of the basic message of Christianity to share it with someone else. Surely if we have understood the gospel well enough ourselves to be converted, we should know it well enough (even if as yet we know nothing else about the faith) to tell someone else how to be converted.

We should also acknowledge the common objection of the lack of time. Between job, family, and church responsibilities, there simply isn't enough time to "go witnessing." Before we adopt this objection to evangelism, let's think of this: Do we really want to say that we are too busy to fulfill the Great Commission of Jesus Christ to make disciples of unbelievers (Matthew 28:19-20)? Do we expect that at the Judgment Jesus will excuse us from the single most important responsibility He gave to us because we say, "I didn't have time"?

Let's work from the assumption that most, even all, of the time-consuming responsibilities that we believers have are God-given ones. And, for the sake of argument, let's accept the explanation that we don't have time for one more regularly scheduled activity on our calendar. But even if God is the Author of all that, He is also the Author of the Great Commission; He still intends for each of His followers to find ways to share the gospel with unbelievers. In whatever context the Lord places us to live our lives, God calls us to find ways to fulfill the Great Commission in that context, however limiting it might be. Raising children in the "training and instruction of the Lord" (Ephesians 6:4) is one way of fulfilling the Great Commission. Supporting the work of a church and its missionaries financially is another. But what about those unbelievers outside our families? And who is there to do the evangelistic ministry of a church but people like you who comprise the membership of that church?

Isn't the main reason we don't witness because we don't *discipline* ourselves to do it? Yes, there are those wonderful, unplanned opportunities "to give the reason for the hope that you have" (1 Peter 3:15) that God brings unexpectedly. But I maintain there is a reason for most Christians to make evangelism a Spiritual Discipline.

As a pastor, I can spend twenty-four hours a day, seven days a week with Christians and never finish the work. In preparing to preach, in counseling, in committee meetings, in Bible studies, in hospital visits, and the like, I could spend all my time around professing believers only (except for large group settings or in cases where unbelievers ask to meet with me privately). And since my ministry with God's people is never done, I could "justify" as easily as anyone my lack of individual contact with nonChristians. But what is my potential for personal evangelism if I'm never with unbelievers? Zero. When am I ever going to share the gospel with a lost person except when it's part of my job? Never. That can't be right.

The Christian homemaker who is rarely with anyone except her children and her friends from church is in the same situation.

"That's not *my* problem!" laughs someone. "At work I'm surrounded all day long by the most worldly pagans you can imagine." Assuming you don't try sharing the gospel with them on company time, when will you? The point is not so much how many unbelievers you see every day, but how often you are with them in an appropriate context for sharing the gospel. Despite the important work-related conversations you may have throughout the day, how often do you have the kinds of meaningful conversations with coworkers where spiritual issues can be raised? If you never have an opportunity to talk about Christ, it doesn't matter how many nonChristians you are around, your potential for evangelism is no better than mine might be.

That's why I say evangelism is a Spiritual Discipline. Unless we discipline ourselves for evangelism, it is very easy to excuse ourselves from ever sharing the gospel with anyone.

Notice in Colossians 4:5-6 the terminology indicating that disciplined thought and planning should go into evangelism: "Be *wise* in the way you act toward outsiders; *make the most* of every opportunity. Let your conversation be always full of grace, seasoned with salt, so that you may *know* how to answer everyone" (emphasis mine). We must think about evangelism whenever we talk with outsiders—wisely making the most of every opportunity. Knowing how to respond to people as individuals implies reflection and preparation. These principles can be applied in as many specific ways as there are witnessing opportunities. But in general they support the idea that in addition to its spontaneous element, evangelism is a Spiritual Discipline.

For me that means I discipline myself to be with unbelievers. Sometimes Caffy and I schedule a meal with neighbors who don't know Christ. We make sure to take food or a housewarming gift to the new family on the street and spend time getting to know them. I try to focus on outsiders at social events in our church, even though I have more in common with the Christians there and usually receive more in conversations with them. Again, the key is not just to rub shoulders with unbelievers, but to dialogue with them in such a way that their hearts and minds might be opened to the gospel.

Disciplined evangelism might also involve having private lunches with neighbors or coworkers periodically and learning to ask good questions about the personal side of their lives. The same kinds of opportunities might arise at company-sponsored athletic or social events, or during informal times while traveling on business with fellow workers. Through conversation and good listening, you will discover their felt needs, and hopefully, explore with them their deepest need, their need for Christ.

Whether with someone you're around frequently or with someone you've met for the first time, the best way I've found to turn the conversation toward spiritual matters is to ask the person how you can pray for him or her. Although it's almost routine to the Christian, most nonChristians don't know of anyone who is praying for them. I've discovered that unbelievers are often deeply moved by this unusual expression of concern. I had a neighbor for more than seven years with whom I'd been largely unsuccessful in discussing the things of God. But the first time I told him I frequently prayed for him and wanted to know how I could pray more specifically, he began to disclose some family problems I never knew existed. I once went through my neighborhood asking for needs our church could pray for that night in a special service. At almost every home I was amazed by people's response and their unprecedented openness to talk about spiritual issues.

But the point in all these possibilities is that you will have to discipline yourself to bring them about. They won't just happen. You'll have to discipline yourself to ask your neighbors how you can pray for them or when you can share a meal with them. You'll have to discipline yourself to get with your coworkers during off-hours. Many such opportunities for evangelism will never take place if you wait for them to occur spontaneously. The world, the flesh, and the Devil will do their best to see to that. You, however, backed by the invincible power of the Holy Spirit, can make sure that these enemies of the gospel do not win.

As mentioned earlier, I don't want to leave the impression that the Discipline of evangelism requires that we all share the gospel in exactly the same ways. Throughout this chapter you may have had a picture of certain methods of evangelism that seem terrifying to you. But the preconceived style of evangelism you may fear is not necessarily the best way for you to help make disciples for Christ.

In one of his letters, the Apostle Peter divides all spiritual gifts into the two broad categories of serving gifts and speaking gifts (1 Peter 4:10-11). Some find that they evangelize more through serving, others more through speaking. Evangelistic serving might involve hosting a meal and living the gospel in front of your guests. As they see the distinctives in your home and family life, immediate or eventual opportunities to voice the gospel may arise. Perhaps you might cook a meal or grill some burgers to provide an open door for your spouse to share his or her faith. I'm told that every family averages a "crisis" once every six months. During that time of illness, job loss, financial crunch, birth, death, etc., being a Christlike servant to that family frequently demonstrates the reality of your faith in a way that piques their interest. Through serving you may have a chance to give evangelistic literature or to fulfill the Great Commission in more imaginative ways.

For the past several years, people in our church have hosted home evangelism meetings. They invite neighbors, coworkers, and friends into their home for the expressed purpose of hearing a guest talk about Jesus Christ and answering their questions about Christianity and the Bible. The hosts may not feel confident about their ability to articulate the gospel, especially to groups of people, but by serving through hospitality, they are providing an opportunity for evangelism by someone whose strength *is* a verbal presentation of the gospel. By opening their home and working with another believer, evangelism takes place that wouldn't have happened otherwise. But this kind of evangelistic serving still requires as much discipline as any other. It still requires the discipline to put the date on the calendar, to invite the people, to cook the meal, to pray for the gathering, and so on. Without such discipline, evangelistic serving never happens.

On the other hand, some are more adept at communicating the gospel directly. As I've pointed out, if you're better at speaking than serving, you may be able to work with someone who specializes in evangelistic serving in ways that will provide more witnessing opportunities than you've had before. However, just as servers may need to serve in order to open a door for speaking the gospel themselves, so those whose strength is in speaking may need to discipline themselves to serve more so they will have chances to speak. In short, speakers often need to serve so they can speak the gospel, and evangelistic servers must eventually speak it. Regardless of how shy or unskilled we may feel about evangelism, we must not convince ourselves that we cannot or will not verbally share the gospel under any circumstances.

I heard the story of a man who became a Christian during an evangelistic emphasis in a city in the Pacific Northwest. When he told his boss about it, his employer responded with, "That's great! I am a Christian and have been praying for you for years!"

But the new believer was crestfallen. "Why didn't you ever tell me?" he asked. "You were the very reason I have not been interested in the gospel all these years."

"How can that be?" the boss wondered. "I have done my very best to live the Christian life around you."

"That's the point," explained the employee. "You lived such a model life without telling me that it was Christ who made the difference, I convinced myself that if you could live such a good and happy life without Christ, then I could too."

The Bible says in 1 Corinthians 1:21 that "God was pleased through the foolishness of what was preached to save those who believe." Often it is the message of the Cross *lived and demonstrated* that God uses to open a heart to the gospel, but it is the message of the Cross *proclaimed* (by word or page) through which the power of God saves those who believe its content. No matter how well we live the gospel (and we must live it well, else we hinder its reception), sooner or later we must communicate the *content* of the gospel before a person can become a disciple of Jesus.

Before closing this section, I want to emphasize that the Discipline of evangelism also applies to the support of missions. For the same reasons we should discipline ourselves for sharing the message of Christ with those around us, we also should discipline ourselves to help those who are fulfilling the Great Commission in places far from us. Disciplining ourselves to support missions by giving, praying, informing ourselves, and being open to go if God calls (or to let our children go if God calls them) are actions Jesus would surely practice.

MORE APPLICATION

Since evangelism is expected, will you obey the Lord and witness?
There is a sense, of course, in which every Christian is always witnessing. By our words and lives, we are at every moment a testimony—good or bad—to the power of Jesus Christ. But I am speaking now of witnessing by design, not by default.

Are you willing to obey Jesus Christ and to set about witnessing *intentionally*? Intentional evangelism will necessarily be customized by your spiritual gift, talents, personality, schedule, family situation, location, etc. But having taken all that into consideration, every believer must realize that it is sinful not to seek ways to spread the message about our Lord Jesus.

Please don't get the impression that because I've written this chapter and shared some experiences that I am a super witness. I am ashamed to say there are many times when I should have spoken about Christ and did not, usually because of fear. But I believe we can find a long-term solution to our failures and frequent lack of witnessing if we will discipline ourselves for evangelism.

Since evangelism is empowered, will you believe God can use your words in the salvation of others? God blesses words, the words of the gospel. It was the *words* of the Lord Jesus, the *words* of Peter, and the *words* of Paul that God blessed in the conversion of people in New Testament times, and it's what He still blesses today. He will bless your words when they are the words of His powerful gospel.

Some fear witnessing because they don't feel confident enough in their persuasive powers or their ability to answer all imaginable objections to the gospel. But the power for evangelism is not in our ability; it is in His gospel. You may have never imagined that an unbeliever could actually be born again by hearing of Christ from your lips. But that's not humility. It's doubt, a denial of God's blessing upon His gospel just because it is spoken by you. Don't doubt the power of God to add His blessing upon your words when you speak of Christ.

Throughout his life, John Bunyan, author of *The Pilgrim's Progress*, insisted that the conversation of some poor women, talking of the things of God while sitting in a sunlit doorway, was a critical turning point in his coming to Christ. Believe that the Lord can use what *you* say as the catalyst in a conversion.

I contend that many Christians *want* to speak to others about the Lord but do not for fear that the observable, daily sin in their lives is too contradictory for them to witness. "How can I ever witness to my boss," such thinking goes, "after I angered him so much?" Or, "I'll never be able to tell my neighbor about the power of Christ now that she's seen me yell at my children."

If God does not use people like these—like *us*!—as His witnesses, there will be no human witnesses. Since there are no perfect people, there are no perfect witnesses. This does not change the fact that the more Christlike our lives, the more convincing our words about Christ. We need to do what we can to eliminate any sin that makes our words look inconsistent. But while attempting to do that we must be convinced that we cannot delay our witnessing until we reach sinless perfection. Otherwise, we would never share the gospel! Part of the beauty of our message is that God saves sinners, sinners like us. In fact, the Holy Spirit can make it possible to turn an occasion of sin into an opportunity to talk about the Savior. I've known Christians who returned to those who observed or were victims of their sin and by confessing the sin and asking forgiveness were able to give a powerful witness. That is the evidence of a changed life that gets the unbeliever's attention. That boss has a lot of people who anger him, that neighbor sees a lot of women yell at their children, but when you humble yourself and acknowledge that as wrong, that demonstrates a difference. Do you see the point? The practice of consistent Christian living does empower evangelism, but a Christian recovery from your own *un*Christian living strengthens your witness in another, very believable way. Through your failures and weaknesses Christ can be made strong.

Since evangelism is a Discipline, will you plan for it? While preaching to his London congregation in 1869 about the responsibility of evangelism, C. H. Spurgeon said,

> If I never won souls, I would sigh till I did. I would break my heart over them if I could not break their hearts. Though I can understand the possibility of an earnest sower never reaping, I cannot understand the possibility of an earnest sower being content not to reap. I cannot comprehend any one of you Christian people trying to win souls and not having results, and being satisfied without results.[3]

If you are not content with your reaping of souls for Christ's sake, will you plan for more disciplined sowing? Will you calendar a date that will be devoted to evangelism? Will you set up a lunch meeting at work or with a neighbor? How about scheduling a home evangelistic meeting? Where can you get some evangelistic literature to give away? Who can you ask to pray for? Will you commit yourself to *at least one way* of intentional evangelism in the near future?

The following is a paraphrase of 1 Corinthians 13 by Dr. Joseph Clark, quoted in *Today's Evangelism* by Ernie Reisinger.

Though I speak with the tongues of scholarship, and though I use approved methods of education, and fail to win others to Christ, or to build them up in Christian character, I am become as the moan of the wind in a Syrian desert.

And though I have the best of methods and understand all mysteries of religious psychology, and though I have all biblical knowledge, and lose not myself in the task of winning others to Christ, I become as a cloud of mist in an open sea.

And though I read all Sunday School literature, and attend Sunday School conventions, institutes, and summer school, and yet am satisfied with less than winning souls to Christ and establishing others in Christian character and service, it profiteth nothing.

The soul-winning servant, the character-building servant, suffereth long and is kind; he envieth not others who are free from the servant's task; he vaunteth not himself, is not puffed up with intellectual pride.

Such a servant doth not behave himself unseemly between Sundays, seeketh not his own comfort, is not easily provoked. Beareth all things, believeth all things, hopeth all things.

And now abideth knowledge, methods, the Message, these three: but the greatest of these is the Message.[4]

The more we are like Christ, the more we will tell of Christ and His message. But we must discipline ourselves to do this. May we discipline ourselves to live so that we can say with the Apostle Paul, "I do all this for the sake of the gospel, that I may share in its blessings" (1 Corinthians 9:23).

NOTES

1. See J. I. Packer, *Evangelism and the Sovereignty of God* (Downers Grove, IL: InterVarsity Press, 1979), pages 37-57.
2. As quoted in *Discipleship Journal*, issue 49, page 40.
3. C. H. Spurgeon, "Tearful Sowing and Joyful Reaping," in *Metropolitan Tabernacle Pulpit* (London: Passmore and Alabaster, 1869; reprint, Pasadena, TX: Pilgrim Publications, 1970), vol. 15, page 237.
4. As quoted in Ernest C. Reisinger, *Today's Evangelism: Its Message and Methods* (Phillipsburg, NJ: Craig Press, 1982), pages 142-143.

CHAPTER SEVEN

SERVING...
FOR THE PURPOSE OF GODLINESS

❖❖❖

The spiritual disciplines are not to be seen as a
pretext for separation and isolation from the world.
Rather they should be regarded as a means to
conquest over the world. Not the renunciation of the
world but service in the world—this is the purpose
of the disciplines of the spirit as seen in the Bible.

Donald G. Bloesch
The Crisis of Piety

It's been gone for more than a century. Yet, if it weren't for TV commercials, more people probably would have heard of the Pony Express than of Federal Express.

The Pony Express was a private express company that carried mail by an organized relay of horseback riders. The eastern end was St. Joseph, Missouri, and the western terminal was in Sacramento, California. The cost of sending a letter by Pony Express was $2.50 an ounce. If the weather and horses held out and the Indians held off, that letter would complete the entire two-thousand-mile journey in a speedy ten days, as did the report of Lincoln's Inaugural Address.

It may surprise you that the Pony Express was only in operation from April 3, 1860, until November 18, 1861—just seventeen months. When the telegraph line was completed between two cities, the service was no longer needed.

Being a rider for the Pony Express was a tough job. You were expected to ride seventy-five to one hundred miles a day, changing horses every fifteen to twenty-five miles. Other than the mail, the only baggage you carried contained a few provisions, including a kit of flour, cornmeal, and bacon. In case of danger, you also had a medical pack of turpentine, borax, and cream of tartar. In order to travel light and to increase speed of mobility during Indian attacks, the men always rode in shirtsleeves, even during the fierce winter weather.

How would you recruit volunteers for this hazardous job? An 1860 San Francisco newspaper printed this ad for the Pony Express: "WANTED: Young, skinny, wiry fellows not over 18. Must be expert riders willing to risk daily. Orphans preferred."

Those were the honest facts of the service required, but the Pony Express *never* had a shortage of riders.

We need to be honest with the facts about the Discipline of serving God. Like the Pony Express, serving God is not a job for the casually interested. It's costly service. He asks for your life. He asks for service to Him to become a priority, not a pastime. He doesn't want servants who will give Him the leftovers of their life's commitments. Serving God isn't a short-term responsibility either. Unlike the Pony Express, His Kingdom will never go under, no matter how technological our world gets.

The mental picture we have of the Pony Express is probably much like the one imagined by the young men of 1860 who read that newspaper ad. Scenes of excitement, camaraderie, and the thrill of adventure filled their heads as they swaggered over to the Express office to apply. Yet few of them envisioned that excitement would only occasionally punctuate the routine of the long, hard hours and loneliness of the work.

The Discipline of serving is like that. Although Christ's summons to service is the most spiritually grand and noble way to live a life, it is typically as pedestrian as washing someone's feet. Richard Foster puts it starkly: "In some ways we would prefer to hear Jesus' call to deny father and mother, houses and land for the sake of the gospel, than His word to wash feet. Radical self-denial gives the feel of adventure. If we forsake all, we even have the chance of glorious martyrdom. But in service we are banished to the mundane, the ordinary, the trivial."[1]

The ministry of serving may be as public as preaching or teaching, but more often it will be as sequestered as nursery duty. It may be as visible as singing a solo, but usually it will be as unnoticed as operating the sound equipment to amplify the solo. Serving may be as appreciated as a good testimony in a worship service, but typically it's as thankless as washing dishes after a church social. Most service, even that which seems the most glamorous, is like an iceberg. Only the eye of God ever sees the larger, hidden part of it.

Beyond the church walls, serving is baby-sitting for neighbors, taking meals to families in flux, running errands for the homebound, providing transportation for the one whose car breaks down, feeding pets and watering plants for vacationers, and—hardest of all—having a servant's heart in the home. Serving is as commonplace as the practical needs it seeks to meet.

That's why serving must become a Spiritual Discipline. The flesh connives against its hiddenness and sameness. Two of the deadliest of our sins—sloth and pride—loathe serving. They paint glazes on our eyes and put chains on our hands and feet so that we don't serve as we know we should or even as we want to. If we don't discipline ourselves to serve for the sake of Christ and His Kingdom (and for the purpose of Godliness), we'll "serve" only occasionally or when it's convenient or *self*-serving. The result will be a quantity and quality of service we'll regret when the Day of Accountability for our service comes.

In *The Spirit of the Disciplines*, Dallas Willard says rightly that not all serving will, or even should be, disciplined serving. However, those who want to train themselves for Christlike spirituality will find it one of the surest and most practical means of growth in grace.

> Not every act that *may* be done as a discipline *need* be done as a discipline. I will often be able to serve another simply as an act of love and righteousness, without regard to how it may enhance my abilities to follow Christ. There certainly is nothing wrong with that, and it may, incidentally, strengthen me spiritually as well. But I may also serve another to train myself away from arrogance, possessiveness, envy, resentment, or covetousness. In that case, my service is undertaken as a discipline for the spiritual life.[2]

But lest we begin to think that serving is merely an option, let's chisel this into the cornerstone of our Christian life:

EVERY CHRISTIAN IS EXPECTED TO SERVE

When God calls His elect to Himself, He calls no one to idleness. When we are born again and our sins forgiven, the blood of Christ cleanses our conscience, according to Hebrews 9:14, in order for us to "serve the living God!" "Serve the LORD with gladness" (Psalm 100:2, NASB) is every Christian's commission. There is no such thing as spiritual unemployment or spiritual retirement in the Kingdom of God.

Of course, motives matter in the service we are to offer to God. The Bible mentions at least six motives for serving.

Motivated by Obedience

In Deuteronomy 13:4 Moses wrote, "It is the LORD your God you must follow, and him you must revere. Keep his commands and obey him; serve him and hold fast to him." Everything in that verse relates to obedience to God. In the midst of this cluster of commands on obedience is the mandate, "serve him." We should serve the Lord because we want to obey Him.

John Newton, the slave-trader who became a pastor following his conversion to Christ and wrote such hymns as "Amazing Grace," illustrates obedient service as follows:

> If two angels were to receive at the same moment a commission from God, one to go down and rule earth's grandest empire, the other to go and sweep the streets of its meanest village, it would be a matter of entire indifference to each which service fell to his lot, the post of ruler or the post of scavenger; for the joy of the angels lies only in obedience to God's will.[3]

Can you imagine one of those angels refusing to serve? It's unthinkable. It was the unwillingness to serve God that once turned some angels into demons. Then how can any professing Christian think it is okay to sit on the spiritual sidelines and watch others do the work of the Kingdom? Any true Christian would say that he or she wants to obey God. But we disobey God when we are not serving Him. Not to serve God is sinful.

Motivated by Gratitude

The prophet Samuel exhorted the people of God to service with these words: "But be sure to fear the LORD and serve him faithfully with all your heart; consider what great things he has done for you" (1 Samuel 12:24). It is no burden to serve God when we consider what great things He has done for us.

Do you remember what it is like not to know Christ, to be without

God and without hope? Do you remember what it is like to be guilty before God and unforgiven? Do you remember what it is like to have offended God and to have His anger burning toward you? Do you remember what it is like to be only a heartbeat away from hell? Now do you remember what it is like to see Jesus Christ with the eyes of faith and to understand for the first time who He really is and what He has done by His death and resurrection? Do you remember what it was like to experience forgiveness and deliverance from judgment and hell? Do you remember what it was first like to have the assurance of Heaven and eternal life? When the fire of service to God grows cold, consider what great things the Lord has done for you.

He has never done anything greater for anyone, nor could He do anything greater for you, than bring you to Himself. Suppose He put ten million dollars into your bank account every morning for the rest of your life, but He didn't save you? Suppose He gave you the most beautiful body and face of anyone who ever lived, a body that never aged for a thousand years, but then at death He shut you out of Heaven and into hell for eternity? What has God ever given anyone that could compare with the salvation He has given to you as a believer? Do you see that there is nothing God could ever do for you or give to you greater than the gift of Himself? If we cannot be grateful servants of Him who is everything and in whom we have everything, what *will* make us grateful?

Motivated by Gladness

The inspired command of Psalm 100:2 is, "Serve the LORD with gladness" (NASB). We are not to serve God grudgingly or grimly, but gladly.

In the courts of ancient kings, servants were often executed for nothing more than looking sad in the service of the king. Nehemiah, in 2:2 of the book that bears his name, was grieving over the news he'd heard that Jerusalem was still in ruins despite the return of many Jews from the Babylonian exile. As he was serving food to King Artaxerxes one day, the king said to him, "Why does your face look so sad when you are not ill? This can be nothing but sadness of heart." Because of what that could mean for him, Nehemiah writes, "I was very much afraid." You don't mope or sulk when you serve a king. Not only does it give the appearance that you don't want to serve the king, but it is a statement of dissatisfaction with the way he's running things.

Something is wrong if you can't serve the Lord with gladness. I can understand why the person who serves God only out of obligation doesn't serve with gladness. I can understand why the person who serves God in an attempt to earn his way to Heaven doesn't serve with gladness. But the Christian who gratefully acknowledges what God has done for him for eternity should be able to serve God cheerfully and with joy.

For the believer, serving God is not a burden, it's a privilege. Suppose God let you serve in any political or business position in the world, but wouldn't let you serve in His Kingdom? Suppose He let you choose anyone in the world to serve and know intimately, but wouldn't let you serve Him? Or suppose He let you serve yourself, doing anything you wanted with your life and with no needs or worries, but you could never know God? Even the best of these things is miserable slavery in comparison with the glad privilege of serving God. That's why the psalmist could say, "Better is one day in your courts than a thousand elsewhere; I would rather be a doorkeeper in the house of my God than dwell in the tents of the wicked" (Psalm 84:10).

Do you serve on that church committee with gladness or with gloom? Do you serve your neighbors willingly or reluctantly? Do your kids get the impression from you that serving God is something you really enjoy or merely endure?

Motivated by Forgiveness, Not Guilt

In Isaiah's famous vision of God, notice his response once God had forgiven him: "Then one of the seraphs flew to me with a live coal in his hand, which he had taken with tongs from the altar. With it he touched my mouth and said, 'See, this has touched your lips; your guilt is taken away and your sin is atoned for.' Then I heard the voice of the Lord saying, 'Whom shall I send? And who will go for us?' And I said, 'Here am I. Send me!'" (Isaiah 6:6-8). Like a dog on a leash, Isaiah was straining out of his skin to serve God in some way, *any* way. Because he felt guilty? No! Because God had taken his guilt *away*!

That pulpit lion of London, C. H. Spurgeon, moved with some of Isaiah's emotion, said in a sermon on September 8, 1867,

> The heir of heaven serves his Lord simply out of gratitude; he
> has no salvation to gain, no heaven to lose; . . . now, out of love
> to the God who chose him, and who gave so great a price for

his redemption, he desires to lay out himself entirely to his Master's service. O you who are seeking salvation by the works of the law, what a miserable life yours must be! . . . you have that if you diligently persevere in obedience, you may *perhaps* obtain eternal life, though, alas! none of you dare to pretend that you have attained it. You toil and toil and toil, but you never get that which you toil after, and you never will, for, "by the works of the law there shall no flesh living be justified." . . . The child of God works not *for* life, but *from* life; he does not work *to be* saved, he works *because* he is saved.[4]

The people of God do not serve Him in order *to be* forgiven but *because we are* forgiven. When believers serve only because they feel guilty if they don't, it's as though they serve with a ball and chain dragging from their ankles. There's no love in that kind of service, only labor. There's no joy, only obligation and drudgery. But Christians aren't prisoners who should serve in God's Kingdom grudgingly because of guilt. We can serve willingly because Christ's death freed us from guilt.

Motivated by Humility
Jesus was the perfect Servant. His greatness is seen in the lowliness He was willing to experience in order to serve the most basic needs of His twelve friends.

When he had finished washing their feet, he put on his clothes and returned to his place. "Do you understand what I have done for you?" he asked them. "You call me 'Teacher' and 'Lord,' and rightly so, for that is what I am. Now that I, your Lord and Teacher, have washed your feet, you also should wash one another's feet. I have set you an example that you should do as I have done for you. I tell you the truth, no servant is greater than his master, nor is a messenger greater than the one who sent him. Now that you know these things, you will be blessed if you do them." (John 13:12-16)

With astonishing humility, Jesus, their Lord and Teacher, washed the feet of His disciples as an example of how all His followers should serve with humility.

In this life there will always be a part of us (the Bible calls it the *flesh*) that will say, "If I have to serve, I want to get something for it. If I can be rewarded, or gain a reputation for humility, or somehow turn it to my advantage, then I'll give the impression of humility and serve." But this isn't Christlike service. This is hypocrisy. Richard Foster calls it "self-righteous service":

> Self-righteous service requires external rewards. It needs to know that people see and appreciate the effort. It seeks human applause—with proper religious modesty of course. . . . Self-righteous service is highly concerned about results. It eagerly wants to see if the person served will reciprocate in kind. . . . The flesh whines against service but screams against hidden service. It strains and pulls for honor and recognition. It will devise subtle, religiously acceptable means to call attention to the service rendered.[5]

By the power of the Holy Spirit we must reject self-righteous service as a sinful motivation, and serve "in humility," considering "others better" than ourselves (Philippians 2:3).

Can you serve your boss and others at work, helping them to succeed and be happy, even when they are promoted and you are overlooked? Can you work to make others look good without envy filling your heart? Can you minister to the needs of those whom God exalts and men honor when you yourself are neglected? Can you pray for the ministry of others to prosper when it would cast yours in the shadows?

In the Discipline of service, the issue is not always how well you serve, for even the world serves well when it leads to profit. But the Christian serves with humility because it leads to Christlikeness.

Motivated by Love

At the heart of service, according to Galatians 5:13, should be love: "You, my brothers, were called to be free. But do not use your freedom to indulge the sinful nature; rather, serve one another in love."

There is no better fuel for service that burns longer and provides more energy than love. There are things I do in the service of God that I would not do for money, but I am willing to do them out of love for God and others. I read of a missionary in Africa who was asked if he really liked what he was doing. His response was shocking. "Do I like this work?" he said. "No. My wife and I do not like dirt. We have reasonably refined sensibilities. We do not like crawling into vile huts through goat refuse. . . . But is a man to do nothing for Christ he does not like? God pity him, if not. Liking or disliking has nothing to do with it. We have orders to 'Go,' and we go. Love constrains us."

When Christ's love controls or constrains people, the result is that they "no longer live for themselves but for him who died for them and was raised again" (2 Corinthians 5:14-15). They serve God and others, but it's a service motivated by love. Jesus said in Mark 12:28-31 that the greatest commandment is to love God with all you are, and the next most important one is to love your neighbor as you love yourself. In light of these words, surely the more we love God the more we will live for Him and serve Him, and the more we love others the more we will serve them.

EVERY CHRISTIAN IS GIFTED TO SERVE

Spiritual Gifts

At the moment of salvation when the Holy Spirit comes to live within you, He brings a gift with Him. We're told in 1 Corinthians 12:4,11 that there are many different varieties of gifts, and the Holy Spirit determines by His sovereign will which gift goes to which believer: "There are different kinds of gifts, but the same Spirit. . . . All these are the work of one and the same Spirit, and he gives them to each one, just as he determines." Even more specific is 1 Peter 4:10, which certifies that each Christian is specially gifted and that the purpose for that gift is service: "Each one should use whatever gift he has received to serve others, faithfully administering God's grace in its various forms."

You may already know that the subject of spiritual gifts is a matter of ongoing controversy in many parts of the Church. My particular persuasion is that every Christian has one of the seven spiritual gifts listed in Romans 12:4-8. The ministries God gives us are themselves gifts from God (1 Corinthians 12:5, Ephesians 4:7-13). And as we minister with our spiritual gift, the fruitful effects the Holy Spirit works in the lives of others are to them another kind of spiritual gift (1 Corinthians 12:6-11). Other significant passages on spiritual gifts are 1 Corinthians 12:27-31, 1 Corinthians 14, and 1 Peter 4:11. I encourage you to read them all prayerfully.

Regardless of your theology of spiritual gifts, the two most important points about them remain those given in 1 Peter 4:10, namely, (1) if you are a Christian you definitely have a spiritual gift, and (2) God's purpose in giving you that gift is for you to serve with it for His Kingdom.

If this is among the first times you have heard about spiritual gifts, then you probably have no idea what your gift is. Relax. Many Christians serve God faithfully and fruitfully for a lifetime without ascertaining their specific gift. I'm not suggesting you shouldn't try to identify your gift; I'm saying that you aren't relegated to bench-warmer status in the Kingdom of God until you can name your gift. Study the biblical material on spiritual gifts and carefully choose some of the best books from the torrent of tomes written on the subject. But by all means, don't be discouraged from serving, for you may still serve well without knowing the name of your gift. J. I. Packer reminds us, "The most significant gifts in the church's life in every era are ordinary natural abilities sanctified."[6]

Stay in balance. God has given you a spiritual gift, and it is not the same as a natural ability. That natural talent, rightly sanctified for God's use, often points toward the identity of your spiritual gift. But you should find out the special gift God has given you while you're serving as diligently as you can without that definite information. In fact, in addition to the study of Scripture, the best way to discover and confirm which spiritual gift is yours is through serving. If you have an inclination to teach, you may never know if your gift is teaching until you accept that class and try. You may discover through a ministry to hurting people that your gift is mercy. On the other hand, through involvement in a particular ministry you may confirm what your gift is *not*. Years ago I thought I had one gift until through serving it became painfully clear that I had an entirely different gift.

I encourage you to discipline yourself to serve in a regular, ongoing ministry in your local church. It doesn't necessarily have to be in a recognized or elected position. But find a way to defeat the temptation to serve only when it's convenient or exciting. That's not disciplined service. Those with a servant's heart and eyes will find themselves compelled by love to serve in ways and times beyond the bounds of their "official" ministry, but they will not neglect the ongoing ministry of the local Body of Christ.

You may feel overlooked, you may be limited by an unusual schedule, you may be physically incapacitated, but there's still a way for you to serve. People with unusual schedules or physical limitations often make powerful intercessors in a prayer ministry. Despite their limitations, those with a heart to serve always have a way to serve.

A flight attendant in our church works overseas routes. When she's on the job she's gone for several days at a time. And she's not on a regular Monday-through-Friday schedule. She had always been one who wrote letters of encouragement and gave away books as a ministry, but when she joined our fellowship she looked for a disciplined way to serve with other believers rather than just individually. But how to do this with her schedule? It soon became apparent that her spiritual gift was service, that is, meeting practical needs. She also excels at hospitality. Now she is part of a ministry team in our church that specializes in hospitality. Because it is a group ministry, she doesn't have to be there every time they serve. When she is in town, she contributes her part.

Spiritual gifts are for using in service. If God didn't intend for your gift to be used, there would no longer be any purpose for your life. Why would God allow us to live beyond any usefulness to Him? In His wisdom and providence He has gifted each believer to serve and kept each of you alive to serve.

The point of this chapter, however, is a call for *disciplined* serving, with the goal that we may be more like Jesus. Some spiritual gifts incline toward ministries that are out of the spotlight and often go unappreciated by the masses. And yet, like Jesus, no matter how much public recognition we gain in ministry, we're also called to times of service in the shadows as well. "Some have the gift of helping, and these actions come more naturally," writes Jerry White. "For most Christians, serving requires a conscious effort."[7] He might have said it this way: "serving requires discipline."

Serving Is Often Hard Work

Some teach that once you discover and employ your spiritual gift, then serving becomes nothing but effortless joy. But that's not New Testament Christianity. The Apostle Paul wrote in Ephesians 4:12 of "the equipping of the saints for the *work* of service" (NASB, emphasis mine). Sometimes serving God and others is nothing less than hard work.

In Scripture Christians are called not only the children of God, but also servants of God. Recall how Paul typically starts his letters by referring to himself as a servant of God (as in Romans 1:1). Every Christian is a servant of God, and servants *work*.

Paul describes his service to God with these words in Colossians 1:29: "To this end I labor, struggling with all his energy, which so powerfully works in me." The word *labor* means to work to the point of exhaustion, while from the Greek word translated "struggling" comes our word *agonize*. So for Paul to serve God was "to agonize to the point of exhaustion." That doesn't mean it was miserable toil; in fact, the reason Paul worked so hard was because the only thing he loved more than serving God was God Himself. God supplies us with the power to serve Him. We struggle in service "with all his energy, which so powerfully works" in us. True ministry is never forced out by the flesh. But the result of His power working mightily in us is "labor."

That means when you serve the Lord in a local church or in any type of ministry, it will often be hard. If you are like Paul, sometimes it will be agonizing and exhausting. It will take time. There will always be more entertaining things you could be doing. And if for no other reason, serving God is hard work because it means serving people.

But remember that service costing nothing accomplishes nothing. And even though serving God can be agonizing and exhausting work, it is also the most fulfilling and rewarding kind of work. In John 4:34 we read where Jesus has been talking with the woman of Samaria. He's been walking all day. He's tired, thirsty, and hungry. And it's all because He's been serving His Father. While He's resting at the well near Sychar, this Samaritan woman comes to the well. They talk and her life is changed forever. As she goes back into Sychar to tell others about Jesus, His disciples return from town, where they've been to buy food. When they offer some to Him He says, "My food . . . is to do the will of him who sent me and to finish his *work*" (emphasis mine).

The work of serving God was so satisfying and fulfilling to Jesus that He called it His food. Serving God often made Him so tired He would fall asleep during a storm in an open boat. It once meant forty days without eating. Service for Jesus meant frequent nights of sleeping outside on the ground. It meant getting up before daylight to have any time alone. But in the midst of all the weariness, hunger, thirst, pain, and inconvenience, Jesus said that the *work of serving God* was so meaningful that it was like *food*! It nourished Him, it strengthened Him, it satisfied Him, and He devoured it!

Serving God is work, but there's no work so rewarding.

Disciplined service is also the most *enduring* kind of work. Unlike some things we may do, service to God is never done in vain. The same Paul who agonized to the point of exhaustion while serving God reminds us, "Therefore, my dear brothers, stand firm. Let nothing move you. Always give yourselves fully to the work of the Lord, because you know that your labor in the Lord is not in vain" (1 Corinthians 15:58).

You don't have to serve God long to be tempted to think your work is in vain. Thoughts come that your service is a waste of time. Results are hard to find. Regardless of what you think and see, God promises that your work is never in vain. That doesn't mean you'll ever see all the fruit of your labors you'd hope for, or that you won't frequently feel nothing has come of all your efforts. But it does mean that even if you can't see the proof, your service to God is *never* in vain.

God sees and knows of your service to Him, and He will never forget it. He will reward you in Heaven for it because He is a faithful and just God. I love Hebrews 6:10: "God is not unjust; he will not forget your work and the love you have shown him as you have helped his people and continue to help them."

Disciplined service to God is work, hard and costly labor sometimes, but it will endure for all eternity.

MORE APPLICATION

Worship empowers serving; serving expresses worship. Godliness requires a disciplined balance between the two. Those who can maintain service without regular personal and corporate worship are serving in the flesh. It doesn't matter how long they've been serving that way or how well others think they serve, they are not striving according to *God's* power, as Paul did, but their own.

In worship we find fresh reasons and desire to serve. Isaiah didn't say, "Here am I. Send me!" until after his vision of God. That's the order—worship, then worship-empowered service. As A. W. Tozer put it, "Fellowship with God leads straight to obedience and good works. That is the divine order and it can never be reversed."[8] The work of service is too hard without the power we receive for it through worship.

At the same time, one measure of the authenticity of worship (again, both personal and corporate) is whether it results in a desire to serve. Isaiah is the classic example here also. Tozer again says it best: "No one can long worship God in spirit and in truth before the obligation to holy service becomes too strong to resist."[9]

Therefore, we must maintain that to be Godly, we should discipline ourselves for both worship and service. To engage in one without the other is, in reality, to experience neither.

You are expected to serve and gifted to serve, but are you willing to serve? The Israelites knew without a doubt that God *expected* them to serve Him, but Joshua once looked them in the eye and challenged them on their *willingness* to serve: "But if serving the LORD seems undesirable to you, then choose for yourselves this day whom you will serve. . . . But as for me and my household, we will serve the LORD" (Joshua 24:15).

When I think of a faithful willingness to serve, I remember a quiet little man from a church where I was a staff member. On Sundays his arrival was always unnoticed, for he would come long before anyone else. Yet he burrowed his old car into an obscure corner of the parking lot to leave the best places for others. He unlocked all the doors, got the bulletins, and then waited outside. When you walked up he'd give you a bulletin and a big smile. But he couldn't talk. He was embarrassed when newcomers asked him questions. Something had happened to his voice long ago. When I met him he was into his sixties and living alone. When he had car trouble, which was often, he never let anyone know and so would walk more than a mile to the church. Because of his vulnerability he was robbed and beaten several times, at least twice during the three years I was in that church. Some long-time church members told me they suspected he lost his voice as the result of being beaten years before. He had extensive arthritis, which stooped his shoulders and prevented him from turning his neck. It made hard work of unlocking doors and handing out bulletins. But he was always there, always smiling, even though he couldn't speak a word. Everything about his life worked to keep him unheralded and in the background, even his name—Jimmy Small. Yet despite his drawbacks, setbacks, handicaps, and a plethora of potential excuses, he willingly served God. And he served in a disciplined way, which in the sight of God, was neither small nor in vain.

The Lord Jesus was always the servant, the servant of all, the servant of servants, *the Servant.* He said, "I am among you as the one who serves" (Luke 22:27). If we are to be like Christ, we must discipline ourselves to serve as Jesus served.

WANTED: Gifted volunteers for difficult service in the local expression of the Kingdom of God. Motivation to serve should be obedience to God, gratitude, gladness, forgiveness, humility, and love. Service will rarely be glorious. Temptation to quit place of service will sometimes be strong. Volunteers must be faithful in spite of long hours, little or no visible results, and possibly no recognition except from God in eternity.

NOTES

1. Richard Foster, *Celebration of Discipline* (San Francisco, CA: Harper & Row, 1978), page 110.
2. Dallas Willard, *The Spirit of the Disciplines* (San Francisco, CA: Harper & Row, 1989), page 182.
3. E. M. Bounds, *The Essentials of Prayer* (Grand Rapids, MI: Baker Book House, 1979), page 19.
4. C. H. Spurgeon, "Serving the Lord with Gladness," in *Metropolitan Tabernacle Pulpit* (London: Passmore and Alabaster, 1868; reprint, Pasadena, TX: Pilgrim Publications, 1989), vol. 13, pages 495-496.
5. Foster, pages 112, 114.
6. John Blanchard, comp., *More Gathered Gold* (Welwyn, Hertfordshire, England: Evangelical Press, 1986), page 291.
7. Jerry White, *Choosing Plan A in a Plan B World* (Colorado Springs, CO: NavPress, 1986), page 97.
8. Harry Verploegh, comp., *Signposts: A Collection of Sayings from A. W. Tozer* (Wheaton, IL: Victor Books, 1988), page 183.
9. Verploegh, page 183.

CHAPTER EIGHT

STEWARDSHIP . . .
FOR THE PURPOSE OF GODLINESS

❖❖❖

*How often do we hear about the discipline of the Christian
life these days? How often do we talk about it? How often
is it really to be found at the heart of our evangelical
living? There was a time in the Christian church when this
was at the very centre, and it is, I profoundly believe,
because of our neglect of this discipline that the church is
in her present position. Indeed, I see no hope whatsoever of
any true revival and reawakening until we return to it.*

D. Martyn Lloyd-Jones
Faith: Tried and Triumphant

Think for a moment. What events have produced the greatest stress in
your life today? This past week? Haven't they involved some feeling
of being overloaded with responsibilities at home, work, school, church,
or all of the above? Paying bills? Running late for an appointment? Balancing your checkbook? Waiting in a traffic jam on the highway or runway? Facing unexpected car repair or medical expenses? Going with
too little rest? Running short of cash before payday?

Each of these anxiety-producers has to do with either time or
money. Think of how many day-to-day issues involve the use of one of
these two. The clock and the dollar are such substantial factors in so
many parts of life that their role must be considered in any serious discussion of Godly living.

THE DISCIPLINED USE OF TIME

Godliness is the result of a disciplined spiritual life. But at the heart of
a disciplined spiritual life is the Discipline of time.

If we are going to be like Jesus, we must see the use of our time as
a Spiritual Discipline. Having so perfectly ordered His moments and
His days, at the end of His earthly life Jesus was able to pray to the

Father, "I have brought you glory on earth by completing the work you gave me to do" (John 17:4). As with Jesus, God gives us both the gift of time and work to do during that time. The more we are like Jesus, the more we will understand why the disciplined use of the time God gives us is so important. Here are ten biblical reasons (many of which were made clear to me in the reading of Jonathan Edwards's sermon on "The Preciousness of Time and the Importance of Redeeming It").[1]

Use Time Wisely "Because the Days Are Evil"

To use time wisely "because the days are evil" is a curious phrase embedded in the inspired language of the Apostle Paul in Ephesians 5:15-16: "Therefore be careful how you walk, not as unwise men, but as wise, making the most of your time, because the days are evil" (NASB). Paul may have exhorted the Christians at Ephesus to make the most of their time because he and/or the Ephesians were experiencing persecution or opposition (such as in Acts 19:23—20:1). In any event, we need to use every moment with wisdom "because the days are evil" still.

Even without the kind of persecution or opposition known by the Christians of Paul's day, the world we live in is not conducive to using time wisely, especially for purposes of spirituality and Godliness. In fact, our days are days of *active* evil. There are great thieves of time that are the minions of the world, the flesh, and the Devil. They may range in form from high-tech, socially acceptable preoccupations to simple, idle talk or ungoverned thoughts. But the natural course of our minds, our bodies, our world, and our days leads us toward evil, not toward Christlikeness.

Thoughts must be disciplined, otherwise, like water, they tend to flow downhill or stand stagnant. That's why in Colossians 3:2 we're commanded, "Set your minds on the things above." Without this conscious, active, disciplined setting of the direction of our thoughts, they will be unproductive at best, evil at worst. Our *bodies* are inclined to ease, pleasure, gluttony, and sloth. Unless we practice self-control, our bodies will tend to serve evil more than God. We must carefully discipline ourselves in how we "walk" in this *world*, else we will conform more to its ways rather than to the ways of Christ. Finally, our *days* are days of active evil because every temptation and evil force are active in them. The use of time is important because time is the stuff of which days are made. If we do not discipline our use of time for the purpose of Godliness in these evil days, these evil days will keep us from becoming Godly.

Wise Use of Time Is the Preparation for Eternity

You must prepare for eternity in time. That statement can be taken two ways, both of which are true. It means that during time (that is, in this life) you must prepare for eternity, for there will be no second chance to prepare once you have crossed eternity's timeless threshold.

I recently had an unforgettable dream that soberly reminded me of this reality. (I place no great weight or prophetic value on the dream; I mention it only because it illustrates my point.) Along with some other Christians, I was in a place of persecution. After a trial we were escorted to a room where our persecutors were putting each believer to death by lethal injection. While waiting my turn I was overcome by the awareness that in moments I was about to enter eternity, and all my preparation for that event was now done. I dropped to my knees and began to pray my last prayers of this life, committing my spirit to the Lord Jesus Christ. At this point in the dream I snapped awake with the adrenaline rush of a man about to be executed. My first conscious thought after realizing it was but a dream was that one day it would *not* be a dream. There is a specific day on the calendar when all my preparation for eternity will be over. And since that day could be any day, I should use my time wisely, for it is all the time I have to prepare for where I will endlessly be beyond the grave.

Do you realize that whether you experience unending joy or eternal agony depends on what happens in moments of your life just like this one? What, then, is more precious than time? For as a small rudder determines the direction of a great ocean liner, so that which is done in time influences eternity.

That leads to the other meaning of preparing for eternity in time—that is, prepare for it before it is too late. The classic scriptural alert is, "Now is the time of God's favor, now is the day of salvation" (2 Corinthians 6:2). Right now is the right time to prepare for where you will spend eternity. If that is an uncertain or unsettled matter with you, now is the time to settle it. You have no guarantee of any more time to prepare for eternity, nor should you put off responding to the One who made you and who gives you this time.

Prepare for eternity by coming in faith to the Eternal Son of God, Jesus Christ. Come to Him in time, and He will bring you to Himself in eternity.

Time Is Short

The more scarce something is, the more valuable it is. Gold and diamonds would be worthless if you could pick them up like pebbles on the side of the road. Time would not be so precious if we never died. But since we are never more than a breath away from eternity, the way we use our time has eternal significance.

But even if you have decades of life remaining, the fact is, "You are a mist that appears for a little while and then vanishes" (James 4:14). Even the longest life is brief in comparison to eternity. In spite of all the time that's passed, you probably can remember happy or tragic events of your childhood or teenage years as vividly as if they happened yesterday. The reason is not simply the strength of your memory, but also because it really hasn't been that long ago. When you think of an entire decade as only 120 months, a great chunk of life suddenly seems short. Even at its longest, life is never long. So regardless how much time you have left to develop more Christlikeness, it isn't much. Use it well.

Time Is Passing

Not only is time short, but what does remain is fleeting. The rest of your life is not like a small block of ice you can take from the freezer and use when you are ready. Instead, time is very much like the sands in an hourglass—what's left is slipping by. The Apostle John put it bluntly: "The world and its desires pass away" (1 John 2:17).

We speak of saving time, buying time, making up time, and so on, but those are illusions, for time is always passing. We should use our time wisely, but even the best use of time cannot put pages back on the calendar.

As a child, time seemed to drag. Now I increasingly find myself saying what I remember my parents saying, "I can't believe another year is over! Where has the time gone?" The older I get, the more I feel as though I'm paddling on the Niagara—the closer I get to the end the faster it comes. If I don't discipline my use of time for the purpose of Godliness now, it won't be any easier later.

The Remaining Time Is Uncertain

Not only is time short and passing, but we do not even know how short it actually is or how quickly it will pass. That's why the wisdom of Proverbs 27:1 is, "Do not boast about tomorrow, for you do not know what a day may bring forth." There are thousands who entered eternity today, including thousands who were younger than you, who yesterday had no idea that today was their last day. Had they known that, their use of time would have become far more important to them.

The sudden death of a promising rookie football player with the Chicago Bears shocked the glitzy world of professional sports this week. Last month two of the junior high students in our church were jolted with the uncertainty of life's time by the death of a close friend. Neither youth nor strength, stardom nor stature obligates God to give us one more hour. Regardless of how long we want to live or expect to live, our times are in *His* hands (Psalm 31:15).

Obviously, we must make certain kinds of plans as though we were going to live for many more years. But there is a very real sense in which we must use our time for the purpose of godliness as though it were uncertain that we would live tomorrow, for that is a very certain uncertainty.

Time Lost Cannot Be Regained

There are many things you can lose but then regain. Many a man has declared bankruptcy, only to amass an even greater fortune later. Time is different. Once it is gone, it is gone forever and can never be regained. Were you to galvanize every person on earth into the purpose, the entire world's efforts, wealth, and technology could not bring back one minute.

God has offered you this time to discipline yourself for the purpose of Godliness. Jesus said in John 9:4, "As long as it is day, we must do the work of him who sent me. Night is coming, when no one can work." The time for the works of God, that is, Godly living, is now, while it is "day." For each of us "night is coming," and none of us is a Joshua who can stop the sun and lengthen his or her day (Joshua 10:12-14). If you misuse the time God offers to you, He never offers that time again.

Many reading these lines may be experiencing grief for wasted years. Despite how you may have misused your time in the past, you can improve the time that remains. The will of God for you now is found in the words of the Apostle Paul: "Forgetting what is behind and straining toward what is ahead, I press on toward the goal to win the prize for which God has called me heavenward in Christ Jesus" (Philippians 3:13-14). Through the work of Christ to repentant believers, God is willing to forgive every millisecond of misused time in the past. And it is pleasing to Him for you to discipline the balance of your time for the purpose of Godliness.

You Are Accountable to God for Your Time

There's hardly a more sobering statement in Scripture than Romans 14:12: "So then, each one of us will give an account of himself to God." The words "each one of us" apply to Christians and nonChristians alike. And though believers will be saved by grace and not by works, once in Heaven our reward there will be determined on the basis of our works. The Lord will "test the quality of each man's work," and for each it will be either that "he will receive his reward" or "he will suffer loss; he himself will be saved, but only as one escaping through the flames" (1 Corinthians 3:13-15). So not only will we be held accountable for our time, but our eternal reward will be directly related to our earthly use of time.

That God will hold us accountable at the Judgment for our use of time in disciplining ourselves for the purpose of Godliness can be illustrated from Hebrews 5:12. In this passage God chastised these Jewish Christians for failing to use their time in a way that would have led to spiritual maturity: "In fact, though by this time you ought to be teachers, you need someone to teach you the elementary truths of God's word all over again. You need milk, not solid food!" If He holds believers responsible on earth for not disciplining their time for Godliness, He will undoubtedly do it at the Judgment in Heaven.

Jesus said, "But I tell you that men will have to give account on the day of judgment for every careless word they have spoken" (Matthew 12:36). If we must give an account to God for every word spoken, surely we must give an account for every hour spent carelessly (that is, wastefully, negligently). And He said in Matthew 25:14-30 that we are accountable for all the talents we have received and how we use them for the sake of our Master. If God will hold us accountable for the talents He has given us, then certainly He will hold us accountable for the use of so precious a talent as time.

The wise response to such truth is to evaluate your use of time now and spend it in a way that you would like to hear at the Judgment. And if you cannot answer your conscience regarding how you use your time in the growth of Christlikeness now, how will you be able to answer God then? Jonathan Edwards suggested living each day as if at the end of that day you had to give an account to God of how you used your time.

Deciding to discipline yourself to use your time for the purpose of Godliness is not a matter for delay and deliberation. Each hour that passes is another you must give account for.

Time Is So Easily Lost

Except for the "fool," no other character in the book of Proverbs draws the scorn of Scripture like the slothful "sluggard." The reason? His lazy and wasteful use of time. When it comes to finding excuses for avoiding his responsibilities and failing to improve his time, the sluggard's creative brilliance is unsurpassed. "The sluggard says," according to Proverbs 26:13-14, "'There is a lion in the road, a fierce lion roaming the streets!' As a door turns on its hinges, so a sluggard turns on his bed." The modern sluggard is the person who won't go to work or church, saying, "Thousands of people are killed on the road each year; I could be killed if I drive out there!" Or he might say, "If I discipline my time for the purpose of Godliness, I might miss interesting things on TV, or become so busy I won't get enough rest!" And he rolls back over in bed.

The sluggard never seems to have time for the things that really matter, especially things that require discipline. But before he realizes it, his time and opportunities are lost. As Proverbs 24:33-34 observes, "A little sleep, a little slumber, a little folding of the hands to rest—and poverty will come on you like a bandit and scarcity like an armed man." Notice that it's just a "little" sleep, a "little" slumber, a "little" folding of the hands to rest that brought the ruin of lost time and opportunity. It's so easy to lose so much. You don't have to do anything to lose time.

Many people value time as silver was appraised in the days of Solomon. It is said of him in 1 Kings 10:27, "The king made silver as common in Jerusalem as stones." Time appears to be so plentiful that losing much of it seems inconsequential. But money is easily wasted as well. And if people threw away their money as thoughtlessly as they throw away their time, we would think them insane. Yet time is infinitely more precious than money because money can't buy time. But you can minimize the loss and waste of time by disciplining yourself for the purpose of Godliness.

We Value Time at Death

As the one who is out of money values it most when it is gone, so do we at death value time most when it is gone.

This assessment comes more tragically for some than for others, especially in the case of those who have rejected Christ. In his dying words, the famous French infidel Voltaire said to his doctor, "I will give you half of what I am worth if you will give me six-months' life." So desperate were his cries when his time was gone that the nurse who attended him said, "For all the wealth in Europe I would not see another infidel die."[2] Similarly, the last words of the English skeptic Thomas Hobbes were "If I had the whole world, I would give it to live one day."[3]

The most important thing to learn from death scenes like these, as mentioned earlier, is to come to Christ while there is still time. But for those who have given their lives to Christ, we should understand this: If additional years were given to us at death, it would profit nothing unless we made a change in how we used our time. So the time to value time is now, and not just at death. The time to pursue Godliness is now, and the way God has provided for those who stand forgiven by grace is through diligence in the Spiritual Disciplines.

The Bible warns believers who pursue a course based more on pleasure than the joy found in the way of God's Disciplines that they will have regrets when their time is gone. Imagine the heartache of dying this way: "At the end of your life you will groan, when your flesh and body are spent. You will say, 'How I hated discipline! How my heart spurned correction! I would not obey my teachers or listen to my instructors. I have come to the brink of utter ruin in the midst of the whole assembly'" (Proverbs 5:11-13). If you suddenly realized you had no more time, would you regret how you have spent your time in the past and how you spend it now? The way you have used your time *can* be a great comfort to you in your last hour. You may not be happy with some of the ways you used your time, but won't you be pleased then for all the times of Spirit-filled living, for all occasions when you have obeyed Christ? Won't you be glad then for those parts of your life that you spent in the Scriptures, prayer, worship, evangelism, serving, fasting, etc., for the purpose of becoming more like the One before whom you are about to stand in judgment (John 5:22-29)? What great wisdom there is in living as Jonathan Edwards resolved to live: "Resolved, That I will live so, as I shall wish I had done when I come to die."[4]

Why not do something about it while you still have time?

Time's Value in Eternity

If there are any regrets in Heaven, they will only be that we did not use our earthly time more for the glory of God and for growth in His grace. If this is so, this may be Heaven's only similarity with hell, which will be filled with agonizing laments over time so foolishly squandered.

In Luke 16:25, the Bible portrays this anguish over a wasted lifetime in the story of the rich man who went to Hades and of Lazarus who went to "Abraham's bosom." Jesus tells how the rich man, being in torment, lifted his eyes and saw Lazarus far away, living in joy with Abraham. The rich man asks Abraham to send Lazarus with water, "But Abraham replied, 'Son, remember that in your lifetime you received your good things, while Lazarus received bad things, but now he is comforted here and you are in agony.'"

What value would those like this man, who have lost all opportunity for eternal life, place on the time we now have? The English pastor-theologian Richard Baxter asked, "Doth it not tear their very hearts for ever, to think how madly they consumed their lives, and wasted the only time that was given them to prepare for their salvation? Do those in Hell now think them wise that are idling or playing away their time on earth?"[5] If those in the merciless side of eternity owned a thousand worlds, they would give them all (if they could) for one of our days. They have learned the value of time by experience. Let us learn it by encountering the truth, and discipline our time for the purpose of Godliness.

THE DISCIPLINED USE OF MONEY

The Bible relates not only the use of time to our spiritual condition, but also our use of money. The disciplined use of money requires that we manage it in such a way that our needs and those of our family are met. In fact, the Bible denounces any professing Christian who fails to care for the physical needs of his family because of financial irresponsibility, slothful mismanagement, or waste as a hypocrite. "If anyone does not provide for his relatives, and especially for his immediate family," 1 Timothy 5:8 says firmly, "he has denied the faith and is worse than an unbeliever." So how we use money for ourselves, for others, and especially for the sake of God's Kingdom is from first to last a spiritual issue.

Why is a biblical use of our money and resources so crucial to our growth in Godliness? For one thing it's a matter of sheer obedience. A surprisingly large amount of Scripture deals with the use of wealth and possessions. If we ignore it or take it lightly, our "Godliness" will be a sham. But as much as anything else, the reason use of money and the things it buys is one of the best indicators of spiritual maturity and Godliness is that we exchange such a great part of our lives for it. Because we invest most of our days working in exchange for money, there is a very real sense in which our money represents *us*. Therefore, how we use it expresses who we are, what our priorities are, and what's in our hearts. As we use our money and resources Christianly, we prove our growth in Christlikeness.

All that has been said about the disciplined use of time also applies to the use of money and possessions (with the exception that unlike time, these things when lost may be replaced). Reviewing each of those truths regarding time and relating them here to the general use of money would be redundant. Instead, let's consider how the Scriptures would have us discipline ourselves "for the purpose of godliness" in the specific area of giving our money for the sake of Christ and His Kingdom.

Growth in Godliness will express itself in a growing understanding of these ten New Testament principles of giving.

God Owns Everything You Own

In 1 Corinthians 10:26, the Apostle Paul quotes Psalm 24:1, which reads, "The earth is the LORD's, and everything in it." God owns everything, including everything you possess, because He created everything. "The whole earth is mine," the Lord says in Exodus 19:5. He says it again in Job 41:11: "Everything under heaven belongs to me."

That means we are managers or, to use the biblical word, *stewards* of the things God has given us. As a slave, Joseph was a steward when Potiphar placed him over his household. He owned nothing, for he was a slave. But he managed everything Potiphar owned on his behalf. The management of Potiphar's resources included the use of them to meet his own needs, but Joseph's main responsibility was to use them for Potiphar's interests. And that's what we are to do. God wants us to use and enjoy the things He has allowed us to have, but as stewards of them we're to remember that they belong to Him and they are primarily to be used for His Kingdom.

The house or apartment you live in, then, is God's house or apartment. The trees in your yard are God's trees. The grass that you mow is God's grass. The garden that you have planted is God's garden. The car you drive is God's car. The clothes you are wearing and those hanging in your closet belong to God. The food in your cabinets belongs to God. The books on your shelves are God's books. All your furniture and everything else inside your home belongs to God.

We don't own anything. God owns everything and we are His managers. For most of us, the house we now call "my house" was called "my house" by someone else a few years ago. And a few years from now, someone else will call that house "my house." Do you own any land? A few years from now, someone else will be calling it "my land." We are just temporary stewards of things that belong to God. You probably believe that in theory already, but your giving will be a reflection of how much you genuinely believe it.

God has specifically said that He owns not just the things we possess, but even the money under our name in the bank and the currency in our wallets. He said in Haggai 2:8, "'The silver is mine and the gold is mine,' declares the LORD Almighty."

So the question is not, "How much of my money should I give to God?" but rather, "How much of God's money should I keep for myself?"

When we put a check or cash in the offering plate, we should give it with the belief that *all* we have belongs to God and with the commitment that we will use *all* of it as He wants.

Giving Is an Act of Worship

In Philippians 4:18, the Apostle Paul thanks the Christians in the Grecian city of Philippi for the financial gift they gave in support of his missionary ministry. He writes, "I have received full payment and even more; I am amply supplied, now that I have received from Epaphroditus the gifts you sent. They are a fragrant offering, an acceptable sacrifice, pleasing to God." He calls the money they gave "a fragrant offering, an acceptable sacrifice, pleasing to God," comparing it to an Old Testament sacrifice people gave in worship to God. In other words, Paul says that their act of giving to the work of God was an act of worshiping God.

Have you ever thought of giving as worship? You know that singing praises to God, prayer, thanksgiving, and listening to Him speak through His Word are all worship, but do you ever think of *giving* to God as one of the biblical and tangible ways of adoring and worshiping Him?

In his book *The Gift of Giving*, Wayne Watts wrote,

> While researching the Biblical principles of giving, I considered the subject of worship. Frankly, I had never before studied worship in detail to find out God's point of view. I have come to the conclusion that giving, along with our thanksgiving and praise, is worship. In the past I made pledges to my church to be paid on a yearly basis. Once a month, I would write a check while in church and drop it in the collection plate. Sometimes I would mail a check from my office. My objective was for the church to get the total pledge before the end of the year. Though I had already experienced the joy of giving, the *act* of making my gift had little relationship to worship. While I was writing this book God convicted me to begin giving every time I went to church. The verse that spoke to me about this was Deuteronomy 16:16—"Do not appear before Me empty-handed." When I started doing this, if a check were not handy, I gave cash. At first I thought about keeping up with the money given. Then God convicted me again. He seemed to say, "You do not need to keep up with the amount of cash. Give to Me simply out of a heart of love, and see how much you enjoy the service." I made this change in giving habits, and it has greatly enhanced my joy in our worship services.[6]

It's common in my tradition for people attending the small-group Bible study before the worship service to give then rather than in the worship hour. If this has been your pattern, you might discover as I have that your giving seems more like worship when you give during the worship service instead.

Most people give as many times each month as they are paid. In other words, if they get a paycheck on the first of the month, they give once a month on the first Sunday of the month. If they are paid on the first and the fifteenth, they give twice each month. In consideration of the Lord's word not to appear before Him empty-handed, you might want to give part of your offering each week, rather than all of it only on the Sunday immediately after each paycheck. Of course, the danger with not giving all at once is spending some of the money you had intended to give the next Sunday. Some people avoid this by writing in one sitting all the giving checks they'll need for that pay period and putting them in their Bible or billfold until the Sunday they are needed. Then, every Sunday they have something tangible in their hands to give as part of their worship to the Lord.

Giving is much more than a duty or an obligation, it is an act of worshiping the Lord.

Giving Reflects Faith in God's Provision
The proportion of your income that you give back to God is one distinct indication of how much you trust Him to provide for your needs.

There's a story of giving and uncommon faith by a poor and very common lady in Mark 12:41-44.

> Jesus sat down opposite the place where the offerings were put and watched the crowd putting their money into the temple treasury. Many rich people threw in large amounts. But a poor widow came and put in two very small copper coins, worth only a fraction of a penny.
>
> Calling his disciples to him, Jesus said, "I tell you the truth, this poor widow has put more into the treasury than all the others. They all gave out of their wealth; but she, out of her poverty, put in everything—all she had to live on."

This poor widow was willing to give "everything—all she had to live on" because she believed God would provide for her.

We will give to the extent that we believe God will provide for us. The more we believe God will provide for our needs, the more we are willing to risk giving to Him. And the less we trust God, the less we will give to Him.

I have a pastor-friend who decided with his wife one month to give their entire salary to the Lord and trust Him to provide for their needs. They were almost out of food when a woman came by with several sacks of groceries. "How did you know?" they asked, since they hadn't told anyone. But she didn't know anything. She simply sensed that the Lord wanted her to take groceries to her pastor.

Your giving can be and is a tangible indication of how much faith you have that God will provide for your needs.

Giving Should Be Sacrificial and Generous

The widow that Jesus commended is one illustration that giving to God is not just for those who, as the world would put it, can "afford it." The Apostle Paul gives another such illustration in 2 Corinthians 8:1-5 when he tells of how the poor Christians in Macedonia sacrificed to give generously to him:

> Now, brothers, we want you to know about the grace that God
> has given the Macedonian churches. Out of the most severe
> trial, their overflowing joy and their extreme poverty welled up
> in rich generosity. For I testify that they gave as much as they
> were able, and even beyond their ability. Entirely on their own,
> they urgently pleaded with us for the privilege of sharing in this
> service to the saints. And they did not do as we expected, but
> they gave themselves first to the Lord and then to us in keeping
> with God's will.

These Macedonians were people Paul described as living in "extreme poverty." And yet "their extreme poverty welled up in rich generosity." They gave not only "as much as they were able," but "even beyond their ability." Like these people, our giving is to be sacrificial and generous.

But let me remind you that giving isn't sacrificial unless it's a sacrifice. Many professing Christians give only token amounts to the work of God's Kingdom. A much smaller number give well, while perhaps only a few actually give sacrificially.

A Gallup Poll from October 1988 shows that the more money Americans make, the *less* sacrificial our giving becomes. Those making less than $10,000 per year give an average of 2.8 percent of their income each year to churches, charities, and other nonprofit organizations.

Those making $10,000 to $30,000 give an average of 2.5 percent, those making $30,000 to $50,000 give 2.0 percent, and those making $50,000 to $75,000 give a total of only 1.5 percent of their income to their church and all other nonprofit groups.[7]

Wouldn't you agree that if we are making more money than ever before but giving a smaller or even the same percentage than we were giving before, then we are not giving sacrificially? We may be giving larger amounts than ever before but actually sacrificing less financially for the Kingdom of God.

I've never known anyone who gave sacrificially—whether through a one-time sacrificial gift or consistent sacrificial offerings— who regretted it. Sure, they missed having some of the things they could have had if they'd spent the money on themselves. But the joy and fulfillment they gained by giving away something they could not ultimately keep was more than worth it. These are the kinds of people who say, "I never made a sacrifice. I always got something greater in return than I gave."

Imagine a mom or dad seeing her or his child graduating from high school or college, or getting married to a Godly spouse, or watching that child do something that makes the eyes wet with tears of joy. If you say to that mom or dad, "Hey, think of all the sleepless nights you had with that child, all the dirty diapers, the tens of thousands of dollars that child cost you that you could've spent on things you wanted, all the time the child cost you when you could have been doing what you wanted," she or he would tell you, "It was worth every so-called sacrifice I made, because what I got in return is worth it all." It's the same way when you give sacrificially and generously. You'll never regret it.

Giving Reflects Spiritual Trustworthiness

This is a startling insight into the ways of God's Kingdom that Jesus reveals to us in Luke 16:10-13:

> "Whoever can be trusted with very little can also be trusted
> with much, and whoever is dishonest with very little will also
> be dishonest with much. So if you have not been trustworthy in
> handling worldly wealth, who will trust you with true riches?
> And if you have not been trustworthy with someone else's
> property, who will give you property of your own?

"No servant can serve two masters. Either he will hate the one and love the other, or he will be devoted to the one and despise the other. You cannot serve both God and Money."

Notice again verse 11, which says that your giving reflects your spiritual trustworthiness: "So if you have not been trustworthy in handling worldly wealth, who will trust you with true riches?"

If we are not faithful with the use of our money, and certainly that includes the giving of our money for Christ's Kingdom, the Bible says God will determine that we are untrustworthy to handle spiritual riches.

Here's the idea: the owner of a lumber company has an employee he wants to take over his business someday. Of course, the owner wants to find out if his employee can handle the business properly. So he gives him a part of the business to manage, the ordering and inspecting of new lumber, to see if he can make it profitable. He watches very closely how the employee runs that part of the business for several months, not really for money's sake, but in order to determine his trustworthiness and abilities. If he doesn't prove to be trustworthy with this small part of the lumber company, the owner won't entrust him with the whole thing. But if he proves to be faithful with it, the owner will entrust him with the true riches of the company, ownership.

The use of your money and how you give it is one of the best ways of evaluating your relationship with Christ and your spiritual trustworthiness. If you love Christ with all your heart, your giving will reflect that. If you love Christ and the work of His Kingdom more than anything else, your giving will show that. If you are truly submitted to the lordship of Christ, if you are willing to obey Him completely in every area of your life, your giving will reveal it. We will do many things before we will give someone else, even Christ, the rights over every dollar we have and ever will have. But if you have done that, it will be expressed in your giving.

That's why it's said that your checkbook tells more about you than almost anything else. If after your death a biographer or your children were to scan your canceled checks for insight into what kind of Christian you were, what conclusion would they come to? What would they reveal about your walk with Christ? Would those checks be tangible evidence of your spiritual trustworthiness?

Giving—Love, Not Legalism

God does not send you a bill. The church does not send you a bill. Giving to God and to the support of the work of His Kingdom isn't done in fulfillment of some "eleventh commandment." Your giving should be motivated by your love to God. How much you give of what you have should be a reflection of how much you love God.

In 2 Corinthians 8, the Apostle Paul is telling the first recipients of this letter, the people of Corinth, about how some of their fellow Greeks in Macedonia were such good and faithful givers. In verse 7 he tells the Corinthians, "But just as you excel in everything—in faith, in speech, in knowledge, in complete earnestness and in your love for us—see that you also excel in this grace of giving." In other words, "see that you excel in this grace of giving just as the Macedonians have." But notice what he says in verse 8: "I am not commanding you, but I want to test the sincerity of your love by comparing it with the earnestness of others." He did not use his authority as an apostle (special messenger) of Jesus to command that the Corinthians give. Instead of dictating a law of giving, he said that giving should be a way of proving your love for God.

He made this principle even more clear in the next chapter. Notice the absence of religious demand as a motive for giving in the first part of 2 Corinthians 9:7 when Paul said, "Each man should give what he has decided in his heart to give."

He said much the same thing to them in 1 Corinthians 16:2 when he told them that each person should give "as he may prosper" (NASB).

Paul never gave them an external, measurable standard of giving. He said that giving to God should be measured in the heart, and the standard is their love to God.

Allow me to adapt an illustration used earlier and apply it this time to our motivation in giving. Suppose I came to Caffy on Valentine's Day and pulled from behind my back a dozen of her favorite yellow roses and said, "Happy Valentine's Day!" And she says, "Oh, they're beautiful! Thank you! You shouldn't have spent so much money." I respond neutrally to her joy with, "Don't mention it. Today is Valentine's Day and as your husband it's my duty to get a gift for you." How do you think she'd feel? Probably like sticking every rose up my nose, thorns and all! Now suppose I do the same thing but say instead, "There's nothing I'd rather do with my money than use it for you because I love you so much." Same money. Same gift. But one gift is motivated by law, the other by love. And it makes all the difference in the world.

God is just like we are in that regard. He wants your giving to be an expression of your love for Him, not of legalism.

Give Willingly, Thankfully, and Cheerfully

Again the verse is 2 Corinthians 9:7, "Each man should give what he has decided in his heart to give, not reluctantly or under compulsion, for God loves a cheerful giver."

God doesn't want you to give with a grudge—that is, you give but you don't want to—resentfully, with a heart that isn't right no matter how much you give. He's not some celestial landlord tapping a greedy, outstretched palm, demanding His due. He doesn't want you to give to Him grudgingly only because you realize He owns it all anyway. He wants you to give because you *want* to.

One man said, "There are three kinds of giving: grudge giving, duty giving, and thanksgiving. Grudge giving says, 'I have to'; duty giving says, 'I ought to'; thanksgiving says, 'I want to.'"[8]

God wants you to *enjoy* giving.

Some people give to God like they give to the IRS after an audit. Others give to God like they give to the electric company. But a few people give to God like they give an engagement ring to their fiance or like they give to their ecstatic four-year-old on Christmas morning.

Some give because they say they can't keep it. Others give because they say they owe it. But there are always those who give because they say *they can't help it!*

I realize we need a reason to give thankfully and cheerfully. Otherwise this sounds like a person who comes when you're down and says, "Cheer up!" Well, when you're down you need a reason to cheer up. But you shouldn't have to think long or hard for reasons to give thankfully and cheerfully. When you think of how God has given you the greatest possible gift in His Son, Jesus Christ, when you think of the mercy and grace He has given you, when you think of how He has provided all you have, and when you think that you're giving to *God*, you should be able to give thankfully and cheerfully.

If one Sunday morning at church the pastor announced, "The head of one of the world's largest drug cartels is here today, and we are going to take up an offering for his army," you probably would not give willingly or cheerfully. But if you were told, "The Lord Jesus Christ is outside in the hallway, and everything you give today will be presented to Him and used by Him for His Kingdom," probably the only thing lighter than your heart after that would be your wallet, because you'd realize you're giving to God.

You don't give grudgingly or under compulsion when you realize you're giving to God. Instead you give willingly, thankfully, and cheerfully.

Giving—An Appropriate Response to Real Needs

There are times when it's right for genuine needs to be made known through the church, and for the members of the church to give spontaneously in response to those needs.

There are at least three instances in the book of Acts where the Christians gave through the church in response to specific needs.

The first happened in the days just after the church was born. In Acts 2:43-45 we read, "Everyone was filled with awe, and many wonders and miraculous signs were done by the apostles. And the believers were together and had everything in common. Selling their possessions and goods, they gave to anyone as he had need."

At Pentecost, when the Holy Spirit came upon believers in Christ and the Church was suddenly born, there were thousands in Jerusalem from all parts of the Roman Empire to celebrate that Jewish feast. Three thousand people, many of them visitors in town, became Christians on Pentecost Sunday. Soon thousands more were added to the Church. Many of these visitors unexpectedly stayed in Jerusalem because of their new faith in Christ. They had no home there, they had no jobs in Jerusalem, and they didn't have the means to provide their needs. So to meet that unique, immediate predicament, all who had believed pooled their resources, sold property, and provided for the needs.

The situation is similar in Acts 4:32-35.

All the believers were one in heart and mind. No one claimed that any of his possessions were his own, but they shared everything they had. With great power the apostles continued to testify to the resurrection of the Lord Jesus, and much grace was upon them all. There were no needy persons among them. For from time to time those who owned lands or houses sold them, brought the money from the sales and put it at the apostles' feet, and it was distributed to anyone as he had need.

It was an appropriate response for the people of the Church to give to meet these real needs.

There's another example in Acts, but this time the need is not a local need. This time those who gave could not actually see the people in need. Read Acts 11:27-30: "During this time some prophets came down from Jerusalem to Antioch. One of them, named Agabus, stood up and through the Spirit predicted that a severe famine would spread over the entire Roman world. (This happened during the reign of Claudius.) The disciples, each according to his ability, decided to provide help for the brothers living in Judea. This they did, sending their gift to the elders by Barnabas and Saul." The Christians in Antioch, three hundred miles to the north of Jerusalem, gave to help feed and meet other needs of their unknown, fellow Christians in Jerusalem.

Here is a biblical basis for our taking special offerings in church, such as offerings for foreign and home missions, world hunger, and so on—for taking a spontaneous offering for any appropriate need. Notice that in none of these cases was anyone compelled to give or told a percentage or amount to give.

There are other guidelines for giving in response to special needs that we don't have time to discuss here, such as making sure you have the facts, knowing how responsibly the money will be used, and so on. As legitimate as such spontaneous giving is, most of our giving should probably not be of this type.

Giving Should Be Planned and Systematic

Notice how the Apostle Paul directs the Christians to give in 1 Corinthians 16:1-2: "Now about the collection for God's people: Do what I told the Galatian churches to do. On the first day of every week, each one of you should set aside a sum of money in keeping with his income, saving it up, so that when I come no collections will have to be made."

This "collection for God's people" was a special offering for the poor Christians suffering in Jerusalem because of the famine. But even though the offering was for a specific need, Paul told them to give toward that need on a weekly basis for quite some time in advance of his coming. He knew that it is better to give in a planned and systematic way than haphazardly whenever a need arises. Since many needs are ongoing—like missions and feeding the hungry and maintaining the ministry of a local church—it is better to give systematically and have occasional special offerings than always to have special offerings.

Quickly notice three things about this planned, systematic giving. He told them to give "on the first day of every week." These people probably were paid every day, if not every week. Most of us are paid every week, every two weeks, or once a month. But is it not possible that there is biblical justification here for all of us to give "on the first day of every week" so that we do not appear empty-handed before the Lord when we come to worship Him? That could mean either systematically dividing your giving by the number of Sundays per pay period and giving equal amounts each Sunday, or giving a small amount of pocket cash on the Sundays when you aren't giving your main gift.

Second, note that he says "each one of you should" do this. All who claim to be believers are to express their stewardship of God's money this way. This means we can't excuse ourselves because we give our time or our talents. To do that is good and right stewardship of those things, but that doesn't teach the stewardship of money. This means we can't excuse ourselves if we are having a difficult time financially, or because we are retired, or because we are teenagers, or because we only work part-time. Remember: God owns all we have, even if He hasn't given us much to manage, and He is the one who tells us how to use it. And also remember: We'll be happiest when we use it God's way. God's way is for us to give in a planned, systematic way.

Third, he says that each is to give "in keeping with his income," or "as he may prosper" (NASB). The more you prosper, the higher should be the proportion of your giving. There is no percentage goal in giving. Giving 10 percent of your gross income does not necessarily mean you have fulfilled the will of God. That's not a ceiling of giving to stop at, but a floor to move from.

I never see what anyone gives, but from personal conversations with them I know one family in our church gives almost 20 percent of its gross income to the Lord, and another regularly gives between 20 and 25 percent. Neither of these families would be considered wealthy by their neighbors or others in the church. I would guess that there are a few more members who give like that. They have children, house payments, and all the bills common to most of us. They haven't always given like this, however. But over the years they have determined to increase systematically the percentage of their giving as they prospered.

Caffy had an aunt who didn't have much, but didn't have many bills either, so she eventually lived on 10 percent of her income and gave 90 percent. R. G. LeTourneau of Peoria, Illinois, did have much as a prosperous Christian businessman and manufacturer of earth-moving equipment. But as the Lord continued to prosper him, he gave until he was giving 90 percent of his income to the work of God's Kingdom. Do you think either of them in Heaven regret doing that?

George Muller asked,

> Are you giving *systematically* to the Lord's work, or are you leaving it to feeling; to impression made upon you through particular circumstances, or to striking appeals? If we do not give from principle *systematically*, we shall find that our one brief life is gone before we are aware of it, and that, in return, we have done little for that adorable One who bought us with His precious blood, and to whom belongs all we have and are.[9]

Whenever you get a raise, unless there are unusual circumstances, plan to give a greater percentage than you're now giving. The percentage increase may be a little or it may be a lot, but you should have as a goal to give systematically more to God every time your income rises.

My parents taught me percentage giving as a little boy when they first started giving me a weekly allowance of fifteen cents. They gave me three boxes—on one was marked "giving," on the second was marked "savings," and on the third was written "spending." Each week a nickel went into the "savings" box, a nickel went into the "giving" box—where it lay until I took it to church on Sunday—and the other nickel never went into the spending box. I immediately rode my bike the mile to the Sterling store downtown and bought a package of baseball cards! But I learned systematic giving.

Hear Muller again:

> Therefore I may affectionately beseech and entreat my beloved Christian friends to take this to heart, and consider that hitherto they have been depriving themselves of vast spiritual blessings,

because they have not followed the principle of giving systematically, and giving as God prospers them, and according to a plan; not merely just according to impulse, not as they are moved by a missionary or charity sermon, but systematically and habitually giving on principle, just as God enables them. If he entrusts to them one pound, to give accordingly a proportion; if they are left a legacy of a thousand pounds, to give accordingly; if he entrusts them with ten thousand pounds, or whatever it may be, to give accordingly. Oh, my brethren, I believe if we realized the blessing, we would give thus on principle; and, if so, we should give a hundred times more than we do now.[10]

Generous Giving Results in Bountiful Blessing

Our Lord Jesus said in Luke 6:38, "Give, and it will be given to you. A good measure, pressed down, shaken together and running over, will be poured into your lap. For with the measure you use, it will be measured to you."

That's not an isolated idea in the New Testament. Go back to 2 Corinthians 9:6-8. The promise of God there is, "Remember this: Whoever sows sparingly will also reap sparingly, and whoever sows generously will also reap generously. Each man should give what he has decided in his heart to give, not reluctantly or under compulsion, for God loves a cheerful giver. And God is able to make all grace abound to you, so that in all things at all times, having all that you need, you will abound in every good work."

If you give to God, God will give to you. If you give bountifully to Him, He will give bountifully to you.

I think the "prosperity theology" popular today is heresy. I don't believe that if you give a lot to God He will make you financially rich here on earth. But I do believe these passages and others indicate that earthly blessings of an unspecified nature will be given to those who are faithful stewards of God's money. The end of verse 8 talks about "having all that you need, you will abound in every good work." That's clearly speaking of earthly blessing. God never says that if you give faithfully He will give you a lot of money, or some other specific earthly blessing. But He does say He will bless you in this life if you love Him enough and trust Him enough to be generous in your giving to Him.

If God really loves us as He says He does (and He demonstrated the depth of His love at the Cross), then we must believe that He will tell us how to use our money in ways that ultimately benefit us the most and will bring us greater joy than we would receive using our money our way. But the world wants God's money. Advertising tells us that. We also have the same desire everyone else does—the Bible calls this desire the flesh—to spend money selfishly. And the Devil would have us waste money because he is our Enemy and the Enemy of God's Kingdom, and he wants to ruin our life and the work of God. But God tells us how to manage His money in ways that will ultimately benefit us most and bring us greater joy than using our money our way.

Most of God's blessing for our giving, however, will not come in this life. And it takes faith to believe that giving money here on earth lays up treasure in Heaven. It takes faith to believe Jesus rightly said, "It is more blessed to give than to receive" (Acts 20:35). But if these passages are true (and they are!), we can believe that there will come a definite time in a real place when God is actually going to reward us bountifully for what we have given generously and cheerfully.

Regardless of your interpretation of these passages, regardless of how much God rewards you here and in Heaven for your giving, the bottom line is clear: God will bless you bountifully if you give generously.

MORE APPLICATION

Are you prepared for the end of time? A popular musician-songwriter of the early seventies was Jim Croce. One of his most famous recordings was "Time in a Bottle," a love song about his desire to save time in a bottle in order to spend it later with someone he loved. The eerie thing about that piece was that by the time it hit the airwaves, Jim Croce was dead. Had he been able to save time in a bottle, I'm sure he would have used it to prolong his life. But of course he wasn't able to do that. And even if he had, it would have been used up long ago anyway.

There are only so many sands in everyone's hourglass, and they all run out sooner or later. Even while writing this chapter I was called to the home of someone whose father had just died. If Christ does not come back first, someday your time will come and go too, and you will go with it.

Are you prepared for that? You may have written your will, planned and paid for your funeral, and have plenty of insurance, but you are not prepared unless the account of your sins before God has been settled. You are not prepared, in fact you *cannot* be prepared, to give an account of the time you have wasted in living for yourself instead of God, the time you spent in disobedience to God, the time you squandered on worldly pursuits that were destined to perish with the world itself, time that you could have spent investing in the work of the Kingdom of God.

You are not prepared to stand before God unless you have taken the time to come to Christ and confessed the misuse of your entire life. You are not prepared for death until you have asked for God to forgive you based on the death of Christ. You are not prepared for time to stop unless you have given the control of the rest of your time to the risen Christ.

"Today if you hear his voice," says Hebrews 4:7, "do not harden your hearts." Hell is full of people who hardened their hearts while they still had time to repent and believe in Christ. Hell is full of people who hardened their hearts because they thought they had plenty of time or thought they would come to Christ at another time. Hell is full of people who would not harden their hearts if they only had the opportunity you have right now. Hell is full of people who would give the world if they could to have one more opportunity as you do to respond to the gospel. Hell is full of people who cry out in agreement with Hebrews 4:7 to those who are outside of Christ, "Today if you hear his voice, do not harden your hearts."

Are you using your time as God would have you use it? Evaluate your use of time in each of these areas and ask yourself if you are spending your time in them as God would have it (remembering that there are extremes on both sides of these): work, work in and around your home, hobbies, TV, sports, the Lord's Day, family, exercise, recreation, sleep, Bible intake, prayer, and showering and dressing for the day.

Maybe your use of time requires some fine tuning. Maybe God is calling for a major adjustment. But remember that a disciplined life is impossible without the Discipline of time. Don't miss the positive implications of those questions. A disciplined life *is* possible through the Discipline of time.

Let me insert a word here to correct some possible misunderstandings. The disciplined use of time described in these pages should not be understood as promoting a relentless, unresting, burnout-prone lifestyle. After reading the biography of Jonathan Edwards, I'm convinced he consistently lived in accordance with the biblical principles regarding the use of time described in this chapter. And yet his biographer never portrays him as a distracted and breathless man, hurtling through his day, always behind schedule. Neither was he icy and calculating, less concerned about people than "producing." It was his custom most days to take long rides with Sarah, and to ride alone each evening to the woods and pray. He spent time with his many children and knew how to laugh with them. He did all those things because they were right and it pleased God for him to do them.

At the heart of the biblical Discipline of time is doing the will of God when it ought to be done. "There is a time for everything," says Ecclesiastes 3:1, "and a season for every activity under heaven." There is a time for the specific kinds of Disciplines mentioned in this book, but there is also a time to discipline ourselves to rest, to replenish our physical and emotional resources through the right kinds of recreation, and to cultivate relationships. Though Jesus often ministered long hours and frequently under conditions that produced great demands on Him, nevertheless He was a Man who rested, recreated (perhaps while He walked everywhere He went), and cultivated relationships. He never used an hour uselessly, yet we never read of Him acting rushed. And He is our Model in the disciplined use of time.

A more Christlike life really *is* possible for you through a Spirit-filled Discipline of time. God doesn't dangle growth in grace before you like a spiritual lure that's always enticing but never enjoyed. He has said that actual progress in Godliness is possible and the Spiritual Disciplines are the means. And the practical step behind each of the Spiritual Disciplines is the Discipline of time.

Are you willing to accept God's principles for giving? You've read them and thought about them, but do you believe them and accept them as God's will for you?

Are you giving like you mean it? Does your use of money—that which you exchange so much of your life for—make clear that you are following Christ and pursuing Godliness? Will you resolve that from this day forward your giving will show that Jesus Christ is at the center of your life?

In the Centennial Edition of *The Wall Street Journal* (June 23, 1989) was the article "A Gallery of the Greatest." It was about several men the *Journal* considered business and financial successes, men like Andrew Carnegie, Henry Ford, J. P. Morgan, and others. In spite of their multiple millions, in spite of all the benevolent and philanthropic uses they made of their money, most of the men in this article did not use their money as God wanted. But you can. It's too late for them, but not for you. No matter how much or little you have, as a believer you can discipline yourself to use your money for the greatest purposes on earth: for the glory of God and "for the purpose of godliness."

NOTES

1. Jonathan Edwards, *The Works of Jonathan Edwards*, rev. Edward Hickman (1834; reprint, Edinburgh, Scotland: The Banner of Truth Trust, 1974), vol. 2, pages 233-236.
2. Herbert Lockyer, *Last Words of Saints and Sinners* (Grand Rapids, MI: Kregel, 1969), page 133.
3. Lockyer, page 132.
4. Edwards, vol. 1, page xxi.
5. Richard Baxter, *The Practical Works of Richard Baxter in Four Volumes, A Christian Directory* (1673; reprint, Ligonier, PA: Soli Deo Gloria Publications, 1990), vol. 1, page 237.
6. Wayne Watts, *The Gift of Giving* (Colorado Springs, CO: NavPress, 1982), pages 35-36.
7. "Plain Talk," *USA Today*, December 23, 1988.
8. Robert Rodenmeyer, as quoted in John Blanchard, comp., *Gathered Gold* (Welwyn, Hertfordshire, England: Evangelical Press, 1984) page 113.
9. Roger Steer, ed., *The George Muller Treasury* (Westchester, IL: Crossway Books, 1987), page 183.
10. Roger Steer, ed., *Spiritual Secrets of George Muller* (Wheaton, IL: Harold Shaw; and Robesonia, PA: OMF Books, 1985) page 103.

CHAPTER NINE

FASTING...
FOR THE PURPOSE OF GODLINESS

❖❖❖

Self-indulgence is the enemy of gratitude,
and self-discipline usually its friend and generator.
That is why gluttony is a deadly sin. The early desert
fathers believed that a person's appetites are linked:
full stomachs and jaded palates take the edge
from our hunger and thirst for righteousness.
They spoil the appetite for God.

Cornelius Plantinga, Jr.
quoted in *The Reformed Journal (November 1988)*

Quick. What do people who fast look like? What kinds of people come to your mind? Do they appear a bit strange? Are they John the Baptist types? Legalists? Health nuts?

Does Jesus come to your mind when you think of fasting and "fasters"? Jesus both practiced and taught fasting, you know. And yet, fasting is the most feared and misunderstood of all the Spiritual Disciplines.

One reason fasting is feared is that many believe it turns us into something we don't want to become and causes things to happen that we don't want to happen. We fear that fasting will make us hollow-eyed fanatics or odd for God. We're afraid that it will make us suffer dreadfully and give us a generally negative experience. For some Christians, fasting for spiritual purposes is as unthinkable as shaving their head or walking barefoot across a fire pit.

The reason fasting is so misunderstood is due to the famine of contemporary awareness of it. Even though there's more interest in fasting today than during the last half of the nineteenth and first half of the twentieth centuries, how many people do you know who regularly practice fasting? How many sermons have you heard on the subject? In most Christian circles you will rarely hear fasting mentioned, and few will have read anything about it. And yet it's mentioned in Scripture more times than even something as important as baptism (about seventy-seven times for fasting to seventy-five for baptism).

Christians in a gluttonous, denial-less, self-indulgent society may struggle to accept and to begin the practice of fasting. Few Disciplines go so radically against the flesh and the mainstream of culture as this one. But we cannot overlook its biblical significance. Of course, some people, for medical reasons, cannot fast. But most of us dare not overlook fasting's benefits in the disciplined pursuit of a Christlike life.

FASTING EXPLAINED

A biblical definition of fasting is a Christian's voluntary abstinence from food for spiritual purposes. It is *Christian*, for fasting by a nonChristian obtains no eternal value because the Discipline's motives and purposes are to be God-centered. It is *voluntary* in that fasting is not to be coerced. Fasting is more than just the ultimate crash diet for the body; it is abstinence from food for *spiritual* purposes.

There is a broader view of fasting that is often overlooked. This is the approach Richard Foster takes when he defines fasting as "the voluntary denial of a normal function for the sake of intense spiritual activity."[1] So then, fasting does not always deal with abstinence from food. Sometimes we may need to fast from involvement with other people, or from the media, from the telephone, from talking, from sleep, etc., in order to become more absorbed in a time of spiritual activity.

Martyn Lloyd-Jones concurs with this wider definition of fasting.

To make the matter complete, we would add that fasting, if we conceive of it truly, must not only be confined to the question of food and drink; fasting should really be made to include abstinence from anything which is legitimate in and of itself for the sake of some special spiritual purpose. There are many bodily functions which are right and normal and perfectly legitimate, but which for special peculiar reasons in certain circumstances should be controlled. That is fasting. There, I suggest, is a kind of general definition of what is meant by fasting.[2]

Strictly speaking, however, the Bible only refers to fasting in terms of its primary sense, that is, abstinence from food. In this chapter I will limit my remarks to that kind of fasting.

The Bible distinguishes between several kinds of fasts. Although it doesn't use the labels we frequently employ today to describe these fasts, each of the following may be found:

A *normal fast* involves abstaining from all food, but not from water. We're told in Matthew 4:2, "After fasting forty days and forty nights, he [Jesus] was hungry." It says nothing about Him becoming thirsty. Furthermore, Luke 4:2 says that He "ate nothing during those days," but it does not say He drank nothing. Since the body can normally function no longer than three days without water, we assume that He drank water during this time. To abstain from food but to drink water or perhaps fruit juices is the most common kind of Christian fast.

A *partial fast* is a limitation of the diet but not abstention from all food. For ten days Daniel and three other Jewish young men only had "vegetables to eat and water to drink" (Daniel 1:12). It is said of the rugged prophet John the Baptist that "his food was locusts and wild honey" (Matthew 3:4). Historically, Christians have observed partial fasts by eating much smaller portions of food than usual for a certain time and/or eating only a few simple foods.

An *absolute fast* is the avoidance of all food and liquid, even water. We're told that Ezra "ate no food and drank no water, because he continued to mourn over the unfaithfulness of the exiles" (Ezra 10:6). When Esther requested that the Jews fast and pray on her behalf, she said, "Go, gather together all the Jews who are in Susa, and fast for me. Do not eat or drink for three days, night or day" (Esther 4:16). After the Apostle Paul was converted on the road to Damascus, Acts 9:9 tells us, "For three days he was blind, and did not eat or drink anything."

The Bible also describes a *supernatural fast*. There are two instances of these. When Moses wrote of his meeting with God on Mount Sinai, he said, " I stayed on the mountain forty days and forty nights; I ate no bread and drank no water" (Deuteronomy 9:9). First Kings 19:8 may be saying that Elijah did the same thing when he went to the site of Moses' miraculous fast: "So he got up and ate and drank. Strengthened by that food, he traveled forty days and forty nights until he reached Horeb, the mountain of God." These required God's supernatural intervention into the bodily processes and are not repeatable apart from the Lord's specific calling and miraculous provision.

A *private fast* is the one referred to most often in this chapter and what Jesus was speaking of in Matthew 6:16-18 when He says we should fast in a way not to be noticed by others.

Congregational fasts are the type found in Joel 2:15-16: "Blow a trumpet in Zion, declare a holy fast, call a sacred assembly. Gather the people, consecrate the assembly." At least a part of the congregation of the church at Antioch was fasting together in Acts 13:2, as evidenced by Luke's words "While they were worshiping the Lord and fasting."

The Bible also speaks of *national fasts*. The response of King Jehoshaphat to an invasion in 2 Chronicles 20:3 is to call a national fast: "Alarmed, Jehoshaphat resolved to inquire of the LORD, and he proclaimed a fast for all Judah." The Jews were called to a national fast in Nehemiah 9:1 and Esther 4:16, and the king of Nineveh proclaimed a fast in response to the preaching of Jonah (3:5-8). Incidentally, during the early days of our nation, Congress proclaimed three national fasts. Presidents John Adams and James Madison each called all Americans to fast, and Abraham Lincoln did so on three separate occasions during the War Between the States.[3]

There was one *regular fast* that God commanded under the Old Covenant. Every Jew was to fast on the Day of Atonement (Leviticus 16:29-31). While they were in Babylon, the leaders of the Jews instituted four other annual fasts (Zechariah 8:19). The Pharisee in Luke 18:12 congratulates himself in prayer for keeping the tradition of the Pharisees by saying, "I fast twice a week." Although without biblical warrant, it is well known that John Wesley would not ordain a man to the Methodist ministry who did not regularly fast every Wednesday and Friday.

Finally, the Bible mentions *occasional fasts*. These occur on special occasions as the need arises. This was the kind of fast Jehoshaphat, as well as Esther, called for. This is the kind of fast implied by Jesus in Matthew 9:15: "How can the guests of the bridegroom mourn while he is with them? The time will come when the bridegroom will be taken from them; then they will fast."

The most common fast among Christians today would fall under the categories of normal (abstaining from food but drinking water), private, and occasional fasts.

FASTING IS EXPECTED

To those unfamiliar with fasting, the most surprising part of this chapter may be the discovery that Jesus expected that His followers would fast.

Notice Jesus' words at the beginning of Matthew 6:16-17: "And *when* you *fast*. . . . But *when* you *fast*. . . ." By giving us instructions on what to do and what not to do when we fast, Jesus assumes that we will fast.

This expectation is even more obvious when we compare these words with His statements about giving in that same passage, Matthew 6:2-3: "So *when* you *give*. . . . But *when* you *give*. . . ." Compare also His words about praying in the same section, Matthew 6:5-7: "But *when* you *pray*. . . . *When* you *pray*. . . . And *when* you *pray*. . . ." No one doubts that we are to give and to pray. In fact, it is quite common to use this passage to teach Jesus' principles on giving and praying. And since there is nothing here or elsewhere in Scripture indicating that we no longer need to fast, and since we know that Christians in the book of Acts fasted (9:9, 13:2, 14:23), we may conclude that Jesus still expects His followers to fast today.

Plainer still are the words of Jesus in Matthew 9:14-15. Immediately after calling Matthew the tax collector to follow Him, Jesus was the guest at Matthew's house for a meal. The Pharisees came and asked how Jesus could eat with such a sinner. The disciples of John the Baptist had a problem with this too. Like John, they were single-minded men with coarse and simple diets. They shared in a ministry that called people to repentance, and fasting was a part of that. If they were to point people to Jesus as John did, it confused them how He could feast when they were supposed to fast. So they came to Him and asked, "'How is it that we and the Pharisees fast, but Your disciples do not fast?' Jesus answered, 'How can the guests of the bridegroom mourn while he is with them? The time will come when the bridegroom will be taken from them; *then they will fast*" (emphasis mine).

Jesus said that the time would come when His disciples "will fast." That time is now. Until Jesus, the Bridegroom of the Church returns, He expects us to fast.

The only instructions He left in addition to those already mentioned are in Matthew 6:16-18. There Jesus gives us a negative command, a positive command, and a promise. The negative command is first:

"When you fast, do not look somber as the hypocrites do, for they disfigure their faces to show men they are fasting. I tell you the truth, they have received their reward in full." When you fast, you aren't to look like you're fasting. Don't look miserable. Don't look like you're suffering. And don't neglect your appearance.

The positive command is next: "But when you fast, put oil on your head and wash your face, so that it will not be obvious to men that you are fasting, but only to your Father, who is unseen." Instead of looking like a hungry scavenger, present yourself so well that no one can tell by your appearance that you are fasting. The only Observer of your fast should be the Secret One. No one else should know that you are fasting unless it is absolutely unavoidable or necessary.

Then Jesus gives us a promise about fasting: "And your Father, who sees what is done in secret, will reward you." As sure and as certain as any promise in Scripture is the promise that God will bless you and reward your fast when it's done according to His Word.

It's interesting that Jesus gives us no command regarding how often or how long we should fast. Just like all the other Spiritual Disciplines, fasting is not to be a legalistic routine. It is a privilege and an opportunity to seek God's grace that is open to us as often as we desire.

How long should we fast? It's up to you and the leadership of the Holy Spirit. In the Bible are examples of fasts that lasted one day or part of a day (Judges 20:26; 1 Samuel 7:6; 2 Samuel 1:12, 3:35; Nehemiah 9:1; Jeremiah 36:6), a one-night fast (Daniel 6:18-24), three-day fasts (Esther 4:16, Acts 9:9), seven-day fasts (1 Samuel 31:13, 2 Samuel 12:16-23), a fourteen-day fast (Acts 27:33-34), a twenty-one day fast (Daniel 10:3-13), forty-day fasts (Deuteronomy 9:9, 1 Kings 19:8, Matthew 4:2), and fasts of unspecified lengths (Matthew 9:14; Luke 2:37; Acts 13:2, 14:2-3).

FASTING IS TO BE DONE FOR A PURPOSE

There's more to a biblical fast than abstaining from food. Without a spiritual purpose for your fast it's just a weight-loss fast. You'll be just like the man who told one writer on fasting,

> I've fasted on several occasions; and nothing happened. I just got hungry. . . . Several years ago I heard a couple of pastors

discussing fasting. On their recommendation I tried my first fast. They said it was commanded in the Bible and should be practiced by every Christian. Being a Christian, I decided to try it. After putting it off for several days, I mustered up enough courage to start. I couldn't go to the breakfast table with my family because I didn't think I would have enough willpower to abstain from eating, so I went on to work. The coffee break was almost unbearable, and I told a little white lie about why I didn't go with the group. All I could think about was how hungry I was. I said to myself, "If I ever get through this day, I'll never try this again." The afternoon was even worse. I tried to concentrate on my work, but all I could hear was the growling of my stomach. My wife prepared a meal for herself and our child, and the aroma of the food was all I could bear. I figured that if I could make it till midnight, I would have fasted all day. I did—but immediately after the striking of the hour of twelve, I dug into food. I don't think that day of fasting helped me one bit.[4]

Of course, he was probably right. This man had no purpose for his fast. And without a purpose, fasting can be a miserable, self-centered experience.

There are many purposes for fasting given in Scripture. I've condensed them into ten major categories. Whenever you fast, you should do so for at least one of these purposes. (Notice that *none* of the purposes is to earn God's favor. We cannot use fasting as a way to impress God and earn His acceptance. We are made acceptable to God through the work of Christ Jesus, not our work. Fasting has no eternal benefit for us until we have come to God through repentance and faith. See Ephesians 2:1-10 and Titus 3:5-7.)

To Strengthen Prayer
"Whenever men are to pray to God concerning any great matter," wrote John Calvin, "it would be expedient to appoint fasting along with prayer."[5]

There's something about fasting that sharpens the edge of our intercessions and gives passion to our supplications. So it has frequently been used by the people of God when there is a special urgency about the concerns they lift before the Father.

When Ezra was about to lead a group of exiles back to Jerusalem, he proclaimed a fast in order for the people to seek the Lord earnestly for safe passage. They were to face many dangers without military protection during their nine-hundred-mile journey. This was no ordinary matter to be brought to God in prayer. "So we fasted and petitioned our God about this," says Ezra 8:23, "and he answered our prayer."

The Bible does not teach that fasting is a kind of spiritual hunger strike that compels God to do our bidding. If we ask for something outside of God's will, fasting does not cause Him to reconsider. Fasting does not change God's hearing so much as it changes our praying. In his book *God's Chosen Fast*, Arthur Wallis remarked,

> Fasting is calculated to bring a note of urgency and importunity into our praying, and to give force to our pleading in the court of heaven. The man who prays with fasting is giving heaven notice that he is truly in earnest. . . . Not only so, but he is expressing his earnestness in a divinely-appointed way. He is using a means that God has chosen to make his voice to be heard on high.[6]

God is always pleased to hear the prayers of His people. But He is also pleased when we choose to strengthen our prayers in a way He has ordained.

Nehemiah (in 1:4) "fasted and prayed before the God of heaven." Daniel (in 9:3) devoted himself to plead with God "in prayer and petition, in fasting." In a direct command through the prophet Joel, Israel was told, "'Even now,' declares the LORD, 'return to me with all your heart, with fasting and weeping and mourning'" (Joel 2:12). It wasn't until after "they had fasted and prayed" that the church in Antioch "placed their hands" on Barnabas and Saul of Tarsus and "sent them off" on the first missionary journey (Acts 13:3).

The most important aspect of this Discipline is its influence on prayer. You'll notice that in one way or another, all the other biblical purposes of fasting relate to prayer. Fasting is one of the best friends we can introduce to our prayer life. Despite this potential power, however, it seems that very few are willing to enjoy its benefits. To quote Wallis again,

In giving us the privilege of fasting as well as praying, God has added a powerful weapon to our spiritual armory. In her folly and ignorance the Church has largely looked upon it as obsolete. She has thrown it down in some dark corner to rust, and there it has lain forgotten for centuries. An hour of impending crisis for the Church and the world demands its recovery.[7]

To Seek God's Guidance

There is biblical precedent for fasting for the purpose of more clearly discerning the will of God.

In Judges 20 the other eleven tribes of Israel prepared for war against the tribe of Benjamin. The soldiers gathered at Gibeah because of a shocking sin committed by the men of that Benjamite city. They sought the Lord before going into battle, and even though they outnumbered the Benjamites by fifteen to one, they lost the battle and twenty-two thousand men. The next day they sought the Lord with prayer and tears, but again they lost the battle and with thousands of casualties. Confused, the third time they not only sought guidance from the Lord in prayer and with tears, but they also "fasted that day until evening" (verse 26). "Shall we go up again to battle with Benjamin our brother, or not?" they asked. Then the Lord made His will plain: "Go, for tomorrow I will give them into your hands" (verse 28). Only after they sought Him with fasting did the Lord give Israel the victory.

According to Acts 14:23, before Paul and Barnabas would appoint elders in the churches they founded, they first prayed with fasting to receive God's guidance.

David Brainerd prayed with fasting for the Lord's leadership regarding his entry into ministry. On Monday, April 19, 1742, he recorded in his journal: "I set apart this day for fasting and prayer to God for His grace; especially to prepare me for the work of the ministry, to give me divine aid and direction in my preparations for that great work, and in His own time to send me into His harvest."[8] He said of his experience during that day,

I felt the power of intercession for precious, immortal souls; for the advancement of the kingdom of my dear Lord and Saviour in the world; and withal, a most sweet resignation and even consolation and joy in the thoughts of suffering hardships, distresses,

and even death itself, in the promotion of it. . . . My soul was
drawn out very much for the world, for multitudes of souls. I
think I had more enlargement for sinners than for the children of
God, though I felt as if I could spend my life in cries for both. I
enjoyed great sweetness in communion with my dear Saviour. I
think I never in my life felt such an entire weanedness from this
world and so much resigned to God in everything.[9]

Fasting does not *ensure* the certainty of receiving clear guidance
from God. Rightly practiced, however, it does make us more receptive
to the One who loves to guide us.

To Express Grief

Three of the first four references in the Bible to fasting connect it with
an expression of grief. As mentioned in Judges 20:26, one of the reasons the Israelites wept and fasted before the Lord was—not only to
seek His guidance—but to express their grief for the forty thousand
brothers they had lost in battle. When King Saul was killed by the
Philistines, the men of Jabesh Gilead walked all night to recover the
bodies of the king and his sons. After the burial, 1 Samuel 31:13 says
they mourned when they "fasted seven days." The next chapter gives
the response of David and his men when they heard the news: "Then
David and all the men with him took hold of their clothes and tore them.
They mourned and wept and fasted till evening for Saul and his son
Jonathan, and for the army of the LORD and the house of Israel, because
they had fallen by the sword" (2 Samuel 1:11-12).

Grief caused by events other than a death also can be expressed
through fasting. Christians have fasted because of grief for their sins.
We are not required to pay for our sins, because we cannot and because
Christ has done that once for all (1 Peter 3:18). God has promised that
"if we confess our sins, he is faithful and just and will forgive us our
sins and purify us from all unrighteousness" (1 John 1:9). But that does
not mean that confession is a light and easy thing, a simple mouthing of
words, a verbal ritual. Mere admission is not confession. Christ is dis-
honored by a frivolous view of confession that does not appreciate how
much our sin cost Him. Although it is not a spiritual self-flagellation,
biblical confession does involve at least some degree of grief for the sin
committed. And inasmuch as fasting can be an expression of grief, it is

never inappropriate for fasting to be a voluntary, heartfelt part of confession. There have been a few occasions when I grieved so deeply over my sin that words alone seemed powerless to say to God what I wanted. And though it made me no more worthy of forgiveness, fasting communicated the grief and confession my words could not.

Fasting also can be a means of expressing grief for sins of others, such as for the sins of people within your church or for sins by your country. When a jealous King Saul was trying unjustly to kill David, the response of his son Jonathan, according to 1 Samuel 20:34, was that "on that second day of the month he did not eat, because he was grieved at his father's shameful treatment of David."

Caffy and I have a friend who has been a Christian just a few years. When she veered away from her profession of faith, we expressed our grief and prayed for her through a mutual fast of several days. Although we'd confronted her about her situation several times, she said, after being restored, that knowing we fasted for her was one of the main turning points in returning to fellowship. Our church has observed some occasional fast days together, partially to express our grief to the Lord over the sins of our nation.

Since fasting is often a means of expressing to God the depth of our feelings, it is as appropriate for grief-stricken prayers to be accompanied by fasting as by tears.

To Seek Deliverance or Protection
One of the most common fasts in biblical times was a fast to seek salvation from enemies or circumstances.

After being notified that a vast army was coming against him, King Jehoshaphat was afraid and "resolved to inquire of the LORD, and he proclaimed a fast for all Judah. The people of Judah came together to seek help from the LORD; indeed, they came from every town in Judah to seek him" (2 Chronicles 20:3-4).

We've already read of the fast called by Ezra when he led a group of exiles back to Jerusalem. There we noticed that they fasted in order to strengthen their praying. But notice from the larger context of Ezra 8:21-23 that the reason they prayed with fasting was for God's protection:

There, by the Ahava Canal, I proclaimed a fast, so that we
might humble ourselves before our God and ask him for a safe

journey for us and our children, with all our possessions. I was ashamed to ask the king for soldiers and horsemen to protect us from enemies on the road, because we had told the king, "The gracious hand of our God is on everyone who looks to him, but his great anger is against all who forsake him." So we fasted and petitioned our God about this, and he answered our prayer.

The best known cooperative fast in Scripture is likely the one in Esther 4:16. It was called by Queen Esther as a part of her appeal to God for protection from the king's wrath. She planned to enter the court of King Xerxes uninvited in order to appeal to him for the protection of the Jews from mass extermination. She said to her uncle Mordecai, "Go, gather together all the Jews who are in Susa, and fast for me. Do not eat or drink for three days, night or day. I and my maids will fast as you do. When this is done, I will go to the king, even though it is against the law. And if I perish, I perish."

When our church has a day of fasting in grief for the sins of our country, we also include prayers asking the Lord to protect and deliver us from enemies that might result from our sins. We realize that He often disciplined Israel for her sins by allowing national enemies to gain advantage over her militarily or economically. Perhaps we don't think as often of the reality of national sin as we should, and how Christians will experience part of any national judgment that comes, even though we did not contribute directly to the national sin.

But not all fasts to seek from God deliverance or protection are corporate fasts. David wrote Psalm 109 as an appeal for personal relief from a group of enemies and their leader in particular. A private fast was accompanying his prayer, as indicated by verse 24: "My knees give way from fasting; my body is thin and gaunt." Apparently this was an unusually long fast.

Fasting, rather than fleshly efforts, should be one of our first defenses against "persecution" from family, schoolmates, neighbors, or coworkers because of our faith. Typically we're tempted to strike back with anger, verbal abuse, counteraccusations, or even legal action. But instead of political maneuvering, gossiping, and imitating the worldly tactics of our enemies, we should appeal to God with fasting for protection and deliverance.

To Express Repentance and the Return to God

Fasting for this purpose is similar to fasting for the purpose of expressing grief for sin. But as repentance is a change of mind resulting in a change of action, fasting can represent more than just grief over sin. It also can signal a commitment to obedience and a new direction.

The Israelites expressed repentance through fasting in 1 Samuel 7:6 when "they drew water and poured it out before the LORD. On that day they fasted and there they confessed, 'We have sinned against the LORD.'"

In Joel 2:12, the Lord specifically commanded His people to signify their repentance and their return to Him by fasting: "'Even now,' declares the LORD, 'return to Me with all your heart, with fasting and weeping and mourning.'"

Surely the most thorough fast ever recorded is the one in Jonah 3:5-8, and it is a fast to express repentance. After God blessed Jonah's preaching with a great spiritual awakening,

> The Ninevites believed God. They declared a fast, and all of them, from the greatest to the least, put on sackcloth. When the news reached the king of Nineveh, he rose from his throne, took off his royal robes, covered himself with sackcloth and sat down in the dust. Then he issued a proclamation in Nineveh: "By the decree of the king and his nobles: Do not let any man or beast, herd or flock, taste anything; do not let them eat or drink. But let man and beast be covered with sackcloth. Let everyone call urgently on God. Let them give up their evil ways and their violence."

Not only can fasting express repentance, but it can also be in vain *without* repentance. As with all Spiritual Disciplines, fasting can be little more than a "dead work" if we have persistently hardened our hearts to God's call to deal with a specific sin in our lives. We must never try to immerse ourselves in a Spiritual Discipline as an attempt to drown out God's voice about forsaking a sin. It is a perversion of fasting to try to use it to balance self-punishment for a sinful part of life we want to continue feeding. One of the stalwart Puritan pastor-writers, Thomas Boston, said,

> In vain will ye fast, and pretend to be humbled for our sins, and make confession of them, if our love of sin be not turned into

hatred; our liking of it into loathing; and our cleaving to it, into a longing to be rid of it; with full purpose to resist the motions of it in our heart, and the outbreakings thereof in our life; and if we turn not unto God as our rightful Lord and Master, and return to our duty again.[10]

To Humble Oneself Before God

Fasting, when practiced with the right motives, is a physical expression of humility before God, just as kneeling or prostrating yourself in prayer can reflect humility before Him. And as there are times when you feel the need to express humility by praying on your knees or on your face before the Lord, so there are times when you may want to express a sense of humility before the Lord in every activity throughout the day by fasting.

Many who are accustomed to expressing humility in prayer by kneeling might ask why we would want to express humility all day by fasting. Conversely, John Calvin asked a better question: Why not? "For since this [fasting] is a holy exercise both for the humbling of men and for their confession of humility, why should we use it less than the ancients did in similar need? . . . What reason is there why we should not do the same?"[11]

One of the most wicked men in Jewish history, King Ahab, eventually humbled himself before God and demonstrated it by fasting: "When Ahab heard these words, he tore his clothes, put on sackcloth and fasted. He lay in sackcloth and went around meekly. Then the word of the LORD came to Elijah the Tishbite: 'Have you noticed how Ahab has humbled himself before me? Because he has humbled himself, I will not bring this disaster in his day, but I will bring it on his house in the days of his son'" (1 Kings 21:27-29).

On the other hand, one of Israel's godliest men humbled himself before the Lord in exactly the same way. King David wrote, "I put on sackcloth and humbled myself with fasting" (Psalm 35:13).

Remember that fasting itself is not humility before God, but should be an *expression* of humility. There was no humility in the Pharisee of Luke 18:12, who bragged to God in prayer that he fasted twice a week. Author David Smith, in *Fasting: A Neglected Discipline*, reminds us,

By this we must not conclude that the act of fasting has some virtuous power, and that *we* have made ourselves more humble;

there is no virtue in fallen man by which he can make himself more godly; there is, however, virtue in the divinely appointed means of grace. If we, by the power of the Holy Spirit, mortify the deeds of the body (through fasting), we shall grow in grace, but the glory of such change will be God's alone.[12]

To Express Concern for the Work of God

Just as a parent might fast and pray out of concern for the work of God in the life of a child, so Christians may fast and pray because they feel a burden for the work of God in a broader scope.

A Christian might feel compelled to fast and pray for the work of God in a place that has experienced tragedy, disappointment, or apparent defeat. This was the purpose for Nehemiah's fast when he heard that despite the return of many Jewish exiles to Jerusalem, the city still had no wall to defend it. "They said to me, 'Those who survived the exile and are back in the province are in great trouble and disgrace. The wall of Jerusalem is broken down, and its gates have been burned with fire.' When I heard these things, I sat down and wept. For some days I mourned and fasted and prayed before the God of heaven" (Nehemiah 1:3-4). After his fast, Nehemiah then went to work to do something tangible and public to strengthen this work of God.

Daniel was also burdened for the return of the Jews from exile and the restoration of Jerusalem and he, too, expressed this by fasting: "So I turned to the Lord God and pleaded with him in prayer and petition, in fasting, and in sackcloth and ashes" (Daniel 9:3).

A devoted believer in this Discipline, David Brainerd's concerns for the work of God frequently found expression in fasting and prayer. In his journal entry for June 14, 1742, he demonstrated his concern for the work he believed God had called him to do.

I set apart this day for secret fasting and prayer, to entreat God to direct and bless me with regard to the great work I have in view, of preaching the gospel. . . . God enabled me to wrestle ardently in intercession for absent friends. . . . The Lord visited me marvelously in prayer; I think my soul never was in such an agony before. I felt no restraint, for the treasures of divine grace were opened to me. I wrestled for absent friends, for the ingathering of souls, for multitudes of poor souls, and for many that I thought were the children of God, personally, in many distant places.[13]

Obviously we can't fast continually, but may the Lord at least occasionally give us a concern for His work so great that our normal concern for food will seem secondary in comparison.

To Minister to the Needs of Others

Those who think the Spiritual Disciplines foster tendencies of introspection or independence should consider Isaiah 58:6-7. In the most extensive passage in Scripture dealing exclusively with fasting, God emphasizes fasting for the purpose of meeting the needs of others. The people originally addressed in this section had complained to the Lord that they had fasted and humbled themselves before Him, but He had not answered them. But the reason why He had not heard them was their disobedience. Their lives were in hypocritical contrast to their fasting and praying. "Yet on the day of your fasting," says the Lord in verses 3-4, "you do as you please and exploit all your workers. Your fasting ends in quarreling and strife, and in striking each other with wicked fists. You cannot fast as you do today and expect your voice to be heard on high." Fasting cannot be compartmentalized from the rest of our lives. The Spiritual Disciplines do not stand alone. God will not bless the practice of any Discipline, including fasting, when we reject His Word regarding relationships with others.

What should we do? How does God want us to fast? "Is not this the kind of fasting I have chosen," the Lord asks in verses 6-7, "to loose the chains of injustice and untie the cords of the yoke, to set the oppressed free and break every yoke? Is it not to share your food with the hungry and to provide the poor wanderer with shelter—when you see the naked, to clothe him, and not to turn away from your own flesh and blood?" In other words, the kind of fasting that pleases God is one that results in concern for others and not just for ourselves.

"But," someone objects, "I'm so busy meeting my needs and those of my family that I don't have the time to minister to other people." That's where you can fast for the purpose of ministering to the needs of others. Fast for one meal or for one day and use that time for ministry. That way you haven't lost any of the time you say you must give to your other commitments. Several months ago I started scheduling a regular fast each week and devoting one of the mealtimes during that day to meet for counseling or discipleship with others. I've been amazed at how convenient and preferable that late-afternoon period is for many people. The result is that this fasting time has become my single most productive, need-meeting, one-on-one ministry slot all week.

There are other ways of fasting to meet the needs of others. Many fast so that they can give to the poor or to some ministry the money they would have spent on food during that period. How could you minister to the needs of others with the extra time or money fasting could provide?

To Overcome Temptation and Dedicate Yourself to God

Ask Christians to name a fast by a biblical character and most will probably think first of the supernatural fast of Jesus prior to His temptation in Matthew 4:1-11. Verse two of that familiar passage tells us that Jesus fasted "forty days and forty nights." In the spiritual strength of that prolonged fast He was prepared to overcome a direct onslaught of temptation from Satan himself, the strongest He would face until Gethsemane. It was also during that fast that He privately dedicated Himself to the Father for the public ministry He would begin soon thereafter.

Nowhere in Scripture are we asked to fast for forty days, or for any specific length of time. But that doesn't mean there is nothing from Jesus' unique experience for us to apply to ourselves. One principle we learn from Jesus' example is this: Fasting is a way of overcoming temptation and of freshly dedicating ourselves to the Father.

There are times we struggle with temptation, or we *anticipate* grappling with it, when we need extra spiritual strength to overcome it. Perhaps we are traveling (or our spouse is traveling) and temptations for mental and sensual unfaithfulness abound. At the start of school or a new job or ministry there may be new temptations, or it may seem appropriate to dedicate ourselves anew to the Lord. Often we face decisions that place unusual temptations before us. Do we take a new job that will mean much more money but much less time with the family? Do we accept the promotion that includes a transfer that would end a significant ministry in our local church or when it means going where our family's spiritual growth may suffer? In times of exceptional temptation, exceptional measures are required. Fasting for the purpose of overcoming the temptation and of renewing our dedication to God is a Christlike response.

To Express Love and Worship to God

By now you may have associated fasting only with dire circumstances and great troubles. But the Bible also says that fasting may be an act of sheer devotion to God.

In Luke 2 there is an unforgettable woman whose entire eighty-four years are flashed before us in just three quick verses. Her name is Anna. The summary of her life is found in Luke 2:37: "She never left the temple but worshiped night and day, fasting and praying." Although Anna's story has its primary significance in the context of Mary and Joseph presenting the newborn Jesus at the Temple, how she lived from day to day is what concerns us here. Anna was married for only seven years before being widowed. Assuming she married as a young lady, this Godly woman devoted at least half a century, night and day, to a worship of God characterized by "fasting and praying."

Fasting can be an expression of finding your greatest pleasure and enjoyment in life from God. That's the case when disciplining yourself to fast means that you love God more than food, that seeking Him is more important to you than eating. This honors God and is a means of worshiping Him as God. It means that your stomach isn't your god as it is with some (see Philippians 3:19). Instead it is God's servant, and fasting proves it because you're willing to sublimate its desires to those of the Spirit.

Christians throughout history have fasted for this purpose in preparation for the Lord's Supper. In addition to the elements of repentance and humility before God in this kind of fast, it is also intended to help the person focus on adoring the One who is represented in the Supper.

Another way of fasting to express love and worship to God is to spend your mealtime in praise and adoration of God. A variation is to delay eating a particular meal until you have had your daily time of Bible intake and prayer. Just remember that your fast is a privilege, not an obligation. It is the acceptance of a divine invitation to experience His grace in a special way. If you can't fast with the faith that you will find more satisfaction and joy at that time than in delaying a meal, then freely eat in faith first (Romans 14:22-23). But may we yearn for days when God will cause us to crave the spiritual banquet of worship more than any smorgasbord.

Fasting must always have a spiritual purpose—a God-centered purpose, not a self-centered one—for the Lord to bless our fast. Thoughts of food must prompt thoughts for God. They must not distract us, but instead remind us of our purpose. Rather than focusing the mind on food, we should use the desire to eat as a reminder to pray and to reconsider our purpose.

There is no doubt that God has often crowned fasting with extraordinary blessings. Biblical, historical, and contemporary testimonies bear witness to God's delight in providing unusual blessings to those who fast. But we should be careful not to have what Martyn Lloyd-Jones called a mechanical view of fasting. We cannot manipulate God to do our bidding by fasting any more than we can by any other means. As with prayer, we fast in hope that by His *grace* God *will* bless us as we desire. When our fast is rightly motivated, we can be sure that God will bless us, but perhaps not in the way we wanted.

Again David Smith has it right.

Any blessing which is bestowed by the Father upon His undeserving children must be considered to be an act of grace. We fail to appreciate the mercy of the Lord if we think that by our *doing something* we have forced (or even coerced) God to grant that blessing which we have asked for. . . . All of our fasting, therefore, must be on this basis; we should use it as a scriptural means whereby we are melted into a more complete realization of the purposes of the Lord in our life, church, community, and nation.[14]

While fasting recently over concern for the work of God in the church I pastor, I began to pray about several critical matters. Suddenly I realized that while I *thought* I was praying in God's will about these things, it was possible that my understanding of things needed readjusting. So I asked the Lord to show me how to pray according to His will on these matters and to grant me contentment with His providences. This, I think, is what Smith meant by fasting being "a scriptural means whereby we are melted into a more complete realization of the purposes of the Lord." Fasting should always have a purpose, and we must learn to elevate His purposes over ours.

God-centered fasting is taught in Zechariah 7:5. A delegation was sent from Bethel to Jerusalem to inquire of the Lord. At issue was the continuance of two fasts the Jews had held to commemorate the destruction of the Temple. For seventy years they had kept these fasts in the fifth and seventh months, but now they wondered if God wanted them to continue the fasts since they had been restored to their land and were building a new temple. The Lord's response to them was, "Ask all the people of the land and the priests, 'When you fasted and mourned in the fifth and seventh months for the past seventy years, was it really for me that you fasted?'" In reality, these fasts had become empty rituals, not God-centered experiences. Matthew Henry's comments on this passage are useful for our own fasting.

> Let them all take notice that, whereas they thought they had made God very much their Debtor by these fasts, they were much mistaken, for they were not acceptable to Him, unless they had been observed in a better manner, and to better purpose. . . . They were not chargeable with omission or neglect of the duty, . . . but they had not managed [it] aright. . . . They had not an eye to God in their fasting. . . . When this was wanting, every fast was but a jest. To fast, and not to fast to God, was to mock Him and provoke Him, and could not be pleasing *to Him*. . . . If the solemnities of our fasting, though frequent, long, and severe, do not serve to put an edge upon devout affections, to quicken prayer, to increase Godly sorrow, and to alter the temper of our minds, and the course of our lives, for the better, they do not at all answer the intention, and God will not accept them as performed to Him.[15]

Before we fast we must have a purpose, a God-centered purpose. But even at our best we do not deserve what we desire, nor can we force God's hand. Having said that, however, let's balance that truth with the incontestable promise of Jesus in Matthew 6:17-18, "But when you fast, put oil on your head and wash your face, so that it will not be obvious to men that you are fasting, but only to your Father, who is unseen; and your Father, who sees what is done in secret, will reward you." God will bless a biblical fast by any of His children. And whether or not you receive the blessing you hope for, one thing is sure: If you knew what God knew, you would give yourself the identical blessing that He does. And none of His rewards is worthless.

MORE APPLICATION

Will you confess and repent of any fear of fasting? There's something about saying, "I'm not going to eat today," that causes anxiety in many Christians. It seems that most believers would rather give an offering of money than give up food for a day. Do you have a mild case of fasting-phobia? It's silly when you put it in perspective. We think about missing a meal or two for the sake of becoming more like Jesus and we get anxious. And yet we willingly miss meals sometimes while shopping, working, recreating, or otherwise occupied. Whenever we believe another activity is at that moment more important, we will go without food fearlessly and without complaint. We need to learn that there are times when it can be not only more important, but much more rewarding to feast on God than food (Matthew 4:4). We should not fear the blessings of fasting.

Will you fast as the Holy Spirit directs? Are you willing to obey God when He prompts you to fast? Because Jesus expected that His followers would fast, I believe that from time to time His Spirit will direct you to fast. Will you determine in advance that you will be obedient to His voice?

One of the ways the Holy Spirit prompts us to fast is through a need in our lives. If you need stronger prayer about a matter, that's an invitation from the Lord to fast. If you need God's guidance in an issue in your life, that's an encouragement to fast. If you need deliverance or protection, that's a time to fast. Will you do it? Or will you miss the unique opportunities for grace that He would extend to you through fasting?

Remember to get medical counsel where necessary. If you're planning an extended fast, or if you are expecting, nursing, diabetic, or have a physical condition that depends on a regular diet, talk to your doctor before starting your fast. And if you've never fasted before, start with a one-, two-, or at most three-meal fast. But start somewhere. Don't look for loopholes to avoid it. Look for ways to experience God's grace through fasting. Remember that God thought it was good enough to command every Israelite to fast for one whole day each year on the Day of Atonement, and that would have included people in all conditions and circumstances.

Like all the Spiritual Disciplines, fasting hoists the sails of the soul in hopes of experiencing the gracious wind of God's Spirit. But fasting also adds a unique dimension to your spiritual life and helps you grow in Christlikeness in ways that are unavailable through any other means. If this were not so, there would have been no need for Jesus to model and teach fasting.

Will you plan a fast of dedication now as an expression of your willingness to fast from now on? Before you go any further, why not set a time of fasting soon that will symbolize your dedication to the Lord and your willingness to discipline yourself to fast in the future?

NOTES

1. LaVonne Neff, et al., ed., *Practical Christianity* (Wheaton, IL: Tyndale House, 1987), page 300.
2. D. Martyn Lloyd-Jones, *Studies in the Sermon on the Mount* (Grand Rapids, MI: Eerdmans, 1960), vol. 1, page 38.
3. R. D. Chatham, *Fasting: A Biblical-Historical Study* (South Plainfield, NJ: Bridge, 1987), pages 96-97, 161-181.
4. Andy Anderson, *Fasting Changed My Life* (Nashville, TN: Broadman, 1977), pages 47-48.
5. John Calvin, *Institutes of the Christian Religion*, ed. John T. McNeil, trans. and indexed by Ford Lewis Battles (Philadelphia, PA: Westminster, 1960), vol. 2, page 1242.
6. Arthur Wallis, *God's Chosen Fast* (Fort Washington, PA: Christian Literature Crusade, 1968), page 42.
7. Wallis, page 43.
8. Jonathan Edwards, ed., *The Life and Diary of David Brainerd*, revised edition ed. by Philip E. Howard, Jr. (Chicago: Moody Press, 1949), page 80.
9. Edwards, page 81.
10. Thomas Boston, *The Works of Thomas Boston*, ed. Samuel McMillan (London: William Tegg and Company, 1853; reprint, Wheaton, IL: Richard Owen Roberts, 1980), vol. 11, page 347.
11. Calvin, pages 1243-1244.
12. David R. Smith, *Fasting: A Neglected Discipline* (Fort Washington, PA: Christian Literature Crusade, 1954; American ed., 1969), pages 46-47.
13. Edwards, page 88.
14. Smith, page 44.
15. Matthew Henry, *A Commentary on the Whole Bible* (New York: Funk and Wagnalls, n.d.), vol. 4, page 1478.

CHAPTER TEN

SILENCE AND SOLITUDE ...
FOR THE PURPOSE OF GODLINESS

❖❖❖

The word discipline has disappeared from our minds,
our mouths, our pulpits, and our culture. We hardly
know what discipline means in modern American
society. And yet, there is no other way to attain
godliness; discipline is the path to godliness.

Jay Adams
Godliness Through Discipline

My favorite short story is "The Bet," by Anton Chekhov, a Russian writer of the last half of the nineteenth century. The plot involves a wager between two educated men regarding solitary confinement. A wealthy, middle-aged banker believed that the death penalty was a more humane penalty than solitary confinement because "an executioner kills at once, solitary confinement kills gradually." One of his guests at a party, a young lawyer of twenty-five, disagreed, saying, "To live under any conditions is better than not to live at all."

Angered, the banker impulsively responded with a bet of two million rubles that the younger man could not last five years in solitary confinement. The lawyer was so convinced of his endurance that he announced he would stay fifteen years alone instead of only five.

The arrangements were made, and the young man moved into a separate building on the grounds of the banker's large estate. He was allowed no visitors or newspapers. He could write letters but receive none. There were guards watching to make sure he never violated the agreement, but they were placed so that he could never see another human being from his windows. He received his food in silence through a small opening where he could not see those who served him. Everything else he wanted—books, certain foods, musical instruments, etc.—was granted by special written request.

The story develops with a description of the things the lawyer asked for through the years and the observations of the guards who occasionally stole a glance through a window. During the first year the piano could be heard at almost any hour, and he asked for many books, mostly novels and other light reading. The next year the music ceased and the works of various classical authors were requested. In the sixth year of his isolation he began to study languages and soon had mastered six. After the tenth year of his confinement, the prisoner sat motionless at the table and read the New Testament. After more than a year's saturation of the Bible, he began to study the history of religion and works on theology. During the last two years his reading broadened to cover many subjects in addition to theology.

The second half of the story focuses on the night before the noon deadline when the lawyer will win the bet. The banker is now at the end of his career. His risky speculations and impetuosity had gradually undermined his business. The once self-confident millionaire was now a second-rate banker and to pay off the wager would destroy him. Angry at his foolishness and jealous of the soon-to-be-wealthy man who was now only forty, the old banker determines to kill his opponent and frame the guard with the murder. Slipping into the man's room he finds him asleep at the table and notices a letter the lawyer has written to him. He picked it up and read the following:

> Tomorrow at twelve o'clock I shall be free, . . . but before leaving this room, . . . I find it necessary to say a few words to you. With a clear conscience, and before God, who sees me, I declare to you that I despise freedom and life and health and all that your books call the joys of this world. For fifteen years I have studied attentively the life of this world. It is true that I neither saw the earth nor its peoples, but in your books I lived . . . . I sang songs, I hunted the deer and the wild boar in the forests. . . . In your books I climbed to the summit of Elburz and Mont Blanc, and I saw from those heights the sun rise in the morning, and at night it shed its purple glow over the sky and the ocean and the mountain-tops. I saw beneath me the flashing lightning cut through the clouds. I saw green fields,

forests, rivers, lakes and towns. I heard the song of the sirens and the music of the shepherd's reed-pipes. I felt the touch of the wings of beautiful [angels] who had flown to me to talk about God. . . . Your books gave me wisdom. All that had been achieved by the untiring brain of man during long centuries is stored in my brain in a small compressed mass. . . . I know I am wiser than you all. . . . And I despise all your books, I despise all earthly blessings and wisdom. All is worthless and false, hollow and deceiving like the mirage. You may be proud, wise and beautiful, but death will wipe you away from the face of the earth, as it does the mice that live beneath your floor; and your heirs, your history, your immortal geniuses will freeze or burn with the destruction of the earth. You have gone mad and are not following the right path. You take falsehood for truth, and deformity for beauty. To prove to you how I despise all that you value I renounce the two millions on which I looked, at one time, as the opening of paradise for me, and which I now scorn. To deprive myself of the right to receive them, I will leave my prison five hours before the appointed time, and by so doing break the terms of our compact.

The banker read these lines, replaced the paper on the table, kissed the strange, sleeping man and with tears in his eyes quietly left the house. Chekhov writes, "Never before, not even after sustaining serious losses on change, had he despised himself as he did at that moment." His tears kept him awake the rest of the night. And at seven the next morning he was informed by the watchman that they had seen the man crawl through a window, go to the gate, and then disappear.[1]

I don't recommend that we separate ourselves in this way, and I don't affirm all the lawyer's conclusions, but I do believe Chekhov looks into a room where every Christian sometimes dreams of living.

There is something both appealing and transforming about silence and solitude. Other than Jesus Christ, perhaps the greatest men under each Covenant—Moses and the Apostle Paul—were both transformed through years of virtual isolation in a remote wilderness. And there are moments in our pressure-cooker lives when years of escape to some hidden place sounds wistfully compelling to the Christian spirit.

When we think with balance we realize that it would be neither right nor desirable to be cloistered from our God-given responsibilities involving other people. Biblical reality calls us to family, fellowship, evangelism, and ministry for the sake of Christ and His Kingdom. And yet through the Holy Spirit, "deep calls to deep" (Psalm 42:7) in such a way that there is a part of our spirit that craves silence and solitude. Just as we must engage with others for some of the Disciplines of the Christian life, so there are times when we must temporarily withdraw into the Disciplines of silence and solitude. In this chapter we will explore what these twin Disciplines are, find biblical reasons for practicing them, and conclude with some sensible suggestions for starting.

EXPLANATION OF SILENCE AND SOLITUDE

The Discipline of silence is the voluntary and temporary abstention from speaking so that certain spiritual goals might be sought. Sometimes silence is observed in order to read, write, pray, and so on. Though there is no outward speaking, there are internal dialogues with self and with God. This can be called "outward silence." Other times silence is maintained not only outwardly but also inwardly so that God's voice might be heard more clearly.

Solitude is the Spiritual Discipline of voluntarily and temporarily withdrawing to privacy for spiritual purposes. The period of solitude may last only a few minutes or for days. As with silence, solitude may be sought in order to participate without interruption in other Spiritual Disciplines, or just to be alone with God.

Three brief thoughts before proceeding in depth. First, think of silence and solitude as complementary Disciplines to fellowship. Without silence and solitude we're shallow. Without fellowship we're stagnant. Balance requires them all.

Second, silence and solitude are usually found together. Though they can be distinguished, in this chapter we will think of them as a pair.

Third, recognize that Western culture conditions us to be comfortable with noise and crowds, not with silence and solitude. In her book *Finding Focus in a Whirlwind World*, Jean Fleming observed, "We live in a noisy, busy world. Silence and solitude are not twentieth-century words. They fit the era of Victorian lace, high-button shoes, and kerosene lamps better than our age of television, video arcades, and joggers wired with earphones. We have become a people with an aversion to quiet and an uneasiness with being alone."² Therefore be careful not to let the world prejudice you against the biblical witness on these matters. "He who has ears, let him hear" (Matthew 11:15).

VALUABLE REASONS FOR SILENCE AND SOLITUDE

There are many biblical reasons for making priorities of the Disciplines of silence and solitude.

Follow Jesus' Example

The Scriptures teach that Jesus practiced silence and solitude. Note these four references:

1. Matthew 4:1, "Then Jesus was led up by the Spirit into the desert to be tempted by the devil." The Holy Spirit led Jesus into this lengthy period of fasting and solitude. In Luke's account of this experience, it's interesting to observe that he says Jesus was "full of the Holy Spirit" (Luke 4:1) when He was led into this particular Discipline, but that afterward He returned to Galilee "in the power of the Spirit" (Luke 4:14).

2. Matthew 14:23, "After he had dismissed them, he went up on a mountainside by himself to pray. When evening came, he was there alone." He sent both the seeking multitudes and His disciples away so He could be alone with the Father.

3. Mark 1:35, "Very early in the morning, while it was still dark, Jesus got up, left the house and went off to a solitary place, where he prayed." The previous verses tell us that after dark "the whole town" gathered at the door of the house where Jesus was staying. There He healed many people and cast out demons. But before it was daylight again, He went to spend time alone. Jesus knew that had He waited until the morning hours He could never have had time for silence and solitude.

4. Luke 4:42, "At daybreak Jesus went out to a solitary place. The people were looking for him and when they came to where he was, they tried to keep him from leaving them." Put yourself in Jesus' sandals for a moment. People are clamoring for your help and have many real needs. You are able to meet all those needs. Can you ever feel justified in pulling away to be alone? Jesus did. We love to feel wanted. We love the sense of importance/power/indispensability (pick one) that comes from doing something no one else can do. But Jesus did not succumb to those temptations. He knew the importance of disciplining Himself to be alone.

By now the point should be obvious: To be like Jesus we must discipline ourselves to find times of silence and solitude. Then we can find spiritual strength through these Disciplines, as Jesus did. Dallas Willard makes the same point when he says,

> We must reemphasize, the "desert" or "closet" is the primary place of *strength* for the beginner, as it was for Christ and for Paul. They show us by their example what we must do. In stark aloneness it is possible to have silence, to be still, and to *know* that Jehovah indeed is God (Ps. 46:10), to set the Lord before our minds with sufficient intensity and duration that we stay centered upon Him—our hearts fixed, established in trust (Ps. 112:7-8)—even when back in the office, shop, or home.[3]

To Hear the Voice of God Better

One of the more obvious reasons for getting away from earthly noise and human voices is to hear the Voice from Heaven better. Biblical examples of this include Elijah going to Mount Horeb where he heard the gentle whisper of God's voice (1 Kings 19:11-13), Habakkuk standing on the guard post and keeping watch to see what God would say to him (Habakkuk 2:1), and the Apostle Paul going to Arabia after his conversion so he could be alone with God (Galatians 1:17).

Of course, it isn't absolutely necessary to get far away from noises and people in order to hear God speak, otherwise we'd never perceive His promptings in the course of everyday life, or even in peopled worship services. But there are times to eliminate the voices of the world in order to hear the undistracted the voice of God.

According to Jonathan Edwards, this was a secret of the Godliness of his wife, Sarah. In his first record of her, penned while his future wife was still a teenager, he wrote, "She hardly cares for anything, except to meditate on Him. . . . She loves to be alone, walking in the fields and groves, and seems to have someone invisible always conversing with her."[4] Where Sarah had "fields and groves," we may have to walk in the park, around the block, or find another place for regular solitude. Wherever it is, we need to find a place to be alone to hear the voice of Him whose presence is unseen yet more real than any other.

Many of us need to realize the addiction we have to noise. It's one thing to listen to the television, tape player, or radio while ironing or doing other chores, but it's another thing habitually to turn one of these on immediately upon entering a room just to have sound. Even worse is to feel that it's necessary to have background noise during Bible intake or prayer. I believe the convenience of sound has contributed to the spiritual shallowness of contemporary western Christianity. The advent of affordable, portable sound systems, for instance, has been a mixed blessing. The negative side is that now we don't have to go anywhere without human voices. As a result we are less frequently alone with our own thoughts and God's voice. Because of this, and because we are the most urban, noise-polluted generation ever, we have an unprecedented need to learn the Disciplines of silence and solitude.

To Express Worship to God
The worship of God does not always require words, sounds, or actions. Sometimes worship consists of a God-focused stillness and hush. Scriptural precedent for this includes texts like Habakkuk 2:20, "But the LORD is in his holy temple; let all the earth be silent before him," and Zephaniah 1:7, "Be silent before the Sovereign LORD." It's not just a silence that's enjoined, but a silence "before him," "before the Sovereign Lord." That's the silence of worship. There are times to speak to God, and there are times simply to behold and adore Him in silence.

Recorded in the journals of George Whitefield is an incident of silent worship that he once had in the solitude of his home. He wrote that in the experience "God was pleased to pour into my soul a great spirit of supplication, and a sense of His free, distinguishing mercies so filled me with love, humility, and joy and holy confusion that I could at last only pour out my heart before Him in an awful silence. I was so full that I could not well speak."[5]

Worshiping God in silence may occur because your heart, like Whitefield's here, is so full that words cannot express your love for Him. At other times you may feel just the opposite, so passionless that any words seem hypocritical. Regardless of the state of your emotions, there is always a place for wordless worship.

To Express Faith in God
The simple act of silence before the Lord, as opposed to coming to Him in a wordy fret, can be a demonstration of faith in Him.

Twice in Psalm 62 David displays this kind of faith. In verses 1-2 he affirms, "My soul waits in silence for God only; from Him is my salvation. He only is my rock and my salvation, my stronghold; I shall not be greatly shaken" (NASB). Then in verses 5-6 he says again, "My soul, wait in silence for God only, for my hope is from Him. He only is my rock and my salvation, my stronghold; I shall not be shaken" (NASB).

A favorite verse of many, Isaiah 30:15, connects silence before God with faith in Him: "This is what the Sovereign LORD, the Holy One of Israel, says: 'In repentance and rest is your salvation, in quietness and trust is your strength.'" Faith is frequently expressed through prayer. But sometimes it is exhibited through a wordlessness before the Lord which, by its quiet absence of anxiety, communicates trust in His sovereign control.

I discovered a real-life illustration of this in the life of the early American missionary to the Indians, David Brainerd. He wrote in his journal on Wednesday, April 28, 1742,

> I withdrew to my usual place of retirement in great peace and tranquility; spent about two hours in secret duties and felt much as I did yesterday morning, only weaker and more overcome. I seemed to depend wholly upon my dear Lord, wholly weaned from all other dependences. I knew not what to say to my God, but only lean on His bosom, as it were, and breathe out my desires after a perfect conformity to Him in all things. Thirsting desires and insatiable longings possessed my soul after perfect holiness. God was so precious to my soul that the world with all its enjoyments was infinitely vile. I had no more value for all the favor of men than pebbles. The Lord was my ALL; and that He overruled all greatly delighted me. I think my faith and dependence upon God scarce ever rose so high. I saw Him such a fountain of goodness that it seemed impossible I should distrust Him again, or be any way anxious about anything that should happen to me.[6]

We may not be able to express ourselves in a journal as well as Brainerd, but we can express our faith to God in ways He thinks are beautiful through seasons of eloquent silences.

To Seek the Salvation of the Lord

A time of silence and solitude to seek the salvation of the Lord can refer either to a nonChristian seeking salvation from sin and guilt in Christ or to a believer seeking God's salvation from certain circumstances. The words of Jeremiah in Lamentations 3:25-28 are appropriate in either case: "The LORD is good to those whose hope is in him, to the one who seeks him; it is good to wait quietly for the salvation of the LORD. It is good for a man to bear the yoke while he is young. Let him sit alone in silence, for the LORD has laid it on him."

In a sermon on this text, C. H. Spurgeon said the following of this method of seeking God:

> I commend solitude to any of you who are seeking salvation, first, that you may study well your case as in the sight of God. Few men truly know themselves as they really are. Most people have seen themselves in a looking-glass, but there is another looking-glass, which gives true reflections, into which few men look. To study one's self in the light of God's Word, and carefully to go over one's condition, examining both the inward and the outward sins, and using all the tests which are given us in the Scriptures, would be a very healthy exercise; but how very few care to go through it![7]

Since Spurgeon's day, some have apparently come to believe that the only time a person will seriously seek salvation is during a postsermon hymn when there is the sound of an organ or piano and a singing church congregation. We shouldn't minimize the value of silence before God to help avoid distractions when considering the state of the soul. Solitude and silence can help us come to grips with the realities of our sin, death, judgment, etc., themes that are frequently drowned out of our consciousness by sounds of everyday life. We need to encourage seekers more to get "alone with God" and, in Spurgeon's words, "to study one's self in the light of God's Word."

To Be Physically and Spiritually Restored

Everyone has a regular need for restoring the resources of both the inward and outward person. It was true even for those who lived most closely with Jesus. After spending themselves in several days of physical and spiritual output, notice the means of replenishment Jesus prescribed for His disciples, "Come with me by yourselves to a quiet place and get some rest" (Mark 6:31).

We all need times to unstring the bow of our routine stresses and enjoy the restoration that silence and solitude can provide for our body and soul.

One evening in October, 1982, I saw a news report about the life and recent death of pianist Glenn Gould. He was described as a miraculous musician when he burst onto the music scene as a teenager during the fifties. He toured the world and amazed listeners with his skills. But in 1964 he quit playing in public. From then on, even though he was one of the world's greatest pianists, Gould played only in private and for recording. And even his recording sessions were done in complete privacy. He was convinced that *isolation* was the only way to create. There's a monkishness about Gould's practice we would not want to imitate completely. However, don't overlook the physically and spiritually *re*-creative qualities about silence and solitude that are deeply therapeutic.

To Regain a Spiritual Perspective

There's no better way to step back and get a more balanced, less worldly perspective on matters than through the Disciplines of silence and solitude.

When Zechariah was told by the angel Gabriel that he and his elderly wife would miraculously have a son, he doubted. In response Gabriel said, "And now you will be silent and not able to speak until the day this happens, because you did not believe my words, which will come true at their proper time" (Luke 1:20). And what happened to Zechariah's perspective about these things during this time of enforced silence? When the baby was born, Luke 1:63-64 says, "He asked for a writing tablet, and to everyone's astonishment he wrote, 'His name is John.' Immediately his mouth was opened and his tongue was loosed, and he began to speak, praising God." A negative illustration, perhaps, but it shows how closing our mouths can help us open our minds.

One of the most famous and life-changing events in the life of Billy Graham happened in August 1949, immediately prior to the Los Angeles crusade that thrust him into national prominence. Many who weren't around at that time may not know that for a short period the unofficial title of North America's most prominent evangelist fell on a man named Chuck Templeton. However, by this time Templeton was coming under the influence of men who doubted the inspiration of Scripture, and this eventually led to his complete denial of the faith. He began to share the books and ideas that were shaping him with Graham. And only days before Graham drove to California, Templeton told him that by continuing to believe the Bible the young evangelist was committing intellectual suicide.

While speaking at a youth conference in the San Bernardino Mountains, Graham knew he had to get God's perspective on the matter, and he found it through solitude. Here's how he describes that night: "I went back alone to the cottage and read in my Bible for a while, and then I decided to take a walk in the forest." There he recalled that phrases such as "the Word of the Lord came" and "thus saith the Lord" were used more than two thousand times in Scripture. He meditated on the attitude of Christ, who fulfilled the law and the prophets, who quoted from them constantly and never indicated that they might be wrong. As he walked he said, "Lord, what shall I do? What shall be the direction of my life?" He saw that intellect alone couldn't resolve the question of the Bible's inspiration and authority. Beyond that it ultimately became an issue of faith. He thought of the faith he had in many everyday things that he did not understand, such as airplanes and cars, and asked himself why it was only the things of the Spirit where such faith was considered wrong. "So I went back and got my Bible," he continues, "and I went out in the moonlight. And I got to a stump and put the Bible on the stump, and I knelt down, and I said, 'Oh, God; I cannot prove certain things. I cannot answer some of the questions Chuck is raising and some of the other people are raising, but I accept this Book by faith as the Word of God.'"[8] And through that time of solitude and the spiritual perspective he gained that night, Billy Graham was shaped into the man the world has known since.

Graham's experience demonstrates what the prolific Puritan theologian John Owen said of our solitudes, "What we are in them, that we are indeed, and no more. They are either the best or the worst of our times, wherein the principle that is predominant in us will show and act itself."[9]

To Seek the Will of God

Perhaps one of the most common reasons believers have a time of silence and solitude with God, at least on occasion, is to discern His will about a matter. Jesus did this in Luke 6:12-13 when deciding whom to choose as the disciples who would travel with Him: "One of those days Jesus went out to a mountainside to pray, and spent the night praying to God. When morning came, he called his disciples to him and chose twelve of them, whom he also designated apostles."

Christian history is rich with memorable stories of men and women who secluded themselves from all others in order to seek the will of Him who matters most. A favorite of these stories involves Hudson Taylor, a young, exhausted missionary to China. In 1865, while back in England to rest and continue some medical studies, he struggled with a decision. He sensed that God might be leading him to start a new mission work that no one else was doing—taking the gospel to the vast, unreached millions in the interior of China. For decades, almost all missionaries worked only in the coastal cities, rarely going inland. But Taylor was fearful of leading such a great enterprise, knowing that the burden of enlisting missionaries, as well as finding and maintaining their financial support, would rest on his shoulders.

By the quiet summer Sunday of June 25, Hudson Taylor could stand the uncertainty no longer. Worn out and ill, he had gone to rest with friends at Brighton. But instead of enjoying their company he knew he must have silence and solitude, and he wandered out along the sands left by the receding tide. Although the scene was peaceful, he was in agony. A decision had to be made. He must know God's will. As he walked, the thought came,

> "Why, if we are obeying the Lord, the responsibility rests *with Him*, not with us! *Thou*, Lord, *Thou* shalt have all the burden! At Thy bidding, as Thy servant I go forward, leaving results with Thee." "How restfully I turned away from the sands," he said, recalling the deliverance of that hour. "The conflict ended, all was joy and peace. I felt as if I could fly up the hill to Mr. Pearse's house. And how I did sleep that night! My dear wife thought Brighton had done wonders for me, and so it had."[10]

And so, on the hinge of seeking His will through silence and solitude, God opened the door for the China Inland Mission. That same work continues to be used of God and has grown into the Overseas Missionary Fellowship, one of the world's great missionary endeavors.

God often makes His will clear to us in public, but there are times when He discloses it only in private. To discover it requires the Disciplines of silence and solitude.

To Learn Control of the Tongue

Learning to keep silent for extended periods of time can help us control our tongue all the time.

There's no doubt that learning control of the tongue is critical to Christlikeness. The Bible says that the religion of the person with no tongue control is worthless (James 1:26). Proverbs 17:27-28 relates the Christlike qualities of Godly knowledge, understanding, wisdom, and discernment to the power to rein in words: "A man of knowledge uses words with restraint, and a man of understanding is even-tempered. Even a fool is thought wise if he keeps silent, and discerning if he holds his tongue."

There is Old-Covenant precedent for disciplined seasons of solitary silence in Ecclesiastes 3:7, which says there is "a time to be silent and a time to speak." Learning the Discipline of the former can help you develop control in the latter, for the one who doesn't know how or when to be silent doesn't know how or when to speak.

In the New Testament, James 1:19 also indicates a relationship between learning silence and learning control of the tongue: "My dear brothers, take note of this: Everyone should be quick to listen, slow to speak and slow to become angry."

How can the Disciplines of silence and solitude teach tongue control? On a long fast you discover that much of the food you normally eat is really unnecessary. When you practice silence and solitude, you find that you don't need to say many things you think you need to say. In silence we learn to rely more on God's control in situations where we would normally feel compelled to speak, or to speak too much. We find out that He is able to manage situations in which we once thought our input was indispensable. The skills of observation and listening are also sharpened in those who practice silence and solitude so that when they do speak there's more of a freshness and depth to their words.

In a final Scripture passage, James 3:2, we find this teaching: "We all stumble in many ways. If anyone is never at fault in what he says, he is a perfect man, able to keep his whole body in check." Practicing the Discipline of silence leads to Christlikeness because it helps develop control of the tongue. And here we see that control of the tongue also promotes a Christlike control of "the whole body." Because of this potential for a life-wide impact, no wonder Dallas Willard refers to silence and solitude as "the most radical of the disciplines for life in the spirit."[11]

One reason why the dual Disciplines of silence and solitude can be so thoroughly transforming is because they can help us with the other Spiritual Disciplines. They should normally be a part, for example, of individual Bible intake and prayer. They are a necessary component of private worship. In silence and solitude we can maximize time for Disciplines such as learning and journaling. It's common to practice fasting during times of silence and solitude. But more than anything else, the Disciplines of silence and solitude can be so transfiguring because they provide time to think about life and to listen to God. The plain fact is that most of us don't do that enough. Generations ago most of our forebears would have spent their days working in the fields or in the home where the only other sounds were those of nature or human voices. Without electronic media there were fewer distractions from the voice of conscience and the still, small voice of God. This is not to glamorize the supposed "good old days" (a sinful practice; see Ecclesiastes 7:10) or suggest we try to return to them. I'm simply reaffirming what we've said from the beginning of this chapter: One of the costs of technological advancement is a greater temptation to avoid quietness. While we have broadened our intake of news and information of all kinds, these advantages may come at the expense of our spiritual depth if we do not practice silence and solitude.

Remember that the great purpose for engaging in these Disciplines is Godliness, that we may be like Jesus, that we may be more holy. In *The Still Hour*, Austin Phelps wrote,

> It has been said that no great work in literature or in science was ever wrought by a man who did not love solitude. We may lay it down as an elemental principle of religion, that no large growth in holiness was ever gained by one who did not *take* time to be often long *alone with God*.[12]

SUGGESTIONS FOR SILENCE AND SOLITUDE

Some people enjoy the Disciplines of silence and solitude like they enjoy reading or watching some great adventure. Instead of developing these practices for themselves, they enter into them only vicariously and admire them from afar. They dream about these Disciplines, but they don't do them. Here is some practical help for making silence and solitude more of a reality and a habit.

"Minute Retreats"

A Christian radio station in my area has a thirty-second spot emphasizing the benefits of silence. Then it provides ten silent seconds to make its point. As simple as it sounds, the impact of that unexpected quiet moment is remarkable.

It's possible to provide that same kind of refreshment on occasion throughout your day. A moment at a traffic light, in an elevator, or in the line at the drive-thru bank can become a "minute retreat" when you consecrate it as a time of silence and solitude. Use the time of prayer at a meal for a spiritual pause. On the phone, see how quiet your thoughts can become while on "hold."

I can't provide suggestions for every person's circumstances. But I can encourage you to find ways to turn the routine into the holy, to find those "minute retreats" that can punctuate and empower even the busiest days.

Of course, the key is not just taking a breath and settling down, as important as that is. What I'm advocating is looking to Christ and listening to His Spirit. It's practicing what we sing in the hymn, "Take my *moments* and my days, let them flow in ceaseless praise" (emphasis mine). Seize these unexpected opportunities given you and concentrate exclusively on Him and life in the Spirit. Even if you are provided with only a few seconds, even if it's not an absolutely quiet or completely solitary place, enjoy the restoration found in the conscious presence of Jesus Christ.

A Goal of Daily Silence and Solitude

Without exception, the men and women I have known who make the most rapid, consistent, and evident growth in Christlikeness have been those who develop a daily time of being alone with God. This time of outward silence is the time of daily Bible intake and prayer. In this solitude is the occasion for private worship.

This daily devotional habit is not easy to develop because we lead busy lives and have an Enemy aware of the stakes involved. Missionary martyr Jim Elliot knew of the battle: "I think the devil has made it his business to monopolize on three elements: noise, hurry, crowds. . . . Satan is quite aware of the power of silence."[13] Our days are usually filled with more than enough noise, plenty of hurry, and demanding people. Unless we *plan* for daily times of solitary silence before God, these other things will rush in to fill our time like water into the *Titanic*.

These daily times are the lifeblood of the Disciplines of silence and solitude. Those who practice silence and solitude well on a daily basis are more likely to discipline themselves to enjoy them on an occasional basis, such as on "minute retreats," the Lord's Day, and on extended periods. The person who rarely exercises struggles with both a brief climb up the stairs and a mile run. The one who jogs every day has no trouble with either. In the same way the person who has a time of daily spiritual exercises is the one who most enjoys both "minute retreats" and extended periods of silence and solitude.

Getting Away for Solitude and Silence

"Getting away" for an extended time of silence and solitude may be nothing more than finding an empty room in your church in which to spend an afternoon, an evening, or a Saturday. Or it may involve spending a night or a weekend at a retreat center, lodge, or cabin.

On some of these getaways you may want to take nothing but your Bible and a notebook. On others you might want to devour a book you believe will have a dramatic impact on your life. Such retreats are a good time to plan and evaluate your goals.

If you've never spent an entire evening, half a day, or longer in silence and solitude, you may be wondering what you would do with all that time. I would advise you to prepare a schedule either in advance or first thing upon arrival, because you'll be surprised at how quickly the time will pass. Don't feel as though you must stick slavishly to your schedule. Even if it's not an overnight event, sleep if you need to. But a plan can help you use your time for the intended purposes rather than inadvertently misspending it.

Although overnight getaways at distant places are wonderful, don't wait for times when you can go like Elijah to Mount Horeb for forty days before you start practicing silence and solitude. Remember that, generally speaking, all the Spiritual Disciplines, including these two, are intended for common practice in the places where we live our daily lives.

Special Places

Locate special places that can be used for silence and solitude. Find them within the home, within walking distance, within a few minutes' drive, and for overnight or longer retreats.

The prophetic Welsh preacher Howell Harris, a friend of George Whitefield, had a special place for silence and solitude in a church building. Writing about the time before the Welshman's evangelistic ministry, Whitefield's biographer, Arnold Dallimore, says,

> Harris's knowledge of Divine things during these days was small. He simply knew he loved the Lord and wanted to love Him more, and in this pursuit he sought out quiet places where he could be secluded with Him in prayer. One of his favourite retreats was the church at Llangasty—the village in which he then taught school—and on one occasion shortly after his conversion he climbed into its tower to be more alone with the Lord. There, as he remained in intercession for some hours, he experienced an overwhelming sense of the presence and power of God. That lonely church tower became to him a holy of holies, and afterwards he wrote, "I felt suddenly my heart melting within me, like wax before the fire, with love to God my Saviour; and also felt, not only love and peace, but a longing to be dissolved with Christ. There was a cry in my inmost soul which I was totally unacquainted with before, 'Abba, Father!' . . . I knew I was His child, and that He loved and heard me. My soul being filled and satiated, cried, 'It is enough! I am satisfied! Give me strength and I will follow Thee through fire and water.'"[14]

Jonathan Edwards found solitude in an open field. While traveling on the Connecticut River he recorded, "At Saybrook we went ashore to lodge on Saturday, and there kept the Sabbath; where I had a sweet and refreshing season, walking alone in the fields."[15] More commonly he retreated to the woods for silence and solitude with God: "I rode out into the woods for my health, . . . having alighted from my horse in a retired place, as my manner commonly has been, to walk for divine contemplation and prayer."[16] You may not live near fields or woods, but there may be a park not far away that could provide a place to walk and think and pray with few distractions. A pharmacist in my church with four young children frequently stops at a park two blocks from where he lives for a few minutes of silence and solitude before going home in the evening. My favorite spot is the Morton Arboretum near my home.

Dawson Trotman routinely walked to a knoll at the end of his street. "Here he spent precious hours alone, praying aloud, singing praise to the Lord, quoting Scriptures of promise and challenge that flooded his mind—now wrestling in urgent prayer, now pacing the hillside in silence."[17] One of my best friends takes the index cards containing his prayer concerns and walks for blocks in his neighborhood while silently pouring his heart out before God.

Susanna Wesley, mother of John and Charles, had a very large family and for many years times of physical isolation were scarce. It is well known that when she needed silence and solitude she would bring her apron up over her head and read her Bible and pray underneath it. Obviously that did not block out all noise, but it was a sign to her children that for those minutes she was not to be bothered and the older ones were to care for the younger.

Like Susanna Wesley's, your place may not be ideal, and it may have to change from time to time, but it is possible to locate some singular spot for you to pursue Godliness through silence and solitude. Where is your special place?

Trade Off Daily Responsibilities

Arrange a trade-off system of daily responsibilities with your spouse, or a friend when necessary, in order to have the freedom for extended times of silence and solitude.

Your initial response to the suggestion of extended times in these Disciplines may have been, "You don't know my situation! I have a family to feed and take care of. I can't just leave them and go off by myself for hours at a time." Most people, including those who practice silence and solitude, have similar obligations that can't be neglected. The most practical, inexpensive method of overcoming this problem is to ask your spouse or a friend to temporarily assume your responsibilities in order to give you time alone. Then return the favor by providing the same or another service. Mothers of young children tell me this is the best, most workable way they've found for getting extended time for these Disciplines.

One word of warning: Reality can hit especially hard when you come home again. A mother of five told me she cushions the shock by preparing a meal in advance for the microwave or in a slow-cooker. If things are disorderly around the home when she returns, she can make her adjustment without having to worry about cooking right away. As tough as it is sometimes to come back, the rigors of reality only prove how much we need the refreshment of silence and solitude.

MORE APPLICATION

Will you seek daily times of silence and solitude? When Solomon's Temple was erected, "no hammer, chisel or any other iron tool was heard at the temple site while it was being built" (1 Kings 6:7). In like manner, our personal temple of the Holy Spirit (1 Corinthians 6:19) needs to be built up with interludes of silence and solitude. Schedule such a retreat for every day. The busier you are, the more hectic your world, the more you need to plan daily spaces of silence and solitude. A. W. Tozer expanded on this by saying,

> Retire from the world each day to some private spot, even if it be only the bedroom (for a while I retreated to the furnace room for want of a better place). Stay in the secret place till the surrounding noises begin to fade out of your heart and a sense of God's presence envelops you. . . . Listen for the inward Voice till you learn to recognize it. Stop trying to compete with others. Give yourself to God and then be what and who you are without regard to what others think. . . . Learn to pray inwardly every moment. After a while you can do this even while you work. . . . Read less, but more of what is important to your inner life. Never let your mind remain scattered for very long. Call home your roving thoughts. Gaze on Christ with the eyes of your soul. Practice spiritual concentration. All the above is contingent upon a right relation to God through Christ and daily meditation on the Scriptures. Lacking these, nothing will help us; granted these, the discipline recommended will go far to neutralize the evil effects of externalism and to make us acquainted with God and our own souls.[18]

As sleep and rest are needed each day for the body, so silence and solitude are needed each day for the soul. These Disciplines have a way of airing out the mind and ironing out the wrinkles of the soul. Plan to come to the quiet every day to meet God in His Word and through prayer.

Will you seek extended times of silence and solitude? Plan for them. Put them on the calendar. The routine and responsibilities of daily living will expand to fill all your time and keep you from spending protracted periods alone with God unless you act decisively.

You may need an extended time to settle your doubts or reestablish your spiritual moorings. That's what the late Francis Schaeffer did during a critical period of silence and solitude in 1951. He came to a crisis about reality that had two parts. He described his struggle this way:

> First, it seemed to me that among many of those who held the orthodox position one saw little reality in the things that the Bible so clearly said should be the result of Christianity. Second, it gradually grew on me that my own reality was less than it had been in the early days after I had become a Christian. I realized that in honesty I had to go back and rethink my whole position.[19]

This was a crisis important enough for extended times of silence and solitude. Of this period of days and days he said, "I walked in the mountains when it was clear and when it was rainy I walked back and forward in the hayloft of the old chalet where we lived. I walked, prayed, and thought through what the Scriptures taught as well as reviewing my own reasons for being a Christian."[20] Gradually he began to see that his problem was a lack of understanding what the Bible says about the meaning of the finished work of Christ for our present lives. And gradually, Schaeffer said, the sun came out again and the song came back. Those days of silence and solitude were a major turning point in his life and the foundation upon which the rest of his unique and now-famous ministry in L'Abri, Switzerland, was built.

Perhaps you need to get alone with God and deal with some doubts and questions. Maybe you have come to a crisis of faith that needs time for prayer, deep thinking, and much soul searching. There's too much at stake to neglect the matter or to deal with it superficially. If your body had an emergency, you would take the necessary time to deal with it. Don't do any less for an emergency of the soul.

But don't think of extended periods of silence and solitude as times only for dealing with doubts or for spiritual urgent care. The memoir of the first missionary from America, Adoniram Judson, tells this story:

> Once, when worn out with translations, and really needing rest, he went over the hills into the thick jungle, far beyond all human habitation. . . . To this place he brought his Bible, and sat down under the wild jungle trees to read, and meditate, and pray, and at night returned to the "hermitage" [a bamboo house he'd built at the edge of the jungle].[21]

Judson spent an incredible forty days like this in the dangerous jungle of Burma. But of this lifestyle, we are told, "He only adopted it *for a time.*" Why would he break his routine for this prolonged period of silence and solitude? His biographer says it was "as a means of moral improvement by which the whole of his future life might be rendered more in harmony with the perfect example of the Saviour whom he worshipped."[22] Judson engaged in this extended time of silence and solitude for purposes of rest, his future usefulness, and "for the purpose of godliness." Shouldn't you seek to do the same (even though forty hours may be more realistic for you than forty days)?

Will you start now? The time for silence and solitude will rarely be easy to chisel out of your schedule. The world, the flesh, and the Enemy of your soul will see to that. But if you discipline yourself to do it, your only regret will be that you didn't start sooner.

Don't expect each time of silence and solitude to have the same effect on your life as some of those quoted here from Christian history. There are not always dramatic results or intense emotions involved. More often than not, they are emotionally simple and serene. However, as with all the Spiritual Disciplines, silence and solitude are profitable even though sometimes you conclude them feeling "normal." Why not begin these refreshing Disciplines now?

These words from Jonathan Edwards are an appropriate concluding reminder:

> Some are greatly affected when in company; but have nothing that bears any manner of proportion to it in secret, in close meditation, prayer and conversing with God when alone, and separated from

the world. A true Christian doubtless delights in religious fellow-ship and Christian conversation, and finds much to affect his heart in it; but he also delights at times to retire from all mankind, to converse with God in solitude. And this also has peculiar advantages for fixing his heart, and engaging his affections. True religion disposes persons to be much alone in solitary places for holy meditation and prayer. . . . It is the nature of true grace, however it loves Christian society in its place, in a peculiar manner to delight in retirement, and secret converse with God.[23]

Will you commit yourself to the Disciplines of silence and solitude? If you've experienced God's saving grace, then silence and solitude will be, in the words of Edwards, a "delight," a faithful fountain of refreshment, joy, and transformation.

If I had them, I would almost bet you two million rubles on it.

NOTES

1. Anton Chekhov, "The Bet," in *Introduction to Literature* (New York: Rinehart and Company, 1948), vol. 2, pages 474-480.

2. Jean Fleming, *Finding Focus in a Whirlwind World* (Dallas: Roper Press, 1991), page 73.

3. Dallas Willard, *The Spirit of the Disciplines* (San Francisco, CA: Harper & Row, 1988), page 161.

4. Iain Murray, *Jonathan Edwards: A New Biography* (Edinburgh, Scotland: The Banner of Truth Trust, 1987), page 92.

5. George Whitefield as quoted from his Journals, in Arnold Dallimore, *George Whitefield: The Life and Times of the Great Evangelist of the Eighteenth-Century Revival* (Westchester, IL: Cornerstone Books, 1979), page 194.

6. Jonathan Edwards, ed., *The Life and Diary of David Brainerd*, revised edition ed. by Philip E. Howard, Jr. (Chicago: Moody Press, 1949), pages 83-84.

7. C. H. Spurgeon, "Solitude, Silence, Submission," in *Metropolitan Tabernacle Pulpit* (London: Passmore and Alabaster, 1896; reprint, Pasadena, TX: Pilgrim Publications, 1976), vol. 42, page 266.

8. John Pollack, *Billy Graham: The Authorized Biography* (London: Hodder and Stoughton, 1966), pages 80-81.

9. John Owen, *The Works of John Owen* (London: Johnstone and Hunter, 1850–1853; reprint, Edinburgh, Scotland: The Banner of Truth Trust, 1965), vol. 5, page 455.

10. Dr. and Mrs. Howard Taylor, *Hudson Taylor and the China Inland Mission: The Growth of a Work of God* (Singapore: China Inland Mission, 1918; special anniversary ed., Singapore: Overseas Missionary Fellowship, 1988), pages 31-32.

11. Willard, page 101.

12. Austin Phelps, *The Still Hour or Communion with God* (1859; reprint, Edinburgh, Scotland: The Banner of Truth Trust, 1974), page 64.

13. John Blanchard, comp., *More Gathered Gold* (Welwyn, Hertfordshire, England: Evangelical Press, 1986), page 295.

14. Dallimore, page 239.

15. Murray, page 53.

16. Murray, page 100.

17. Betty Lee Skinner, *Daws: The Story of Dawson Trotman, Founder of the Navigators* (Grand Rapids, MI: Zondervan, 1974), page 257.

18. Warren Wiersbe, comp., *The Best of A. W. Tozer* (Grand Rapids, MI: Baker Book House, 1978), pages 151-152.

19. Francis Schaeffer, *True Spirituality* (Wheaton, IL: Tyndale House Publishers, 1971), page ix.

20. Schaeffer, page ix.

21. Francis Wayland, *A Memoir of the Life and Labors of the Rev. Adoniram Judson*, D.D. (London: James Nisbet and Company, 1853), vol. 1, page 435.

22. Wayland, page 437.

23. Jonathan Edwards, *The Works of Jonathan Edwards*, rev. Edward Hickman (1834; reprint, Edinburgh, Scotland: The Banner of Truth Trust, 1974), vol. 1, pages 311-312.

CHAPTER ELEVEN

JOURNALING...
FOR THE PURPOSE OF GODLINESS

❖❖❖

*That there is a crying need for the recovery
of the devotional life cannot be denied. If anything
characterizes modern Protestantism, it is the absence
of spiritual disciplines or spiritual exercises.
Yet such disciplines form the core of the life of
devotion. It is not an exaggeration to state that this is
the lost dimension in modern Protestantism.*

Donald Bloesch
The Crisis of Piety

More than almost any other Discipline, journaling has a fascinating
appeal with nearly all who hear about it. One reason is the way journaling blends biblical doctrine and daily living, like the confluence of
two great rivers, into one. And since each believer's journey down life's
river involves bends and hazards previously unexplored by them on the
way to the Celestial City, something about journaling this journey
appeals to the adventuresome spirit of Christian growth.

Although the practice of journaling is not commanded in Scripture, it is modeled. And God has blessed the use of journals since
Bible times.

EXPLANATION OF JOURNALING

A *journal* (a word usually synonymous with *diary*) is a book in which
a person writes down various things. As a Christian, your journal is a
place to record the works and ways of God in your life. Your journal
also can include an account of daily events, a diary of personal relationships, a notebook of insights into Scripture, and a list of prayer
requests. It is where spontaneous devotional thoughts or lengthy theological musings can be preserved. A journal is one of the best places

for charting your progress in the other Spiritual Disciplines and for holding yourself accountable to your goals.

Woven throughout this fabric of entries and events are the colorful strands of your reflections and feelings about them. How you respond to these matters, and how you interpret them from your own spiritual perspective, are also at the heart of journaling.

The Bible itself contains many examples of God-inspired journals. Many psalms are records of David's personal spiritual journey with the Lord. We call the journal of Jeremiah's feelings about the fall of Jerusalem the book of Lamentations.

As you read this chapter, think prayerfully about joining these and others of God's people who have taken up the penned Discipline of journaling "for the purpose of godliness." Remember, the goal of becoming more like Jesus should be the main reason for beginning any Spiritual Discipline, including this one. With that fresh in your mind, consider the words of the United Kingdom's Maurice Roberts about journaling.

The logic of this practice is inevitable once men have felt the urge to become molded in heart and life to the pattern of Christ. No one will keep a record of his inward groans, fears, sins, experiences, providences and aspirations unless he is convinced of the value of the practice for his own spiritual progress. It was this very conviction which made it a commonplace practice in earlier times. We suggest the practice should be revived and something needs to be said in its defense.[1]

VALUE OF JOURNALING

Using a journal not only promotes spiritual growth by means of its own virtues, but it's a valuable aid to many other aspects of the spiritual life as well.

Help in Self-Understanding and Evaluation

In Romans 12:3 we're encouraged to have a balanced self-image: "Do not think of yourself more highly than you ought, but rather think of yourself with sober judgment." Journaling is certainly no guarantee against either conceit or self-abasement. But the simple discipline of recording the events of the day and noting my reactions to them causes me to examine myself much more thoroughly than I would otherwise.

This is no minor point or small need in our lives. A more God-centered theologian never lived than John Calvin, yet even he wrote on the first page of his monumental *Institutes*: "Without knowledge of self there is no knowledge of God."[2] Through the knowledge of ourselves and our condition, he explained, we are aroused to seek God. A journal can be the means by which the Holy Spirit shows us areas of sin or weakness, the emptiness of a path we have chosen, insight into our motives, or other things that can transform the journal page into an altar of seeking God.

At an 1803 meeting of the "Eclectic Society," where evangelical ministers of London met each week to sharpen their minds and deepen their fellowship by discussing theological issues, Josiah Pratt noted the value of a journal in self-examination.

> The practice of keeping a diary would promote vigilance. The lives of many are spent at a sort of hazard. They fall into certain religious habits: and are perhaps under no strong temptations. They are regular at church and sacrament, and in their families. They read the Bible and pray daily in secret. But here it ends. They know little of the progress or decline of the inner man. They are Christians, therefore, of very low attainments. The workings of sin are not noticed, as they should be, and therefore grace is not sought against them: and the genial emotions of grace are not noticed, and therefore not fostered and cultivated. Now, a diary would have a tendency to raise the standard to such persons by exciting vigilance.[3]

One of the ways the "progress or decline of the inner man" can be noted through journaling is by the observation of patterns in your life you've not seen before. When I review my journal entries for a month, six months, a year, I see myself and events more objectively. I can analyze my thoughts and actions apart from the feelings I had at the time. From that perspective it's easier to observe whether I've made spiritual progress or have backslidden in a particular area.

Journaling is not a time for navel gazing, however. Nor is it an excuse for becoming self-centered at the expense of a needy world. Writing on the Puritans and their relationship to society, Edmund S. Morgan cites an entry from the journal of a Godly young man during an illness from which he died in the late 1600s. In it the young man evaluates whether he had shown sufficient love to others. Then says Morgan,

> The fact that many Puritans kept diaries of this kind helps to explain their pursuit of social virtue: diaries were the reckoning books in which they checked the assets and liabilities of their souls in faith. When they opened these books, they set down lapses of morality with appropriate expressions of repentance and balanced them against the evidences of faith. Cotton Mather made a point of having at least one good action to set down in his diary on every day of the week.[4]

Used appropriately, instead of drawing us more into ourselves, a journal can actually become a means of propelling us into action for others.

The journal can be a mirror in the hands of the Holy Spirit in which He reveals His perspective on our attitudes, thoughts, words, and actions. Since we will be held accountable for each of these at the Judgment, evaluating them by *any* means is wisdom.

Help in Meditation

It seems as though more Christians are interested in biblical meditation (cf. Joshua 1:8, Psalm 1:1-3) than ever before. However, meaningful meditation requires a concentration not often developed in our fast-paced, media-distracted society.

I read the tale of a New England man convinced that nowhere in the world was fog any thicker than at his coastal home. Once while roofing his house, he claimed to be in a cloud so dense that he unknowingly continued on past the edge of the roof, "shingling off into the fog." Without pen in hand, I can get so distracted in meditation that I begin tacking one unrelated thought to another until I'm shingling off into the fog of daydreams instead of thinking in the light of Scripture. The discipline of writing down my meditations in my journal helps me concentrate.

Sitting with pen and paper also heightens my expectation of hearing from God as I think on Him and His words in the passage before me. I always listened better in school when I was taking notes. I'm the same way with hearing a sermon; I listen more attentively when I'm writing down the more significant thoughts of the message. The same principle transfers to journaling. When I record in a journal my meditations on a passage of Scripture, I can follow more closely the still, small voice of God as He speaks through the text.

Help in Expressing Thoughts and Feelings to the Lord

No matter how close the friendship or how intimate the marriage, we can't always tell others what we think. And yet sometimes our feelings are so strong and our thoughts so dominant that we *must* find some way to give them expression. Our Father is always available and willing to listen. "Pour out your hearts to him," says Psalm 62:8.

A journal is a place where we can give expression to the fountain of our heart, where we can unreservedly pour out our passion before the Lord.

Since human thoughts and emotions range between the extremes of exhilaration and despondency, we can expect to find both within the pages of our journal. That's true in all the well-known journals of church history. Notice the depths in which David Brainerd found himself in this entry:

> Lord's Day, December 16, 1744. Was so overwhelmed with dejection that I knew not how to live. I longed for death exceedingly; my soul was sunk into deep waters and the floods were ready to drown me. I was so much oppressed that my soul was in a kind of horror. I could not keep my thoughts fixed in prayer for the space of one minute, without fluttering and distraction. It made me exceedingly ashamed that I did not live to God. I had no distressing doubt about my own state, but I would have cheerfully ventured (as far as I could possibly know) into eternity. While I was going to preach to the Indians, my soul was in anguish. I was so overborne with discouragement that I despaired of doing any good, and was driven to my wit's end. I knew nothing what to say, nor what course to take.[5]

A short time later, on the other hand, his journal reveals this profound expression of joy:

> Lord's Day, February 17, 1745. I think, I was scarce ever enabled to offer the free grace of God to perishing sinners with more freedom and plainness in my life. Afterwards, I was enabled

earnestly to invite the children of God to come renewedly and drink of this fountain of water of life, from whence they have heretofore derived unspeakable satisfaction. It was a very comfortable time to me. There were many tears in the assembly and I doubt not but that the Spirit of God was there, convincing poor sinners of their need of Christ. In the evening I felt composed and comfortable, though much tired. I had some sweet sense of the excellency and glory of God; and my soul rejoiced that He was "God over all, blessed forever"; but was too much crowded with company and conversation and longed to be more alone with God. Oh, that I could forever bless God for the mercy of this day, who "answered me in the joy of my heart."[6]

Perhaps you read Brainerd's words with the same sense of distance from your own experience as I do. Was he odd? Did he live on some higher spiritual plane inaccessible to Christians like myself? Can the difference between his experiences with God and mine be explained exclusively by the difference in our times? Because I am unable to express in writing the kinds of emotions toward God that he did, am I the one who is strange?

I think it is possible for every child of God to experience more of what Brainerd expresses here, and a journal can help make the difference. Maurice Roberts explains,

A spiritual diary will tend to deepen and sanctify the emotional life of a child of God. There is great value to us of becoming more deeply emotional over the great issues of our faith. Our age is not deep enough in feelings. Biblical men are depicted as weeping copious tears, as sighing and groaning, as on occasion rejoicing with ecstasy. They were ravished by the very idea of God. They had a passion for Jesus Christ—His person, offices, names, titles, words and works. It is our shame to be so cold, unfeeling and unemotional in spite of all that God has done to us and for us in Christ. . . . The keeping of a diary might help to put us right in this respect also.[7]

By slowing us down and prompting us to *think* more deeply about God, journaling helps us *feel* more deeply (and biblically) about God.

It provides an opportunity for the intangible grays of mindwork and heartwork to distill clearly into black and white. Then we're better able to talk to God with both mind and spirit.

Help in Remembering the Lord's Works
Many people think God has not blessed them with much until they have to move it all to a new address! In the same way, we tend to forget just how many times God has answered specific prayers, made timely provision, and done marvelous things in our lives. But having a place to collect all these memories prevents their being forgotten.

A journal helps us to be like Asaph in Psalm 77:11-12, who said, "I will remember the deeds of the LORD; yes, I will remember your miracles of long ago. I will meditate on all your works and consider all your mighty deeds." Even the kings of Israel were required by the Lord to write for themselves a copy of the Law of Moses to help them remember what God had said and done in the lives of the Patriarchs (Deuteronomy 17:18).

The testimony of Luci Shaw, widow of the late Christian publisher Harold Shaw, illustrates how a journal is not only helpful but *essential* when remembering that the works of the Lord are important to you.

> All my life long I've thought I should keep a journal. But I never did until a few years ago, when the discovery that my husband, Harold, had cancer suddenly plunged us into the middle of an intense learning experience, facing things we'd never faced before. Confronted with agonizing decisions, we would cry out to the Lord, "Where are you in the middle of this?" It suddenly occurred to me that unless I made a record of what was going on, I would forget. The events, details, and people of those painful days could easily become a blur. So I started to write it all down.[8]

Francis Bacon put it bluntly, "If a man write little, he had need have a great memory."[9]

One of the greatest benefits of keeping a record of the works of the Lord is the encouragement it can be to faith and prayer. C. H. Spurgeon, the lionhearted British Baptist preacher in the last half of the 1800s, said, "I have sometimes said, when I have become the prey of doubting thoughts, 'Well, now, I dare not doubt whether there be a God, for

I can look back in my Diary, and say, On such a day, in the depths of trouble, I bent my knee to God, and or ever I had risen from my knees, the answer was given me."[10]

"How worthy it is to remember former benefits," said Stephen Charnock, author of the classic *The Existence and Attributes of God*, "when we come to beg for new."[11] A journal is one of the best ways to keep fresh the memory of the Lord's "former benefits."

Help in Creating and Preserving a Spiritual Heritage

Journaling is an effective way of teaching the things of God to our children and transmitting our faith into the future (cf. Deuteronomy 6:4-7, 2 Timothy 1:5).

We may never know the future spiritual impact of something we write today. My dad died suddenly on August 20, 1985. He was the manager of a small-town radio station. Each morning he hosted a thirty-minute program of music and local news. On his desk I found the devotional material he had used to begin his final broadcast. He had read the words to William Cowper's hymn, "God Moves in a Mysterious Way." Finding his initials and "8/19/85" written beside these lines of faith has given me more comfort and spiritual strength than anything said to me by anyone else. After his death his old guitar became one of my most cherished possessions. His early days as an announcer came during the time when almost everything on radio was broadcast live. He had a popular show of his own in which he played this guitar and sang. On my first Thanksgiving Day without a dad I was rummaging around in the guitar case. In it I found more than a dozen old letters postmarked within a few days after my birth. Every one of them was from his listeners writing to rejoice with him that my mother and I had survived a difficult birth. They noted that it was obvious he was very proud of me and referred to remarks he had made on the air about his gratitude to the Lord for my safe arrival. I sat in the floor by the open case with these scraps of my heritage and wept tears of thanksgiving to the Lord for this remnant of his life. How precious it would be if only more of his walk with God were recorded for me in a journal.

Never underestimate the power of a written record of faith acting as a spiritual time capsule. The writer of Psalm 102:18 recognized it when he said of his experience with God: "Let this be written for a future generation, that a people not yet created may praise the LORD."

Help in Clarifying and Articulating Insights and Impressions
An old adage says that thoughts disentangle themselves when passed through the lips and across the fingertips. While reading makes a full man, and dialogue a ready man, according to Francis Bacon, *writing* makes an *exact* man. I've discovered that if I write down the meditations of my quiet time with the Lord, those impressions stay with me much longer. Without journaling, by day's end I usually can remember little from my devotional time.

The great champion of prayer and faith, George Muller, used his journal to articulate insights into Scripture and spiritual impressions.

July 22, 1838. This evening I was walking in our little garden, meditating on Hebrews 13:8, "Jesus Christ is the same yesterday and today, and forever." Whilst meditating on His unchangeable love, power and wisdom, and turning all as I went into prayer respecting myself; and whilst applying also His unchangeable love, power, and wisdom both to my present spiritual and temporal circumstances—all at once the present need of the orphan houses was brought to my mind. Immediately I was led to say to myself, "Jesus in His love and power has hitherto supplied me with what I have needed for the orphans, and in the same unchangeable love and power He will provide me with what I may need for the future." A flow of joy came into my soul whilst realising thus the unchangeableness of our adorable Lord. About one minute after, a letter was brought me enclosing a cheque for twenty pounds. In it was written: "Will you apply the amount of the enclosed cheque to the objects of your Scriptural Knowledge Society, or of your Orphan Establishment, or in the work and cause of our Master in any way that He Himself, on your application to Him, may point out to you. It is not a great sum, but it is a sufficient provision for the exigency of today; and it is for *today's* exigencies that ordinarily the Lord provides. Tomorrow, as it brings its demands, will find its supply."[12]

When insights from my quiet time are clearly fixed in my mind through journaling, I've also found them ready to use later in conversation, counseling, encouraging, and witnessing (see 1 Peter 3:15).

Help in Monitoring Goals and Priorities

A journal is a good way to keep before us the things we want to do and emphasize. Some put a list of goals and priorities in their journal and review it every day. I draw a small rectangle at the beginning of each journal entry. With one horizontal line and two vertical lines I divide the box into six tiny squares. Each square represents a particular spiritual accomplishment I want to do every day, such as encouraging at least one person. Before I make a journal entry for a day, I turn to the entry for the previous day and color in the appropriate squares for the daily goals I accomplished. Some may see this as legalism. For me it's a way of reminding myself to do some things I want to do as part of pressing on toward the goal of Christlikeness (Philippians 3:12-16).

The resolutions made by young Jonathan Edwards are still well known to many Christians today. They included the resolve of his soul concerning the use of time, temperance in eating, growth in grace, duty, self-denial, and other matters dealt with in seventy resolutions. These were much more than today's halfhearted New Year's resolutions. They became Edwards's lifelong spiritual goals and priorities. What isn't so well known is how he evaluated his conduct daily by these resolutions and recorded the results in his journal. On Christmas Eve, 1722, he wrote, "Higher thoughts than usual of the excellency of Christ and his kingdom. Concluded to observe, at the end of every month, the number of breaches of resolutions, to see whether they increase or diminish, to begin from this day, and to compute from that the weekly account my monthly increase, and out of the whole, my yearly increase, beginning from new-year days."[13] An example of this use of his journal is found in the entry of the following January 5: "A little redeemed from a long, dreadful dullness, about reading the Scriptures. This week, have been unhappily low in the weekly account:—and what are the reasons of it?—abundance of listlessness and sloth; and, if this should continue much longer, I perceive that other sins will begin to discover themselves."[14]

The ocean-hopping evangelist of the Great Awakening, George Whitefield, is best remembered for his inimitable, passionate preaching. Like his contemporary Edwards, Whitefield's *Diary* reveals that his spirituality was at least as deep as his influence was wide. The book begins with a list of criteria that he used each night as a basis of self-examination.

Have I,

1. Been fervent in prayer?
2. Used stated hours of prayer?
3. Used ejaculatory prayer each hour?
4. After or before every deliberate conversation or action, considered how it might tend to God's glory?
5. After any pleasure, immediately given thanks?
6. Planned business for the day?
7. Been simple and recollected in everything?
8. Been zealous in undertaking and active in doing what good I could?
9. Been meek, cheerful, affable in everything I said or did?
10. Been proud, vain, unchaste, or enviable of others?
11. Recollected in eating and drinking? Thankful? Temperate in sleep?
12. Taken time for giving thanks according to (William) Law's rules?
13. Been diligent in studies?
14. Thought or spoken unkindly of anyone?
15. Confessed all sins?[15]

Each day's entry in Whitefield's *Diary* is in two parts, one page per part. On the first page he would list the specific activities of his day, then evaluate each on the basis of his fifteen questions. On the second page, according to his biographer, Arnold Dallimore, "He records any unusual activity throughout the day, but above all, gives expression to his inner self. The longings of his soul, a searching of his motives, severe self-reproach for the slightest wrong and bursts of praise to God, are all recorded without inhibition."[16]

How did men like Edwards and Whitefield become so unusually conformed to the image of Christ? Part of their secret was their use of the Spiritual Discipline of journaling to maintain self-accountability for their spiritual goals and priorities. Before we give all the reasons why we cannot be the kind of disciples they were, let us try doing what they did.

Help in Maintaining the Other Spiritual Disciplines

My journal is the place where I record my progress with all the Spiritual Disciplines. For instance, I also use some of these small squares to keep myself accountable with Disciplines like Scripture memory. It's very easy for me to become lazy and slip away from memorizing God's Word, which the Bible says is so essential to holiness (Psalm 119:11). Once I return to the habit of *not* memorizing Scripture, momentum keeps me there. However, when I have a daily prompter such as my journal, where I find a reminder to "discipline myself for the purpose of godliness," I can more easily reverse the momentum.

The flesh, our natural inclination toward sin, does not contribute to our spiritual growth. Unless we *labor* to put to death the misdeeds of the body (Romans 8:13), our progress in Godliness will be very slow. Unless we find *practical* ways to cooperate with the Holy Spirit against our congenital tendency toward spiritual sloth, we will not build ourselves up in the faith (Jude 20); we will drift toward spiritual entropy instead.

This fact was affirmed by Maurice Roberts in an article, "Where Have the Saints Gone?"

> There will be no marked growth in Christian holiness if we do not labor to overcome our natural disinclination towards secret spiritual exercises. Our forefathers kept honest diaries where the soul's battles were recorded. Thomas Shepherd, Pilgrim Father and founder of Harvard, wrote in his private papers, "It is sometimes so with me that I will rather die than pray." So is it with us all. But this honesty is not commonplace. Such men climbed high only as they labored with sweat and tears to cultivate the soul. We, too, must "exercise ourselves unto godliness" (1 Timothy 4:7).[17]

Missionary Jim Elliot used his now-famous journal to irrigate the practice of the Disciplines in his life when the tide of zeal for them ran low. On November 20, 1955, less than two months before he was killed by Auca Indians in Ecuador, he wrote,

> Also read parts of *Behind the Ranges* and am resolute to do something about it in my private devotional and prayer life. In studying Spanish I left off English Bible reading, and my devotional reading pattern was broken. I have never restored it. Translation and preparation for daily Bible lessons is not

sufficient to empower my soul. Prayer as a single man was difficult, I remember, because my mind always reverted to Betty. Now it's too hard to get out of bed in the morning. I have made resolutions on this score before now but not followed them up. Tomorrow it's to be—dressed by 6:00 a.m. and study in the Epistles before breakfast. So help me, God.[18]

Apparently the desire to revitalize his devotional life had surged through Elliot's mind and emotions many times before. Transferring that desire to paper, however, seemed to channel it like water into a turbine, so that what was once mere fluid desire began producing power.

Recording the joys and freedom I experience through the Spiritual Disciplines is another way journaling helps maintain my involvement with them. When I review my journal and read in my own handwriting of my inexpressible delight in sharing the gospel with elderly people in the bush of Kenya who have never heard of Jesus, or of preaching and seeing Brazilian teenagers repent of involvement in spiritism, I am resolved to maintain the Discipline of evangelism in overseas missions projects regardless of the cost. Reviewing the sense of victory I recorded during a day of fasting creates in me a hunger for another such day of spiritual feasting.

The Christian life is, by definition, a living thing. If we can think of the Discipline of Bible intake as its food and prayer as its breath, many Christians have made journaling its heart. For them it pumps life-maintaining blood into every Discipline connected with it.

WAYS OF JOURNALING

How is it done? "Your way of keeping a journal is the right way. . . . There are no rules for keeping a journal!"[19]

Today I was in a local Christian bookstore and noticed at least a dozen books to be used as journals. There were cloth-covered volumes and paperbacks. Some had devotional thoughts or inspirational quotes on each page. Others simply provided blank pages with headings like "Prayer Requests" and "Insights from Scripture" at the top. Numerous bookstores sell beautifully bound, gilt-edged books of empty pages, which work well as journals.

Many Christians find that the most practical approach is to use everyday notebook paper. While some prefer a spiral-bound notebook,

I find loose-leaf pages more workable. Besides being less expensive, using plain paper also does not force you to confine your entries to the designated space of a preprinted journal book. On the other hand, some find that writing in an attractive book gives their journaling a special appeal that stimulates their faithfulness in the Discipline. (This motivation backfires on some people when they feel as though their entries are rather mundane for such a fine depository. They begin writing less frequently and soon stop altogether.)

Another reason I prefer the loose-leaf format is convenience. Although it is handy to carry around a book or spiral-bound notebook to journal in, it's even handier to carry only a few pages of paper. My journal pages are eight-and-a-half by five-and-a-half inches and fit easily into my Bible, briefcase, a book, or almost anything I take with me. In fact, I keep packages of journal paper in my briefcase, my study at home, and my study at church as well. That way I can record any sudden flash of insight, impression, conversation, quotation, etc., I've come across as soon as it happens. I usually let the pages accumulate for about a month. Around the beginning of a new month, I take the collection and put them in a ring binder, which is kept at home. This leads to two other advantages over the book or spiral notebook method: (1) if I ever lose my current journal, I never lose more than a month's worth, and (2) I can easily go back and insert new pages, photocopies, etc., if they pertain to previous entries. But having said that, I return to this maxim: "Your way of keeping a journal is the right way." Use the method that works best for you.

The means you use to actually put the words on paper will also affect the format you choose. I like to make my journal entries on a word processor. That's because I can type faster than I can write, and also because it looks neater when it's printed. Frequently, however, my journaling time occurs when I'm at my church study rather than at home, so I journal on a typewriter. Still other times require that I write by hand. Some feel strongly about only journaling by hand, that it's more spontaneous and expressive. That's not true in my case. I find that the speed of the word processor or the typewriter actually allows me more freedom of expression than does writing script.

With the rise of technology will likely come the increase of using its capabilities for journaling. A *Chicago Tribune* article reported that there is now a Japanese company that uses technology to help busy people with their journaling. For those who feel too busy to write their entries at the end of a day, they simply dial a number and say what they want to enter into their journal. This is tape-recorded. At the end of each month, the customer is sent a printed copy of his or her journal in an attractive binder. Perhaps this will work for those who only want to record the facts and events of the day. But it seems a bit too impersonal to use as a means of interaction with the Lord and of significant spiritual growth. I still find it difficult to imagine expressing my deepest thoughts and feelings to the Lord over the phone, much less doing so as the bill gets higher by the minute! This doesn't even take into account the fact that someone must transcribe the intimacies of your journal from the tape recorder to printed form. Despite technological advances, there will always be a place in journaling for the simple tools of pen and paper.

For those using a medium other than pen and paper, be careful not to confine your journaling only to the times when you have access to your computer or typewriter. Many of the best journal entries are made in times of solitude away from typical circumstances. Many of my most memorable entries are made when I'm traveling and can only write them by hand. These aren't as neat as my typed entries, but I can overlook the variety in the appearance of the pages for the value of what's on them. The general warning is: Don't be bound to only one method of making entries.

As a starting entry for each day, try listing the one verse or idea from your Bible reading that impressed you most. Meditate on that for a few minutes, then record your insights and impressions. From there consider adding recent events in your life and your feelings and responses to them, brief prayers, joys, successes, failures, quotations, etc.

Don't think that "official journaling" (there is no such thing!) means you have to write a certain number of lines every day, or even that you have to write every day. I try to write in my journal daily, but if I don't, I refuse to feel guilty about it. Whenever I seem to be content with needlessly long lapses in making entries, I discipline myself to write at least one sentence per day. Inevitably, that one sentence turns willingly into a paragraph or a page.

MORE APPLICATION

As with all the Disciplines, journaling can be fruitful at any level of involvement with it. Journaling is profitable regardless of how well you think you write, compose, or spell. Whether or not you write every day, whether you write much or little, whether your soul soars like a psalmist's or plods from thought to thought, journaling will help you grow in grace.

As with all the Disciplines, journaling requires persistence through the dry times. The novelty of journaling soon wears off. There will be days when you will have a spiritual version of "writer's block." At other times you just won't have any insights from the Scriptures or your experience with God which seem noteworthy. While it's okay to write little or nothing on a given day or during a longer stretch of time, remember that you must eventually push through this barrier in order to enjoy the long-term benefits of journaling. In other words, don't quit the Discipline entirely just because the excitement of the first day eventually erodes. That will happen. Plan on it. But also plan for persistence.

As with all the Disciplines, you must start journaling before you can experience its value. Irishman Thomas Houston was pastor of a Presbyterian church in Knockbracken, County Down (near modern Belfast), for fifty-four years during the 1800s. At the beginning of his ministry there he began keeping a journal, which he called "A Diary of God's Dealings and Providences with a Most Unworthy Sinner." In his entry for April 8, 1828, he reveals the inward struggle that ultimately resulted in the birth of his Spiritual Discipline of journaling:

> For a considerable period I have been resolved on keeping a register of the dealings and providences of my Heavenly Father towards me, but, what through want of what I considered a fit opportunity, and through what was, I fear, a greater cause, spiritual sloth, I have hitherto neglected it. When I first began to think of this subject, various objections appeared to me to lie against diary writing altogether. It would give room for spiritual pride; it led persons to measure themselves by themselves; and as it is not easy to determine between the motions of the spirit and the natural outworkings of the unrenewed conscience or the artifices of the Deceiver, there is a danger of forming incorrect judgments. These and other reasons kept me a length of time from determining for the thing. Of late I have got over these objections entirely, and am now of the opinion that such a

record may be of much service to an individual to furnish him with matter for prayer and self-examination, and to be a monument to God's faithfulness.[20]

Perhaps you can identify with Houston's struggle. As millions want to begin walking, jogging, biking, or some other form of exercise but never do, so there are many who have wanted to begin the spiritual exercise of journaling but have never done it. It sounds interesting, and you are convinced of its value, but the words never find their way to the paper. There just never seems to be the time, a "fit opportunity" as Houston called it. But in our heart of hearts we know that the "greater cause" is probably the same "spiritual sloth" that clung drowsily to the will of this Irish pastor. Consider journaling, not only "for the purpose of godliness," but also as a way to raise up a "monument of God's faithfulness" in your life.

NOTES

1. Maurice Roberts, "Are We Becoming Reformed Men?" *The Banner of Truth*, issue 330, March 1991, page 5.
2. John Calvin, *Institutes of the Christian Religion*, ed. John T. McNeil, trans. and indexed by Ford Lewis Battles (Philadelphia, PA: Westminster, 1960), vol. 2, page 35.
3. Josiah H. Pratt, ed., *The Thought of the Evangelical Leaders* (James Nisbet, 1856; reprint, Edinburgh, Scotland: The Banner of Truth Trust, 1978), page 305.
4. Edmund S. Morgan, *The Puritan Family* (New York: Harper & Row, 1966), page 5.
5. Jonathan Edwards, ed., *The Life and Diary of David Brainerd*, revised edition ed. by Philip E. Howard, Jr. (Chicago, IL: Moody Press, 1949), page 186.
6. Edwards, page 193.
7. Roberts, page 6.
8. LaVonne Neff, et al., ed., *Practical Christianity* (Wheaton, IL: Tyndale House, 1987), page 310.
9. Ralph Woods, ed., *A Treasury of the Familiar* (Chicago, IL: Peoples Book Club, 1945), page 14.
10. C. H. Spurgeon, *Autobiography, Volume 1: The Early Years, 1834-1859*, rev. ed. in 2 vols., comp. Susannah Spurgeon and Joseph Harrald (Edinburgh, Scotland: The Banner of Truth Trust, 1962), page 122.
11. Stephen Charnock, *The Existence and Attributes of God* (Robert Carter and Brothers, 1853; reprint, Grand Rapids, MI: Baker Book House, 1979), vol. 1, page 277.
12. Roger Steer, ed., *The George Muller Treasury* (Westchester, IL: Crossway Books, 1987), pages 55-56.

13. Jonathan Edwards, *The Works of Jonathan Edwards*, rev. Edward Hickman (1834; reprint, Edinburgh, Scotland: The Banner of Truth Trust, 1974), vol. 1, page xxiv.

14. Edwards, page xxiv.

15. Arnold Dallimore, *George Whitefield: The Life and Times of the Great Evangelist of the Eighteenth-Century Revival* (Westchester, IL: Crossway Books, 1979), vol. 1, page 80.

16. Dallimore, pages 80-81.

17. Maurice Roberts, "Where Have the Saints Gone?" *The Banner of Truth*, October 1988, page 4.

18. Elisabeth Elliot, ed., *The Journals of Jim Elliot* (Old Tappan, NJ: Fleming H. Revell, 1978), page 474.

19. Ronald Klug, *How to Keep a Spiritual Journal* (Nashville, TN: Thomas Nelson, 1982), page 58.

20. Edward Donnelly, ed., "The Diary of Thomas Houston of Knockbracken," *The Banner of Truth*, August-September 1989, pages 11-12.

CHAPTER TWELVE

LEARNING...
FOR THE PURPOSE OF GODLINESS

❖❖❖

We must face the fact that many today are notoriously
careless in their living. This attitude finds its way
into the church. We have liberty, we have money,
we live in comparative luxury. As a result,
discipline practically has disappeared. What
would a violin solo sound like if the strings
on the musician's instrument were all hanging loose,
not stretched tight, not "disciplined"?

A. W. Tozer
quoted in *Christianity Today* (November 20, 1987)

More than a decade ago I pastored a church near a small town with two small universities. One school was the main educational institution of the largest evangelical denomination in the state. Known for producing students zealous for Christ's Kingdom, this university consistently led the dozens of other schools in its denomination in numbers of alumni on the mission field. One complaint I frequently heard from students in the religion department, however, related to the apparent lack of spiritual zeal among two or three of the professors. To many students, these were men with overgrown theological brains and pygmy-like, passionless hearts. We've all heard teachers or preachers who could anchor a theological Mensa Club but whose Christianity seemed as dry and stale as the inside of a basketball. But that just doesn't sound like the Lord Jesus, or even the Apostle Paul, does it?

In this same pastorate a man who was a deacon in his church once said to me, "I never liked school, and I don't want to learn anything when I come to church." Somehow there's something unlike Jesus in that attitude as well, isn't there?

Why do we seem to think we must choose between the two? Why do many Christians live as though they've been told, "Choose you this day whom you will serve: scholarship or devotion"? I maintain that a biblically balanced Christian has both a full head and a full heart, radiating both spiritual light and heat.

If absolutely forced to have only one or the other, we must choose the burning heart. If we have the truth in our head but our hearts are not right with God, an awareness of the truth will only magnify our guilt before Him at the Judgment. But if we have properly responded to the gospel from the heart, in the end we shall be saved even though the rest of our doctrinal understanding is shallow or muddy. Not only would I choose that option for myself, but I would prefer that for those I pastor as well. It's much harder to get a ship out of the harbor than to correct one on the sea that has drifted off course.

But let us be both out of the harbor *and* on course. Christians must realize that just as a fire cannot blaze without fuel, so burning hearts are not kindled by brainless heads. We must not be content to have zeal without knowledge.

Does this mean we must be brilliant to be Christians? Absolutely not. But it does mean that to be like Jesus we must be learners even as He was at only age twelve, "sitting among the teachers, listening to them and asking them questions. Everyone who heard him was amazed at his understanding and his answers" (Luke 2:46-47). Does this mean we must have several diplomas hanging on the wall to be first-rate Christians? It certainly does not. But it does mean that we should discipline ourselves to be intentional learners like Jesus, of whom it was marveled, "How did this man get such learning without having studied?" (John 7:15).

An examination of the word *disciple* reveals that it means to be not only "a follower" of Christ but also "a learner." To follow Christ and become more like Him, we must engage in the Spiritual Discipline of learning.

LEARNING CHARACTERIZES THE WISE PERSON

According to a book of the Bible written specifically to give us wisdom, one of the characteristics of a wise man or woman is a desire for learning. We read in Proverbs 9:9, "Instruct a wise man and he will be wiser still; teach a righteous man and he will add to his learning." Wise and righteous people can never get enough wisdom or knowledge. Those unteachable or prideful about their learning only reveal how shallow they really are. There is humility with the truly wise because they know there is so much they have yet to learn. This verse says that wise and righteous people are teachable. They can learn from anybody, regardless of age. Give one of them instruction and "he will be wiser still and he will add to his learning." Those who are wise are always looking to learn.

In Proverbs 10:14 we're told, "Wise men store up knowledge." The Hebrew word here means to store up like a treasure. Wise men and women love to learn because they realize that knowledge is like a precious treasure.

Imagine the great bulk of knowledge being inaccessible to you. During the mission trip to Kenya I mentioned in chapter 2 that I met a schoolteacher in his early thirties named Bernard. He lived in the back of a store that was one of four buildings in the Kilema community. He walked several miles even further into the bush country each day to the mud-brick elementary school where he taught. He returned home to his "cube," an eight-foot-by-eight-foot-by-eight-foot room where he lived with his wife and infant son. A twin bed was against the back wall with a sheet hanging from the ceiling to separate the "bedroom" from the rest of the cube. Only a small table with one chair occupied the front half. What interested me most was what he had on the cement walls. On every wall were several pages from long-outdated magazines or pictures from old calendars. He explained that they were all he had to read. Though he'd been a Christian for many years, he was too poor even to own a Bible. The only books that ever came into his hands were a few secondhand books the teachers used at the school.

So as he holds his son to get him to go to sleep he reads the words on the magazines for the umpteenth time. While he eats at his table or lays on his bed, he looks at the pictures of far-off people and places and wonders what they are like. As I stood in that concrete cube, looking at a couple of dozen faded pictures and yellowing pages, I realized that before me stood a wise man. Bernard understands that knowledge really is like a rare treasure. Though it is more scarce than gold, he had stored up all he could. That's the attitude all who are wise will have, for "wise men store up knowledge." (Incidentally, some people in our church have since sent Bernard boxes of books and subscribed to a couple of magazines for him.)

Notice Proverbs 18:15: "The heart of the discerning acquires knowledge; the ears of the wise seek it out." Wise people not only "acquire" knowledge, they "seek" it. They desire to learn and discipline themselves to seek opportunities to learn.

One other verse in Proverbs deserves our attention. In 23:12 we're commanded, "Apply your heart to instruction and your ears to words of knowledge." No matter how much you know, especially about God, Christ, the Bible, and the Christian life, you still need to apply your heart to learn, for you haven't learned it all. And no matter how intelligent or slow you may think you are, according to this verse you are to diligently apply your heart and ears to learn.

Learning is a lifelong Discipline, a Spiritual Discipline that characterizes the wise person. Samuel Hopkins, one of the early biographers of Jonathan Edwards, said that when he met Edwards he was impressed by the fact that a man already twenty years in the ministry had still "an uncommon thirst for knowledge . . . he read all the books, especially books of divinity, that he could come at."[1] Edwards had an undeniably superior mind, but he never stopped applying it to learn. It was that, blended with an equally strong devotional zeal, that made him wise and great in the Kingdom of God.

A durable yearning for learning characterizes all those who are truly wise.

FULFILLING THE GREATEST COMMANDMENT

Part of what Jesus said was God's greatest commandment is, "Love the Lord your God . . . with all your mind" (Mark 12:29-30). What God wants most from you is your love. And one of the ways He wants you show love and obedience to Him is by Godly learning. God is glorified when we use the mind He made to learn of Him, His ways, His Word, and His world.

Lamentably, many Christians do not associate learning with loving God. In fact, we live in a very anti-intellectual age. That may sound strange in a day when the world's entire body of knowledge doubles every few years, when there are more advanced academic degrees being awarded than ever before, and when everything is moving toward "high tech." Perhaps it is precisely because of such events that people— including Christian people—are more averse to things intellectual. Kids who are smart may be unpopular just because they are smart. They are the "nerds," and the "underachievers" get the social attention. Our culture glorifies the physical and the material. Nobody sells posters of the top software engineers or architects, much less the leading theologians. Instead we sell posters of ballplayers, some of whom can do everything with a ball except read its label. Some political candidates are now referred to as too intellectual to be electable, almost as though we don't want thinkers running the government. In the Church we want everything to be "relevant," and we tend to think of theology and doctrine as very irrelevant.

There is an intellectual*ism* that is wrong, but it is also wrong to be anti-intellectual. We are to love God just as much with our mind as with our heart and soul and strength. How can it all fit together? As contemporary Christian thinker R. C. Sproul wrote, "God has made us with a harmony of heart and head, of thought and action. . . . The more we know Him the more we are able to love Him. The more we love Him the more we seek to know Him. To be central in our hearts He must be foremost in our minds. Religious thought is the prerequisite to religious affection and obedient action."[2]

Unless we love God with a growing mind, we will be like Christian versions of the Samaritans to whom Jesus said, "You Samaritans worship what you do not know" (John 4:22).

LEARNING—ESSENTIAL FOR INCREASED GODLINESS

How is it that we are to be transformed into Christlikeness? The Bible indicates that one of the crucial elements in the process is learning when it says, "Do not conform any longer to the pattern of this world, but be *transformed* by the renewing of your mind" (Romans 12:2, emphasis mine). Growth in Godliness involves a mental renewal that cannot happen without learning. And the alternative to transformation via learning is conformity to the world.

Think of it this way. How is it that faith is exercised? It is a gift of God that is expressed only after there is the hearing with understanding of a particular message, namely the gospel. Thus Romans 10:14, "And how can they believe in the one of whom they have not heard?" Just as we cannot believe and love Him of whom we have not heard, so we cannot grow in our faith and love of Him if we do not learn more about Him. We will not *grow* much in Godliness if we do not know much of what it means to be Godly. We will not become more like Christ if we don't know more of what Christ is like.

The late London preacher Martyn Lloyd-Jones reminded us, "Let us never forget that the message of the Bible is addressed primarily to the mind, to the understanding."[3] No one is changed by an unread Bible. No one grows into a Godliness he or she knows nothing about. The Word of God must go through our head if it's going to change our heart and our life.

The absence of the Discipline of learning explains why many professing believers seem to grow so little in Godliness. Richard Foster makes the same point, referring to learning as the Discipline of study.

> Many Christians remain in bondage to fears and anxieties simply because they do not avail themselves of the Discipline of study. They may be faithful in church attendance and earnest in fulfilling their religious duties and still they are not changed. I am not here speaking only of those who are going through mere religious forms, but of those who are genuinely seeking to worship and obey Jesus Christ as Lord and Master. They may sing with gusto, pray in the Spirit, live as obediently as they know how, . . . and yet the tenor of their lives remains unchanged. Why? Because they have never taken up one of the central ways God uses to change us: study.[4]

Besides more conformity to the world and a lack of growth in Godliness, those who are not disciplined learners have little spiritual discernment and become prime targets for the cults, New Age influence, and other false prophets.

The Bible tells us to be like Christ, but it also warns us not to be foolish, untaught, naive, or ignorant. Taken together these two strands of truth tell us we must *learn* to be like Jesus.

LEARNING IS MOSTLY BY DISCIPLINE, NOT BY ACCIDENT

As every dustball gets bigger the longer it rolls around under the bed, so every mind picks up at least a little knowledge the longer it rolls around on the earth. But we must not assume that we have learned true wisdom just by growing older. The observation found in Job 32:9 is, "The abundant in years may not be wise" (NASB). Age and experience alone don't increase your spiritual maturity. Becoming like

Jesus doesn't happen incidentally or automatically with the passing of birthdays. Godliness, as 1 Timothy 4:7 says, requires a deliberate discipline.

Those who are not *trying* to learn will only get spiritual and biblical knowledge by accident or convenience. Occasionally they will hear a biblical fact or principle from someone else and profit from it. Once in a while they will get a brief burst of interest in a subject. But this is not the way to Godliness. The Discipline of learning helps us to be *intentional* learners, not accidental learners.

It's a lot easier to be an accidental learner and a convenience learner than an intentional learner. We're born that way. And television spoon-feeds that inclination in megadoses. Watching television is so much easier than choosing a good book, reading words, creating your own mental images, and relating it to your life. Television decides for you what will be presented, speaks the words to you, shows you its own images, and tells you what impact it wants to have on your life, if any. Books are much too demanding for the modern mind. Alas, it takes discipline to become an intentional learner.

Jo H. Lewis and Gordon A. Palmer have demonstrated the need for accidental and convenience learners to become disciplined, intentional learners in their book *What Every Christian Should Know: Combating the Erosion of Christian Knowledge in our Generation.*

> Young people today know Genesis as the name of a rock band or a planetary project in a *Star Trek* film, but not as the first book of the Bible. They know Pepsi and the new generation, but not heaven and the everlasting generation; "L.A. Law," but not God's Law. They know who makes *280 Z's*, but not the Alpha and Omega who made them. They know Nikes and the winning team, but not victory in Jesus. They know how to look at "Days of Our Lives," but not how to look into the days of their lives.[5]

I came across a tragic true-life illustration of this just recently. The Center for Science in the Public Interest conducted a survey of 180 boys and girls ranging in age from eight to twelve who lived in the Washington, D.C. area. On this written survey the children were asked to name as many brands of beer as they could and as many U.S. presidents as they could. The results showed that these children, raised in or near our nation's capitol with all its internationally known presidential memorials, could name more alcoholic beverages than presidents. A ten-year-old girl could only come up with "George Wash" for a president, but named Michelob, Jack Daniel's, and Heineken. One nine-year-old boy listed "gorge Bush" and "prestent ragen" among the presidents, but perfectly spelled Molson Golden. Another nine-year-old boy could name only four of our most famous presidents, but completed all fifteen available spaces provided to list the names of beer products.[6] That may sound shocking, but how would your children do in such a test? How would *you* do? Learning that's mostly by accident does not lead to Godliness. We must become disciplined, intentional learners if we're going to become like Jesus.

Jo Lewis and Gordon Palmer proceed to show that the reason young people are not intentional learners is because their parents aren't.

> Young people are not readers. This is not surprising since their parents rarely prize reading. At one Christian college, a fifth of the students said their parents had never read to them. The lack of reading is partly the result of the strong vocational orientation of Americans: Parents don't read because it doesn't seem practical. They are more concerned with "Can my kid operate computers and get a job?" It fits the American obsession with the bottom line. These parents have never learned for the sake of learning, so neither have their children. In this way the value of education has become attenuated and relativized by the marketplace. So it follows that young people who read little of anything do not read their Bibles. One researcher found that "in the liveliest evangelical churches, people strongly feel they should read their Bible daily, but only around fifteen percent do so." Adults, we should also point out, are affected by many of the same pressures as the youth. If they watch television, listen to pop radio, and go to popular movies, they will imbibe these values that are targeted at teens. The result is that many younger adults in their twenties and thirties are, like their younger counterparts, to some extent dulled in their ability to read and understand the Bible.[7]

The Bible says, "Brothers, stop thinking like children. In regard to evil be infants, but in your thinking be adults" (1 Corinthians 14:20).

LEARNING IN A VARIETY OF WAYS

Since some people have legitimate difficulties with reading, here's a list of other learning methods. Besides, the one who has a desire for learning by reading usually wants to learn by all available means. Consider listening to recorded books. This is a fast-growing market in both Christian and secular bookstores. Most public libraries have a selection of books on tape now and there are several mail-order organizations with hundreds of recorded books you can rent. Listen to cassette tapes. In addition to the Christian bookstores and a few large, free-loan Christian cassette libraries scattered around the country, your church or pastor may have cassettes you can listen to while dressing in the morning, driving, or working around the house. Much the same is true for watching videotapes. Almost all Christian bookstores rent them now. Of course, there's listening to Bible teaching programs on Christian radio. This requires discernment to make sure you're listening to a reputable ministry. But if so, this can be a great way to learn. Don't forget the use of study guides. These are found in Christian bookstores and can direct you into an investigation of any book of the Bible as well as many doctrinal and practical topics.

One of my favorite ways of learning is to plan for meaningful dialogue with, and ask prepared questions of, spiritually mature Christians. Twice in recent weeks I have had the privilege of an all-day car ride with some Godly and experienced men whom I admired. In anticipation of each trip I prepared a list of questions to discuss. On both excursions I learned some valuable lessons and felt confident that I was "redeeming the time" (Ephesians 5:16, KJV) quite well. I frequently do this with a few people by mail also. It makes for much more interesting and profitable correspondence than typical postal fare. Obviously, this could also be done by telephone, and I have a friend who leads a Bible study/discussion with two other men in a cross-country conference call each Monday at 8:00 p.m. It's expensive, but they take turns making the call and say that the personal benefit is always worth the cost.

Having said all that, I still want to return to the emphasis on learning by reading. I've always found it to be true that growing Christians are reading Christians. For some it's a habit they find hard to develop. Others love to read, but because of the demands of their job or because they have small children in perpetual motion, they can't seem to find the time for it. But let me encourage you to find some time to read anyway, even if it's no more than one page per day and one book per year. Jean Fleming, author of *Finding Focus in a Whirlwind World* and mother of three grown children, told me she has observed that women who don't develop devotional disciplines, including reading, when they have young children, rarely tend to develop them once they do have the time. I can think of four women I have pastored who had at least four small children each and who were readers. One of them determined to find the time to read at least one page per day, and though it took several weeks, finished Dallas Willard's *Spirit of the Disciplines* with much profit to her spiritual life. Another read the nine-hundred-plus pages in the two-volume life of George Whitefield by Arnold Dallimore. A third read a steady stream of worthy books every year and even wrote a manual for our vacation Bible school workers on sharing the gospel in a God-centered way with children. When you consider that each woman made the time-consuming commitment to home-school her children, you realize that it is possible for almost anyone with the necessary discipline to make spiritual progress through reading.

Yet studies show that 45 percent of Americans say they *never* read a book. Worse than that, the National Commission on Excellence in Education reported in 1983 that the average *college graduate* does not read one serious book in the course of a year.[8] You have too much to lose by not reading, and too much to gain by disciplined reading.

Discipline yourself to learn by reading, and choose your books well. You will be able to read relatively few books in your lifetime, so read the best books. Suppose you were to read ten books every year between now and when you died, how many books would you read in a reasonable life span? Even if you read a few more or a few less than that, it still doesn't amount to very many, especially when you consider that fifteen hundred books are published in America every day. Don't waste your time on books you'll regret reading when you look back upon them from the perspective of eternity. I believe in recreational reading. I don't maintain that every volume you read should be didactic or even theological. There are books to be read just for relaxation and refreshment. But even these should be edifying and help you in some sense to love God with your mind.

MORE APPLICATION

Will you discipline yourself to become an intentional learner? I read a short account in *Discipleship Journal* of the famous "Greek mathematician Euclid who wrote a formidable thirteen-volume text for the study of geometry. But Ptolemy I, King of Egypt, wished to learn the subject without laboring through so many books. As a king, he was accustomed to having his way made easy by servants, so he asked if there was a shortcut to mastering geometry. Euclid's reply to the throne was terse: 'There is no royal road to learning.'"[9]

The same is true with Godliness. It requires discipline, the discipline of an intentional learner. Are you willing to pray for the grace and to make the effort it takes to break the habits of an accidental and convenience learner?

Where will you start? How will you begin to "apply your heart to instruction" and to "store up knowledge"? What habit will you stop and what habit will you begin? Is there a place in your life for a method of learning you have previously overlooked? What about your reading? Is there something you should *stop* reading because it doesn't build up your life or because it doesn't deserve a place on your life's reading list? Do you need to make the "one page per day" commitment so that you don't lose the Discipline of learning?

When will you start? When does your plan begin?

Let's apply the principle of Proverbs 13:4 here: "The sluggard craves and gets nothing, but the desires of the diligent are fully satisfied." This says that all people crave for something, but only the souls of the diligent are satisfied because they discipline themselves to do something while sluggards do not. There is a sense in which everybody "craves" to learn something and every Christian wants to be more like Jesus. But only those who diligently discipline themselves to learn will satisfy those desires.

Above all, remember that learning has a goal. The goal is Christlikeness. Jesus said in Matthew 11:28-29, "Come to me, all you who are weary and burdened, and I will give you rest. Take my yoke upon you, and *learn* from *me*" (emphasis mine). There is a false or superficial knowledge that "puffs up" (1 Corinthians 8:1), but Godly learning leads to Godly living. John Milton, the Englishman who penned the classic poem "Paradise Lost," wrote, "The end of learning is to know God, and out of that knowledge to love Him and to imitate Him."[10] May God give us an unquenchable desire for the knowledge that leads us to love Him more and that makes us more like Jesus Christ.

NOTES

1. Quoted in Iain Murray, *Jonathan Edwards: A New Biography* (Edinburgh, Scotland: The Banner of Truth Trust, 1987) page 184.
2. R. C. Sproul, "Burning Hearts Are Not Nourished by Empty Heads," *Christianity Today*, September 3, 1982, page 100.
3. John Blanchard, comp., *Gathered Gold* (Welwyn, Hertfordshire, England: Evangelical Press, 1984), page 203.
4. Richard Foster, *Celebration of Discipline* (San Francisco, CA: Harper & Row, 1978), page 54.
5. Jo H. Lewis and Gordon A. Palmer, *What Every Christian Should Know* (Wheaton, IL: Victor Books, 1990), page 74.
6. Bob Greene, "A Controversy Abrewing," *Chicago Tribune*, July 23, 1990, sec. 5, page 1.
7. Lewis and Palmer, pages 80, 82.
8. As quoted in *Discipleship Journal*, issue 23 (1984), page 27.
9. Paul Thigpen, "No Royal Road to Wisdom," *Discipleship Journal*, issue 29 (1984), page 7.
10. As quoted in *Discipleship Journal*, issue 23 (1984), page 16.

CHAPTER THIRTEEN

PERSEVERANCE
IN THE DISCIPLINES . . .
FOR THE PURPOSE OF GODLINESS

✦✦✦

*We must discipline our lives, but we must do so all
the year round, and not merely at stated periods.
I must discipline myself at all times.*

Martyn Lloyd-Jones
Studies in the Sermon on the Mount

As usual, the work week begins about dawn Monday. Very little flex time is built into the schedule of showering, dressing, eating, getting the kids ready, and heading out the door. From then on, most of the day is spent on the run. The kids are taken to school and errands are run and work is done around the house or the yard until the very minute you have to get the kids from school. Or else you battle the traffic to work where you make it just at starting time and plug away relentlessly until the hour when you join the quitting queue on the road again.

Once home, often after a hasty, but necessary stop or two on the way, you find it's more and more common to shove a meal in the microwave while you hurriedly change clothes for your evening responsibilities. One or two nights a week it's a school-related function with the kids. Another night might find the entire family at a midweek service at church. Still another night holds a committee responsibility for someone. Next, throw in an occasional night of working late or doing work at home, work-related travel, or work around the house. Don't forget the nights of bill paying, checkbook balancing, homework helping, community involvement, classes, hobbies, and socializing.

Complicating all this may come the pressures of single parenting, family conflict, illness, job stress, a second job, financial tension, and so on.

Sound familiar? Is your life a testimony to the surveys that tell us—despite all our labor-saving devices and technological advancements—leisure time has decreased dramatically in the last generation?

Then you read this book, which encourages you to practice all these Spiritual Disciplines. And it makes you feel like a tired, staggering juggler on a highwire, trying to keep a dozen eggs in the air with someone else wanting to throw you a half dozen more.

I've come to the conclusion that, with rare exceptions, the Godly person is a busy person. The Godly person is devoted to God and to people, and that leads to a full life. Though never frantic in pace, Jesus was a busy Man. Read Mark's gospel and notice how often the word *immediately* describes the transition from one event in Jesus' life to the next. We read of Him sometimes ministering all day and until after dark, then getting up before dawn to pray and travel to the next ministry venue. The gospels tell of occasional nights when He never slept at all. They tell us He got tired, so tired that He could sleep in an open, storm-tossed ship. Crowds of people pressed upon Him almost daily. Everyone wanted time with Him and clamored for His attention. None of us knows "job-related stress" like the kind He continually experienced. If Jesus' life, as well as that of Paul, were measured against the "balanced life" envisioned by many Christians today, they would be considered workaholics who sinfully neglected their bodies. Scripture confirms what observation perceives: laziness never leads to Godliness.

All this is to say that the Spiritual Disciplines have always been what can make a Godly person out of a busy person. The Spiritual Disciplines aren't intended only for Christians who have a lot of spare time on their hands (where are they?). They are *the* God-given means by which busy believers become like Christ. God offers His life-changing grace to taxi-driving, errand-running moms, to hard-working, over-committed dads, to homework-heavy, extracurricular-busy students, to schedule-packed singles, to responsibility-overloaded single parents—in short, to every believer—*through* the Spiritual Disciplines.

But how can we keep up the pace? For one thing, God's voice regarding priorities can best be heard while practicing the Spiritual Disciplines. The older you grow, the more you tend to accumulate responsibilities like barnacles. The addition and growth of children requires an increase in attention to their lives in school, sports, and transportation. Job advancement brings with it more commitments as well as opportunities. The accumulation of goods and property over the years tends to escalate the time you must devote to their maintenance. All this means that periodically your life will call for an evaluation of priorities. Perhaps through the Discipline of Bible intake, or prayer, or worship, or silence and solitude, or journaling, God might speak to you about which activities are "barnacles" that must be cut away. Instead of seeing the Spiritual Disciplines as additional weight, they are actually one of the ways God uses to help lighten your load and give you smoother sailing.

Even with the consistent evaluation of priorities, the Godly person will continue to be a busy person. However, the busy person is also the one most tempted to lapse in the practice of the very Disciplines that lead to Godliness. Without practicing the Spiritual Disciplines we will not be Godly, but neither will we be Godly without *perseverance* in practicing the Disciplines. Even a slow, plodding perseverance in the Spiritual Disciplines is better than a sometimes spectacular but generally inconsistent practice.

How can we be more persevering in the Disciplines of Godliness? When the emotions that usually accompany the beginning of a Spiritual Discipline have ebbed, how can we stay faithful? There are three things that have been seldom mentioned so far which, when better understood, will help you persevere in the practice of the Spiritual Disciplines. They are the role of the Holy Spirit, the role of fellowship, and the role of struggle in Christian living.

THE ROLE OF THE HOLY SPIRIT

Wherever the Holy Spirit dwells, His presence creates a hunger for holiness. His office is to magnify Christ, and it is He who gives the believer a desire to be like Christ. The natural man has no such passion. But in the Christian, the Spirit of God begins to carry out the will of God to make the child of God like the Son of God (Romans 8:29). And He who began this good work in the life of the believer "will carry it on to completion until the day of Christ Jesus" (Philippians 1:6).

So it is the role of the Holy Spirit to produce within us the desire and the power for the Disciplines that lead to Godliness. That He develops this in every believer is evident from 2 Timothy 1:7: "For God did not give us a spirit of timidity, but a spirit of power, of love and of self-discipline."

Therefore, whether or not your natural temperament or personality inclines toward orderly and disciplined habits, the presence of the Holy Spirit within you equips you with enough of a supernatural "spirit of . . . self-discipline" for you to obey the command to "discipline yourself for the purpose of godliness."

That's why even though there are days when you are tempted to quit Christianity altogether, or to give up on the people of God, or to abandon the Spiritual Disciplines as a waste of time, you still hang in there. It is the Holy Spirit who is causing you to persevere. In those times when you are lazy and have no enthusiasm for any Spiritual Discipline, or when you haven't practiced a particular Discipline as you habitually do, it is the Holy Spirit who prompts you to pick it up in spite of your feelings. Left to yourself you would have forsaken these means of sustaining grace long ago, but the Holy Spirit preserves you by granting to you the grace to persevere in them.

Self-control, according to Galatians 5:23, is a direct product, or "fruit," of the Spirit's control in a believer's life. And when the Christian expresses this Spirit-produced self-control by the practice of the Spiritual Disciplines, the result is progress in Godliness.

To illustrate the role of the Holy Spirit in helping the child of God to persevere in the Disciplines of Godliness, one contemporary writer tells of his struggle and success with the Discipline of prayer.

Recently I read again of a woman who simply decided one day to make such a commitment to pray, and my conscience was pricked. But I knew myself well enough to know that something other than resolve was being called for. I began to pray *about praying*. I expressed to God my frustrated longings, my jaded sense of caution about trying again, my sense of failure over working at being more disciplined and regular. I discovered something surprising happening from such simple praying: I was drawn into the presence of One who had, far more than I did, the power to keep me close. I found my focus subtly shifting away from my efforts to God's, from rigor to grace, from rigidity to relationship. I soon realized that this was happening *regularly*. I was praying much more. I became less worried about the mechanics and methods, and in turn I was more motivated. And God so cares for us, I realized anew, that He Himself helps us pray. When we "do not know what we ought to pray for . . . the Spirit Himself intercedes for us with groans that words cannot express" (Rom. 8:26).[1]

The Bible doesn't explain the mechanics of the mystery of the Spirit's ministry to us. How prayer (or the practice of any other Spiritual Discipline) is prompted and produced by Him on the one hand, and yet on the other hand is our responsibility, is unfathomable. But these two things are clear: (1) He will be ever faithful to help each of God's elect to persevere to the end in those things which will make us like Christ, and (2) we must not harden our hearts, but instead respond to His promptings if we would be Godly.

THE ROLE OF FELLOWSHIP

No one should read of these Disciplines and imagine that by practicing them in isolation from other believers they can be just as Christlike, perhaps even more so, than Christians who are active members of a local Body of Christ. Nothing could be further from the truth than to think of the Spiritual Disciplines as a part of the Christian life unrelated to the fellowship of believers.

To measure progress in Christlikeness only in terms of growth in fellowship with God is an incomplete measurement. Spiritual maturity also includes growth in fellowship with the children of God. The Apostle John juxtaposed these two in 1 John 1:3: "We proclaim to you what we have seen and heard, so that you also may have fellowship with us. And our fellowship is with the Father and with His Son, Jesus Christ." New Testament fellowship is with both the Triune God and with His people. Just as the human maturity of Jesus included growth in favor with both God and man (Luke 2:52), so will the spiritual maturity of those who seek to be like Jesus through the Spiritual Disciplines.

One obvious reason we shouldn't think of taking the Spiritual Disciplines and becoming spiritual recluses is that some Disciplines cannot be practiced without other Christians—public worship, united prayer, serving other disciples, and so on. Furthermore, one of God's purposes of fellowship is to supplement the Spiritual Disciplines and to stimulate our growth in Godliness through them. For example, as studying the Word alone is one Discipline God has given us for growing in grace, so is studying the Word with other believers. The Spiritual Disciplines definitely have some nonpublic applications, but they were never meant to be practiced apart from fellowship in the New-Covenant community.

Christians in Western cultures find it easy to forget the role played by fellowship in the theology and practice of the Spiritual Disciplines. One cause of that oversight is the intense individualism touted in our do-your-own-thing, be-your-own-boss, look-out-for-number-one society.

But there's a more subtle reason: the common Christian failure to distinguish between socializing and fellowship. Although socializing is often both a part of and the context of fellowship, it is possible to socialize without having fellowship. Socializing involves the sharing of human and earthly life. Christian fellowship, New Testament *koinonia*, involves the sharing of spiritual life. Don't misunderstand— socializing is a valuable asset to the church and necessary for a balanced life. But we have gone beyond giving socializing the place it deserves. We have become willing to accept it as a *substitute* for fellowship, almost cheating ourselves of the Christian birthright of true fellowship altogether. When this happens, our practice of the Spiritual Disciplines suffers and our growth in grace is stunted.

It looks like this: two or more Christians can sit together for hours, talking only of the news, weather, and sports while completely ignoring their need to discuss directly spiritual matters. I'm not saying that every conversation between Christians must include references to Bible verses, recent answers to prayer, or insights from today's devotional time. But I've observed that many otherwise committed Christians are so independent in their practice of the Spiritual Disciplines that they almost never talk about such things on a heart level. And without personal interaction about the mutual interests, problems, and aspirations of discipleship, our spiritual lives are impoverished. Then at the end of the day, having merely socialized, we think we have had fellowship. Only Christians can have the rich banquet of *koinonia*, but too often we settle for little more than the fast-food kind of socializing that even the world can experience.

Just as we need to experience the Discipline of modeling and talking of Christ with unbelievers, so we have a need for a similar Discipline with believers. Unlike the Discipline of evangelism, where sharing the life of Christ is unidirectional, fellowship involves abidirectional communication of spiritual life. J. I. Packer defines fellowship as "a seeking to share in what God has made known of Himself to others, as a means to finding strength, refreshment, and instruction for one's own soul."[2] Fellowship can happen in as many ways as Christians can be together socially—worshiping, serving, eating, recreating, shopping, witnessing, commuting, praying, etc. Whatever the social setting in which fellowship happens, it should involve sharing the life of Christ in both word and deed. As we live like Christ when together, we encourage each other in Christian living. As we talk like Christ and about spiritual matters, we also stimulate each other toward Godliness.

This mutual edification is described in Ephesians 4:16, which speaks of "the whole body, being fitted and held together by that which every joint supplies, according to the proper working of each individual part, causes the growth of the body for the building up of itself in love" (NASB). As we grow in grace we can properly contribute to "the proper working of each individual part." As the body of believers experiences the "building up of itself in love," each individual Christian is built up in Godliness as well. Put directly, as each believer disciplines himself for the purpose of Godliness, his or her individual spiritual growth helps to build up the local body of believers when that believer is in fellowship with them. As that body of Christians is built up collectively, the increased strength of this fellowship contributes to the spiritual growth of the individual and encourages his or her pursuit of Godliness through the Spiritual Disciplines. Practicing the Disciplines biblically will strengthen the fellowship of believers. Biblical fellowship will strengthen the practice of the Spiritual Disciplines.

But without true fellowship, even the Christian who is ardently practicing the Spiritual Disciplines will not develop in a spiritually balanced way. The writer of Hebrews 3:13 warns, "But encourage one another daily, as long as it is still called Today, so that none of you may be hardened by sin's deceitfulness." Fellowship is required to "encourage one another." When we are outside the spiritual protection God intends for us to get from fellowship, it is much easier to be deceived by sin. Some of the most sin-deceived people rigidly practice many of the Disciplines. I've known people who studied the Bible and prayed so much on their own that they were convinced they didn't need any of the "unspiritual" people in the church. Without the tempering influence of believers with differing gifts, they confidently asserted twisted views of Scripture, delivered "words from God" for everybody, and were able to justify even gross sin because of their supposed spirituality. Obviously, these are extreme cases, but they illustrate how even those most rigorously exercised in the Spiritual Disciplines need what God intends for them to have only through fellowship.

"Associate with sanctified persons," was the recommendation of the Puritan Thomas Watson, "they may, by their counsel, prayers, and holy example, be a means to make you holy."[3]

THE ROLE OF STRUGGLE

There is an element of struggle in Christian living. Many forces combat the spiritual progress of those still on this side of Heaven. Now, the way of Christ is not always an inner struggle, every moment a battle, but neither is it without lifelong opposition. Therefore, don't be misled into thinking that if you drink of the grace God offers through the Spiritual Disciplines then living the Christian life will be easy.

Strange as it may sound, I'm including this section about the role of struggle in hopes that you will be encouraged to follow Christ and practice the Spiritual Disciplines when it's difficult to do so. While writing the above paragraph I received a phone call from a young woman who has been a Christian for about three years. She expressed frustration over a recent spiritual failure and wondered if others at church who appeared so spiritually mature fought any of the battles she was bleeding from. A fresh and timely reminder that *all* Christians struggle in most of the same ways she does brought both comfort and hope. May it do the same for you.

Avoid those who teach that if you follow certain steps or have a particular experience, you can be freed from all struggle against sins that hinder your holiness. Such promises are a spiritual carrot-on-a-stick, always leading you on but never giving fulfillment.

The idea that practicing the Spiritual Disciplines and progressing in Godliness will be accompanied by struggle is confirmed in the context of our theme verse. Referring to the Godliness mentioned in 1 Timothy 4:7-8, the Apostle Paul writes in verse 10, "And for this we labor and strive." The words *labor and strive* tell us that becoming like Christ involves a lot more than to "let go and let God." The Greek word translated "labor" means to work until one is weary. We get our English word *agonize* from the term rendered here as *strive*. It literally means "to struggle." Does this sound like a theology of works instead of grace? Am I saying that though we begin the Christian life by the Spirit we must become holy by works of the flesh (Galatians 3:3)? Nonsense! This is the same balance found throughout the New Testament's teaching on spiritual growth. Advance in the Christian life comes not by the work of the Holy Spirit alone, nor by our work alone, but by our responding to and cooperating with the grace the Holy Spirit initiates and sustains. Our experience in Christlike development will happen as it did with Paul, who said, "I labor, struggling with all his energy, which so powerfully works in me" (Colossians 1:29). Notice that Paul himself labored and struggled, but it was according to the power of the Holy Spirit working (literally, "agonizing") within him. We've already talked about the role of the Holy Spirit keeping us faithful in the Disciplines and producing Christ's character in us through them. To keep a balanced view of how spiritual progress happens means we must also remember the reality of struggle a forgiven, yet sin-tainted man or woman will have in becoming like Jesus Christ.

This is trenchant New Testament teaching. It warns us of the world, the flesh, and the Devil and how they constantly war against us. The Bible says that because of this trinity of opposition we will have to struggle to overcome sin as long as we are in this body.

While we are in the world it will put its unending pressure on us. Jesus reminds us that the world hated Him, and it will hate us if we discipline ourselves to follow Him (John 15:18-19). John exhorts us, "Do not love the world" (1 John 2:15). Then he goes on to talk about the lust of the flesh, the lust of the eyes, and the boastful pride of life as being part of the world. And there is no experience that can give you a lasting escape from every single one of these worldly temptations except the experience of leaving the world.

One of the more obvious passages on the reality of spiritual struggle relates to our war against the flesh, that indwelling tendency we have toward sin. The stark reality of Galatians 5:17 is that "the flesh sets its desire against the Spirit, and the Spirit against the flesh; for these are in opposition to one another, so that you may not do the things that you please" (NASB). Sometimes it's no problem at all to do what's right, to obey God. There are days when your greatest joy is to get into the Word of God. Occasionally you have experiences in prayer that you wish would never end. Still, you know there are many times when it's a battle to engage in any Spiritual Discipline. The Spirit will prompt you toward Christlikeness and the practice of the Disciplines, and your flesh will rise in defiance at the suggestion. That's because "these are in opposition to one another." But even though disciplining yourself is sometimes difficult and involves struggle, self-discipline is not self-punishment. It is instead an attempt to do what, prompted by the Spirit, you actually want in your heart to do. The struggle comes when "the flesh sets its desire against the Spirit, . . . so that you may not do the things that you please." But rather than thinking of entering this battle as a form of self-punishment, it is more scriptural to see the practice of the Spiritual Disciplines as one way of "[sowing] to the Spirit" (NASB) that Galatians 6:8 encourages. But the biblical fact that the flesh does set its desire against the Spirit affirms that there is no spiritual experience while in this body that will permanently free you from that tension.

Of course, you have a personal Enemy committed to your failure in the Disciplines—the Devil: The Apostle Peter reminds us, "Be self-controlled and alert. Your enemy the devil prowls around like a roaring lion looking for someone to devour" (1 Peter 5:8). If there's some experience we can have whereby we never have to enter spiritual warfare, why aren't we told about it rather than being told to be alert? Why are we commanded in Ephesians 6 to put on the armor of the Holy Spirit? It's because we are in a battle, a conflict, a struggle. And there is no vacation from the struggle that is a part of Christian living.

Where, then, is the victory? The victory over the world, the flesh, and the Devil has long ago been decisively and eternally won by Jesus Christ. That victory is mediated to us by the Holy Spirit. For His part, He preserves us in the grace of God. But part of this preservation includes granting us the grace to be faithful. For our part, we take up the struggle of our cross and follow Christ, living as He did by the Spiritual Disciplines. The victory that we actually experience over the forces opposing our progress in the Disciplines will come, practically speaking, *through the practice of the Disciplines*. In other words, it is through perseverance in the Spiritual Disciplines that we will most consistently experience victory over the enemies of the practice of the Disciplines. If we surrender to these enemies of our soul and forsake the Disciplines, victory will never come. But if we will utilize these spiritual weapons, we will be given the grace and strength to conquer even more. One day, all struggle will be over, all the promises will be fulfilled, and the Spiritual Disciplines will no longer be necessary, for at last "we shall be like him, for we shall see him as he is" (1 John 3:2). So let us face this struggle with Spirit-ignited resolve, for it will be for us as it was for the Puritans whose motto was "*Vincit qui patitur*—he who suffers conquers."[4]

"So we need to remember," advises Packer, "that any idea of getting beyond conflict, outward or inward, in our pursuit of holiness in this world is an escapist dream that can only have disillusioning and demoralizing effects on us as waking experience daily disproves it. What we must realize, rather, is that any real holiness in us will be under hostile fire all the time, just as our Lord's was."[5] The writer of Hebrews (12:3-4) tells us, "Consider him who endured such opposition from sinful men, so that you will not grow weary and lose heart. In your struggle against sin, you have not yet resisted to the point of shedding your blood."

The Holy Spirit, true fellowship, and the recognition of the ongoing struggle in the Christian life will help you persevere in the practice of the Spiritual Disciplines. Apart from such perseverance, the Disciplines are incomplete and ineffective. Notice how perseverance connects discipline, or self-control, with Godliness in 2 Peter 1:6: "and to self-control, perseverance; and to perseverance, godliness." Without perseverance between the two, the relationship between the self-controlled practice of the Spiritual Disciplines and Godliness is like a battery full of power but poorly connected to a light bulb. The light flickers inconsistently and without benefit. But when there is a persevering connection between the two, the light shines brightly. In the same way, the light of the life of Christ will shine more steadily through you the more you persevere in the practice of the Spiritual Disciplines.

MORE APPLICATION

Would you be Godly? Then practice the Spiritual Disciplines in light of eternity. I'm told that Jonathan Edwards would pray: "Oh, God, stamp eternity on my eyeballs!" Imagine how differently we would spend our time and make our choices in life if we saw everything from the perspective of eternity. So much that seems critical now would suddenly become trivial. And many things that get relegated to the "when-I-have-more-time" column of our priority list would quickly take on a dramatic new importance. The practice of the Spiritual Disciplines, when seen through eyes stamped with eternity, becomes a priceless priority because of its intimate connection with Godliness.

To practice the Spiritual Disciplines with eternity in view has always been God's plan. The words of 1 Timothy 4:7 upon which this book has been based, "Discipline yourself for the purpose of godliness," are followed in verse 8 by these: "For physical training is of some value, but godliness has value for all things, holding promise for both the present life and the life to come." To see the Spiritual Disciplines only from the pragmatic and temporal perspective is shortsighted. We need to think bigger about them than to ask only what they can do for us today or even in this life. Discipline-cultivated Godliness "holds promise" worth pursuing in "the present life" to be sure. But the value of Godliness, and the practice of its attendant Spiritual Disciplines, is best seen in light of eternity.

Whether you realize it or not, everything you do is for eternity. Nothing has an impact only in this life. This is evident from the scriptural teaching that we must finally give an account before God of how we have spent our lives (see Romans 14:12) and will suffer reward or loss based upon each of our works in this life (1 Corinthians 3:10-15). Since the weight of all eternity, in the words of the Puritan Thomas Brooks, hangs upon the thin wire of time, let us use our time in ways that are profitable not only in this life, but will best prepare us for eternity as well. Nothing provides a more balanced preparation for living on this earth and the new one to come like the faithful practice of the Spiritual Disciplines.

Would you be Godly? There's no other way but through the Spiritual Disciplines. The scriptural path to Godliness has been made plain. Would you be Godly? Then, says the Lord in 1 Timothy 4:7, "Discipline yourself for the purpose of godliness." That is the way and there is no other.

There are no shortcuts to Godliness. But the flesh broods for an easier way than through the Spiritual Disciplines. It protests, "Why can't the Christian life be more extemporaneous and unstudied? All this talk of disciplining myself sounds legalistic and regimented and harder than I thought being like Christ should be. I just want to be *spontaneous!*"

Evangelist John Guest responds well to this temptation.

"Discipline" has become a dirty word in our culture. . . . I know I am speaking heresy in many circles, but spontaneity is greatly overvalued. The "spontaneous" person who shrugs off the need for discipline is like the farmer who went out to gather the eggs. As he walked across the farmyard toward the hen house, he noticed the pump was leaking. So he stopped to fix it. It needed a new washer, so he set off to the barn to get one. But on the way he saw that the hayloft needed straightening, so he went to fetch the pitchfork. Hanging next to the pitchfork was a broom with a broken handle. "I must make a note to myself to buy a broom handle the next time I get to town," he thought. . . .

By now it is clear that the farmer is not going to get his eggs gathered, nor is he likely to accomplish anything else he sets out to do. He is utterly, gloriously spontaneous, but he is hardly free. He is, if anything, a prisoner to his unbridled spontaneity.

The fact of the matter is that discipline is the only way to freedom; it is the necessary context for spontaneity.[6]

Does the farmer's day remind you of your spiritual life—spontaneous but sporadic? Do you flitter from one thing to another with apparently little effect or growth in grace? Certainly we want spontaneity, but spontaneity without discipline is superficial. I have several friends who can improvise beautiful melodies on a keyboard or a guitar. But the only reason they can play so "spontaneously" is because they have spent years in the disciplines of playing musical scales and other fundamental exercises. Jesus could live so spiritually "spontaneous" because He was in reality the most spiritually disciplined man who ever lived. Do nothing and you will live spontaneously. But if you desire *effective* spontaneity in the Christian life, it must be the fruit of a spiritually disciplined faith.

For many believers the failure to practice the Spiritual Disciplines is not so much a struggle with the desire for spontaneity as it is a struggle with finding time. But if you desire to be Godly, you must face the fact that you will always be busy. To do what God wants most, that is, to love Him with all your heart, soul, mind, and strength, and to love your neighbor as you love yourself (Mark 12:29-31), can't be done in your spare time. To love God and others in deed and in word will result in a busy life. This is not to say that God wants us to live hectic lives, but rather to affirm that Godly people are never lazy people.

So if you are simply waiting until you have more time for the Spiritual Disciplines, you never will. In a card to my wife and me, Jean Fleming wrote, "I find myself thinking, 'When life settles down, I'll. . . .' But I should have learned by now that life *never* settles down for long. Whatever I want to accomplish, I must do with life unsettled." I think that's a marvelous insight to the mundane. Because life never really settles down, because we will always have plenty of things to do, if we are ever going to make progress in Godliness through the Spiritual Disciplines it must be done when life is like it is now.

During my junior high and high school years, anyone with an interest in basketball wanted to be like Pete Maravich. "Pistol Pete," as he was known, scored more points than anyone in college history and was the most electrifying basketball player of his time. Before his day, dribbling between the legs and making behind-the-back passes were considered just for show. Maravich made them commonplace. After his pro career he was inducted into the National Basketball Association Hall of Fame. He became a Christian in his midthirties, and suddenly died in January of 1988 of a heart attack at only age forty.

A year before he died, Maravich said this in an interview:

> The key to my ability was repetition. I practiced and practiced and practiced again. I gave the sport my total-commitment. I tried everything I could in every way I could to perfect my skills. It was like an obsession. It paid off for me as a player. I'm not so sure in life. If I had given that same devotion then to my faith, which is what I do now, I'd have been a better person in the long run.[7]

By disciplining himself to practice shooting, passing, and dribbling, Pete Maravich became one of the greatest basketball players ever. Despite all the money and fame brought to him by the sport, he ultimately regretted giving such productive discipline to anything besides his faith in Christ. Are you willing to discipline yourself in the way he wished he had done? Are you willing to "discipline yourself for the purpose of godliness" as much as he was willing to discipline himself for the purpose of basketball? Does Godliness mean as much to you as basketball once meant to Pete Maravich?

Just as the only way to God is through Christ, so the only way to Godliness is through the Christ-centered practice of the Spiritual Disciplines. Will you "discipline yourself for the purpose of godliness"? Where and when will you begin?

NOTES
1. Timothy K. Jones, "What Can I Say?" *Christianity Today*, November 5, 1990, page 28.
2. J. I. Packer, *God's Words: Studies of Key Bible Themes* (Downers Grove, IL: InterVarsity Press, 1981), page 195.
3. Thomas Watson, *A Body of Divinity* (1692; reprint, Edinburgh, Scotland: The Banner of Truth Trust, 1970), page 249.
4. John Geree, *The Character of an Old English Puritane or Nonconformist* (1646), as quoted in J. I. Packer, *A Quest for Godliness: The Puritan Vision of the Christian Life* (Wheaton, IL: Crossway Books, 1990), page 23.
5. J. I. Packer, *Keep in Step with the Spirit* (Old Tappan, NJ: Fleming H. Revell, 1984), page 111.
6. John Guest, as quoted in *Christianity Today*, April 23, 1990, page 33.
7. *USA Today*, January 18, 1988.

SCRIPTURE INDEX

SUBJECT AND PROPER NAME INDEX

AUTHOR

DONALD S. WHITNEY is the associate professor of spiritual formation at Midwestern Baptist Theological Seminary in Kansas City, Missouri. He holds a doctor of ministry degree from Trinity Evangelical Divinity School in Deerfield, Illinois, and has over twenty-four years of pastoral experience. Don is the author of *How Can I Be Sure I'm A Christian?* (NavPress) and *Spiritual Disciplines Within the Church* (Moody Press). He lives in Kansas City with his wife, Caffy, and daughter, Laurelen Christiana. For more information, please visit Don's website at www.spiritualdisciplines.org.